Maria Mulock

Domestic Stories

Maria Mulock

Domestic Stories

ISBN/EAN: 9783742821126

Manufactured in Europe, USA, Canada, Australia, Japa

Cover: Foto ©Andreas Hilbeck / pixelio.de

Manufactured and distributed by brebook publishing software (www.brebook.com)

Maria Mulock

Domestic Stories

COLLECTION

OF

BRITISH AUTHORS.

VOL. 584.

DOMESTIC STORIES.

IN ONE VOLUME.

TAUCHNITZ EDITION.

By the same Author,

JOHN HALIFAX, GENTLEMAN	In 2 vols.
THE HEAD OF THE FAMILY	In 2 vols.
A LIFE FOR A LIFE	In 2 vols.
A WOMAN'S THOUGHTS ABOUT WOMEN .	In 1 vol.
AGATHA'S HUSBAND	In 1 vol.
ROMANTIC TALES	In 1 vol.
MISTRESS AND MAID	In 1 vol.
THE OGILVIES	In 1 vol.
LORD ERLISTOUN	In 1 vol.
CHRISTIAN'S MISTAKE	In 1 vol.
BREAD UPON THE WATERS	In 1 vol.
A NOBLE LIFE	In 1 vol.
OLIVE	In 2 vols.
TWO MARRIAGES	In 1 vol.
STUDIES FROM LIFE	In 1 vol.
POEMS	In 1 vol.
THE WOMAN'S KINGDOM	In 2 vols.
THE UNKIND WORD	In 2 vols.
A BRAVE LADY	In 2 vols.
HANNAH	In 2 vols.
FAIR FRANCE	In 1 vol.
MY MOTHER AND I	In 1 vol.
THE LITTLE LAME PRINCE	In 1 vol.
SERMONS OUT OF CHURCH	In 1 vol.
THE LAUREL BUSH; TWO LITTLE TINKERS	In 1 vol.
A LEGACY	In 2 vols.

DOMESTIC STORIES.

BY THE AUTHOR OF
"JOHN HALIFAX, GENTLEMAN."

COPYRIGHT EDITION.

LEIPZIG
BERNHARD TAUCHNITZ
1862.

CONTENTS.

	PAGE
THE LAST OF THE RUTHVENS	1
THE ITALIAN'S DAUGHTER	63
THE TWO HOMES	77
MINOR TRIALS	92
PHILIP ARMYTAGE; OR, THE BLIND GIRL'S LOVE	105
ADELAIDE: BEING FRAGMENTS FROM A YOUNG WIFE'S DIARY	138
THE OLD MATHEMATICIAN	152
THE HALF-CASTE	169
MISS LETTY'S EXPERIENCES	217
A BRIDE'S TRAGEDY	263
'TIS USELESS TRYING	296
THE ONLY SON	307
THE DOCTOR'S FAMILY	319
ALL FOR THE BEST	329

DOMESTIC STORIES.

THE LAST OF THE RUTHVENS.

PART I.

"Davie Calderwood! worthy tutor and master! — Davie Calderwood!" The old man made no answer to the call, which he scarce seemed even to hear. He sat not far from the shadow of his college walls, watching the little silvery ripples of the Cam. His doctor's robes hid a homely dress of gray; his large feet, dangling over the river bank, were clumsily shod, and his white close-cropped hair gave him a Puritanical look, when compared with the cavalier air of the two youths who stood behind him.

"Davie Calderwood — wake up, man! News! — great news. And from Scotland!" added the elder lad in a cautious whisper.

It pierced the torpor of the old man: he started up with trembling eagerness.

"Eh, my dear bairn! — I mean, my Lord — my Lord Gowrie!"

"Hush!" said the youth, bitterly; "let not the birds of the air curry that sound. Was it not crushed out of the earth a year ago? Call me William Ruthven, or else plain William, till with my good sword I win back my title and my father's name."

"Willie — Willie!" murmured the younger brother, in anxious warning.

"He's feared — wee Patrick!" laughed William Ruthven. "He thinks that walls have ears and rivers tongues, and that every idle word I say will go with speed to the vain, withered, old hag in London or to daft King Jamie in Edinburgh! He thinks he shall yet see brother Willie's love-locks floating from the top of the Tolbooth beside those of winsome Aleck and noble John."

The elder youth spoke in that bitter jesting tone used to hide keenest suffering; but the younger one, a slight delicate boy of nineteen, clung to his brother's arm, and burst into tears.

"My Lord," said Master David Calderwood, "ye suld be mair tender o' the lad — your ae brother — your mother's youngest bairn! Ye speak too lightly o' things awfu' to tell of — awfu' to mind. Master Patrick," he added, laying his hand gently on the boy's shoulder, "ye are thinking of ilk puir bodie given to the fowls of the air and to the winds of heaven at Stirling, Edinburgh, and Dundee; but ye forget that while man dishonours the helpless dust, evermair God keeps the soul. Therefore think ye thus o' your twa brothers — the bonnie Earl of Gowrie, and noble Alexander Ruthven — that are baith now with God."

As he spoke, the doctor's voice faltered, for nature had put into his huge, ill-formed frame a gentle spirit; and though he had fled from his country, and never beheld it since the year when his beloved lord, the first Earl of Gowrie, and father of these youths, perished on the scaffold, still, amidst all the learning and honours gained in his adopted home, David Calderwood carried in his bosom the same true Scottish heart. Perhaps it yearned more over the boy Patrick, in that he was, like his long-dead father, a quiet retiring student, given to all abstruse philosophy; whereas William, the elder, was a youth of bold spirit, who chafed under his forced retirement, and longed to tread in the footsteps of his ancestors, even though they led to the same bloody end.

"Well, good master," he said, "when you have wept enough with Patrick, hear my news."

"Is it from your mother, the puir hunted dove, auld and worn, flying hither and thither about the ruins of her nest?"

Lord Gowrie's — let us give him this title, borne for three months, then attainted, but which yet fondly lingered on the lips of two faithful friends, David Calderwood and Lettice his daughter — Lord Gowrie's brow reddened, and instinctively he put his hand to where his sword should have hung. Then he muttered angrily, "Ah, I forget I am no earl, no Scottish knight, but only a poor Cambridge student. But," he added, his face kindling, "though the lightning has fallen on the parent trunk and its two brave branches, and though the rest are trodden under foot of men, still there is life — bold, fresh life in the old tree. It shall grow up and shelter her yet — my noble, long-enduring mother — the first, the best, the — No; she shall *not* be the last Lady Gowrie."

While speaking, a flush deeper even than that of youth's enthusiasm burned on the young Earl's cheek, and he looked up to the window where Lettice sat — sweet Lettice Calderwood, sweeter even than she was fair! She at a distance dimly saw the look; she met it with a frank smile — the smile a single-hearted, happy girl would cast willingly on all the world.

"The news — the news!" murmured old David. "My bairns, ye talk and ye rave, but ye dinna tell the news."

"My mother writes that the cloud seems passing from our house; for the Queen Anne — she favours us still, despite her lord — the Queen Anne has secretly sent for our sister Beatrice to court."

"Beatrice, whom brother Alexander loved more than all of us," said Patrick. But the elder brother frowned, and rather harshly bade him hold his peace.

"Patrick is a child, and knows nothing," said the young Earl; "but I know all. What care I for this weak Queen's folly or remembered sin? What care I whether my bold brother Alexander encouraged her erring love or not, if through her means I creep back into my father's honoured seat? Oh, shame! that I *can* only creep; that I must enter Scotland like a thief, and steal in at the court holding on to a woman's robe, when I would fain come with fire and sword, to crush among the ashes of his own palace the murderer of my race!"

He spoke with a resolute fierceness, strange in such a youth; his black brows contracted, and his stature seemed to swell and grow. Simple Davie Calderwood looked and trembled.

"Ye're a Ruthven, true and bold; but ye're no' like the Earl of Gowrie. I see in your face your father's father — him that rose from his dying bed to be a shedder of blood — him that slew Rizzio in Holyrood!"

"And when I stand in Holyrood — whether I creep in there

or force my way with my sword — I will kneel down on that bloody spot, and pray Heaven to make me, too, as faithful an avenger."

Then turning off his passion with a jest, as he often did, Lord Gowrie said gaily to his brother, "Come, Patrick, look not so pale; tell our good master the rest of the news — that to-night, this very night, thou and I must start for bonnie Scotland!"

"Who is talking of bonnie Scotland?" said a girl's voice, young indeed, but yet touched with that inexplicable tone which never comes until life's first lessons have been learned — those lessons, whether of joy or grief, which leave in the child's careless bosom a woman's heart.

Lord Gowrie turned quickly and looked at Lettice, rapturously, yet bashfully, as a youth looks at his first idol. Then he repeated his intention of departure, though in a tone less joyous than before. Lettice heard without emotion, as it seemed, only that her two thin hands — she was a little creature, pale and slight — were pressed tightly together. There are some faces which, by instinct or by force of will, can hide all feeling, and then it is often the hands which tell the tale — the fluttering fingers, the tight clench, the palms rigidly crushed together. But these tokens of suffering no one sees: no one saw them in Lettice Calderwood.

"Do ye no' grieve, my daughter, over these bairns that go from us? Wae's me! but there's danger in ilka step to baith the lads."

"Are both going?" asked Lettice; and her eye wandered towards the younger brother, who had moved a little apart, and stood by the little river, plucking leaves, and throwing them down the stream. "It is a long, severe journey, and Master Patrick has been so ill, and is not yet strong," added the girl, speaking with that grave dignity which, as mistress of the household, she sometimes assumed, and which made her seem far older than her years.

"Patrick is a weakly fellow, to be sure," answered Lord Gowrie, inwardly smiling over his own youthful strength and beauty; "but I will take care of him — he will go with his brother."

"Yes," said Patrick, overhearing all, as it appeared. But he said no more: he was a youth of few words. Very soon Calderwood and the young Lord began to talk over the projected journey. But Patrick sat down by the river-bank, and began idly plucking and examining the meadow-flowers, just as if his favourite herbal and botanical science were the only interests of life.

"Patrick!" whispered Lettice's kind, sisterly voice. She sometimes forgot the difference of rank and blood in her tender compassion for the young proscribed fugitives who had been sent, in such utter destitution and misery, to her father's care — "Patrick!"

"Yes, Mistress Lettice."

"The evening closes cold; take this!" She had brought a cloak to wrap round him.

"You are very kind, very thoughtful — like a *sister*." Saying this, he turned quickly, and looked at her. Lettice smiled. Whether gladsome or sorry, she could always bend her lips in that pale, grave smile.

"Well, then, listen to me, as you always do — I being such a staid, wise old woman —"

"Though a year younger than I."

"Still, listen to me. My Lord Gowrie, your brother, is rash and bold; you must be prudent for the sake of both. When you go from us, Patrick, cease dreaming, and use your wisdom. You have indeed the strength and wisdom of a man; it will be needed. Let not William bring you into peril; take care of him — and of yourself."

Here the lips that spoke so womanly, grave, and calm, began to tremble; and Lettice, hearing her name called, went away.

Patrick seemed mechanically to repeat to himself her last words, whether in pleasure, pain, or indifference, it was impossible to tell. Then his features relapsed into their usual expression — thoughtful, quiet, and passionless. An *old-young* face it was — a mingling of the child with the man of eld, but with no trace of youth between — a face such as we see sometimes, and fancy that we read therein the coming history as plainly written as in a book. So while, as the evening passed, Lord Gowrie's fiery spirit busied itself about plots and schemes, the fate of kingdoms and of kings — and David Calderwood, stirred from his learned equipoise, troubled his simple mind with anxiety concerning his two beloved pupils — Lettice hid all her thoughts in her heart, brooding tremblingly over them there. But the young herbalist sat patiently pulling his flowers to pieces, and ruminating meanwhile, his eyes fixed on the little rippling stream. He seemed born to be one of those meek philosophers who through life sit still, and let the world roll by with all its tumults, passions, and cares. They are above it; or, as some would deem, below it. But in either case it touches not them.

It was the dawn of a September day, gloomy and cold. All things seemed buried in a dull sleep, except the Cam that went murmuring over its pebbles hour after hour, from night till morn. Lettice heard it under her window, as she stood in the pale light, fastening her head-tire with trembling hands. They were just starting — the two young Scottish cavaliers. Both had cast off the dress of the student, and appeared as befitted their birth. Bold, noble, and handsome looked the young Earl William in his gay doublet, with his sword by his side. As he walked with Lettice to the garden (he had half-entreated, half-commanded to have a rose given by her hand), his manner seemed less boyish — more courtly and tender withal. His last words, too, as he rode away, were a gay compliment, and an outburst of youthful hope; alluding to the time when he should come back endowed with the forfeited honours of his race, and choose, not out of Scottish but of English maidens, a "Lady Gowrie."

Patrick, stealing after, a little paler — a little more silent than usual — affectionately bade his master adieu; and to the hearty blessing and good-speed only whispered "Amen." Then he took Lettice's hand; he did not kiss it, as his brother had gracefully and courteously done; but he clasped it with a light cold clasp, saying gently, "Farewell! Lettice, my kind *sister*."

She calmly echoed the farewell. But when the sound of the horses' feet died away, she went slowly up to her little chamber, shut the door, sat down, and wept. Once only, looking at her little hand — holding it as if there still lingered on it a vanished touch — the deep colour rose in her cheek, and over her face there passed a quick, sharp pang.

"His sister — always his *sister*!" She said no more. After a while she dried her tears, wrapped round her heart that veil of ordinary outer life which a woman must always wear, and went down to her father.

"Lettice, what are these torn papers that thou art fastening together with thy needle? Are they writings or problems of mine?"

"Not this time, father," said Lettice, meekly; "they are fragments left by your two pupils."

"That is, by Patrick; William did not love to study, except that fantastic learning which all the Ruthvens loved — the occult sciences. Whose papers are these?"

"Master Patrick's; he may want them when he returns."

"When! Ah, the dear bairn, his puir father's ain son; will I ever see his face again?"

There was no answer save that of silence and paleness. Lettice's fingers worked on. But a dull, cold shadow seemed to spread itself over the room — over everywhere she turned her eyes; duller than the gloomy evening — colder than the cold March rain which beat against the narrow college-windows, that shadow crept over her heart. She looked like one who for many days and weeks had borne on her spirit — not a heavy load, that is easier to bear, but a restless struggle — sometimes pain, sometimes joy — doubt, fear, expectation, faith — wild longing, followed by blank endurance. It was now a long time since she had learned the whole bitter meaning of those words: "The hope deferred which maketh the heart sick."

"My dear lassie," said the old doctor, rousing himself from a mathematical calculation which had degenerated into a mere every-day reverie, "where hae ye keepit the puir young Earl's letter, that said he and Patrick were baith coming back to Cambridge in a week? Can ye no tell how lang it is sin syne?"

Lettice could have answered at once — could have told the weeks, days, hours — each passing slowly like years — but she did not. She paused as though to reckon, and then she said, "It is nigh two months, if I count right."

"Twa months! Alas, alas!"

"Do you think, father," she said, slowly, striving to speak for the first time what had been so long pent up that its utterance shook her whole frame with tremblings — "do you think that any harm has come to the poor young gentlemen?"

"I pray God, no! Lettice, do you mind what our puir Willie — I canna say 'the Earl' — tauld us of their great good fortune through the Queen; how that he would soon be living in Edinburgh as a grand lord, and his brother should end his studies at St. Andrews; only Patrick said he loved better to come back to Cambridge, and to his auld master. The dear bairn! Do ye mind all this, Lettice?"

"Yes, father." Ah, truly poor Lettice did.

"Then, my child, we needna fear for them. They are twa young gentlemen o' rank, and maybe they lead a merry life, and that whiles gars them forget auld friends; but they'll come back safe in time."

So saying, the old doctor settled himself in his highbacked chair, and contentedly went to sleep. His daughter continued her work until the papers were all arranged, and it grew too dark to see; then she closed her eyes and pondered.

Her thoughts were not what may be called love-thoughts, such as you, young modern maidens, indulge in when you dream of some lover kneeling at your feet, or walking by your side, know yourselves adored, and exult in the adoration. No such light emotion ruled Lettice's fancy. Her love — if it *were* love, and she scarce knew it as such — had crept in unwittingly, under the guise of pity, reverence, affection, it had struck its roots deep in her nature; and though it bore no flowers, its life was one with the life of her heart. She never paused to think, "Do I love?" or "Am I loved?" but her whole being flowed into that thought, wave after wave, like a stream that insensibly glides into one channel, leaving all the rest dry.

Lettice sat and thought mournfully over the many weeks of wearying expectation for him who never came. How at first the hours flew, winged with restless joy; how she lay down in hope, and rose in hope, and said to herself, calmly smiling, "To-morrow — to-morrow!" How afterwards she strove to make those words into a daily balm to still fear and pain that would not sleep; how at last she breathed them wildly, hour by hour of each blank day, less believing in them than lifting them up like a cry of despair which *must* be answered. But it never was answered; and the silence now had grown so black and dull around her, that it pressed down all struggles — left her not even strength for fears.

She had feared very much at first. The young Earl William, so sanguine, so bold, might have been deceived. The King's seeming lenity might be but assumed, until he could crush the poor remnant of the Ruthven race. She pondered continually over the awful tale of the Gowrie plot; often at night, in her dreams, she saw the ensanguined axe, and the two heads, so beautiful and young, mouldering away on the Tolbooth. Sometimes beside them she saw another. Horror! she knew *it* well — the pale, boyish cheek — the thoughtful brow. Then she would wake in shudderings and cries; and falling on her knees, pray that wherever he was — whether or no he might gladden her eyes again — Heaven would keep him safe, and have pity upon her.

Again she thought of him in prosperity, living honoured and secure under the glory of the Ruthven line — forgetting old friends, as her father had said. Well, and what right had she to murmur? She did not — save that at times, even against her will, the selfish cry of weak human tenderness would rise up — "Alas, thou hast all things, and I — I perish for want!" But her conscience ever answered, "He neither knows nor sees, so with him there is no wrong."

Night, heavy night, fell down once more. Lettice had learned to long for the dull stupor it brought — a little peace, a little oblivion mercifully closing each blank day. "Is it not time for rest, father?" she often asked long ere the usual hour; and she was so glad to creep to her little bower-chamber, and shut out the moonbeams and the starlight, and lie in darkness and utter forgetfulness, until lulled to sleep by the ripple of the stream close by. There had been a time when she had either sat up with her father, or else lain awake until midnight, listening for steps in the garden — for voices beneath the window — when every summons at the gate made her heart leap wildly. But all this was passed now.

Lettice put down the lamp, took off her coif, and unbound her hair. Before retiring she opened the window, and gazed out into the night, which was cold, but very clear. She half-leaned forward, and stretched out her hands to the north. No words can paint the look her countenance wore. It was yearning, imploring, despairing, like that of a soul longing to depart and follow another soul already gone. In her eyes was an intensity that seemed mighty enough to pierce through all intervening space, and fly, dove-winged, to its desire. Then the lids drooped, the burning tears fell, and her whole frame sank collapsed, an image of hopeless, motionless dejection.

She was roused by a noise — the dash of oars on the

usually-deserted river. She shut the window hastily, blushing lest the lamp should have revealed her attitude and her emotion to any stranger without. The sound of oars ceased — there were footsteps up the garden alleys — there was her father's eager voice at the door, mingled with other well-known voices. They were coming! — They were come!

In a moment all the days, weeks, months of weary waiting were swept away like clouds. The night of her sorrow was forgotten as though it had never been.

"And now that I am returned, thou wilt not give me another flower, Mistress Lettice?" said the young Earl, as he followed her up the garden-walks in the fair spring morning. She had risen early, for sleep had been driven away by joy.

"There are no flowers now, at least none gay enough to be worth your wearing. Daisies and violets would ill suit that courtly dress," said the maiden, speaking blithely out of her full-hearted content.

"Does it displease you, then? Shall I banish my silver-hilted sword, and my rich doublet with three hundred points, and don the poor student's hodden gray? I would do it, fair damsel, and willingly, for thee!" And he smiled with a little conscious pride, as if he knew well that six months passed in the precincts of a court had transformed the bashful youth into an accomplished cavalier — brave, handsome, winning, yet pure and noble at heart, as the young knights were in the golden time of Sidney and of Raleigh.

Lettice regarded him in frank admiration. "Truly, my Lord Gowrie, you are changed. Scarcely can I dare to give you the name you once honoured me by permitting. How shall I call you and Master Patrick my brothers?"

"I wish it not," said the young man, hastily. "As for Patrick — never mind Patrick," as Lettice's eyes seemed wandering to the river-side, where the younger Ruthven sat in his old seat. "You see he is quite happy with his herbal and his books of philosophy. Let him stay there; for I would fain have speech with you." He led her into a shady path, and began to speak hurriedly: "Lettice, do you know that I may soon be summoned back to Scotland — not as a captive, but as the reinstated Earl of Gowrie? And, Lettice" — here his voice faltered, and his cheek glowed, and he looked no more the bold cavalier, but a timid youth in his first wooing —

"dear Lettice, if I might win my heart's desire, I would not depart alone."

"Not depart alone! Then thou wilt not leave Patrick with us, as was planned?" said the girl, uttering the first thought that rose to her mind, and then blushing for the same.

"I spoke not of Patrick — he may do as he wills. I spoke of some one dearer than brother or sister; of her who ——"

"What! is it come to that?" merrily laughed out the unconscious girl. "Is our William, at once, without sign or token, about to bring to Cambridge, and then carry away home, a bonnie Lady Gowrie?"

The Earl seemed startled by a sudden doubt. "It is strange you should speak thus! Are you mocking me, or is it a womanly device to make me woo in plainer terms? Hear, then, Lettice! Lettice that I love! It is you I would win, you whom I would carry home in triumph, my beautiful, my wife, my Lady Gowrie!" She stood transfixed, looking at him, not with blushes, not with maiden shame, but in a sort of dull amaze.

"Do my words startle you, sweet one? Forgive me, then, for I scarce know what I say. Only I love you — I love you! Come to my heart, my Lettice, my bride that shall be;" and he stretched out his arms to enfold her. But Lettice, uttering a faint cry, glided from his vain clasp, and fled into the house.

In their deepest affections women rarely judge by outward show. The young Earl, gifted with all qualities to charm a lady's eye, had been loved as a brother — nothing more. The dreamy Patrick, in whose apparently passionless nature lay the mystery wherein such as Lettice ever delight — whose learning awed, while his weakness attracted tender sympathy — he it was who had unconsciously won the treasure, which a man, giving all his substance, could not gain — a woman's first, best love.

Her wooer evidently dreamed not of the truth. She saw him still walking where she had left him, or passing under her window, looking up rather anxiously, yet smiling. One thought only rose clearly out of the chaos of Lettice's mind — that he must be answered; that she must not let him deceive himself — no, not for an hour. What she should say she mournfully knew — but how to say it? Some small speech she tried to frame; but she had never been used to veil any thought of her innocent heart before him she treated as a brother. It was so hard to feel that all this must be changed now.

Lettice was little more than eighteen years old, but the troublous life of a motherless girl had made her self-dependent and firm. Therefore, after a while, courage came unto her again. Strengthened by her one great desire to do right, she descended into the garden, and walked slowly down the alley to meet the Earl. His greeting was full of joy.

"Did I scare her from me, my bird? And has she flown back of her own accord to her safe nest — her shelter now and evermore?" And he extended his arms with a look of proud tenderness, such as a young lover wears when he feels that in wooing his future wife he has cast off the lightsome follies of boyhood, and entered on the duties and dignities of man.

Lettice never looked up, or her heart would have smote her — that heart which, already half-crushed, had now to crush another's. Would that women felt more deeply how bitter it is to inflict this suffering, and if wilfully incurred, how heavy is the sin! Even Lettice, with her conscience all clear, felt as though she were half guilty in having won his unvalued love. Pale and trembling she began to say the words she had fixed on as best, humblest, kindest — "My Lord Gowrie ——"

"Nay, sweet Lettice, call me William, as you ever used to do in the dear old times."

At this allusion her speech failed, and she burst into tears. "Oh, William, why did you not always remain my brother? I should have been happy then!"

"And now?"

"I am very — very miserable."

There was a pause, during which Lord Gowrie's face changed, and he seemed to wrestle with a vague fear. At last he said, "Wherefore?" in a brief, cold tone, which calmed Lettice at once.

"Because," she murmured, with a mournful earnestness there was no doubting or gainsaying, "I am not worthy your love, since in my heart there is no answer — none!"

For a moment Lord Gowrie drew himself up with all his ancestral pride. "Mistress Lettice Calderwood, I regret that — that ——" He stammered, hesitated, then throwing himself on a wooden seat, and bowing his head, he struggled with a young man's first agony — rejected love.

Lettice knelt beside him. She took his passive hands, and her tears rained over them; but what hope, what comfort could she give? She thought not of their position as maiden and suitor — Lord Gowrie and humble Lettice Calderwood — she only saw her old playmate and friend sitting there overwhelmed with anguish, and it was her hand which had dealt the blow.

"William," she said, brokenly, "think not hardly of me. I would make you happy if I could, but I cannot! I dare not be your wife, not loving you as a wife ought."

"It is quite true, then, you do not love me?" the young Earl muttered. But he won no other answer than a sad silence. After a while he broke out again bitterly — "Either I have madly deceived myself, or you have deceived me. Why did you blush and tremble when we met last night? Why, before we met, did I see you gazing so longingly, so passionately, on the way I should have come? Was that look false, too?"

Lettice rose up from her knees, her face and neck incarnadine. "My Lord of Gowrie, though you have honoured me, and I am grateful, you have no right ——"

"I *have* a right — that of one whose whole life you have withered; whom you have first struck blind, and then driven mad for love! Mistress Calderwood — Lettice ——"

In speaking this beloved name, his anger seemed to disperse and crumble away, even as the light touch shivers the molten glass. When again he said "Lettice," it was in a tone so humble, so heartbroken, that, hearing it, she, like a very woman, forgot and forgave all.

"I never did you wrong, William: I never dreamed you loved me. In truth, I never dreamed of love at all until ——"

"Go on."

"I cannot — I cannot!" Again silence, again bitter tears.

After a while Lord Gowrie came to her side, so changed, that he might have lived years in that brief hour. "Lettice," he said, "let there be peace and forgiveness between us. I will go away: you shall not be pained by more wooing. Only, ere I depart, tell me, is there any hope for me in patience, or long waiting, or constant, much-enduring love!"

She shook her head mournfully.

"Then what was not mine to win is surely already won? Though you love not me, still *you love:* I read it in your eyes. If so, I think — I think it would be best mercy to tell me. Then I shall indulge in no vain hope: I shall learn to endure, perhaps to conquer at last. Lettice, tell me: one word — only one?"

But her quivering lips refused to utter it.

"Give some signal — ay, the signal that used to be one of death! — let your kerchief fall!"

For one moment her fingers instinctively clutched it tighter, then they slowly unclasped. The kerchief fell!

Without one word or look Lord Gowrie turned away. He walked, with something of his old proud step, to the alley's end, then threw himself down on the cold, damp turf, as though he wished it had been an open grave.

When the little circle next met, it was evident to Lettice that Lord Gowrie had told the tale of his rejection to his faithful and loving younger brother. Still Patrick betrayed not his knowledge, and went on in his old dreamy and listless ways. Once, as pausing in his reading, he saw Lettice glide from the room, pale and very sad, there was a momentary change in his look. It might be pity, or grief, or reproach, — none could tell. He contrived so as to exchange no private word with her until the next morning; when, lounging in his old place, idly throwing pebbles into the river, and watching the watery circles grow, mix, and vanish, there came a low voice in his ear:

"Master Patrick Ruthven!"

He started to hear his full name formally uttered by lips once so frank and sisterly.

"Well; what would you, Lettice?"

"It is early morning; there is no one risen but we two; come with me to the house, for I *must* speak with you. And what I say even the air must not carry. Come, Patrick; for the love of Heaven, come!"

Her face was haggard, her words wild. She dragged rather than led him into the room where the two boys had once used to study with her father. There she began speaking hurriedly:

"Did you hear nothing last night? — no footsteps? — no sounds?"

"No: yet I scarce slept."

"Nor I." And the two young faces drooped, unable to meet each other. But soon Lettice went on: "At dawn, as I lay awake, it seemed as if there were voices beneath my window. I did not look: I thought it might be——"

"William sometimes rises very early," said the brother, gravely.

"It was not Lord Gowrie, for I heard these strange voices speak his name. Your hopes from King James were false! Oh, Patrick, there is danger — great danger! I have learned it all!"

"How?" And rousing himself, the young man watched eagerly Lettice's agitated mien.

"I opened the lattice softly and listened. When they went away, I followed stealthily to the water's edge. Patrick, they said that on the night but one after this, they will return and seize you in the King's name! Fly — fly! Do not let me lose for ever both my brothers!"

And she caught his hands as in her childhood she had used to do, when beseeching him to do for her sake many things which, from dreamy listlessness, he would never have done for his own.

"What must I do, Lettice — I, who know nothing of the world? Why did you not tell all this to William?"

"I — tell William!" She blushed scarlet, and seemed struggling with deep emotion.

"Oh, true — true!" Patrick said, and there seemed a faint waking up in his passionless features. "No matter; I will at once go and tell my brother."

Lettice sat down to wait his return. All her murmur was — "Oh, William — poor William! — so truly loving me whom others love not at all! I turned from thee in thy prosperity, but now shall I save thee and lose myself? — shall I sacrifice all to thee?" But instinct rather than wisdom whispered to Lettice, that she who weds, knowing her heart is not with her husband, wilfully sacrifices both. In the sight of heaven and earth she takes a false vow, which, if requited not by man, will assuredly be avenged by God.

Patrick Ruthven came back in much agitation. "He says he will not fly; that he heeds neither the prison nor the block; that he has no joy in life, and death is best! Lettice, go to him: save him — you only can!"

"How can I save him?" mournfully Lettice cried.

"By urging him to fly. We can take horse, and cross the country to Harwich, whence a ship sails for France to-night. I know this, for yesterday I, too, was planning how to depart."

"You?"

"No matter," said Patrick, hurriedly. "Only go to William; compel him to save his life: he will do so at your bidding."

He spoke commandingly, as if fraternal love had transformed the gentle, timid youth into a resolute man. Lettice, wondering and bewildered, mechanically obeyed. She came to Lord Gowrie, who, with the disordered aspect of one who has wasted the night in misery, not sleep, lay on the floor of what had been the boys' play-room. To all her entreaties he only turned his face to the wall, and answered not. At last his brother beckoned Lettice away.

Looking at Patrick, the girl marvelled. All his impassive coldness seemed to have melted from him. His stature appeared to rise into dignity, and there was a nobility in his face that made it beautiful to see. Lettice beheld in him, for the first time, the likeness of what she knew he would one day become — a grand, true man: the man before whom a woman's heart would instinctively bow down in Eve-like submission, murmuring — "I have found thee, my greater self — my head, my sustainer, and guide."

Patrick stood silent awhile, sometimes reading her face, sometimes casting his eyes downward, as it were struggling with inward pain. At last he said, solemnly, "Lettice, this is no time for idle scruple. I know all that took place yesterday. I know, too, that there is one only chance, or William is lost. Is your will so firm that it cannot change? Must he die through loving you — my dear, my noble brother, whom I would give my poor life to save? Lettice, in this great strait I entreat you — even I;" — and he shuddered visibly — "Consider what you do. It is an awful thing to have life and death in your hands. I beseech you, let him love you, and be happy."

Lettice listened. As he spoke, slowly — slowly — the young rich blood faded from her face; she became rigid, white, and cold; all the life left was in her eyes, and they were fixed on Patrick, as it were the last look of one dying.

"Answer me," she said, with a measured, toneless voice — "answer truly, on your soul. Do you desire this of me? Is it *your* wish that I should become your brother's wife?"

"My wish — my wish!" he muttered, and then his reply came clear and distinct as one says the words which fix the sentence of a lifetime, "In the sight of God, yes!"

Lettice gave him her hand, and he led her again to his brother.

"I need not stay," he whispered: "you, Lettice, will say all — better say it at once."

She looked at Patrick with a bewildered, uncertain air, and then began to speak.

"Lord Gowrie — that is, William, I — —"

She said no more, but fell down at Patrick's feet in a death-like swoon.

Lettice lay insensible for many hours. For her there were no farewells; when she awoke, the two brothers were gone. She found on her neck a golden chain, and on her finger a ring, the only tokens of the last passionate embraces which William had lavished on her whom he now considered his betrothed. But she herself remembered nothing. And when they told her, she flung away the ring and chain, and prayed Heaven that she might die before ever Lord Gowrie came to claim her vows.

Of the younger Ruthven, she could learn nothing either from her bewildered father or her old nurse, except that Patrick had forcibly torn his brother away. He had not spoken, save leaving a kind farewell to *his sister*.

In the twilight Lettice rose from her bed. She could not, for any inward misery, neglect her good father. And all her senses had been so stunned, that as yet she was scarce alive either to the present or the future. She sat almost as if nothing had happened, listening to the old man's broken talk, or idly watching the graceful smoke-wreaths of the Virginian weed that Sir Walter Raleigh had just introduced, and with which rare luxury the young knight's friendship had provided David Calderwood.

Oppressed by the sudden events which had greatly discomposed the tenor of his placid existence, the worthy doctor smoked himself to sleep. When with his slumbers Lettice's duties ceased, her bitter grief rose up. It choked her — it

Domestic Stories. 2

seemed to make the air close and fiery, so that she could not breathe. Dark and cold as the March night was, she fled out. But she kept in the thick alleys of the garden — she dared not go near the river, lest out of its cool, cool depths should rise a demon, smilingly to tempt her there.

But at length, when the moon came out from under a black cloud, Lettice thought she would approach and sit in Patrick's old seat by the side of the Cam, where in summer nights they had spent hours — she, with girlish romance, looking up at the stars, and he teaching her all concerning them in his learned fashion, for the boy was a great astronomer.

Was it a vision, that he sat there still, in his old attitude, leaning against the willow-tree, the light slanting on his upturned brow? Her first thought was, that he had met some fearful end, and this was his apparition only. She whispered faintly, "Patrick;" but he neither spoke nor moved. Then she was sure she beheld the spirit of her beloved. Her highly-wrought feelings repelled all fear, and made her take a strange joy in this communication from the unseen world.

Once more she called him by his name, adding thereto words tenderer than his living self would ever hear. Then, seeing that the moon cast his shadow on the water, the conviction that it was no spirit but his own bodily form, made her start and glow with shame. Yet when she approached, he lay quite still, his eyes were closed, and she could almost have believed him dead. But he was only in a deep sleep, overpowered by such heavy exhaustion that he hardly seemed to breathe.

Lettice crept beside him. Scarce knowing what she did, she took his cold hand and pressed it to her breast. There, suddenly awaking, he felt it closely clasped; and met a gaze pure and maidenly, yet full of the wildest devotion — a look such as man rarely beholds, for the deepest tenderness is ever the most secret. Scarce had Patrick seen it, than it melted into Lettice's ordinary aspect; but he *had* seen it, and it was enough.

"When did you come back?" faintly asked Lettice.

"At twilight: a day's hard riding exhausted me, and I suppose I fell asleep here."

"And wherefore did you return?" Mechanical were the questions and replies, as though both spoke at random.

"Why did I return?"

"Yes — to danger. Oh, Patrick, how shall we save you? Why did you not sail with William, if he has sailed?"

"He has. There was a passage for one only — his life was the most precious — he is my elder brother, so I persuaded him to go on board; and then — I left him."

"Patrick — Patrick!" Unconsciously she looked up at him in her old childish, loving way, and her eyes were full of tears.

"Are you glad, Lettice?"

"Glad, because you have done a noble thing. But if through this you should be discovered and taken; if I — that is, we all — should lose you — — Hush!" That instant her quick ear, sharpened by terror, heard down the river the sound of oars. "They are coming — those men I saw last night; they will have brought the King's warrant that I heard them speak of. It is too late. Oh, would that you at least had been saved!"

"I, and not William?" His words spoke grave reproach, but his beaming looks belied his tone.

"I think not of William now. Why did he go and leave you to perish? But I will not leave you; Patrick, I will die with you — I — —"

"Lettice!" He began to tremble violently, took her hand and looked questioningly into her eyes. There seemed a doubt suddenly furling off from his mind, so that all was light and day — ay, even though nearer every minute came the distant sounds which warned him of his danger.

"Hark! they are close upon us;" said Lettice, in an agonized whisper. "They will search the house through: what must be done?"

"I know not," answered Patrick, dreamily.

"But I know: come, come."

She drew him cautiously into a laurel thicket close by, which, lying deep in shadow, furnished a safe hiding-place. Thinking a moment, she took off her black mantle and wrapped it over him, that his light-coloured doublet might not be seen through the boughs.

"We may escape them," she said: "we two have hidden here many a time when we were children."

"Ah, Lettice!" he sighed, "we were happy then! Even now, if William had not loved you — —"

2*

"Hush! they are landing; I hear their steps — keep close." She made him kneel, so that her dress might hide him; and, as fearing that his fair floating curls might catch some stray moonbeam, she put her hands upon his hair.

Footsteps came nearer and nearer; life or death was in each tread. The terrified voice of David Calderwood was heard avouching that, hours since, the Scottish brothers had fled; and still the only answer was "Search — search!"

In their agony, the two young creatures — they were both so young! — drew closer to each other; and Patrick's arms were wrapped round Lettice, as they used to be when she was a child. He whispered, "If I die, Lettice, love me. Better than life — better than aught, save honour, I have loved thee!"

She pressed her cold lips upon his forehead, close and fond. This was the only vow which passed between them. The officers began to search the garden, David Calderwood following, wringing his feeble hands. "Good friends, gin ye seek till dawn, ye'll no find ae thing alive, save my puir bairn, if sae be she is living still. Lettice — Lettice, whar are ye gane?" cried the old man, piteously.

"Go to your father — go!" murmured Patrick; but Lettice was deaf to all love save his now.

"I'll help ye to seek in ilka bush and brake, if only to find my puir lassie; and I pray our sovereign lady Queen Elizabeth" — —

"Our sovereign lord King James of England and Scotland; that's the prayer now — so no treason, old man," said one of the officers, giving him a buffet which made poor Davie stagger. At the sight, Patrick Ruthven started in his hiding-place.

"An owl in the bushes — Hollo there!" shouted the men.

Patrick and Lettice scarcely breathed. In her frenzy, she clasped her arms passionately round his neck; her eyes, stretched out into the darkness, flashed fire; she felt that had she only a weapon at hand, she would have committed murder to save him. Vain — vain — all vain!

A crash in the bushes, a rough hand on Patrick's breast — "Ho! prisoners in the King's name!"

He was taken at last.

Whether she wept, or shrieked, or prayed, whether they took any farewell of one another or no, Lettice never remem-

bered. All that remained in her memory after that awful moment was one sight — a boat gliding down the river in the moonlight; and one sound, words which Patrick had contrived to whisper, "The Tower — the Tower!"

PART II.

ONE day, in mid-winter, when Tower Hill, so often reddened with blood, lay white under many inches of snow, a woman might have been seen taking her way over the portcullis into the Tower. She seemed to belong to the middle class; her hood and kirtle were of humble fashion, black and close. She was a small, insignificant-looking woman too, and seemed to be admitted into the awful state prison, or rather to creep in there, attracting from the warders no more notice than a bird flying in at a captive's window, or a little bright-eyed mouse peering at him in the dark.

Her errand, she said, was to the Governor's lady. Thither she was brought, through gloomy passages that seemed to make her shudder, under narrow-barred silent windows, at which she looked up with a terrified yet eager glance, as if she expected to see appear there the wan face of some wretched prisoner. She reached the Governor's apartments. There air and light were not wanting, though it was in the grim old Tower. From it might be seen the shining Thames, with ships of all nations gliding by. There were plants, too, growing in the heavy embrasures of one window, and in the other was a group of human flowers — a young mother and her beautiful children.

The stranger briefly stated her errand. She had heard that the lady desired an attendant for her daughters, and she came to offer her services, bearing credentials from one whom the Governor's wife knew.

"The name is Scottish: are you from our country?" said the graceful mother, her fair face brightening with kindliness.

"My father was Scots, and so were all my nearest relatives," answered the woman in a low voice, as she pulled her hood closer over her face.

"You say *was* and *were*: are all gone then?"

"Yes, madam: I am quite alone."

"Poor young thing!"

"Nay, I am not young; I am thirty-four years old."

"And you have never been married?"

"No."

"Ah!" sighed the happy young wife of twenty-five, with a sort of dignified compassion. But she was of a kindly nature, and she discerned that the stranger wore a look of great sweetness, and had withal a gentle voice — that truest index of a womanly spirit. She enrolled her in her household at once.

"And you are willing, my good — What did you say was your Christian name?"

"Lettice."

"You are willing to reside in the Tower? It is at best but a dreary place for us, as well as for the poor prisoners: though, thanks to our merciful King James, we have had but few executions here lately."

Lettice faintly shuddered — perhaps it was to hear such gentle lips speak so indifferently of these horrors — but she answered, "I am quite satisfied, madam: even this prison seems a home to one who has just lost the only home she ever knew, and who has now none in the wide world."

She spoke with great simplicity, and in the calm manner of a woman who has been taught patience by long suffering. Nevertheless, when the Governor's lady bade her take off her mantle and hood, and the three little maidens, summoned from the inner room, came gathering round her, and, won by her sweet looks, offered childish kisses, Lettice's self-control failed, and a few tears began to fall from her eyes.

"Nay, take heart, my countrywoman," said the young matron, kindly: "We will make you very happy here; and perhaps find you for husband a brave yeoman-warder with a good estate: King James takes care his Scottish subjects shall thrive in merry England."

And quite satisfied that in a wealthy marriage she had thus promised the chief good of life, the lady departed.

That night Lettice saw the stars rise and shine, not on the limpid Cam, not on the quaint old garden where her childish feet had played, and where afterwards — all earlier memories blotted out by those of one terrible night — she had walked patiently, bearing the burden of her sorrow for sixteen years.

Sixteen years! It was thus long since Patrick Ruthven had disappeared, and yet no tidings had ever been heard of or from him. She had exerted all energies, exhausted all schemes — so far as she dared without endangering her father's safety, or leaving him in his helpless age — but could gain no clue as to the after-fate of her lover. Whether he still languished in prison, or had been freed by escape or death, all was mystery: her only certainty was, that he had not perished on the public scaffold, otherwise she would have known.

And so praying for him day and night, and loving him continually, this faithful woman had lived on. The days and years of her youth had glided from her like the waves of a river, uncounted, for no light of love rested on them. Their onward course she neither watched nor feared.

She saw the young men and maidens of her own age pass away into the whirl of life, marry, and gather round them a third generation, while she remained the same. Wooers she had, for when sorrow comes in early youth, and fails to crush, it sometimes leaves behind a tender charm beyond all beauty, and this made Lettice not unsought. Some women — good women, too — can love in their simple, easy-hearted fashion, twice, thrice, many times. Others pour out their whole soul in one love, and have no more left to give ever after. Lettice Calderwood was one of these.

Her father lingered many years in great bodily weakness, and in an almost fatuous old age. She tended him unweariedly until he died. Then when she had no kindred tie left in the wide world, no duty to perform, none to love, and none to obey, she formed a resolution over which she had been long brooding with an intensity of persevering will such as few women have, but which no human being ever has *except* a woman.

That resolution planned, maturely guided, carried through many hindrances, formidable indeed, but which fell like straws before the might of her great love, Lettice found herself at last an inmate of the Tower. If detained there, as in all human probability he was, unless no longer of this world, she should certainly discover Patrick Ruthven. Farther plans she saw not clear, still doubtful as she was of his very existence. But as she sat by herself in the silent midnight, within a few yards, it might be, of the spot where, if living, he still dragged on his mournful days; or where, if dead, his spirit had parted from his body, there came upon her a conviction which often clings to those whose portion is somewhat like to hers.

"He is not dead," Lettice murmured, "else he would have come to me; he knew I should not have feared. No; he is still living; and if living, I will find and save him."

So, praying for her Patrick with the woman's pale, faded lips, as the girl had prayed sixteen years before, Lettice fell asleep.

It was a dangerous thing for the free inhabitants of the Tower to inquire too closely about the prisoners. The days of Guy Fawkes and Sir Thomas Overbury were not so long past but that all who had any interest in the enemies of King James knew it was wisest to keep a silent tongue and close-shut eyes. Lettice Calderwood had dwelt for weeks within the walls where perchance lay her never-forgotten lover, and yet she had neither heard nor spoken the name of Patrick Ruthven.

Her whole time was spent with the Governor's children. They, happy creatures, played merrily outside the cells wherein was concealed misery and despair. Sometimes they talked about the "prisoners" with a light unconsciousness, as if speaking of cattle, or things inanimate. Poor little ones! how could they understand the meaning of the word!

"Do you ever see the — the *prisoners?*" Lettice ventured to ask of them one day.

"Oh, yes; a few are allowed to walk on the leads, and then we peep at them from below. We are very good friends with one or two — our father says we may."

"What are their names, my child?" If the little girl could have known the strong convulsion that passed over Lettice's heart while she put this simple question!

"We don't call them anything: they are only prisoners. They have been here a great many years, I believe. One lives there, in the Beauchamp Tower: he is always writing; and when we go in to see him, for he likes us to come, he does nothing but puff, puff, puff!" and the laughing child put her finger in her mouth, and began mimicking a smoker to perfection.

"Mabel," said the elder sister, "you should not laugh at him, for our father says he is a good man, and the King is not very angry with him, any more than with the other man who is shut up in the Bell Tower. You should see him, Mrs. Lettice; he is my favourite, because he is so gentle. They say he walks on the leads between his room and the Beauchamp Tower, night after night, watching the stars; and he plays with us children, and gets us to bring him quantities of flowers, out of which he makes such wonderful medicines. He cured Mabel of the chin-cough, and father of the ague, and —"

"Hush, Grace; Mistress Lettice is quite tired with your chatter. See how white she looks!"

"No; go on, my darlings; talk as much as you will," murmured Lettice; and rousing herself, she contrived to learn from them what this prisoner was like.

A little, bent man, very old the children thought, because his hair was quite gray, except a few locks behind that were just the colour of Grace's. Lettice, holding the child on her knee, had often secretly kissed the soft fair curls; she did so now with passionate tenderness. Yet could it indeed be Patrick — so changed! The thing seemed scarcely possible.

Next time the children went to see this prisoner, she hid herself, where, from below, she could watch the leads on which he was accustomed to walk. There appeared the figure of a man, moving with the heavy, stooping, lounging gait of long captivity. Could it be that Patrick's youth had been crushed into such a pitiable semblance as this? He came and leaned on the breastwork or boundary of his narrow walk. In the distance the features were indistinct; but something in the wavy falling of the hair reminded her of Patrick. She half uttered a cry of recognition, suppressed it, sank back, and wept. His name — if she could only learn the captive's name! But there was great mystery kept about that. The children said, "he had none, he had been in the Tower so many years." Grace added, that she had once asked him, and he answered, "that he had almost forgotten it." Alas, poor soul!

One day Lettice, impelled by a wild hope, fastened in Grace's dress a little childish ornament that she herself had used to wear: it had been broken, and the boy Patrick's rude workmanship in the repairing was on it still. If this man were indeed Patrick, it might catch his eye, and bring back to his dulled memory the days of his youth.

The "prisoner" noticed and touched the brooch, Grace said; observed that it was pretty; that he thought he had once seen one like it, he could not tell where; and then his dull mood came over him, and he would not talk any more.

Lettice's eager hope sank; but on it she lived yet longer;

and day by day she watched tearfully the poor captive, who, if not Patrick, had suffered Patrick's doom.

The child Grace fell sick. Lettice grieved, for she loved the little girl; but this trouble seemed helping to work out her one great aim of life. Then, at least, she might hear more of the prisoner whose skill in medicine had won the deep gratitude of both the Governor and his lady. But Grace improved, and still of the invisible physician nothing was disclosed. At length one night, when the anxious mother and Lettice were watching the child, together and alone, there arose an emergency.

"The potion will be needed at dawn; 'tis near midnight, and I have not sent to — to the Bell Tower," said the mother. "What must be done? Who can I trust?" She looked at Lettice, whom she and all the household had already learned to love — "I will trust you."

She explained briefly that the child's physician was a state prisoner, who had acquired his skill during sixteen years' captivity; that his durance was now greatly softened by the King's order; but that still, except the Governor's family, he was allowed to see no one, nor to hold any communication with the outer world. "And" said the lady, "if I send you to him, you must keep silence on all concerning him, for he and his have been greatly hated by King James; and no marvel. He is Patrick, the last of the Ruthvens."

What dizzy, tumultuous joy rushed to the heart of the faithful woman, who, after long silent years, again heard the music of that name! But she stood still and mute, and gave no sign.

"Lettice, will you go?"

"I will:" and she went.

There was not a foot heard, not a breath stirring, in the grim old Tower. As, bearing the ponderous keys, she unfastened door after door, the sound of the opening locks was startling and awful. At the foot of the Bell Tower Lettice paused. Sixteen years seemed all swept away; her heart throbbed, and her pale brow of middle age flushed like a young girl's. Would he know her? Would she not appal him, standing suddenly, like a spectre, by his side? She pulled her hood over her face, and resolved to feign her voice, lest the shock might overpower his strength. Thinking of his emotion, she soon calmed her own, and came with firm step to the outer door. There gleamed a faint ray through some worm-eaten fissure; the Governor's wife had told her that he always studied until late in the night. Lettice pictured him as at the old home at Cambridge, as in perpetual youth he dwelt ever in her memory. She saw him, leaning over his books, with his pale boyish features, his fair curls, his dreamy-lidded eyes. She opened the door, and saw — a gray-headed man, withered and bent, quaint and careless in dress, writing by lamp-light. He momentarily raised his head; the face had a strange old world look, mingled with an aspect half vacancy, half abstraction. Lettice shrank aghast. It seemed as if the former Patrick were dead, and this a phantom risen up to mock her. But when he spoke, it was his own true voice.

"Ah, you come for the child Grace's potion?" said he. "'Tis all prepared; wait a moment — listen!"

He rose, put the medicine into her hand, and proceeded to give various directions concerning it. Then he sat down again, and prepared to resume his reading. Lettice stood silent; that he did not recognise her she plainly saw, yet this was what she had desired. Why should she feel pain?

She put back her hood, and approached him — "Master Patrick Ruthven!"

He started, but it could only be to hear the long unused Christian name; for looking up at her face, now turned fully on him, *his* expressed blank unconsciousness. He did not know her!

"Madam, pardon me; I have not seen you before, but I suppose you come from little Grace. If I have omitted anything, or forgotten — One forgets everything here."

Lettice groaned.

The poor captive looked disturbed, bewildered; restlessly he moved his papers about, and she saw his hands, long, white, and woman-like, whose delicacy William used to mock and Lettice to admire; the same hands she had clasped and kissed in her last frenzied agony of parting. She did so now.

"Patrick, Patrick; have you forgotten me — even me?"

He looked at her again, and shook his head. "I have seen you somewhere I think, perhaps in the old time before I came hither; but my memory is poor, very poor. What is your name?"

"Lettice!"

A light came into his face for a moment, and faded. "It is a sweet name. I used to love it once, I believe; some one I knew bore it; but, as I said, I forget so many things now. Lettice, Lettice!" He repeated the name, as if trying to call back images of a long-past life.

Lettice's first horror passed. She discerned all now — she saw what he had become: how, shut up from youth to manhood in that fearful prison, his life had withered there; how, as the slow vacant years crawled by, passion, affection, feeling of every kind, had grown dull. Wreck as he was — the wreck captivity had made him — her never-dying love encompassed him still.

"Patrick," she said gently, though her tears were flowing fast, "look at me, and try to think of the past — my father, who taught you when you were a boy: and I, Lettice Calderwood, who used to be your playfellow; the old house at Cambridge — the river-bank where you liked to sit — the garden, and the laurel-trees."

His features began to quiver.

"It is dim, very dim; but I think I do remember all this, ay and you, Lettice! I am glad to see you once more."

He trembled a good deal, and looked at her many times, as though, in comparing his old recollection of her with her present likeness, the difference puzzled him.

Lettice said, faintly smiling, "You know I am old now — one changes much in sixteen years." But the smile brought back somewhat of her former self, and Patrick's mind seemed to grow clearer.

"I think," he said, with a mournful simplicity, "I think I must have loved you once. I never forgot you even here, until" — and he shuddered — "until they put me into that dark, damp cell, where I heard no sound and saw no living face, for I know not how long; I forgot everything then."

Lettice's heart was bursting; she pressed his hands to her breast, and sobbed aloud. At first he seemed troubled by her emotion, and then, as if unable to resist, his own gray hair drooped on Lettice's shoulder, and the poor prisoner also wept. By slow degrees Patrick's memory wakened to the things of the past and of the living world; but they seemed to touch him little. He heard of David Calderwood's death with a quiet sigh — all keen sense of human pain being apparently obliterated from his mind. After a pause he asked, though still indifferently, "There was my brother, too — tell me something of William."

"William acted nobly, and so acting, ceased to be unhappy!" said Lettice, in a confused voice.

"Unhappy!" repeated the captive, vacantly. "Ah, yes; I had forgotten: we had much sorrow in our youth — he, and you, and I —"

"Hush, Patrick! we will not speak of that. I wrote to William, and told him all: he freed me from my promises. Time brought him comfort! he remained abroad, married, and last year — grieve not, Patrick, for while living he had great happiness — last year he died."

"Poor William dead! — my last brother dead!" Patrick said, thoughtfully; and sat a long time wistfully gazing in the air, now and then uttering broken words, which showed his mind was recalling incidents of their boyish days. At last he said, "And you, Lettice — what of yourself?"

"I am as you left me — poor Lettice Calderwood; in nothing changed but years." She murmured this with her eyes cast down, as if she had need to be ashamed that she had felt a woman's one, pure love; that for it she had given up all sweetness of wifehood and motherhood, and stood there in her faded bloom, speaking no word, but letting her whole life's story speak for her: "See how faithful I have been to thee!"

Perhaps, as Patrick looked on her, some sense of the greatness of this love, so strong in its oneness, so patient in its endurance, dawned upon his bewildered and long paralysed senses. He stretched out his arms to her, crying, "I am unworthy — most unworthy! But, Lettice, love me still: help me — take care of me: do not leave me again!"

He had forgotten, and she too, all worldly things. Waking from that dream, they found that she was only humble Lettice Calderwood, and he a prisoner in the Tower. No matter — one at least had ceased to fear. When a woman once feels that all depends upon the strength of her love — that the power to will and to act of necessity lies in her hands — she gains a courage which nothing can daunt or quell. And as Lettice bade Patrick Ruthven farewell, whispering hope and tenderness which his long-dulled ears would scarcely receive, she felt certain that she should set her beloved free; ay, as certain as though she stood at the head of armies to hurl King James from his throne.

Little Grace recovered; and unto the mother's heart, still trembling with its recent joy, another heart was led to open itself, with all its burden of many years. One day, when both their spirits were attuned to confidence, Lettice told the Governor's wife her whole story. It was a story that would have melted many a one to sympathy: the young Scottish gentlewoman listened even with tears. Ruthven was her countryman, and she had shown him kindness ever since her husband was made Governor; he was her child's preserver, and she determined to try all efforts to obtain his liberty. She exerted secret influence at Court, at first with hope of success; but that year the bugbear treason was loudly dinned into the pusillanimous monarch's ears, and Tower Hill was again watered with its red rain.

One day the little Grace and Mabel loudly lamented that they were forbidden any longer to visit their friend in the Beauchamp Tower. On the next, Lettice and Patrick, walking on the leads (where she had liberty to visit him now), saw the black procession winding past, and heard distantly the heavy sound of the axe's fall. Patrick said, "There dies a just man and a guiltless, and one that Davie Calderwood would have deeply mourned. God receive the soul of Walter Raleigh!"

He spoke calmly, as if such sights had ceased to move him; but Lettice crouched down, hiding her face in inexpressible horror. When they re-entered his narrow prison, she clasped her arms wildly round her betrothed — for they had plighted their troth to one another, whether it were for life or death. She felt that to have him safe, with freedom to see him, to love and comfort him, was blessedness even here.

And so, for a whole year, through fear lest the King's anger should be roused, nothing more was done toward effecting Ruthven's release.

When once a generous purpose roots itself in a leal Scottish heart, especially a woman's, it is not easy to uproot it thence. The Governor's wife came to Lettice one day, and told her that there was hope; since Queen Anne was dead, and the King could now fear no treason from the Ruthven line. She applied to the Court, and answer came that Patrick Ruthven should be set at liberty, if some near friend would solicit his pardon.

"A form — a mere form — only desired to soothe King James's pride," said the plain-speaking Scottish lady; she came from the bold race of Kirkaldy of Grange.

But, form as it was, when Lettice told her lover the tidings, he shook his head in his listless way, and said it could never be.

"I have no friend in the wide world to plead for me, or to crave my pardon; all my kith and kin have died; I am left the last of my race. No, Lettice, it is best as it is! Perchance I would have liked to go once more to the meadows by the Cam where the rare flowers grow; and it would have been a sweet and thankful duty to exercise my skill in healing on the poor and needy. But let be — let be! Do not talk of worldly liberty; we will go and look at the free, free stars that roam, night after night, over this prison, and never tire! Come, my faithful Lettice — come!"

But Lettice groaned in spirit. He, long used to captivity, scarce felt the chain; she, for his sake, writhed under it like a double weight.

"Patrick," she said, leaning by him, and with him watching the few dull lights that were scattered throughout the black city which lay below, while a yellow mist rising from the river, gathered over everything, palely and cold — "My Patrick, would it not be happy to go far away from here into your own clear northern air? Look!" — and she pointed to the barren osier-flats through which the Thames winds seaward — "if instead of that dull line were the mountains you told me of when we were children, rising, height after height, like a good man's life, which grows year by year nearer to heaven, until it melts, cloudlike, into heaven itself at last."

The prisoner sighed, and looked on the blank landscape with glistening eyes that saw — not it, but some dim view beyond.

Lettice continued: — "Ay, and if we were free — both free — if we could hide ourselves in some sweet spot, and live our old childlike life!"

He answered restlessly — "Do not talk of this, or else I shall die of longing; and I had grown so resigned, so content with my books and my herbs. Why did you bring me back to the bitter world?"

"To save thee, my beloved!" she answered, soothingly. "To take thee out of prison, and bring thee back the dew of thy youth. Shall it not be so?"

"How can it, when there is no one who has a right to entreat for my pardon? I have no kindred, no tie in the wide world!"

"Save one."

"Ah, true! — forgive me, my faithful love! But what can you do?"

Lettice hid her face on his shoulder. If she blushed it was not with shame, for she knew her own pure heart, and Heaven knew it too. She rose, and spoke in a quiet, womanly tone, though somewhat trembling the while.

"Patrick, we are neither of us young; all love we bear each other is stilled into the affection that must always exist between two who, having wasted half a life-time in sorrow, hope to spend the poor remainder together and in peace. You will not misjudge what I am going to say?"

"No — no," answered Ruthven in his absent manner.

"There is but one way to obtain your freedom. Dearest, long-lost and found, let *your wife* go and plead for you before the King!"

The young kinswoman of Kirkaldy of Grange had a rebellious yearning, though she was a Governor's lady. She liked to cheat King James of his captives when it could be done with safety. Secretly, in order to avoid all risk to her husband, she introduced a Scottish minister to the dismal chambers of the Bell Tower. There, in that dull prison-house, was celebrated a marriage. Brief it was, and grave; without smiles, without tears. Yet not without love, for they did indeed love one another, those two who, as girl and boy, had clung together so wildly in the garden by the Cam. But their love was not like that of youth: it was deep, solemn, still.

When the marriage was performed, Patrick said, in his dreamy way —

"Is it all done? Am I thy husband, Lettice?"

She answered, "Yes."

"A hard task for thee to fulfil; a weary life to lead! But art thou content?"

She answered, "I am content." And taking his hand, held it fast in that which would now guide him through life.

"Nay, have no fear, friends," cheeringly said the brave Scottish lady who aided them so much. "King James is feeble-hearted, and he has heard the people's outcry against Raleigh's twelve years' imprisonment, sealed at last with blood. He dare not do the like again. Lettice, take comfort; you will soon have your husband free."

Her *husband!* She heard the word — she who had never dreamed of any other life than one of loneliness, over which hung the pale shadow of that early-lost love. Her heart melted under the sense of its great content, and she wept as softly and joyfully as though she had been a young bride.

"Will his Majesty appear to-day, my Lord of Buckingham?" said one of the Scottish attendants of the palace at Whitehall, meeting the twin stars of James's court — "Steenie," and "Baby Charles."

"Wherefore, good Ferguson?"

"Because, my lord, there is a person here craving audience, who has been recommended to me by a countrywoman of my own."

"A woman is it? My prince, let us see!"

The woman rose up and curtsied beneath the gaze of royalty and nobility; but she had nothing in her to attract or retain either. She was pale, low-statured, and of middle age. "Steenie," gave her a mock salutation; Prince Charles, ever chivalrous to women, acknowledged her lowly reverence with his dignified, half-melancholy, Stuart smile, and the two youths passed out.

"The King is coming, Mistress Ruthven; now is your time!" whispered young Allan Ferguson.

He entered — the poor feeble pedant, to whom had dwindled down the ancient line of Scotland's kings. Surrounding him were the great and noble of the day: Gondomar, the gay Spanish ambassador; the Lord-Chancellor Bacon; all the choicest of the English nobility left after the death-sweeping reigns of Mary and Elizabeth; and those of the King's own country whom his conciliatory rule had detached from various factions, to join in fidelity to the one branch of the Stuart family now remaining.

"Hech, sirs, wha's here?" James cried in his sharp,

quavering voice, through which rang the good humour produced by a satisfactory arrangement with Spain, completed that same hour. "Petitioning, my bonnie woman? Aweel, then say your say!"

Lettice told her story in words so broken that they would scarce have been understood save for the earnestness of her eyes. It was a story touching and interesting even to James and his frivolous court. To them it sounded new and curious to hear of a woman who had loved and suffered, waited and hoped, and gone through all trial for one man's sake, for seventeen years. And it so chanced that their possible mockery of her long maiden life was prevented by Lettice always unconsciously saying "my husband," as the Governor's wife had charged her to say, instead of mentioning at once the hated name of Ruthven.

James looked discomposed. "My lords, a king maun do as he wills; ye a' ken the chapters in my 'Basilicon Doron' respecting free monarchies, and the right or prerogative of rulers. But I wadna keep an innocent man — mind ye, an *innocent* man — in prison for saxteen — did she no say saxteen years? Woman, wha may ye be? and why dinna ye tell your husband's name?"

"It is a name — the bearing of which was the only wrong he ever did your majesty: I am the wife of Patrick Ruthven!"

James turned pale, as he ever did at the sound of that dreaded name. He never forgot that it was a Ruthven who acted in that scene of blood which impressed cowardice on the nature of the yet unborn babe: he never forgot the actors in the Gowrie plot, who, for a brief space, caused him, a king by birth and right, to be tied and bound like a felon.

He frowned, and looked round on his courtiers, who kept a discreet silence. Then he said with a pedantic air, "Woman, I will bear thee again on this matter," and passed into the audience-chamber.

Lettice's heart grew cold. It was a horrible thing to reflect that life or death lay on the fiat of that poor, vain, fickle king. No! On the fiat of a King far higher, whose government comprises not kingdoms, but worlds. Kneeling where she had knelt to King James, she knelt to Him, and prayed.

There came, crossing the empty chamber, one of the nobles who had formed one of the monarch's train. He was an old man, tall and pale. His demeanour savoured more of the courtly grace of Elizabeth's reign than the foppish gallantry of James's. He announced his name at once.

"Mistress Ruthven, I am the Earl of Hertford."

She had heard it in the Tower. It had been long chronicled there as a portion of that mournful story of the Lady Catherine Grey, sister to Queen Jane, who, marrying Hertford without Elizabeth's consent, had been imprisoned until her young life's close.

He was an old man now, but something in Lettice's story had touched him with the days of his youth. He came to say that he would plead her cause with the King, and that he thought she had good reason to hope.

"And you have been parted ever since your marriage — seventeen years?"

"We are but newly married, my lord; our bridal was in the Tower," said Lettice, who never said aught but truth.

"Ah! no need to tell the King that: yet it makes a sadder tale still. Where abides your husband in the Tower?"

"In the Bell Tower — a narrow, dreary spot."

"I know — I know!" He turned away, perhaps remembering the poor young mother who had there, in that very Bell Tower, given birth to his two brave sons. He, too, had felt the bitterness of captivity; and as he departed from Lettice, having given her both counsel and cheer, she heard the old nobleman muttering to himself, "Seventeen years! — seventeen years!"

Patrick Ruthven sat in his tower poring over his wealth of books. An August sunbeam quivering in, rested on a bunch of dried flowers, which the herbalist was examining with great earnestness. He scarce lifted up his head when the light footstep warned him of his wife's entrance.

"Lettice," he said, "*Eureka!* — ('I have found it!') This plant must be the veritable hemlock of the ancients — the potion which gave Socrates death. Compare the description — see."

He looked at her; she was trembling all over with joy.

"My husband," she said, breathlessly, "leave these books; come and gaze out in the clear morning air; how fresh it is: how free — free — free!"

She repeated the words that the tidings might dawn upon him slowly, not too bewilderingly. She drew him out upon the prison leads, and bade him look northwards, where in the distant uplands beyond Holborn, the ripening wheatfields shone, wave upon wave, like yellow seas.

"Think, Patrick, to go thither; to sit down under the sheaves like little children, as we used to do; to hear the trees rustling, and see the swallows fly; and then to go home — to a quiet, safe cottage home. Oh, Patrick, my husband, you are free!"

"I am free!" He, the prisoner for seventeen years, neither fell down in a swoon of transport, nor wept, nor grew wild with ecstasy. He only uttered the words in a monotonous incredulous tone — "I am free!" His wife embraced him with passionate joy; he kissed her, stroked her yet fair cheek — fairer still since she had once more known peace — and then went slowly back into his dark room.

There he sat motionless, while Lettice busied herself in putting together the books and scientific matters which had gradually accumulated round the captive. Then she brought him attire suitable for a man of middle rank at that period.

"You must not wear this out in the world, my Patrick," said the wife, touching his threadbare robe of a fashion many years back.

"Must I not?" and he contemplated the dress, which seemed to him gaudy and strange. "Lettice," he murmured, "I am afraid — is the world so changed? Must I give up my old ways?"

But she soothed him with cheerful words, and made ready for his departure. Ere they quitted the Bell Tower, he went into the little closet which had been his bedchamber, and, kneeling down, thanked God, and prayed for all captives a deliverance like his own. As he rose, there peeped at him a bright-eyed mouse.

"Poor fellow-prisoner, whom I have fed so many years, who will feed thee now?" And breaking off some food, he called the little creature to his hand, and gave it its last meal.

Then, leaning on his wife's arm, for he trembled, and seemed feeble as a child, Patrick Ruthven left the Tower.

He had entered it a youth of nineteen; he quitted it a worn-out, prematurely old man of thirty-six. The prime and glory of manhood had been wasted in that gloomy prison. Thank God, there is no such doom for *innocence* now!

Far past what then was London's utmost verge, Lettice Ruthven led her husband. He walked through the streets like one in a dream; all sounds stunned — all sights bewildered him. If a chance eye noticed his somewhat quaint aspect, he clung to Lettice with terror, lest he should again be taken prisoner. She told him there was no fear, that through Lord Hertford's solicitation and the mediation of Prince Charles, the King had granted him a free pardon; nay, the young prince, over kind hearted, had settled on him a pension for life. All this he heard as if he heard it not. Nothing soothed him but Lettice's calm smile.

They came to the place which she had chosen as their first abode. It was a farm-house, planted on one of the hills to the north of London. Above was a great wide heath; below numberless little undulating valleys, with trees and meadows, harvest-fields and streams. There, after sunset, they took their evening walk. He, long used to the close air of the prison, shivered even at the warm summer wind; and his feeble limbs, accustomed to pace their narrow round, could scarcely endure fatigue. But Lettice wrapped him warm, and took him to a soft-wooded bank with a stream running below. There he lay, his head on her lap, listening to the ripple of the water.

He had never heard that sound since he was a boy sitting beside the Cam, on the night his brother sailed from Harwich. Though his memory was dull yet, and he rarely spoke of the past, perhaps he thought of it now, for the tears crept through his shut eyes, and he whispered — "Lettice, you are sure, quite sure, that afterwards William was happy?"

She told him again and again that it was indeed so. She did not tell him how — though William grew renowned abroad — he never sent for tidings of his imprisoned brother. She would not pain the fraternal love which had kept its faith through life so close and true.

"And Patrick, are you happy?"

He answered "Yes!" softly, like a drowsy child. His

wife leaned over him, and her hand fell on his hair, once so beautiful, now quite gray. Something of protection was there in her love for him; the mingling of reverence and tender care, due alike to his great mental power and his almost infantile simplicity in worldly things. All he had, she honoured with her whole soul; all he had not, she, possessing, made his own. She was a fit wife for him. And so, in this deep content and peace, the sun set upon Patrick Ruthven's last day of captivity.

PART III.

A HOUSE, simple, yet not mean, facing the river-side at Chelsea; its upper storeys fanned by that line of majestic trees which you, reader, may still stroll under; and if you are of dreamy mood, I know of no sweeter spot than Cheyne Walk in the moonlight; the river lying silvery and calm; the tall trees rustling among their branches; telling tales of the quaint old mansions they overshadow. But the house of which we were speaking was far humbler than these. Its occupants had chosen it more for the sake of the trees and the river than for any interior show. They lived retired; and when, as now, the master re-entered his own door, he was not met by a troop of domestics, but by one little, old, gentle-looking woman — his wife.

Twenty more years had passed over the head of Lettice Ruthven, yet something of its ancient airiness was in her footstep still; and in her eyes shone the same loving light, for it was kindled at an altar where the fire was never suffered to decay.

"You are late to-night, Patrick?" said she.

"Ay, I have been all through the meadows at Chiswick, in search of herbs for a poor lad down there who is stricken with ague. I stayed late gathering them, and there came by a couple of Roundheads, who hooted at me for a wizard hunting for charmed plants in the moonlight. Ah, me! do I look such a weird creature, Lettice?" asked the old man in a piteous, humble tone.

He certainly had an out-of-the-world aspect, in his long white beard and hair, and his black serge gown, which he wore to indicate his character as physician. And there was a passive gentleness in his voice, which showed how little able he was to assert his own dignity, or to fight his own battles with the hard world. Well for him that neither had been needed; that for twenty years his life had flowed in a quiet stream, he growing continually more absorbed in his favourite studies, and leaving all mundane matters to his faithful helpmate. She did not usually trouble him with any of these latter, but on this day she seemed longing to talk of something else besides the additions he was making to the "Middlesex Flora," or the wonderful cures he had wrought with simples until then unknown; or, what he carefully kept to his wife's ears alone, his discoveries in those abstruse and occult sciences, the love of which seemed inherent in the Ruthven blood.

"I have found it out," he said; "the parchment charm worn by my brother, the Earl John. All these years I have kept it, and never deciphered it until now. It will bring to us and all our children great prosperity."

"All our children!" repeated Lettice, mournfully. She looked at a corner of the room where hung, each in its never changed place, a boy's plumed hat, and beside it a heap of well-worn childish books, mementos of two little sons, who had been sent and taken away, leaving the hearth desolate.

"Ah, I forgot!" said the other with a light sigh. "Bravely did Aleck read his Greek Galen; and as for poor wee Willie, he knew every plant in Battersea-fields. Well might the gossips mock at me, saying, 'Physician, save thyself!' or rather, thy two better selves. But I could not. I am aye good for little, very little."

His wife took his hand affectionately, and said, smiling through her tears — "Nay, there is many a one hereabouts who lifts his hat when Dr. Ruthven passes by. If the vulgar mock, the learned honour thee, my husband. And Patrick," she murmured, with her sweet voice of calm, which hid all sorrow from him, "though our two boys are with God, He has left us our Marie! I saw her to-day."

"Did she come hither?"

"No; she cannot easily leave the Queen's household, you know. But she bade me meet her at a friend's," and a faint expression of pain crossed the mother's face. "Perhaps she was right; I am scarce fit to mingle with court ladies, as Marie does; and Marie is growing as beautiful and as stately as any of them all."

"Is she?" said Dr. Ruthven, absently. He had never felt the same affection for his daughter as he had done for his two lost sons. Marie had in early youth been separated from her family, and taken under the care of the wife of the Lieutenant of the Tower — now become a countess, and in high favour in the Queen's household. Through her means the little girl was afterwards adopted by Henrietta Maria, to be educated at court, and raised to the position due to the last daughter of the direct Ruthven line.

"She had tidings for me, Patrick — tidings that may well make a mother's heart both tremble and rejoice. The Queen wishes to dispose of our daughter in marriage."

Ruthven lifted his eyes, dropped them, and then became intent upon a handful of flowers which he had drawn from the great coarse bag he always carried in his rambles. It was evident he took little interest in the news which had so agitated the mother.

"Do you not wish to know who it is that will wed our Marie — ay, and at once — for all is fixed?"

"I hope it may be some good man. Young women usually marry — I am glad she should do so: but you know, Lettice, I am a quiet, dreamy, old philosopher; I have forgotten all such things."

So spoke, after nearly forty years, the boyish lover who had once sat mournfully by the side of the Cam. But this life is an eternal progression. Young, passionate love must of necessity change its forms. Yet what matters that, if its essence remains the same? Lettice, a wife for many years, keeping in her heart still something of its fresh, womanly romance, neither murmured nor felt pain that with her husband the noon-day of love had gradually dwindled into evening-tide. And as with her, so should it be with all. Never should a maiden promise her troth, never should a bride stand at the altar, unless she can look calmly forward to the time when all romance melts into reality; when youth and passion cease, and even long-assured affection from its very certainty at times grows tame. Never ought a woman to take the marriage-vow unless she can bear to think fearlessly of the time when she will sit an old wife by her old husband's side, while her only influence over him, her only comfort for herself, lies in the strength of that devotion which, saying not alone in words but in constant deeds — "I love thee!" desires and exacts no more.

This picture was Lettice Ruthven in her old age.

She might have sighed to hear Patrick speak so forgetfully of those things which she with great tenderness remembered still — for women cling longer than men to the love-days of their youth — but she never thought of bringing the brightness of that olden dream to contrast painfully with their calm life now. She passed over her husband's words, and kept silence, musing on her daughter's future.

"He is a rich man, and one of great renown, this Sir Anthony Vandyck," she said at last. "Being the King's painter, he saw our Marie frequently at court: no wonder he thought her beautiful, or that he should learn to adore her, as she says he does. I wonder if she loves him!"

"Fret not thyself about that, goodwife, but come and tie up this bundle of herbs for me. There, hang it on the wall, and then sit by me with thy knitting-pins, which I like to watch until I go to sleep. I am so weary, Lettice."

She arranged the cushion under his head: he looked quite old now, far more so than she, though they were nearly equal in years. But he had never recovered the long imprisonment which had dried up all the springs of life. Lettice watched him as he slept — his pale, withered face, his thin hands — and her undying tenderness enfolded him yet. Dearly she had cherished her three children — the two dead boys, the daughter now her sole pride — but this one great love was beyond them all.

Marie Ruthven was one of the beauties of that court, which, whatever its political errors might have been, was then in its inner circle as brilliant as any which England had known. A monarch generous, accomplished, devoted to the arts — a queen, against whom the greatest crime ever alleged was that she exercised undue influence over her husband by means of the warm attachment which she had inspired and returned — a royal circle whose domestic purity knew no stain — these evidences show that, however his political conduct may condemn Charles the King, his domestic life leaves no blot upon the memory of the unfortunate Charles Stuart. Of this court, now gay as if no tempest were near to overthrow it, the chief topic was the marriage of Sir Anthony Vandyck and the Lady Marie Ruthven. The King honoured the bridegroom — the Queen loved the bride. There were great preparations, banquets, and balls. No one ever thought of the old father and mother dwelling in the little house at Chelsea.

But one heart, though sorely stung, yearned over the forgetful daughter. When the beautiful Marie was being attired for her bridal, it was told her that some one wished to see the bride.

"A little old woman, dressed like a Puritan, forsooth!" said the gay waiting-maid.

And creeping in, dazzled by the splendour of the court-dames, who were grouped around the bridal toilet, the mother came to her only daughter's side.

The stately bride uttered no disrespectful disclaimer, for she was a Ruthven; and in ceasing to honour her parents, she would have been disowning her ancient race. But the red flush darkened her brow, and the kiss she gave her mother was forced and cold.

"Marie, my child," murmured Lettice, "why did you not tell me your bridal was to-day? I would not have intruded there — alas! not I. But I would fain have come a little while beforehand to talk with thee, and bless thee, my own, my only child!"

Marie looked round — the apartment was deserted; she fancied she heard the retreating mockery of her companions and her maids. She said, sharply —

"Mother, I meant you no wrong; but the life I lead is so different to yours and my father's: when you gave me up at the Queen's request, it changed all things between us. Therefore, since I knew it would not suit either, I did not invite my parents to my marriage.

"No, no, of course," said the poor mother, humbly. She had long looked upon her daughter as quite a different being from herself — a creature in whom the noble Ruthven race, crushed throughout one hapless generation, was again revived. She scarce could believe that the beautiful majestic woman she now beheld, was the pining babe whom she had nursed in the hill-cottage, where Patrick after his long captivity had slowly returned to his own right self, so as to be fit for intercourse with the world. Yet something like a sense of pride came over her when she thought that, but for the love of poor Lettice Calderwood, the last of the Ruthvens might have perished in his prison. It seemed enough glory to have been Patrick's deliverer — the mother of Patrick's beautiful child.

"And is thy bridegroom worthy of thee, my sweet Marie?" asked Lettice. "Above all, dost thou love him?"

"He is a gay and courteous gentleman," answered the bride, avoiding the question. "People say he is the most renowned artist in Europe: I think him the most graceful courtier, even though he be not very young. He dwells in state at Blackfriars, and he has a country abode at Eltham. Ah, I shall be a great lady as the wife of Sir Anthony Vandyck!"

But the question which came from the mother's heart, "Lovest thou thy husband?" was never answered. Something jarred upon Lettice, as if the nameless division between parent and child were growing wider. How unlike was this courtly bridal to the stolen marriage in the Tower! Yet could she have seen in her daughter's heart some of the emotions which had then touched her own, she would have been more content.

"But," she murmured, "I was a poor, simple maiden always. From my youth up I never thought of anything but love. It may be different with those reared at court."

She stayed a while longer, until Marie grew restless; and then, with many tears, she embraced the bride, and gave her her blessing.

"Your father sends his too, my child," she continued. "Perhaps we would have been less grieved could we have come, as other parents do, to our daughter's wedding. But her Majesty's desire should ever guide yours, and since the Queen does not will it —"

"The Queen *does* will it," said a voice behind.

There had entered, unobserved, a lady of dignified presence, but yet on whose face was written *woman* in every line. It was Henrietta Maria.

"Marie Ruthven," she said, in gentle reproof, "I meant not to overhear, but I am glad it has chanced so. You should have told me this. Madam," and she turned to Lettice, "I believed it was of your own will that you and your husband abstained from court. Let me now say that I, a wife and mother, would never banish parents from the nuptials of their child. In the King's name and my own, I command both your presence at our solemnities."

Men can make queenships, but the sweetness of true womanhood none can give. Years after, when misery had darkened over the hapless Queen, Lettice remembered the words breathed by her now, in calm content — "*I, a wife, and a mother.*" Wretched wife! broken-hearted mother! humble Lettice Calderwood was happier than she.

The marriage was to be celebrated in the chapel at Whitehall. There were gathered all the court, gladly following where royalty delighted to honour; as if any honours could add to those which the illustrious bridegroom already wore — the nobility of genius! As Sir Anthony Vandyck stepped forward in his dignified maturity of fame, it would be hard to say which was most honoured in this friendship — for it was indeed such — the great artist or the king.

"What wait we for, my Lord Strafford?" said Charles, as his favourite Minister, Vandyck's chosen friend, advanced, by the Queen's signal, to delay the ceremony a little. Soon after, the courtly circle was joined by two strangers, the father and mother of the bride.

Patrick Ruthven had cast off the garb of the poor physician, and appeared as became his noble descent. At his side hung his long-unused sword, preserved by one faithful woman's care ever since the day when the two young brothers had fled to Harwich. In his bearing there seemed to have momentarily revived the ancient dignity of his race; and when he had knelt to kiss the King's offered hand, he arose, lifted his white head, and looked around with a mien well beseeming the last of the Ruthvens.

His wife was little noticed and little seen, and she scarcely wished otherwise. It was enough for her to behold her husband resuming his birthright — her daughter wedded in happiness and honour. Her loving, reverent eyes never turned from these two. Except once, when they rested on the countenance of King Charles, already shadowed with the cares of his troublous reign. She thought of the boyish prince who had passed her by in the audience-chamber at Whitehall; and her memory went back twenty years, dwelling thankfully at last in the resting-place which, as she deemed, her life had now found.

The marriage was duly celebrated; Sir Anthony bent graciously for the blessing of his wife's father; and the King, on his departure, smiled so cordially upon Patrick Ruthven, that the courtiers gathered round the poor physician, as though they would fain haste to press under the shadow of another Earl of Gowrie. But the old man's temporary firmness had passed from him; he looked wistfully round for his wife, his only strength.

"Let us go home," he said, wearily; and, so they went home from Whitehall to their peaceful abode at Chelsea.

Arrived there, Patrick laid aside his rich mantle and sword with an air of relief. "Ah, Lettice!" he said, as the long, cool shadows of the trees fell across the physician's garden, "dear wife, we are happier here!"

She might have dreamed loving dreams of his restoration to the honours of his house; but now she saw that that would never be. In him ambition had either never sprung up, or it had been long crushed by calamity. Besides the outward misfortunes of his lot, fate had implanted in him that easy, gentle nature, which had not the power to rise. Born an earl's son, he would die a poor physician.

Lettice was pondering over these things when a guest crossed the threshold. It was a friend of many years — the young Scottish lady who had contrived their marriage. She held high station now in the Queen's household, where, through her, Marie Ruthven had at first been brought. She yet visited occasionally the little house on Cheyne Walk. Thither, too, came at times her daughters, both peeresses by marriage, though often old Dr. Ruthven, forgetting himself, called them Grace and Mabel still.

"I have a welcome mission to-day," said the Countess; "not a formal one, it is true, but one that implies much. It is her Majesty's will that I should ask whether the Master of Ruthven — she knows enough of our Scottish usages to give him that title — whether the Master of Ruthven was pleased with his reception at court, and whether he would desire in future to be the King's good servant?"

"I am so now," answered Ruthven, simply; "God knows I never plotted aught against his Majesty or his father, King James."

The lady smiled half-loftily upon the poor old man, who knew so little of worldly, and especially of courtly ways. "You understand me not, worthy doctor. This message implies that you have only to desire it, and you will be graciously offered, not perhaps your confiscated honours, but a rank equivalent. The King has already planned a peerage wherein to revive your ancient name. What say you, Lettice, will you be Lady Ruthven of Ettrick?"

"*Lord* Ruthven of Ettrick!" the wife repeated, unconsciously altering a word. She went up to her husband, and her voice trembled as she said "Patrick, do you hear? The ancient glory may be restored, my beloved! I may live to see thee in great honour yet: shall it be so?"

"What?" he said. He had been dreamily watching the swallows skim over the river, and had not heard a syllable of what was passing.

Lettice repeated the tidings.

He shook his head restlessly: "Good wife, these dreams only weary me. What should I do as Lord Ruthven? Then I could not go out in the fields with my wallet, nor sleep at peace in the chimney-corner. No; I am happier as now."

The Countess became rather indignant. "Mistress Ruthven, urge him still; 'tis a mournful and a shameful thing that the last descendant of one of the noblest families in Scotland should waste his life in obscurity. Bid him think of his ancestors — of the honour of his name. He may yet be Earl of Gowrie."

Patrick Ruthven rose, and something of that dignity which so rarely appeared in him was visible now. "My Lady Countess, I am already by right Earl of Gowrie, heir to all which the poor title has brought to the Ruthven line — the heritage of blood. My father, the first Earl, perished on the scaffold; my brother John, the second, was slaughtered in his own house; my brother William, the third, died forgotten in exile; I am the last. Tell his Majesty I thank him, but I desire no title save that one which I still possess, though I never claim. What matter, since it will cease with me?" As he spoke, his eye caught the memorials of his two sons, and the old man's voice faltered. "Ten years ago I might not have answered thus — now, I have nothing more to say."

He rose from his seat at the window, and walked feebly across the room to the apartment set apart for his especial use.

There in a few minutes they saw him, his passing emotion having subsided, sitting in his old dreamy way buried among his books.

"Are all arguments lost upon him?" said the surprised Countess. "Even you, Lettice, have you for yourself no ambition — no pride?"

"None," she answered. "All I ever had was only for him — and for these."

She looked first at her husband, and then at the mementos of her lost children. Though she spoke sadly, there was great composure in her demeanour; insomuch that the court lady, already somewhat shaken by the first rude breath of the political storm then just beginning to rise, regarded her half-enviously and sighed. Ere departing, however, she tried once more to urge her friend to come to court.

"No," answered Lettice; "Patrick said right — he is happier here; for me, I stay with him always."

So saying, she went back to her husband.

Lettice Ruthven sat anxiously in her house at Chelsea. She looked considerably older, and, alas! her face wore not the placid content which best becomes old age. It is very sad to see cares creeping on when life's declining energy requires all cherishing. Youth can endure — sometimes can grow stronger — while tossed about on life's billows; but old age needs a quiet haven, where the chiefest happiness is rest.

Many cares had come upon the ancient couple at Cheyne Walk. The awful civil commotions which now shook England to its base had touched even them. Their pension had failed, and that they were in great necessity was plain from the changed appearance of the household. Its little luxuries of furniture were absent, and its bare chambers were swept and ordered by the feeble hand of the mistress alone.

When Dr. Ruthven entered, Lettice's own hands were preparing the evening meal. "Nay, wife," he said, restlessly, "come and sit by me and talk. Leave all else to Marjory."

"Marjory is gone," answered Mistress Ruthven, smiling. "Lettice will be henceforth your serving-woman."

She never wearied him with any domestic troubles; and he, so that he had his simple fare at the customary hour, and the house kept quiet for his evening study, rarely questioned more. He did not now.

But after a while Lettice began with a seemingly careless air, yet with evident anxiety —

"Patrick, you have not told me about your day's adventures. Have you found any patients in your wanderings?" For the poor physician had been obliged to wander, as a peripatetic herbalist, through London streets, in order to win his daily bread.

"Patients? Oh, yes! There was a poor lad at Charing trodden on by one of the Guard's horses — it took me two hours to make fomentations for him; and there was a beggar woman, with a child in convulsions; and a sick old gipsy near Battersea. I have expended all my herbs, and must spend two whole days in collecting more."

"But the money, dear husband," said Lettice, hesitatingly. "Did any patients give money? You know, alas! we must needs ask for payment now."

"I never asked — I forgot; and I could not *sell* my herbs to those poor souls."

"No — no," answered Lettice Ruthven's kind heart.

But she thought sorrowfully of the empty coffers, of the fast-coming poverty; not only poverty, but positive want. Against it there was no resource, for Patrick's unworldly ways made him helpless as a child. With a great pang, Lettice had induced him to try this life of a wandering physician; but day by day, when he came in, weary and dispirited, longing for his ancient country rambles, every unconscious complaint of his stung his wife to the heart. Gladly would she even have begged for him, but it was impossible; he would not have suffered it. And besides, humble as she herself was, Lettice never forgot that she was the wife of the Last of the Ruthvens.

"Husband," she said, compelling herself to speak to him on a subject she dreaded — "dear husband, you know we are very poor."

"Are we, Lettice?" he answered, absently.

"I am afraid, if the pension is not paid, our money will not last for many days. Suppose I were — just to ask about the pension, you know — to go again to Marie?"

"To *Lady Vandyck?*" And anger gave a momentary life

to the old man's dull eyes. "I thought I told you our Marie was to be henceforth dead. Call her Lady Vandyck only."

"I cannot, Patrick — I cannot! Though she has been ungrateful, and though she does, as it were, shut the door on her poor old mother, still she is our Marie; and she will be kind to us. I pray you, Patrick, let me go!"

"No!" he said. He, otherwise so feeble, was resolute on this one subject only. Therein was compressed his last lingering remnant of pride — the pride of a man and a father.

But in Lettice the strong yearnings of a mother's heart overcame all pride. She tried still to win her husband to consent.

"It is not that I may entreat of our daughter that bounty which we might well claim. No, Patrick; if you desire, I will ask of her nothing. But I long to see her. She is a widow now, and trouble may have changed her heart. She has a child — and not till then does one truly feel what it is to have had a mother. Do you remember how, when little Marie was born, I wept, thinking of my own mother, whom I never saw? Be sure that same Marie will now welcome me."

Ruthven made no answer to these gentle entreaties, but, after a while, relapsed into his usual quiet mood.

"I will try again to-morrow," thought Lettice, as she obeyed his signal, and came to sit beside him while he took his twilight doze. He often did so, holding one of her hands like a child.

But on the morrow he left early; and she, spending the day alone in the dull house, could not suppress her yearning to see her daughter. Some hope, too, she had that that daughter's tenderness might be reawakened. And if Lady Vandyck did offer shelter and help to her parents in their old age, from whom might they so well receive it?

Lettice arranged her household affairs, examined her remaining store; alas, it was brief work to count the coins! She had thought to walk to Blackfriars — where, in Vandyck's former house, still abode his young widow, left widowed in less than two years from the bridal — but her strength failed; so she took a boat, and was rowed up the Thames to her destination.

Strange was the aspect of London in those times: Westminster without a parliament; Whitehall without a king; the whole city divided against itself. Lettice took little heed of what was passing in the world outside; and as she glided along the half deserted river, she was bewildered to see, along the streets diverging from the Thames, crowds of excited Roundheads.

"Down with the King!" shouted the boatman from his place. "Hurrah for the victory of Marston Moor!"

And Lettice trembled; for she knew that with the King's fall must sink all her hopes of Patrick's spending his old age in peace and undisturbed by poverty. Landing at Blackfriars she took out her purse. It was one which, some time ago, had come filled with the bounty of the good Queen Henrietta Maria, and on it was worked a royal crown.

"Ho, ho — here are Cavaliers!" cried the man, snatching at it. "Fair madam, I take this in the name of the State." With a satirical grimace he poured the few coins left into his pouch, and threw the empty purse to the bottom of the river.

Lettice entered her daughter's house, knowing herself to be utterly penniless.

It was a wealthy, luxurious abode, for apparently the political convulsions of the time had not touched the peaceful follower of the arts. In its halls still hung many of Sir Anthony's works — even some royal portraits. But the one which most charmed Lettice was that of her own beautiful Marie — which picture remains to this day — a token of Vandyck's admiration for his young wife, and a memorial of the wondrous beauty possessed by the last daughter of the Ruthven line. Looking on its sweet features, the mother forgot the cruel neglect which now kept her waiting a full hour in the anteroom of her own child.

There passed by a nurse carrying a babe of some twelve months old. At the sight of it, the love which nature causes to revive so strongly towards the third generation, awoke in the aged mother's heart. As yet she had never thought much of her grandchild; but now there came a great longing for this new tie, which might bind up all those that were lost or broken. The nurse was surprised to be stopped by a little old woman, trembling and in tears, who begged to see the child.

"Give it to me — into my own arms: the mother would not forbid," she said, imploringly. And close to her breast Lettice pressed her daughter's child. "What is its name?" was her question, half ashamed, poor soul! that she had to ask it.

"Justina. It was given to her the day her father died," said the Dutch nurse, somewhat pettishly. "If poor Sir Anthony could see how things are now ——"

Further revelations were stopped by a message that Lady Vandyck was now visible. Lettice once more embraced her grandchild, and was ushered into her daughter's presence.

Marie was not alone: there lounged about the apartment a young man, who seemed a Puritan proselyte. His sombre dress was jauntily worn, and his demurely-worded speech ran "trippingly on the tongue." His close-cropped hair was daintily perfumed, and his embroidered frills bespoke the Roundhead far less than the Cavalier. But Lettice Ruthven saw nought of this: she only saw her daughter. She ran eagerly to meet the gracefully-extended hand of Lady Vandyck, who looked fair and stately in her youthful matronhood.

"Wilt thou not embrace me, Marie?" said the mother, half-entreatingly.

"Honour thy father and mother, that thy days," &c., &c., droned out the Puritan gentleman.

Marie stooped, and gave her mother one cold, brief kiss. A few formal inquiries she made, ever looking with a sort of timid doubt to her sanctimonious companion, whose approbation seemed to be the rule of all her actions.

The mother also regarded him with more than curiosity. "My child," she murmured, "I thought to see thee alone; but this young cavalier ——"

"Nay, good madam, give me not that unholy title," answered the stranger. "I have disowned the pomps and vanities of the world, together with a baronetage two hundred years old. You now behold in me plain John Pryse, the servant of the Lord and of the Parliament: and so, ladies, I will retire. Fairest Marie, a brief adieu."

He kissed the hand of the young widow with an air anything but Puritanical, and vanished.

The mother and daughter passed an hour alone. Marie talked gaily of herself and her household; and then, as the time wore on, she seemed to grow wearied and restless. Still Lettice sat and listened, and had not strength to tell what was in her heart. Had it been but to whisper in a loving ear —

4*

"Child, thy mother has need!" — but to this woman, so stately, so wrapped up in herself, it would be like asking charity. Yet it must be done. Tremblingly she began by telling the story of her stolen purse.

"Ah, then, you will need some few coins for your journey homeward," said Lady Vandyck. She summoned an attendant, and, with an air of careless ease, desired him to find and present to "that lady" a small purse of silver pieces.

For a moment Lettice's fingers drew back, the coins seemed to burn under her touch; but her motherly heart, finding excuses to the last, whispered that Marie meant kindly, and in manner only erred. So she took the purse. How could her daughter guess that it was the last resource of the aged parents against positive want?

Still — still the bitter truth remained untold. Marie seemed struggling between discomfort and a sense of duty, when there was heard without Sir John Pryse's heavy footstep and his loud whistle subdued into a psalm-tune. Lady Vandyck rose.

"Marie, dearest, let us have one instant more alone; I have somewhat to say to thee," cried the poor mother.

"Say on then quickly: Sir John might come."

"A word will explain all. It grieves me bitterly, my child, to speak of this; but these troubled times have brought care even upon your father and me. Our pension from the King has ceased."

"Well, mother, I regret it; but what of that? I can offer neither counsel nor influence. Since Sir Anthony's death, I have kept entirely aloof from the court, which will soon have ceased to be a court at all. And if I might advise, speak as little as you can about King Charles; and let the pension rest."

"You know not all, Marie." And even the careless daughter was startled to see the bitter expression on Lettice Ruthven's face. "You consider not that when the pension ceases your father and I must starve."

"Starve, my mother? What a disagreeable word! Pray do not use it."

"It is the truth."

Some conviction of this seemed forced upon Marie. She rose from her seat, and came beside her mother.

"You do not mean this: it cannot be that you and my father are in want. You know I would never suffer that."

The words were kind, though there was pride in the tone; but Lettice clung to the sweet, and perceived not the bitter. She clasped her daughter's hands and wept.

"I knew she would not forsake us — my only daughter — my darling! I said so when my husband forbade my coming."

"Did he, indeed? Well, he was always strange, and cared little about me," answered Lady Vandyck, indifferently. "But come, mother, we must plan for the future. Of course you both will trust to me for subsistence. The world shall never say that Marie Vandyck left her parents to starve," she continued, and her beautiful face had in it more of haughtiness than filial sympathy. "Perhaps, you might both come and live with me; but" (here she faintly coloured) "I will consult Sir John Pryse."

"Do not, I pray you. Why should a stranger come between parent and child? And — forgive me, Marie — but I cannot like that man."

Marie smiled half contemptuously.

"I grieve to differ with you; but 'that man' has, by his influence with the Parliament, preserved to me my whole possessions, where the widow of King Charles's favourite might well have lost all. Still more I grieve, seeing that in nine days Sir John Pryse will be my husband."

"Thy husband!" echoed Lettice, incredulously.

"It seems to have startled you, mother; yet, nevertheless, it is the fact. My first marriage was of her Majesty's will, my second is of my own. Nay, while you recover from this somewhat unflattering astonishment, I will go seek my betrothed." And with a proud step, Lady Vandyck quitted the room.

She re-entered ere long, leaning on her bridegroom's arm. The mother sat as she had left her, having neither looked up nor stirred. Lettice rose now, however, and scanned with thirsty eagerness the mien and countenance of the man who was to be her second son-in-law, and on whom her daughter's future peace must rest. Her glance fell, and she sighed.

"Sir John, I have explained all. Greet my mother Mistress Ruthven," said Lady Vandyck, in a tone as if she desired to throw the veil of her own dignity round the humble obscurity of her parent. And Sir John Pryse with a valorous condescension, kissed the little withered hand.

But Lettice felt that she stood there a stranger on her daughter's hearth — a pensioner on the charity of her daughter's lord. Yet still, though colder and colder sank her heart, she murmured, "It must and shall be borne, since, husband, it is for thee."

"My fair Marie has told me," began the young Roundhead, "that you, excellent madam, are in want of the good things of this world. Now, by my halidome — I mean by the ordination of Providence — for children to succour their parents is a virtuous and godly deed. Therefore, count on us, madam — count on us! Have I satisfied my charming bride?"

Marie smiled, and he smiled too, with marvellous self-content. And Lettice, her wan cheeks crimsoning, thought how bitter was an old age of dependence.

"Our plan, Mistress Ruthven, is this. Shall I explain it, Marie?" She acquiesced. "That you should abide with your daughter, or at least in her household. Such an easy life may best suit your years, and you can take care of your grandchild. Do you consent?"

"I know not. My husband loves quiet and freedom: he might not choose to dwell in this great house."

"Which he will never be required to enter. Madam, the offer was meant for yourself alone. John Pryse, the servant of the Parliament, could not venture to endanger his safety by harbouring a Royalist, a pensioner and follower of Charles Stuart."

Lettice was dumb with amazement.

"It is said," continued the bridegroom elect, "that Dr. Ruthven has long dealt in unholy charms and spells, which are blasphemous, and not to be allowed. Therefore, ere farther harm come to him, let him retire to some country village, where I will see that he shall not need."

Having delivered himself of all this generosity, Sir John Pryse lounged to the window, and gazed out listlessly on the Thames.

Lettice paused, breathed hard, and then rushed up to her daughter.

"Marie, say this is not true, or that you have not desired it!"

"What! Is there anything so marvellously wicked in this plan? I thought it for your good. You must have trouble enough with my old father, if what I have heard be true. Well, mother, why do you look so strange?"

"Go on!"

"I have little else to say," answered the lady, carelessly. "Sir John knows best; I abide by his decision. As to the danger he would run, he is certainly right in that; and you know I could not give up a husband for the sake of a father."

"Yet you would have me give up *my* husband — and for whom? Not for my daughter. Alas! I have no daughter," moaned the aged mother, struck with a grief worse than that of the childless. Suddenly she roused herself, and came up to Marie. With a fixed sorrow, far deeper than when she looked on her two dead sons, she gazed into the beautiful face of the living lost.

"Marie, you have been a wife, you are a mother; hear now a tale you never wholly heard before. There was once a girl who learned to love with her whole soul one who was brought up with her from a child. They were parted. For sixteen years, she never saw or heard of him, yet she loved on. She sought him out through all his miseries; Heaven helped her, and gave her power to save him. They were wedded — 'twas not like your gay bridal, for it was in a prison. He was somewhat changed — grown old before his time, perhaps a little feeble and wayward. But she kept the troth of her youth and her marriage-vow. She has 'loved, honoured, and cherished him' for nearly thirty years. She will do so until the end."

As Lettice spoke, the dignity of this great love, which had been the soul and centre of her life, seemed to encompass her round, so that even the haughty daughter quailed before it.

"I said nought to pain you, mother; I know you have been a good wife to my father. But for any other plan than this of Sir John's, it cannot be. Let us talk no more on the matter," she added, coldly, playing with her jewelled rings, and glancing less with affection than with the coquettish jealousy of wooing days to where her future lord was idly amusing himself.

Lettice pressed her hand upon her heart, where the last pulses of a mother's love — so long crushed, so keenly wounded — were ebbing into eternal silence. Then she said, speaking slowly and very calm, "Years ago, when I was past my youth, when I had thought to go childless to my grave, God sent me a daughter. We were poor then. I often toiled all day, and lay awake at night nursing my sickly babe. But I smiled, and said she would repay it all to my old age —"

"Mother, I cannot endure romance, but I wish to do all that I believe is my duty to do. As for affection — you know, parted as I was from you in my very childhood —"

"Ay, there is the grief again! I said to myself, 'What am I, simple Lettice Calderwood, to rear a daughter of the noble Ruthven line?' So I crushed my heart down, and gave up my darling. I wish now that I had then given her unto God, that she might be lying at peace in the grave, with her two brothers, rather than I should live to look on her as I look this day, and say — '*I have no child.*'"

Sir John approached. "Your mother seems excited, sweet Marie. Surely her mind wanders?" And he smiled. Marie exchanged glances with him, and smiled too. There was neither anger nor pain on her brow; smooth and polished it was as marble, an emblem of her own nature.

Lettice regarded her beautiful daughter once more with that long, long gaze which one gives, knowing it to be the last; and then she turned to the door. Lady Vandyck followed her with graceful courtesy.

"You will depart thus, mother? At least let me aid you in some way."

There was no answer.

"Do not let the world, or even Sir John, suppose there is bitterness between parent and child. Give me your hand, mother."

Lettice gave it. There was a light, cold pressure, and it fell. The lady went back to her lover; the mother passed out, walking slowly, like one whose eyes are bound. Once, twice, she paused and looked back, as if she heard herself called. But it was only the light echo of a laugh, the same as the little Marie had once laughed beside her mother's knee. Lettice closed her ears, and, half-staggering as she moved, passed out of the house to the river side.

Gliding, gliding down the quiet Thames, it seemed as if her whole life passed by her like a vision: the merry childhood; the long years of melancholy maidenhood, sad vigil to a brief day of joy; the time of full content, when the house rang with children's voices, and the future almost blotted out the dreary past; last of all, the still, but not sorrowful old age, when they two were left alone, husband and wife, waiting calmly for the next great change — the only one that, as it seemed, could come. It was a life which contained much sorrow, as all human lives must; but it had been full of love. No woman would look back upon it and grieve.

Lettice Ruthven entered her own house, and sat long in meditation. Then she rose up as usual, and made ready for her husband's return. He came up wearied out; but he poured into her lap, with an almost childish pride, a handful of silver, his fees as a wandering physician. When he was not observing her, Lettice took one of the coins, replaced it in lieu of that she had taken from her daughter's gift, and put Marie's purse aside, to be touched no more. Then she came to her husband, and her aged arms embraced his neck as she murmured, "Now I have no one but thee, no one but thee!"

PART IV.

"I have been young, and now am old, yet never saw I the righteous forsaken, nor his seed begging their bread."

This is the experience of good men, and of wise observers of life throughout all time.

Patrick Ruthven and his wife were not "forsaken." True, they were very poor — sometimes even positive need stood at their cottage-door, but it never entered. Some invisible hand always came between, and the spectre passed. They lived in great peace; for Patrick, growing feebler and more dreamy year by year, had few wants, few desires. To sit in the sun, or stroll about the meadows at Battersea, where their cottage was, now and then wandering on towards London — thus passed his quiet existence. Sometimes he gained a little money as a physician; at other times their dependence was on gifts brought by the Scottish lady who had contrived their marriage in the Tower, and whose husband had readily changed sides, and gone over to the Commonwealth. She, with her daughters, Grace and Mabel, sometimes visited them. But the old man and his wife were, as it were, childless: Marie, lady of Sir John Pryse, never crossed their threshold.

One day, when the January twilight was fast closing in, Lettice sat waiting for her husband. He had been absent since morning, having journeyed to London with a young boy whose life he had once saved in a fever, and who often-times faithfully guarded the old physician's failing steps. Lettice waited and waited, until it grew dark. The slow pulse of age is not easily stirred with the quick fears of youth. Yet she was growing alarmed, when she heard a well-known step, and Patrick Ruthven tottered in.

"My husband, what is this?" cried Lettice, for his aspect was wild and disordered. He trembled violently, and kept continually his hand before his eyes. At last he slowly removed it, and looked fearfully around.

"I think I shall not see it here; I have seen it all the way home — the axe, the block — even the snow on the hedge-side seemed dyed with blood! Oh, Lettice, Lettice, it was horrible!"

She, in her seclusion, knew nothing of what had happened on that fatal day, which she had spent calmly sitting in her quiet cottage — the 30th of January, 1649. She thought her husband's mind was wandering, as it well might, to the horrors of his youth and middle age. She tried to soothe him, but in vain. Some great shock had evidently overwhelmed the old man's feeble powers. As he sat in his arm-chair, shudder after shudder came over him. Often he clutched his wife's hand convulsively, or muttered broken exclamations. At last he said, speaking somewhat more connectedly, "I will tell thee all, Lettice. This day I went to London; the streets were crowded with people, thronging, as it seemed, to some great sight. I asked a soldier if it were so. He laughed, and said there was indeed at Whitehall a rare show — a royal show. I thought it was the King restored, so I said with gladness, 'God bless King Charles!' Then the soldier smote me down. Look, Lettice!"

He held up his bruised arm, and his wife turned pale.

"Nay, it is nothing; for the people rescued me soon, and one man cried, 'We shall have blood enough on our heads this day.' So the crowd bore me on with them till we came to Whitehall."

Lettice ever changed countenance at that word, which brought back the great crisis in her life, when she came to the palace to plead for her husband's freedom. She said anxiously, "And what didst thou see there, Patrick?"

"A black scaffold, an axe, a block — sights I knew well!" he answered, shuddering.

His wife came closer to him, but could not calm his rising agitation.

"Yes," he cried, "it was indeed a royal show — it was the murder of a king!"

Lettice cried out, "Have they done it then? Alas! for the good king — the gentle king! He it was who gave me back my husband — the noble Prince Charles."

Patrick continued, unheeding:

"He came forth, stepping from his own palace-window to the scaffold. When he appeared women shrieked, even men wept. For me, the strength of my youth seemed restored; I lifted my voice in the crowd — 'I am Patrick Ruthven! The King's father sent my father to the block, slew my two brothers, imprisoned me for seventeen years; yet would I not take life for life. God defend King Charles!' But the people crushed round, and silenced me. There was an awful hush; then I saw the axe shining — saw it fall."

The old man gasped, shivered, and was seized with a convulsion. All night he raved of things long past, of the scenes of blood which had marked his childhood, of those he had witnessed in the Tower. Towards morning these paroxysms ceased, and with ebbing strength there came over him a great calm. He tried to rise, and walked, with Lettice's help, to their fireside. But he staggered as he moved, and sinking in his arm-chair, said piteously, "I am so weary — so weary!" then fell into a quiet slumber.

While he slept, there entered the Scottish countess. She was attired in black, her countenance full of grief and horror. She came hastily to say she was going abroad, to join her unhappy mistress. Her heart seemed bursting with its load of indignant sorrow.

"Look you," cried she, "I never loved the Stuart line: I believe that, as a king, the King erred; but I would have given my right hand to save the life of Charles Stuart. And I wish that I may yet see this vile England flow with blood, to atone for his which rests upon it this day! But, Lettice, you are calm — these horrors touch not you!"

And then mournfully Lettice told of what had befallen her husband.

The lady stepped quickly and noiselessly to look at Dr. Ruthven. He still slept, but over his face had come a great change. The temples had fallen in, there were dark lines round the eyes; yet over all was a sweetness and peace like that of childhood. Lettice almost thought she saw in him the image of the boy Patrick, her playfellow by the Cam. She said so to her friend, who answered nothing, but stood steadfastly gazing a long time. Then she took Lettice's hand, and looked at her solemnly, even with tears.

"I shall come back here to-morrow, Lettice; my journey can be deferred a day," she muttered, and departed.

Lettice Ruthven went to her husband's side, and watched him until he awoke. It was with a quiet smile. "What think you, dear wife? I have been dreaming of the old time at Cambridge. How long is that ago?" She counted, and told him, more than fifty years. "It seems like a day. How happy we were, Lettice — you, and William, and I! How we used to sit by the river-side on summer nights, and play by moonlight among the laurels! I think, when I gain strength enough, we will go and see the old place once more."

So he talked at intervals, all day referring to incidents which had vanished even from Lettice's memory. For thirty years he had not spoken of these things; and Lettice, while she listened, felt a vague awe stealing over her. Something she remembered to have heard, that at life's close the mind often recurs vividly to childhood, while all the intermediate time grows dim. Could it be so now?

At night Patrick did not seem inclined for rest. He said he would rather stay in his arm-chair by the fireside. There, sometimes talking, sometimes falling into slumber, the old man lay, his wife watching over him continually. Gradually the truth dawned upon her — that on the path they had long trodden together *his* step would be the soonest to fail. To the eternal land, now so near unto both, he would be the first to depart.

"It is well!" she murmured, thinking not of herself, but only of his helplessness — as a mother thinks of a child whom she would fain place in a safe home rather than leave in the bitter world alone. "All is best thus. It is but for a little while." And she ceased not to comfort herself with these words — "A little while — a little while!"

When Patrick woke his mind had begun to wander. He fancied himself in the old house at Cambridge; he talked to his aged wife as if she were the girl Lettice, whom he had loved. More especially, he seemed to live over again the night when he was taken prisoner.

"I will hide here, but I will not see Lettice — William's Lettice! I could not take away Lettice and break poor William's heart. If I suffer, no one shall know. Hark, how the laurels are shaking! We must keep close. I clasp thee, love — I clasp thee! Why should I fear?"

Thus he continued to talk, but gradually more incoherently, until, just before dawn, he again slept. It was a winter's morning, pale but clear. There was something heavenly in the whiteness of the snow; Lettice, looking at it, thought of the shining robes — white "such as no fuller on earth can whiten them" — with which those who have gone through much tribulation shall be clothed upon one day. That day seemed near — very near, now.

She heard her husband call her. He had awakened once more, and in his right mind.

"Is it morning?" he asked, faintly. "I feel so strangely weak to-day. Lettice, take care of me."

She came to him, and laid his head on her breast.

Patrick looked up, and smiled. "Dear wife, my comforter and sustainer! I have been happy all my life — I am happy now."

He closed his eyes, and his features sank into an expression of perfect rest. Once or twice he murmured his wife's name, those of his two boys, and another — unuttered for years — the name of *Marie*. Then, and not till then, the cruelly-forsaken mother wept.

The old man's breathing grew fainter — the solemn hour was nigh. He said, softly, "Lettice, pray!" She knelt beside him, still holding his hands, and prayed. When she arose, his soul was just departing. He whispered, smiling, "Come soon!" And Lettice answered, "Yes, love — yes!" It was all the farewell needed for a parting so peaceful and so brief.

Thus Patrick Ruthven died.

"You will come abroad with me, my poor Lettice," said the Scottish lady, affectionately. But Lettice refused, saying it was not worth while changing her way of life for such a little time.

"Alas, a mournful life has yours been! It is always the good who suffer!" bitterly said the lady. "How strange appear the inequalities of this world!"

Lettice Ruthven lifted her aged face, solemn yet serene! "Not so! I loved, I have spent my whole life for him I loved; I have been very happy, and I thank God for all." These were the only words that she would say.

Patrick Ruthven and his wife have long been forgotten; even their very burial-place is unknown. But I think there lives not one true heart that, in pondering over their history, would not say, "These two were not unhappy, for they feared God, and loved one another."

THE ITALIAN'S DAUGHTER.

A TRUE STORY OF THE ENGLISH POOR.

In one of the midland counties of England there is a district, the name of which we shall not give, but merely allude to its characteristics. It has risen up within the last century, until, from a few clusters of poor cottages, the seat of a manufacture of trifling importance, it has become one of the wealthiest, most populous, and most intelligent communities within the three kingdoms. The five or six small hamlets have grown into towns, whose boundaries meeting, have all merged into one mass of habitations; so that, but for the diversity of name which each portion still preserves, it might be considered as one large city of manufactures, such as Manchester or Birmingham. But like most newly-risen places, this region still presents an anomalous mixture of town and country; for instance, between two colonies where the manufacture is carried on, a few green meadows yet unbuilt upon, will intervene; and the tall chimney of "the works" sometimes casts its smoke upon a puny corn-field or a blackberry hedge. Alternately the eye views green wooded undulations and hills covered with red brick houses, as if town and country were struggling together for the mastery. But as soon as the habitations are left behind, the ruralities of the place triumph, and the naturally beautiful face of the country is seen in all its luxuriousness.

On a little hill up which the road winds, just without the town, was — perhaps is — a row of cottages inhabited by working people. But with one only have we to do. Its inmates sat or lolled outside the door, enjoying the cool summer evening. They were a mother and some half-dozen children, of all sizes and ages. Mrs. Sutton was a comfortable-looking, middle-aged woman, clad with tolerable neatness. Whether she had ever been pretty, was a matter entirely traditional: probably she had, for the neighbourhood to which she belonged is remarkable for the good looks of its damsels; but the wear and tear of eight-and-thirty years had entirely obliterated Mrs. Sutton's beauty, if she ever had any. She stood tossing her youngest hope, a baby of three months old, and watching the two others playing at marbles. They were sturdy boys, save that their faces had the paleness which was the result of their occupation; a circumstance which never fails to strike a visitant to this region, where the workpeople all acquire the same pallid hue. Yet it is not unhealthy; and it gives the young girls a delicate complexion, which, though fleeting, is still very attractive while it lasts. Mrs. Sutton's little maidens were an evidence of this fact: two fairer blossoms never grew up in a poor man's home than did the twins, Edna and Keziah.

And here — to account for such extraordinary appellations — we must premise that Scripture names of the most out-of-the-way character are at a premium in the neighbourhood of which we write — the boys being all Enochs, Calebs, or Obadiahs; the girls all Miriams, Jemimas, or Naomis, with a sprinkling of such ultra-romantic cognomens as Thyrza, Zillah, or Rosanna. One cannot but observe how these things mark the character of the early inhabitants of a region which was once the stronghold of Wesley and Whitfield; how, whether or no the descendants of these saintly-named children have kept up their progenitors' Christian zeal, they have certainly kept up their Christian names.

But we are wandering from Mrs. Sutton. She, good soul, was wandering too, at least her eyes were, for she was watching up the hill a couple who seemed both weary and waysore; — a young woman, and a man who might have been any age from twenty to forty, for he had the hard sallow features which never show the progress of time. Still less would years be marked on his low and ungainly figure, which was stunted and slightly deformed — a strong contrast to the tall and upright form of his companion. This ill-matched pair came near Mrs. Sutton's door, and then the man, after whispering to his fellow-traveller, addressed the good dame in broken English, which she could not understand. She looked inquiringly at the woman.

"My husband"— Mrs. Sutton could not help a slight start,

and glance of surprise at the man, as the young creature said this — "my husband means that we are very tired, and would be glad of a lodging for the night, if you can give us one, or direct us elsewhere. We can pay you," she added, with a half smile, seeing the doubtful expression of Mrs. Sutton's face. But to do the latter justice, we must say that it was caused as much by her surprise at hearing the young wife speak in the good vernacular tongue, mingled with a natural feminine curiosity to know the reason that any Englishwoman could marry such a man.

Perhaps this latter quality, added to her good-nature, made her assent to their request.

"You can sit down and rest," she said, "and I'll get you some supper; but I can't promise more till my 'master' comes home" — *master* being the S——shire equivalent for husband; and, alas! sometimes the title is only too true. But in this case it was a mere form of speech, as every one knew that Mrs. Sutton was both master and mistress herself in her own house.

So the two wanderers sat down, and soon the cottage-hearth was blazing with a friendly brightness which is at the will of the poorest labourer in this plentiful land of coal. Oh, there are no such fires out of S——shire! The foreigner bent over his supper in hungry taciturnity, occasionally darting glances from his large, bright, black eyes, that seemed the more piercing from the bushy eyebrows under which they gleamed, and, in conjunction with the long, matted hair and the yellow skin, made Mrs. Sutton feel rather uncomfortable. She hated foreigners; but her motherly and womanly sympathy was excited by the weary and sickly look of the young wife, who had all an Englishwoman's claims to compassion; and Mrs. Sutton inly resolved that, whatever her "master" said, these strange wayfarers should remain for a night's shelter under her roof.

They did remain, and before noon on the following day, Pietro Ponti — that was his name, he said — had so ingratiated himself with the children, as to win a few kindly opinions from the mother herself; while his gentle wife was liked so much, that Mrs. Sutton almost felt it a relief when, after paying for their lodging, they requested to occupy it for another day or so.

"She is such a mild, soft-spoken young creature," was Mrs. Sutton's confidential observation to her husband John, after the first day passed with their inmates — "she seems almost a lady. I wonder what on earth could have made her marry that ugly little fellow!"

And probably the good dame's curiosity would have led her on to direct questionings instead of vague wonderment, had she not been withheld by a certain reserve and refinement which marked the young woman's deportment, and caused the mechanic's wife to treat her with unconscious deference. Yet she was not proud, for she always helped Mrs. Sutton in her domestic duties without any reluctance or awkwardness.

At last Pietro spoke of proceeding onwards; and then the anxious looks of his wife loosened Mrs. Sutton's tongue. She boldly asked whither they intended going.

"I — I hardly know," said the wife, timidly. Ponti, in his broken English, explained that he was an Italian, who gained his living by catching bullfinches and larks, and teaching them to sing, in the hope of meeting purchasers.

"A pretty way of making a fortune!" thought Mrs. Sutton; and then she said, "Well, master, if such is your trade, you may as well follow it here as anywhere: you will find plenty of birds in the fields hereabouts: and as your wife seems comfortable, why, suppose you were to stay with us a little longer?"

This proposal caused a consultation between the husband and wife, if a consultation it could be called, where Pietro had all the talk to himself, and his helpmate meekly acquiesced. It ended in an assent to the offer, and the Italian and his wife were fairly established in the Sutton family.

"I am really glad you are not going, Mrs. Ponti," was the hearty exclamation of the kindly hostess to her young friend the first time they happened to be alone. "I wonder your husband could think of dragging you up and down the country."

"He never thought about it, I believe," was the deprecating reply. "But" added the wife, while her cheek flushed and her head drooped, "I am glad to stay here — for the present. I would not like going among strangers now."

"Ah, no, no, poor girl!" quickly answered Mrs. Sutton; "but have you no mother to be with you?" She repented of her words ere they were well uttered; for the girl burst into a fit of weeping so violent, that all the consolatory endearments that women of all classes instinctively use to one another in time of affliction were employed by Mrs. Sutton in vain. At last the wife of the Italian grew calmer, and said without tears, though in accent of the deepest sorrow, "I have no relatives, no friends in the wide world, except my husband."

"Poor thing — poor thing! But you know, my dear, a good husband is something, and he seems very fond of you." Mrs. Sutton tried hard to say this, as if she really believed the fact.

"Yes — yes, Pietro is very kind," answered the young woman, faintly smiling. "I thought so, or I would not have married him. Shall I tell you how it was?"

Now this was the climax of all Mrs. Sutton's wishes; but she had self-denial enough to say, "Not if it troubles you, Mrs. Ponti."

"I wish you would call me Anne," said the girl, taking her hand: "you are the first woman who has seemed to love me since my mother died." And here she began to weep afresh, but soon recovered herself so as to tell her story: how that she came from York; that she was an only child, and fatherless, and had been left utterly friendless and helpless on her mother's death.

"It was during her illness," Anne continued, "that Pietro Ponti, who lived in the same house, showed us much kindness. He was so much older than I, he treated me as a father would a child, and helped me out of all my troubles. When I was quite broken-hearted, I heard that he was going away on his usual rounds, and I went to him to ask his advice as to how I could support myself. My poor mother had been a dressmaker; but I was too young to take her business, for I was only seventeen. I felt that I must starve or beg, for I had no money. Then Pietro talked to me quietly and seriously, and told me that there was but one way in which he could maintain me, and save me from poverty — if I would marry him. He said this doubtingly, almost afraid that I would be angry; but I was not, for I saw tears in his eyes when he spoke of my youth and beauty being thrown away on a poor deformed creature like himself. I knew it was all his kindness: and I told him how grateful I was, and that, if he would let me think of it for a week, I would see if I could not make up my mind to

5*

be his wife. Pietro asked me if I had any other lover — any one I preferred to him? But I said no; there was no one who seemed to me so good and kind as he. And so, at the end of the week, I married him; and he has ever been a good husband to me. I fear I hardly love him as he deserves; but indeed I try; and I do obey him in all things."

To this long story Mrs. Sutton had listened without a word. As Anne ended, the good woman pressed her hand, bade "God bless her!" in rather a husky voice, and muttering a hope that she would stay long with them, and be very happy, went about her household business. But all that day Mrs. Sutton's voice — at times raised sharply enough — sounded softer than usual; and when Pietro Pouti came into supper, the best portion of the meal, and the warmest corner of the fireplace, were kindly, though abruptly, bestowed on the little deformed Italian.

Two or three months passed, and Ponti and his wife became like members of the family. The birdcatcher pursued his trade successfully, being taken to the woodland haunts for miles round by the younger Suttons, with whom he was an especial favourite. They Anglicised his name into Peter, which appellation was soon given him by the whole family. And ten times better than even they liked Peter did they all love the pretty Anne, who seemed so young that she was almost a playmate for the children. But a continual pensiveness darkened her face, though not detracting from its mild beauty. Her husband was always kind, yet still there was a perpetual yearning — a restless void in the girl's heart. How could it be otherwise? She never uttered a word of complaint, or even of sadness; but often, when she sat preparing for the little being that was soon to give her new ties of love, Anne would let the work fall from her hands, while her dark-blue eyes, so dreamy in their depths, were fixed on vacancy, as if looking wistfully into the dim future. Good, plain Mrs. Sutton, could not understand these fancies, and sometimes wished that Anne would think less and talk more — it would be much better for her.

Birth and death came hand in hand together. The babe lived — the mother died! Kind-hearted Mrs. Sutton closed the eyes of the poor young creature who had so twined round her honest heart. She had tended her with a mother's care until the last; when she saw how peaceful and beautiful the dead face looked, the good woman dried her tears.

"Poor thing! — poor thing! She has nothing to trouble her now! Perhaps it is as well — God knows best!"

And then Mrs. Sutton heard the wail of the little motherless babe, and for a time forgot the dead in her care over the living.

"Charley is six months old now," she said to her husband. "He is strong and healthy; I shall turn him away, and take this poor little creature, who wants the most."

So she nursed the babe, and became a mother to it in the stead of her who had now no need of the comfort of a child. Many a time, when the little one grew older, and began to laugh and crow in her arms, Mrs. Sutton would think of its dead mother; how Anne's heart would have leaped to feel the bliss of maternal love — the tiny, twining fingers — the kiss of the little soft lips. But then she would remember that a child's love is not all-sufficient, and that, perhaps, it was well for poor Anne that she lived no longer.

Whether the widower grieved much for the loss of his sweet young wife it was impossible to tell. The Italian was always of a reserved disposition; and when the first shock was over, he seemed to return to his old habits much as if nothing had happened. His taciturnity increased; and sometimes, after spending the day out in the fields, he came home, silently took his place in his own warm corner, and uttered not a syllable until it was time to go to rest. He rarely noticed his child, except that when Mrs. Sutton began to talk to him about the name of the babe, hinting that, as a matter of course, the little one should be christened Anne, Pietro shrank from her with an expression of acute pain, and at once said, "No: — that the child should be called Ginevra."

"Jenny what?" cried Mrs. Sutton, aghast at this foreign appellation.

"Ginevra!" said the Italian, lingering on the melodious syllables as if it were a name long unuttered, but most dear, and saying it over and over again, coupled with the tender and musical diminutives of his own language. All this was incomprehensible to the worthy woman, and she tried again to protest against "so unchristian and heathenish a name." But the only answer she gained was the distinct repetition of the name, in a tone so firm that she saw it was useless to dispute the father's will. As a contest of words between herself and the foreigner would have been highly unprofitable to both, Mrs. Sutton wisely yielded her point, probably for the first time in her life. So the babe was christened Ginevra; but Mrs. Sutton, determined to make the baptismal name void, gave to her nursling the pet diminutive of Jenny; and Jenny she was called evermore by the household.

The child grew up as a younger sister in the family: no one seemed to look upon her in any other light. She learned to call her nurse "mother," and John Sutton "father;" while her own father was "Peter," as he was called by the rest of the children. Nor did the Italian seem to care for the abolition of these parental ties; he treated his own daughter just as he did the little Suttons, with neither more nor less regard than he had ever shown to them. Only he always called her Ginevra; sometimes adding to it sweet diminutives, but these seemed less meant for the child than recollections awakened by the name she bore.

In truth, as the little girl grew older, no one could have guessed her Italian descent. She was in all respects an English child, with her soft blue eyes and brown hair, like her mother's – her true mother — now so utterly forgotten, that her very existence was unknown to the child whose life had been her death. Once or twice, smitten in conscience, Mrs. Sutton tried to explain the truth to Jenny; but the mystery was too great for the little girl's mind. And besides, Mrs. Sutton loved her nursling so much, it was a pain to remember she was not her own child — so at last she let the matter rest.

Time passed on; Jenny became of an age to go to school and to school she was accordingly sent, with her foster-brother Charley — Pietro Ponti never interfering in the matter at all. Indeed, from the child's birth, he had seemed to give her up entirely to the Suttons. She was clothed and fed by the honest labourer with his own children; and not a murmur did worthy John Sutton and his equally worthy helpmate utter with regard to the little one thus quartered on them, and dependent on their bounty. In everything she was to them as their own. Oh, there are noble hearts in the dwellings of the English poor! and good deeds, of which the greatest philanthropist might be proud, are often concealed under thatched roofs, and highways, and hedges, unknown and unchronicled, except by the All-seeing.

When Jenny was ten years old, her father died. They found him one morning lying dead in his bed, in the little room where he slept, and where he taught his birds; rising up at daybreak, whistling and talking to them in his own tongue. The little birds were now warbling joyously, carolling in the sunshine over the pillow of the dead man. Poor Pietro! in life they had been his only companions, and they were the only witnesses of his death. The same kind hands which had laid his wife in her grave now laid her husband beside her; but there was little mourning for him. He had come a stranger, and remained a stranger to the last. For some time Pietro's trade had not prospered, and he had owed his very subsistence to the charity of those whose inmate he had been so long. Now, but for John Sutton, the Italian might have found a parish grave.

The only treasures left by Pietro Ponti were his birds, a silver crucifix, and a little Italian story-book, in which was written a name — the name he had given his daughter — Ginevra. It might have been his mother's, a sister's, perhaps some early memory still dearer; for the human heart is the same all over the world. But nothing more was ever known of the father of Ginevra Ponti. After a time, Mrs. Sutton explained to her adopted child as much of her history as she knew herself, and then, clasping Jenny in her arms, told her that she need think of it no more, for that she was henceforth her own daughter.

Two years or more passed away; the sons and daughters of Mrs. Sutton grew up: one girl married; two boys went away — another turned out ill, and gave many a gnawing care to his parents. It was a hard time for trade, and anxieties came heavily upon John Sutton, yet he never complained of the additional burden which he had in his adopted child: the idea never crossed his mind, nor his wife's either. They seemed to think that Jenny was always to live with them; to send her away would be like parting with their own. That any one should claim her was equally improbable; but strange things happen sometimes.

One day a visitor, who appeared not exactly a lady, though she was very well dressed, came to inquire for Mrs. Sutton.

"I wanted to speak to you," she said abruptly. "My name is Dalton. — Miss Dalton." Mrs. Sutton started. "You seem to know the name!"

"I have heard it before," answered Mrs. Sutton, briefly and rather grimly, being struck with a presentiment which was either pleasure or dread — she knew not which.

"I don't belong to these parts," continued Miss Dalton, in a tone that, if not exactly refined, sounded honest and straightforward; "but in crossing that churchyard, I saw a stone with the name of Anne Meredith Ponti. Now, I have been long looking for my brother's child, of whom I only know that her name was Anne Meredith Dalton, and that she married a wandering Italian called Ponti. The sexton sent me to you for information."

Though incensed at the imperative tone of her visitor, Mrs. Sutton honestly related all she knew.

"It must have been my niece," said Miss Dalton, musingly. Mrs. Sutton began to speak of poor Anne — what she was like in person; but the latter stopped her quickly — "You need not describe her, as I never saw her; but let me look at the child."

Jenny came, was much admired, and at last acknowledged in favour of her mouth and chin, which were, the lady avouched, exactly those of a Dalton. She at once declared her intention of taking away her niece, to educate and adopt.

Mrs. Sutton was perfectly overwhelmed! To part with Jenny, her darling Jenny, was a thing dreadful even to imagine. She burst into tears, snatched the child to her bosom, and ran away with her out of the house.

But with calm reflection came a dread of the injury she might be doing to Jenny's interests in thus keeping her to share the poverty which was coming darkly on, when she might be made a lady of by one to whom she was bound by ties of kindred. The simple-hearted but upright woman thought of all this, until she was well-nigh bewildered; and then she had to convince her husband, too. But Mary Sutton was a woman who, through prejudice and ignorance, possessed that rare faculty of seeing *the right*, and of acting up to what she saw. The end was, that within a week the adopted parents of the little Jenny consented to Miss Dalton's proposition.

"If she should come to any harm," cried the poor woman, folding her darling to her heart in the agony of a parting which Jenny could hardly comprehend — "if you do not teach her what is right, and be kind to her, I shall never forgive myself."

Miss Dalton promised, with an earnestness and sincerity which was proved by her moistened eyes and softened voice, that she would try to be as good a mother to the orphan as the excellent woman who had nurtured Jenny for so many years. Then she took the child away; and Jenny's sweet face was seen no more among those of her adopted brothers and sisters. From the far distant home to which she was taken came her childish letters, every line of which was wept over, though with some self-reproach, since Jenny said she was "so happy!" But year by year they grew less frequent; and at last altogether ceased. A neighbour once passing through the town, tried to get a sight of her, but failed; and though the circumstance brought a few tears to Mrs. Sutton's eyes, and a pain to her heart, at the thought of her darling having forgotten her, still the regret soon passed away. The poor have no time for much sentiment, and Mrs. Sutton was engrossed by her own thickly-gathering cares.

It is all very well for political economists and theoretical philanthropists to talk about the wisdom of laying up for old age, and providing against the evil day; but for a labouring man, whose weekly earnings only suffice to provide weekly food for the many little mouths that must be filled, the matter is extremely difficult. Many and many an honest man, who has brought up a large family, which has not requited his care, is thrown upon parish charity in his old age. It was not quite so bad as this with John Sutton; but still, when all their young nestlings were fledged, and had gone out into the wide world — some for good, and some for evil — the parents were left, aged, solitary, and poor.

"Ah, if Keziah had but stayed!" lamented the poor old mother, when the prettiest of the twins stole away one fine morning, and secretly married a worthless young man, leaving her parents deprived of the few comforts which her earnings, as the last of the flock, had brought them.

"Children always turn out so," angrily said John Sutton. "And we that were fools enough to bring up another body's child, too; much good *she* has been, either."

"Don't say that, John," answered Mrs. Sutton, and her voice was gentler than it had once been: trouble is a great softener sometimes. "I will never believe it was poor Jenny's fault; and anyhow, we did what was right, and that ought to be a comfort to us."

It was years since the name of the Italian's daughter had been mentioned by the Suttons. The wounded feelings of the old man had brought up the subject now, and his wife could not drive it from her mind. Her own daughter's unkindness made her think of the little gentle creature whom she had loved so much, and who had ever been willing and dutiful, far more so than her own wild troop of children. As the old woman knelt before her hearth, kneading the dough for the one loaf which was sufficient now for their weekly need, her thoughts went back twenty years, wandering, by a natural train of ideas, to the pile of bread she had used to bake when the cottage was filled with merry children, now scattered far and wide. In fancy, she saw little Jenny standing by her side, burying her round, rosy arms in the dough, as she was so fond of doing — and the good woman stopped to wipe her eyes, which these old memories made dim.

"Poor Jenny, if she could but come back, and be as she used to be. But that's quite impossible," thought Mrs. Sutton with a heavy sigh.

Life is more full of strange coincidences than we are aware. How often, on meeting unexpectedly some dear, long-lost friend, do we remember that our thoughts had, only the day before, with a curious wilfulness, persisted in bringing up the very face we were so soon to see, and we laugh, and say, "What an odd chance it was!" As if there were such a thing as chance in this world!

Little did Mrs. Sutton think, as she got the tea ready, that when she and her good man went to rest that night it would be with the happy knowledge that the dear lost Jenny was once more sleeping under their roof. But so it was.

While they sat at their homely meal the latch was lifted, a young girl's face appeared, and a sweet voice said, "May I come in, *mother?*"

"*Mother!*" — Who could it be? Alas, not the erring Keziah; nor yet the other twin, Edna — her home was beyond the Atlantic. It was the child of their adoption, the long lost Jenny.

What a tea-drinking that was! The old couple forgot all their cares in the delight of welcoming her. They were never weary of looking at and admiring Jenny, now grown a tall and graceful woman, like what her mother had been. But the sadness that had darkened the face of poor Anne was not found in her daughter's.

After the first delight was passed, Mrs. Sutton said mournfully, "But we shall not have you long, Jenny: you are a rich lady now, I suppose?"

Jenny put her arm round the neck of her old nurse, and whispered, merrily, "Dear mother, I am not a lady; and I am as poor as Job: and I will never go away from you again, if you will let me stay."

And then she told at length, what we must relate in a few words, how her aunt, who was a prosperous dressmaker in a large city, as Jenny grew a woman, had made her cease all communication with the Suttons. They were "not respectable enough." It was only the accident of the neighbour's inquiring for her that brought to Jenny any news of them or their troubles.

"Then," said the young girl, deeply blushing, "I thought how wicked and ungrateful I must seem to you; and I asked my aunt to let me come and see you, but she refused. I could not rest; I was very miserable. But she fell ill, and I thought it would be wrong to leave her — so I tended her six months, until she died."

"And what became of the business?" asked Mrs. Sutton, who had not lost her prudence, especially for those she loved. "She promised me to provide for you, Jenny. How comes it you're 'as poor as Job?'"

Jenny hung her head. "She told me I should have all she had — if — if I would never come near you again. So" — added the girl simply, clinging fondly to her adopted parents — "she left her money and the business to some one else, and I have got to earn my living. Never mind — I am a capital dressmaker. I'll make a fortune, now I am come back to you."

"And how did you come — all alone, poor child?"

"I walked almost all the way, for I had hardly any money. Oh, mother, don't cry — I am so happy! You shall never want a child, nor I a mother, any more!" Nor did they — one or other of them. Jenny worked skilfully at the dressmaking; and though she never "made a fortune," she kept the aged pair in plenty till they died. It was none of their own children, but the adopted one, who closed their eyes.

And, as afterwards it came to pass that Jenny, like many another of the good women — nay, the best women of this world — never married, she, in her turn, adopted a desolate baby — Keziah's orphan child. Thus the blessing of a good deed came down even to the third generation.

THE TWO HOMES.

A STORY FOR WIVES.

Our story begins — as most other stories terminate — with a wedding. Mr. Stratford, the rich banker, gave away at the marriage altar on the same day, his only daughter and his niece. The fortunate bridegroom who won the former was Sir Francis Lester, a baronet of ancient and honourable family. The husband of the latter was of lower standing in society — plain Henry Wolferstan, Esq., a gentleman whose worldly wealth consisted in that often visionary income, a "small independence," added to an office under Government which yielded a few hundreds per annum. These were the two who carried away in triumph the beautiful heiress and the graceful but portionless niece of Mr. Stratford.

With the usual April tears, the two young brides departed. A carriage-and-four conveyed Sir Francis and Lady Lester to the abode of a noble relative; while the humbler railway whirled Henry and Eunice Wolferstan to the quiet country-house where a new father and sisters awaited the orphan. And thus passed the honeymoon of both cousins, different, and yet the same; for in the lordly domain and in the comfortable dwelling of an English squire, was alike the sunshine of first, young, happy love.

In a few weeks the two couples came home. How sweet the word sounded, "our home!" What a sunny vista of coming years did it open to the view, of joys to be shared together, and cares divided — that seem, when thus lightened, no burden at all. Sir Francis Lester forgot his dignity in his happiness as he lifted his young wife from her downy-cushioned equipage, and led her through a lane of smiling, bowing, white-ribboned domestics, up the noble staircase of his splendid house in —— Square. Hand in hand the young pair wandered through the magnificent rooms, in which taste refined the luxuries of wealth. Isabel was never weary of admiring, and her husband only looked in her eyes for his delight and reward. At last, sated with pleasure, Lady Lester threw herself on a sofa. "I can do no more to-day; I am quite wearied."

"Wearied of home — or of me?" said Sir Francis, smiling.

"No, no," answered the bride, looking proudly and fondly at her husband; "only wearied with being so happy."

"I hope you may always have that excuse, dearest. But now we must not give way to laziness: my mother is coming to-night, you know; and I want my Isabel to be brilliant and beautiful — more than usual, if possible."

"Indeed I do not care: all the mothers in the world would not induce me to rise and have the fatigue of dressing and dining in state to-night."

Sir Francis looked regretful; but he had been married too short a time to do more than look. "As you will, Isabel," he said; "but I wished ——"

There was something in his tone that made the wife look up. She saw the expression and repented. "If you wished — nay, I will do anything you wish, now and always," whispered her beautiful lips in his ear, and the shadow was gone from between the two — swept away by the touch of love.

Half a mile from the abode of Sir Francis Lester was the home of Mr. and Mrs. Wolferstan. It was one of those pleasant houses that a generation now past used to erect in the suburbs of London. White staring terraces and formal squares have risen up around, but the old houses still remain here and there, with their barrier of trees, or low privet hedges, shutting out the dusty road; their little gardens and verandahs covered with ivy, or woodbine, or thick-leaved vines. To one of these pretty dwellings Henry Wolferstan brought home his bride.

It was an evening in September, chilly enough to make a fire welcome, when Henry and Eunice sat for the first time by their own hearth together. The ruddy firelight gleamed on the young wife's face as she presided at the tea-table; while her husband, resting at his ease in an arm-chair, watched with his affectionate eyes every movement of the delicate little hand that flitted about in matronly dignity. How happy they were! After all the trials of a love whose course had been often ruffled by worldly cares and hindrances, to find themselves at last in a still haven — a happy, wedded home! Eunice looked round the cheerful room, hung with well-chosen prints, silent, beautiful companions, which they both loved so much; on either side book-shelves and an open pianoforte — all seemed to speak of future comfort and happiness. And then she saw beside her the face that had been for years the sunshine of her life, and knew that he was her husband; that they would never be parted more; that the love between them would be as an ever-living fountain, daily springing up anew to freshen and brighten their united life. All this came upon the full heart of the young wife, and she fairly burst into tears. Happy blessed tears they were, quickly kissed away, and changed into smiles!

Many and many a time in after-years did the young couple call to mind that first evening in their own home — how they looked over their treasures, their household gods! Eunice tried her new piano, and sang; but her voice trembled; so at last they came and sat by the fireside — like John Anderson and his spouse, as Henry laughing said — and built castles in the air; the jests always ending in seriousness, for they were too happy to be very mirthful.

Time glides away fast enough with every one, and most of all with those whose life is untroubled. Eunice had been married six months before she began to think how long it was since she had resigned her hand into Henry's loving keeping. Yet short as the time seemed, it was sufficient to make the former life of both appear like a dream. They had already settled down into a calm, sedate married pair. Sometimes people jested with them upon restricted freedom and marriage fetters; but Henry Wolferstan only laughed — he was ever of a merry mood — and asked if any man or woman, single or not, could ever truly say they had their *liberty*. And in good truth it is well it should be so; for such liberty would be a sore burden sometimes.

Mrs. Wolferstan still kept up her intercourse with her cousin, for Isabel was of too generous a disposition to make the difference in position a bar to such old friendship. Still there was externally a distinction between the wife of a rich baronet and of a gentleman of limited income: and still more than this, there was the difference of habits, thoughts, feelings, which the diverse fortunes of the two cousins naturally brought about; so that, if the intercourse of the two wives gradually narrowed, it was scarcely surprising. Eunice never returned from Lady Lester's house, which breathed the very atmosphere of gaiety and splendour, without feeling a sense of relief on entering the quiet precincts of her own home.

One day she came earlier than usual to visit Isabel, whom she found still in her apartment, seemingly half asleep; but when Eunice drew aside the curtains, and let in the warm noon sunshine, she saw the pale face and swollen eyes that were beneath the rich lace cap. Before she had time to speak, Lady Lester observed, "Well, Eunice, my husband and I have had our first quarrel."

"I am sorry — truly sorry. And Sir Francis ——"

"Do not mention him: he is unkind, proud, obstinate."

"Hush!" said Eunice, laying her finger on Emily's lips; "you must not speak of him thus — not even to me."

"Nay — I will not be contradicted," answered the young beauty, resolutely. And Mrs. Wolferstan thought that to listen would perhaps be the wisest course, though she knew the evil of such confidences in general.

"My husband gives me nothing of his society," continued Isabel. "He is always going out — not with me, but alone, or with that disagreeable mother of his, whom I hate to see in my house; yet she makes it like her own, and I am thought nobody — I, the wife of Sir Francis Lester! I entreated him this morning not to invite her so much, that he and I might be alone together, if he would stay at home a little more. But he was very angry; not passionate, for that he never is — I often wish he were — it would be better than his cold, formal manner when he is displeased."

"Was that all?" asked Eunice.

"Not quite. I told him he ought not to leave me so much — that I would not suffer it. And he answered in his quiet way, 'It is in Lady Lester's own power to make her society more pleasant to her husband.' And so he went away. I will make him repent it, though," said Isabel, while the hot flush mounted on her brow. Eunice saw at once that it was no time for even gentle reproofs, and, besides, her cousin was not all in the wrong; there was much to be laid to the charge of the husband also. Scarcely had Mrs. Wolferstan succeeded in calming her, and just as she was beginning to think how she might best frame salutary but tender advice, the elder Lady Lester entered.

The hasty greeting between the wife and mother of Sir Francis showed mutual dislike. Eunice contrasted the tall, harsh-voiced, frigid lady before her with the gentle woman who was Henry's mother — and her own, too, in love, which made the formidable title of mother-in-law but a name for a most sweet bond. Thinking of this, how much she pitied Isabel! Had she not heard the confession of her cousin, the one half-hour during which she listened painfully to the abrupt, coldly polite, or sarcastic speeches that passed between the lady and her son's wife, was enough to convince Eunice that she was in a house of strife. She rose to depart; for it was vain to hope for more conversation with Isabel. As she bade her cousin adieu in the ante-room, Eunice could just find time to whisper, "Isabel, when I married, a wise and true friend said to me, 'Take care of the *first* quarrel!' I did so; Henry and I have not had our first quarrel yet. Dear girl, at all risks, end yours; make any sacrifices to do so; and never, never have another. God bless and help you! and good-bye."

The wise Solomon says, "The beginning of strife is like the letting out of water." Alas! if they who first open the fountain did but know into what a fearful river of woe it soon swells, sweeping away everything in its overwhelming tide! Isabel Lester was wise enough to follow her cousin's advice; she did "make up" the quarrel, as a loving and still beloved wife almost always can, if she chooses. But Sir Francis, though gifted with many high qualities, was a difficult temper to bear with. His character and pursuits were fixed before he married; his wife had to mould her habits to his, for he would never bend his to hers. He loved Isabel fondly, but, probably from the difference in their years, he regarded her more as a plaything than an equal. After the silken fetters of the lover were broken, he would never brook the shadow of control. To give him an idea that he was ruled, was to lose that influence for ever. Isabel had truly called him obstinate; for the same quality that made him firm in a good purpose, hardened him in an erring one. To seek to thwart, was but to strengthen his iron will. Yet he was a man of high principle and generous feeling; but he required to be lured by smiles to a cheerful home, instead of being driven away by frowns and complainings.

Let us pass over another year, and again visit the two

homes. A mother's bliss had come to both: the heir of Sir Francis Lester was received with triumphant joy, and cradled in satin and down; while the first-born of Henry Wolferstan was laid in its mother's bosom with a tearful but not less happy welcome. Life had become very sweet to Henry and Eunice; their cup of joy was running over. Too much bliss is a snare to the wisest; and therefore, perhaps, it was for the best that, before many months had passed over the babe whose advent had given so much happiness, a shadow gathered on the path of the young parents.

Eunice sat waiting for her husband's daily return from town. Sleep had closed the eyes of her little Lily — the child's name was Lavinia, but they called her Lily, and very like was she to that sweet flower, especially now as she lay asleep. Eunice's fingers were busy in fabricating a christening robe for her darling; and the mother's heart kept pace with their quick movements, travelling over future years, until she smiled at herself to think how earnestly she had been considering the making of the bridal dress of the babe three months old that lay unconsciously sleeping by her side.

A little later than his accustomed hour — for he was generally very punctual — Henry came in. He looked pale, and his eye was troubled, but he kissed his wife with his usual affection, perhaps even more. Still, Eunice saw that all was not right. She waited for him to tell her: he always did; but this night he was silent. A few passing questions Eunice put, but they were answered so shortly, that the wife saw that that plan would never do; so she tried to distract his attention by speaking of Lily and the christening.

"See, Henry, how beautiful she will look in her robe — the darling!" said the mother, unfolding and displaying the delicate fabric.

Henry covered his face. "Take it away!" he said, in tones of deep pain. "I cannot think of such things. Eunice, I ought to tell you, and yet I dare not."

"What is it you dare not tell me, my own Henry?" said Eunice, softly putting her arm round his neck. "Nothing wrong, I am sure; and even if so, you know I will forgive."

"I have not done wrong, Eunice; it might be foolish, but it was not wrong."

"What was it, Henry, love?" said a voice so low, that it

might have only been that of his own heart urging the confession.

"I will tell you. You know my brother George, how wild he is, and always was? Well, he came to me a year ago: he had a good situation offered him, but they required a surety; and he asked me to aid him: I did so for the honour of the family. I was bound for him to the extent of our little all — poor Lily's fortune — and he has just fled to America — defrauding his master, and me. Eunice, we have now only my salary to live upon. This is the trouble that weighs me down."

"Is that all?" said the wife. "It is nothing — nothing," and she smiled through her tears.

Her husband looked surprised. "But do you know that we shall be much poorer than we are now? that we must give up many comforts? and the poor babe growing up too. Oh, how thoughtless I have been!"

"Never mind the past now, dear Henry; I have only one thing to complain of — that you did not tell me sooner."

"You have indeed a right to complain," said Henry, slowly and painfully. "I have sacrificed my wife and child to a brother that deserved nothing. It is all my fault that you are reduced to poverty."

Eunice looked at her husband with eyes overflowing with love. "Henry," she answered, "since you speak thus, I also must think of myself. I must remember that I brought you no fortune; that I owe all to you. When I consider this, what right have I to complain of reduced luxuries — nay, even of want?"

"You are my own noble-minded wife," cried Henry, folding her in his arms. "The richest treasure I ever had was the loving heart you brought me."

Thus even adverse fortune without could only throw a passing shadow on that blessed, united home.

The birth of their son drew a little nearer the hearts of Sir Francis Lester and his wife, but their life had been too long a troubled current to receive more than a temporary calm. When Sir Francis stooped from his usual dignified reserve to fondle his child, with the pride of a new-made father, these caresses, after the first pleasure was over, gave a pang to Isabel's heart. She was absolutely jealous of the babe, attributing her husband's more frequent society to his delight in his son and heir. She even doubted the increased fondness of manner that he evinced towards herself; until, repulsed by her coldness, he again sought abroad the comfort that was denied him in his splendid but joyless home.

From that home Sir Francis became more and more estranged. His wife rarely saw him in the day, and midnight often found him absent. If she complained, or questioned him whither he was going, or where he had been, his sole answer was silence or haughty reserve. In the early days of their marriage, Isabel had often had her way, even against her husband's will, by tears or caresses. But the former were useless now: the power of the latter she scorned to try. Only the shadow of her olden love lingered in the wife's heart, and in its stead had come distrust, and jealousy, and wounded pride.

One morning daybreak saw Lady Lester returning from a ball alone, for her husband now seldom accompanied her. As she entered, her first inquiry was, if Sir Francis had returned? He had not; and this was only one of many nights that he had outstayed the daylight. Lady Lester compressed her lips in anger, and retired; but she had scarcely gained her room ere Sir Francis entered.

"You are out late?" said the wife. He made no answer.
"Where have you been?"
"Nowhere, Isabel, that can signify to you."
"Sir Francis Lester, excuse me," answered Isabel, trying to speak calmly, though she trembled violently, "I have a right to know where you go and what you do — the right of a wife."
"Do not let us discuss unpleasant topics; I never interfere with your proceedings."
"Because you know there is no evil in them. I have nothing to hide. You have."
"How do you know that?"
"Ah — I see. I was right," cried the wife, startled by his sudden and violent change of manner. "Shall I tell you what I think — what the world thinks? That you gamble!"
"The world lies!" cried Sir Francis, the words hissing through his lips; but he became calm in a moment. "I beg your pardon, Lady Lester; I will bid you good-night."
"Answer me, Francis!" said his wife, much agitated. "Where do you go, and why? Only tell me."

"I will not," replied he. "The ignoble curiosity of a suspicious wife is not worth gratifying. Good-night."

Isabel pressed her throbbing forehead against the cushions of a sofa, and wept long. Ere morning dawned upon her sleepless eyes, she had resolved what to do. "I *will* know," muttered the unhappy wife, as she pondered over the plan on which she had determined. "Come what may, I will know where he goes. He shall find I am equal to him yet."

Two days after, Sir Francis Lester, his wife, and mother, were seated at the well-lighted dinner table. There was no other guest — a rare circumstance, for any visitor was ever welcome, to break the dull tedium of a family *tête-à-tête*. Alas for those homes in which it is so! Silently and formally sat Lady Lester at the head of her husband's table. How cheerless it was in its cold grandeur! with the servants gliding stealthily about, and the three who owned this solemn state exchanging a few words of freezing civility, and then relapsing into silence. When the servants had retired, Sir Francis uttered a few remarks in his usual tone — perhaps a little kinder than ordinary — to his wife; but she made no effort to reply, and he turned to his mother. They talked a while, and then the elder Lady Lester rose.

Isabel's pale cheek grew a shade whiter as she said, "Before we retire I have a word to say to my husband."

Sir Francis looked up, and his mother observed sharply, "Perhaps I had better leave you together?"

"As you will," Lady Lester replied with a bitter emphasis, oh, how different from sweet Isabel Stratford of old! "But it might be an unpleasant novelty to Sir Francis to listen to his wife without his mother's presence."

"What is all this?" coldly said the husband.

"Merely, that what you refused to tell me, I have otherwise learned. I know where, and how, you pass the evenings in which your wife is not deemed worthy to share your society. I know also where you spent last night. A noble thing, a very noble thing for Sir Francis Lester to be squandering his own — ay, and his wife's — fortune, in a gaming-house!"

Sir Francis started from the table. "It is false!" he said, while the blue veins rose like knots on his forehead.

"It is true," Isabel answered. "I discovered it."

"May I ask how?"

"By the evidence of one who saw you enter the house."

"And shall I tell you, Francis, how that evidence was gained?" said his mother in the biting tone she well knew how to use. "I now see why Lady Lester gave yesterday and to-day two such long audiences to her father's old servant, and why she needed his assistance so much — to make him a spy upon her husband!"

Sir Francis clenched his hands involuntarily, and looking keenly at his wife, said, in a tone so low and suppressed that it became almost a whisper, "Isabel Lester, is all this true?"

Much as Lady Lester had erred, she was not yet so far advanced in the ways of wrong as to hide that error with a falsehood; she answered steadily, though a deep blush spread itself over her face and neck, "It is quite true!"

Her husband, to Isabel's great surprise, did not answer a syllable. His head was bent, and his features immoveable. He offered no justification, uttered no reproaches, and his silence irritated her beyond all bounds. Amidst violent bursts of sobbing, she poured out a torrent of recriminations: all her forced calmness had departed, and she upbraided Sir Francis with the bitterness of an injured wife.

"I have endured too long — I will endure no more," she cried. "You trust me not, and therefore you cannot love me. I will go to one who does both — my kind, dear father. I will leave you — we must part."

"We *will* part," said Sir Francis, in a tone of freezing coldness, that went like an ice-bolt to Isabel's heart. Her husband rose up, walked slowly and firmly to the door; but when he reached it, he staggered, and felt about for the handle, like one who was blind. In another minute the hall-door closed, and he was gone.

His wife sat as he had left her, but her tears flowed no longer: she was as still and white as a marble statue. The mother-in-law stormed, sneered, reviled; but she might as well have talked to the dead. At last she went away. When the servants entered to remove the dessert, they found their mistress still in her seat, half-leaning on the table, but perfectly insensible.

Eunice Wolferstan was roused from the contemplation of her own reverses to soothe the unfortunate Isabel. For two days, during which her delirium lasted, no news of Sir Francis came to his wife. His supposed guilt became as nothing compared to the fear lest he should take her wild words in earnest, and that they should part. But this fear soon became an agonizing certainty. In a letter to Isabel's father, Sir Francis declared his intention to return no more to the home his wife occupied; that all her own fortune, and a portion of his, should be settled upon her, but that henceforth they must be separated. In vain the poor old father, his natural anger subdued by witnessing the agony of his child, pleaded for her. Sir Francis was resolute. That his wife should have dared to discover what he chose to conceal, was a deep offence in his eyes; but that she should have set a servant to watch him — no power on earth would have made the haughty Sir Francis Lester forgive that!

The desolate wife implored her cousin to try her power to soften his obstinate will; for Sir Francis had ever respected Eunice. She went to him: her words moved him a little as she could see by the changing of his countenance. He bore more from her than from any one; for a man will sometimes yield to a high-souled, pure-minded woman, when he will not listen for a moment to one of his own sex. Eunice pleaded Isabel's sorrow and repentance; but all failed to move Sir Francis. Then she spoke of the child; and at the mention of his boy, she saw the very lips of Sir Francis quiver.

"You will not take him away from her? Poor Isabel's heart will break to lose both husband and child."

"Mrs. Wolferstan, I wish to be just to myself — not cruel to her. I shall not take the child from his mother. Though it is hard, very hard, to part with my boy." And the father's voice trembled, until, erring as she thought him, Eunice felt compassion for the stern, unyielding, yet brokenhearted man.

Sir Francis continued, "When Lady Lester and myself are separated, I could wish the world to know as little about the fact as possible. Keep it altogether secret — or assign any cause you choose; but let there be no shadow cast on her fair fame — or mine."

"Isabel need fear none," answered Eunice. "And you —"

Sir Francis drew up his tall figure proudly — "Nor I, neither, Mrs. Wolferstan. To a wife who insults her husband by mean suspicions, no explanations are due. But I owe it to myself to say, and I wish you to know also, that your cousin was deceived; that I never stooped to a vice so detestable as gambling; and that the nights I spent in torture amidst scenes I loathe, were devoted to the attempt to save from ruin a friend whom I had loved as a brother. Now judge me as you will."

Eunice could only mourn that the little cloud which had arisen between the husband and wife, had so darkened the vision of both. But it was passed now: no peace-making could restore the alienated love.

Once only did Sir Francis and his wife meet: it was on the signing of the deed of settlement. A cold bend of salutation was all that passed between the two who had once loved so fondly. Sir Francis preserved his old reserve and calmness of manner; Isabel strove to maintain equal composure, and the excitement of her mind gave her strength. Sir Francis placed his signature on the fatal parchment, and then her father led Isabel to the table. She gave one wild imploring look at her husband — but his face seemed passionless as stone: there was no hope. She took the pen, wrote her name — her fingers, her whole frame, collapsed — and, without a sigh or moan, dropped down. But he had already departed.

It was over: Sir Francis went abroad; and the young wife, widowed by her own deed, was left alone. Save for the babe who remained to cling round her neck, and look at her with eyes like those of the husband whom she had lost, Isabel's reason would have left her. The magnificent house was closed; and she took up her abode in the home from which she had been taken, a beautiful and happy bride. Thither the loving care of Eunice followed her still; and she gradually became calmer, and wiser, and better, under the guidance of her cousin.

Eunice's own path was far from smooth. In her first high-hearted fearlessness of poverty, her very ignorance had made her brave. Now she came to experience how bitter are those trifling but gnawing cares which those who have known the comfort of easy circumstances feel so keenly; how wearying is the constant struggle to spin a sovereign into the longest thread of gold-wire possible. The grim ogre, Poverty, whom Eunice had at first repulsed so cheerfully and boldly, took his revenge by all sorts of sly assaults on her peace. But in time she bore them better, and felt them less: and it was a balm to all sorrow to know how much she was loved, ay, and reverenced too, as a good and virtuous wife, "whose price is above rubies," ought to be, by her husband. And day by day were their hearts more knitted together. She, in willing obedience, yielding honour where honour was due, and he guiding and protecting her, as the stronger should the weaker, in a union in which neither ought to strive for the pre-eminence, unless it be the pre-eminence of love.

For two years only was Eunice fated to know the soreness of altered fortunes. Conscience overtook the brother whose crime had caused so much misery: he died, and, dying, made restitution to the master whom he had defrauded. The master was a just man, and dealt equally well with Henry Wolferstan. His income restored, he left the small house where Eunice had learned the hard lesson of poverty, and returned to the same pleasant home where he had brought his bride.

There, after four years had passed over her head, let us look at Eunice, now in the summer of womanhood, wifehood, motherhood. It was high summer, too, on the earth; and through the French windows of the room where Eunice sat, came the perfume of roses from the garden. Bees hummed among the leaves of the mulberry-tree, luring sweet Lily from her A B C to her favourite seat under its boughs. The child looked wistfully towards her little cousin, Sidney Lester, who was sporting among the flowers, and all her mother's words failed to attract her attention, until the lesson was happily broken in upon by a visitor. Lily scampered away — the unannounced guest entered — and Eunice looked upon the face of Sir Francis Lester!

She had never seen him since the day of the signing of the deed of separation; and time, travel — it might be suffering also — had changed him much. He looked now like a man whose prime was past; his hair was turning gray, and he had lost much of his stately carriage. When he spoke too, there was a new softness in his voice; perhaps it was because of the emotion which Eunice evinced at seeing him so unexpectedly.

He said, he had come on urgent business to England; he should soon return to Italy, and had been unwilling to go without seeing Mrs. Wolferstan. After a while he asked after his boy — and then after his wife; but very formally, and as he spoke he walked away to the window. It was to meet a sight which startled him. He hastily turned to depart.

"Excuse me — I understood — I heard — that Lady Lester was in the country?"

"She and Sidney returned to-day, but I feared to tell you they were here," answered Eunice, softly.

"Is that my boy? I must see him;" and the father's eyes eagerly returned to where Sidney stood on the garden seat, supporting himself by one rosy arm thrown round his mother's neck, as he pulled the mulberry-leaves within his reach. Isabel sat still — not the brilliant Isabel of yore, but calm, thoughtful, subdued: even the light of a mother's love could not altogether remove the soft sadness from her face. How little she knew whose eyes were gazing upon her now! "I must speak to my little Sidney," at last said Sir Francis in changed and broken accents. "Will you bring him to me?"

"They are coming now," Eunice answered.

"Then I will retire to the other room: I cannot, I will not see her." And Sir Francis, with his freezing manner of old, walked away just before his wife entered with her child.

"Sidney, come with me to the library," said Eunice, stooping over the boy to hide her agitation; "some one wants to see you."

"Who is it?" asked Lady Lester.

"An old acquaintance; that is, a stranger," hurriedly said Mrs. Wolferstan, so new in the art of stratagem, that her cousin at once guessed the fact. She trembled violently, and sat down; but when Eunice took Sidney's hand to lead him away, the mother interposed.

"Not so, Eunice; you cannot deceive me," she said, firmly. "I see it all; and no one but myself shall take Sidney to his father." She lifted the boy in her arms, suffered Eunice to open the door, went in, and closed it after her.

For a whole half-hour, which seemed a day in length, did Eunice sit without, waiting for the result of that interview on which joy or misery, life or death, seemed to hang. She heard no sound; all was still. She hardly dared to hope; she could not even think; only her affectionate heart lifted up a wordless aspiration, too indistinct to be even a prayer.

At last the child's voice within called loudly and fearfully,

"Aunt Eunie — Aunt Eunie; come!" Eunice went trembling. Isabel had fainted; but she lay in her husband's arms; her face rested on his shoulder, and heavy tears were falling on that poor pale cheek from the stern eyes of Sir Francis Lester.

They were reconciled! Love had triumphed over pride, wrath, obstinacy; and the husband and wife were again reunited, with an affection even passing that of bride and bridegroom, for it had been tried in the furnace of suffering, and had come out the pure gold of patient, long-enduring love.

In the home to which Sir Francis once more brought his loving and now worthily beloved wife there was no more coldness, no dull weariness, no estrangement. Perhaps it was a fortunate thing for the married pair that the mother of Sir Francis — who had doubtless originated most of his faults of character, by being to him, and his wife afterward, little or nothing of a mother except the name — now slept beneath a marble monument, as frigid, and stately, and hollow as she herself in life had been.

Perfect bliss is never known in this world; yet if there can be a heaven upon earth, it is that of a happy home, where love — not girlhood's romantic folly, but strong, deep, all-hallowing, household love — is the light that pervades everything within it. With this blessed sunshine resting upon them both, let us take our last look at the Two Homes.

MINOR TRIALS.

A STORY OF EVERY-DAY LIFE.

The prick of a pin is often more painful than the gash of a lancet. So, as we pass through life, our minor trials are frequently harder to bear than our great afflictions. The latter either deaden our sense of suffering by the violence of the blow, or else excite an unwonted and unnatural strength, which enables us to stand firm against them. But the former annoy us — irritate us: we chafe against them, and can neither patiently endure, nor manfully fight them. And thus it is that we often see those whom we had most reverenced for having nobly borne great trials, the first to sink ignobly under lesser ones.

But enough of this moralizing strain. There is no sermon so good as example, and a simple story often does more service than all the essays on morality that ever came from old Wisdom's pen. So here is one.

It was on a fine May morning, that a bride was brought home to the small village of Woodmanslea. It was a gay procession; green boughs were nodding over the horses' heads, and girls were strewing flowers on the road; for the bridegroom was no less a personage than the young rector, the Rev. Owen Thornton, who had brought to his English home a Scottish wife. Katharine was that rare sight — a truly beautiful woman. Not to a common taste, which generally prefers mere prettiness. Her tall stature, purple-black hair, and aquiline, rather strongly marked features, her eyes —

> "Her dark and intricate eyes,
> Orb within orb, deeper than sleep or death," —

made her beauty more noble than loveable; so that the village girls who clustered around her carriage were in some degree awed, until the inexpressible sweetness of her smile chased away all their shyness. The bridegroom was, as is nearly always the case, totally unlike his wife; mild in face and manner, with irregular but pleasing features, which, amidst all their amiability of expression, bore a certain character of indecision. Quiet and gentlemanlike in his deportment, of disposition according with his kindly looks, not particularly clever, but possessing considerable acuteness of perception, united with almost womanly tenderness of feeling — Owen Thornton was really an excellent man, and no unworthy type of that very harmless and often useful member of society, an English country clergyman.

The carriage wound slowly up the wooded hill, on the top of which stood the church and the rectory. The road through which they passed was bounded by thick hedges, out of which sprang noble trees — oak, elm, and chestnut with its fragrant white flowers. At times a break in these verdant boundaries showed glimpses of a lovely, wide extended landscape. But when they had passed the old church, and came to the summit of the hill, how beautiful was the scene before them! For miles and miles, as far as the eye could reach, lay a rich undulating valley; sunny slopes, of the graceful curve which is peculiar to the part of the country we describe; white mansions glimmering through trees, dark woods here and there; and the river winding amidst all, like a silver thread, now seen, now lost, until it hid itself in the distant hills that bounded the whole; and above all hung the deep blue arch of heaven, resplendent with the glorious sunshine of May.

Katharine Thornton looked on this scene, and her beautiful lip trembled. She took her husband's hand, and said in a sweet voice, which a slight northern intonation only made more musical, "And is this your sunny England? It is beautiful, most beautiful."

"And you will love it for my sake?" answered the delighted bridegroom.

Her answer was audible to him alone; but the evident pleasure of the young bride had gratified all; and as the carriage turned to enter the heavy gates of the old rectory, the villagers and tenants rent the air with their shouts. And such was Katharine Thornton's welcome home.

A few weeks passed by, and the bride became settled in her new abode, and entered cheerfully on her new duties. It was in every way a great change for Katharine. True, she had no distant home to cling to and regret, for she was an orphan; and then she loved her husband so entirely! But yet everything she met seemed new and strange to the young Highland girl, thus suddenly transformed into an English clergyman's wife. Still she was happy — most happy! She moved about her beautiful garden on the slope of the hill, and amused herself with the arrangement of her pretty home, which Owen's care had filled with everything that could please his beloved wife. The housekeeping, too — she felt such delight in her new dignity, when she took the head of her husband's table as the mistress of the establishment. It was a girlish feeling; but she was so young — not out of her teens. And then Katharine had to welcome and visit her new relatives — her husband's mother, and brother, and sisters. Her heart was overflowing with love for them all, for she had no kindred of her own; and even before her marriage, she had looked forward to these new ties with intense pleasure. But when the young wife actually met them, though their greeting was not unkind, she fancied it was cold. It might have been fancy — she tried to hope so — yet it weighed on the young warm heart a little.

Mrs. Thornton was an English gentlewoman of the old school, such as exist in the nooks where the manufacturing whirlpool has not yet swallowed up and mingled the gradations of ancient gentry, yeomen, and farmers. Dignified, reserved, but not forbidding — kind to the poor from nature and from custom — loving her children with a deep but not openly-shown affection, the sole remaining tie of a long-widowed heart — such was Owen's mother. John Thornton, her eldest son, the squire of the village, was the very opposite of his brother — bold, manly, reckless — the best hunter and best fox-hunter for miles round. Devoted to these sports, he lived unmarried with his mother and sisters at the Hall. Of these three sisters we must now speak, for it was to them that Katharine chiefly looked for society and affection.

Miss Thornton, the eldest, was — an old maid. She might once have been handsome, but her younger sisters never remembered her otherwise but as she now appeared — a gentle and ladylike woman of middle age. There had been some shadow over her youth, Owen told his wife — but no one ever spoke of it now. A broken heart is rare — blessings to old Time, the benevolent healer of all sorrows, for the same! And if some coldness was left in Elizabeth Thornton's heart, which gave a slight tinge to her manners, it was all that now remained of her early sorrows.

Agnes, the second sister, was one of those every-day characters that are constantly met with — neither plain nor pretty, neither disagreeable nor particularly winning; but Florence, the youngest, was a beautiful and accomplished girl, and Owen's darling sister. Of her Katharine had often heard, and had longed to see her; but when they really met, she was disappointed. There was an evident constraint in her sister-in-law's manner towards her. Florence seemed to watch so eagerly every word, every action, of her brother's wife; and then Owen thought so much of Florence. Every new ornament in the house, or improvement in the garden, was the result of her taste, until the young wife became wearied of hearing "Florence did that," "Florence planned this," "Florence thought so and so." Foolish Katharine! she was absolutely becoming jealous; while Florence, on her part, apparently found it hard — for alas! it *is* rather hard to sink from being a pet sister to the secondary position of sister-in-law to a favourite brother's beautiful wife.

Now came various trifling vexations, which jarred on the spirit of the young bride, and often contracted her fair brow with a frown, at which she herself was the first to laugh and blush when the trivial cause that brought it thither was past. Katharine had borne nobly the loss of parents, of home, and many other sorrows too heavy for one so young; but now, in the midst of her happiness, innumerable minor things arose to annoy her. She was so anxious that her sisters should love her; and yet it seemed that they always happened to visit the rectory when its young mistress was chafed by some household disaster; and Agnes looked grave, and praised English ways and habits in a tone which made Katharine's Highland blood rush to her brow, while Florence laughed, and Miss Thornton talked of the advantages of patience and the beauty of gentleness of temper. And, in truth, this latter quality was what Katharine sorely wanted. She was a high-spirited woman, of strong deep feelings, but she wanted that meek, loving spirit "which endureth all things;" and she felt too keenly those chance words and looks in which even the best of people will at times indulge, not knowing how very bitterly some of them rankle in the memory of another.

Katharine certainly loved Mrs. Thornton; much more than

she did her new sisters. It might be that she saw a likeness to Owen in his mother's face; or that his mother's strong and evident attachment to her son touched the wife's generous heart; so that in Owen their two loves met, without one feeling of jealousy or pain. Still, Katharine's sensitive temper questioned towards herself the reserved and sedate manner of Mrs. Thornton.

"How I would love her if she would let me!" thought the young wife many a time. "But I fear she never will."

There is nothing so chilling, so repulsive to affection, as this doubt concealed in the heart; and Katharine's manner grew colder, and her visits at the Hall less frequent; so that her sisters, whose slight prejudices a little patient forbearance would have melted into warm regard, began to look upon Owen's wife as a stranger who could not share in any of their pursuits or enjoyments.

However, Katharine had her husband still: his love was unchanged. Hers had been gained, not by outward beauty or dazzling talent, but, as the dear old song says, "his gentle manners won her heart;" and those "gentle manners" and that innate goodness of heart could never alter in Owen Thornton. Some might have said that the young rector's wife was superior to himself; in some things, perhaps, she was; but the thought never entered Katharine's mind. Had it done so, she would have shrunk away from it in fear and shame; for there is nothing so bitter to a wife's peace as to think meanly of him whom she ought to reverence with her whole soul. If all the world had seen Katharine's superiority to her husband, alas for her on the day when it should be discovered to her own eyes!

The honeymoon was over, but many long, sweet evenings — almost lover-like — did Owen and Katharine spend together in the pretty room which overlooked the sloping hill-side. The husband and wife were still lingering in the shadow of the romance of courtship; and they loved to sit in autumn evenings and watch the brown and changing woods, and talk of the mountains and lakes, and wild, beautiful moors, where Owen had first met and wooed his Highland bride. One night the quick-coming twilight found them still here. Katharine had been talking to her husband of her own young days, long before she knew that such a person as Owen Thornton existed. These childish memories left a vague sadness behind; and when Owen brought her harp, and asked her to sing away all old thoughts, she sat down and poured forth her whole heart in the deep pathos of the "Flowers of the Forest."

When she finished the last line, which seems to die away like the last sigh of nature's summer or of youth's hope — "The flowers o' the forest are a' wede away" — Katharine remained some moments silent. Her husband, too, did not speak. She turned towards him — Owen had fallen fast asleep during her beautiful song!

A sudden chill struck on Katharine's heart. She had felt so much, sung with such fervour, and all was lost upon Owen! Poor Katharine! She did not think how many times her gentle husband had listened to songs which his own different associations made him feel far less than she did, and which he entered into solely from his love for her. She had forgotten, too, that he had ridden five-and-twenty miles that morning to administer baptism to a dying child, and to comfort the last moments of a poor widow. No wonder that he was wearied, and had sunk to sleep even in the midst of his wife's sweet music.

When Owen awoke an hour after, there was no smile on Katharine's face to greet him, and a slight pout sat on her lips, which gave to their very loveliness that expression of all others the most odious on a woman's face — mingled scorn and sullenness. Katharine's good angel had fled — but it was only for a time. In the silence of night all this rose up against her, and floods of contrite tears washed away all the hardness and unkindness which had entered her heart.

Next morning, Katharine's loving care seemed determined to make amends for the unexplained and unconfessed error into which she had fallen. Owen's chair was placed close to the bright fire, which made the misty autumn morning seem cheerful; his favourite flowers, yet wet from the dew whence Katharine's hand had gathered them, were beside him; the breakfast which he liked best was provided; and Katharine, fresh and rosy as the morning itself, sat behind the ever-musical urn awaiting her husband.

Owen came in with an open letter in his hand. It was from his mother, asking them to one of her old-fashioned dinner parties. Owen was all cheerfulness; he was always pleased to go over to the Hall — almost too pleased, his wife thought sometimes.

Domestic Stories. 7

"My mother complains that they have not seen you so much of late, Katharine love," said Owen.

She looked rather confused. "It is certainly a good while since I went; but I have so many things to keep me at home; and then the girls seldom come here: it is their fault too."

"Perhaps so. Well, we must go oftener in future, and go to-morrow in particular; and you must make my mother happy by looking well, and singing your best," said the husband, gayly.

Katharine felt anything but willing; but the mention of singing reminded her of her sins against poor Owen the evening before, and she knew atonement was needed. So she assented cheerfully, and they went together to the Hall the day following.

Mrs. Thornton's was one of those formal entertainments so uninteresting to a stranger, when neighbours meet and discuss the public and private affairs of the country. All this was very dull to Katharine; but she looked across the table to Owen's happy face, as he talked to an old college friend. So she bore bravely with her own prosy neighbour, and strove with all her heart to take an interest in names, and persons, and places, of which she had never heard before. Florence, too, was merry, for she had her betrothed husband at her side; and Elizabeth Thornton's rare smile flitted more than once over her mild features as she talked to one who sat next her — a sweet-looking woman, whose pale golden hair, and delicate, almost transparent, complexion, made her at first sight seem scarcely out of girlhood.

When the dinner was over, and Katharine sat with Florence in a little recess in the drawing-room window, out of hearing of the rest, she could not resist inquiring who was the stranger that had attracted her so much?

"Do you really not know?" said Florence, surprised. "Did my brother never speak of Mary Wynn?"

"No, indeed: is that her name?"

"Yes: she was Owen's first love."

An uneasy sensation made the young wife start, and look fixedly at "Owen's first love;" but then she laughed, and asked Florence to tell her the story.

"I hardly know if I ought," said the mischief-loving girl. "It happened years ago; Owen was very young; and I do not suppose he long remembered her, though he certainly loved her at the time; but," added Florence, gravely, "I know how much she loved him, and how deeply she suffered; for she was, and is, my dearest friend. However, she may have forgotten him now. She seemed pleased to see you, and speaks cheerfully to Owen. Poor Mary! I hope she has forgotten her 'first love,' as he has forgotten her."

No more was said about Mary Wynn, but Katharine became thoughtful and silent; not that she doubted Owen's strong affection for herself, but no woman ever really likes to hear that her husband once had a "first love." And yet Florence was right: Owen had entirely forgotten his boyish flame. It is seldom that such endure; and perhaps it is well for the silvery veil of romance and fancy which enshrouds man's first idol, would infallibly, when removed, leave an image far below his ideal standard of perfection. Nevertheless, Katharine, in the happy fulfilment of her own young love, felt much more than perhaps Mary Wynn did herself. Had she known how much deeper and stronger is the love of the man than of the boy, of the woman than of the romantic girl, Katharine would not have so closely watched her husband and Mary Wynn, nor have returned home with such a weight on her heart.

Miss Wynn left the Hall, went home, and was forgotten; but still her visit had left a painful impression on Owen's wife. Katharine thought that much of Florence's distaste to herself — aversion it could hardly be called — arose from her strong love and sympathy for Mary Wynn. Day by day the bond between Katharine Thornton and her sisters-in-law was gradually loosening; and her quick eyes were ever discovering failings, and her mind becoming more alive to unworthy suspicions. Florence's mirth-loving nature was to her full of bitter sarcasm; Elizabeth's gentle gravity, which had interested her so much, appeared only the hypocrisy of self-important goodness; and Agnes's indolence was insupportable. Katharine fancied they tried to make her husband love her less; and even Owen felt the results of her harsh doubts in her changed manner and anxious looks. Husband and wife loved one another still; but the perfect sunshine of all-hallowing, all-forgiving love was gone; and what trifles, what mere shadows, had blotted it out!

In her unhappiness, Katharine's mind turned regretfully

7*

to her old Scottish home, and lingered sinfully on many former joys. At last her over-burdened heart would find vent: she told all the doubts and troubles of her wedded life to an old and dear friend — the wife of her former guardian. In this Katharine was wrong, very wrong. Such trials, even when they amount to real grief, should be hidden in the depths of the heart; no eye should see them — no ear should hear them. True, of her husband himself — the kind, good, affectionate Owen — Katharine had nought to complain. But of his family, the very knowledge that they were his should have sealed her lips.

However, she erred in ignorance; and out of her error, for once, came less evil than good. Her friend, Mrs. Lindsay, was wise as well as kind; and candid, although gentle, was the reproof given to the young wife.

"You are young, and I am old," she wrote, "therefore, Katharine, listen to me with patience. You tell me how much you are tried — ask of your own heart, have you been entirely in the right? Is there in you no discontent — no readiness to compare old things with new — no suspicious quickness in detecting slight failings, that, perchance, would best be passed over with a loving blindness? Child, you came a stranger to your husband's home — your sole resting-place was in his affection; having thus trusted him, you should strive, so far as conscience allows, to love what he loves, think as he thinks, see as he sees. All that are his are yours. When you married, his kindred became *your own*, and you should love them as such; not with jealous comparison, not with eyes eager to detect faults, but with the forbearance that is needful in a family bound together for life. And as for their want of love — if they see that you feel as one of themselves, which, indeed, you are; that, to a certain degree, you 'forget your own people, and your father's house,' to enter into their plans and hopes, and sympathies; and, above all, that you are bent on conquering any slight obstacles to mutual affection — if they see all this, they will soon love you as your heart could wish. And, my Katharine, make no fancied sorrows for yourself. You are a beloved and happy wife — thank God each day for that blessing, so rare to many. Look not for perfection — it is not to be found on earth; but forget the past, and go on in your loving, patient, and hopeful way; it will surely lead to happiness at last."

Mrs. Lindsay's words sank deeply into Katharine Thornton's heart. But ere she had time to guide her conduct by their wise counsel, sickness, that harsh and fearful, yet often kindly monitor, came to her. Thus it happened: Katharine was a wild and fearless rider, and one sad day her high-mettled horse took fright, nor stopped until its burden was thrown senseless at her husband's own gate. Many days she lingered between life and death, and when reason and consciousness returned, Katharine learned that her constant and unwearied attendants, night and day, had been the grave, cold-hearted Elizabeth, and the mirthful and often thoughtless Florence!

"How little I knew them — how deeply I misjudged them!" thought the repentant Katharine. But still she did not know, and it was well that she did not, that the untiring care of the two sisters had sprung at first more from duty than inclination — that Elizabeth's shy and seldom roused feelings, and Florence's remembrance of old prejudices, had struggled long with their natural kindness of heart. Rare, very rare, in real life, is a character even distantly approaching to perfection — the angel nature after which we all unconsciously seek. Most needful is it to bear and forbear; ever seeking to behold the bright half of the nature of all around us. For there are none of the sons and daughters of man — of man made in the image of God — in whom some trace of the divine image does not linger still.

Katharine rose from her sick bed, having learned much. In many a long hour, when she lay in the silence that was necessarily imposed upon her, her thoughts were very busy. Owen's image rose up before her, not as the adoring, enthusiastic lover, who submitted delightedly to all her fancies, and from whom she expected unwearied sympathy of thought and feeling, but as he was now, and would be more as they grew older — a helpmate not free from faults, but still most loveable, and worthy of the strongest trust and affection, with whom she was to pass through — not an enchanted valley of bliss, but a world in which there were sorrows to be borne, and cares to be overcome, and joys to be shared together.

Then Katharine would lie watching the lithe figure of her sister as she flitted about the room, until her growing love cast a charm even over Florence's outward attractions; and the invalid thought how very sweet her smile was, and what a pleasant voice she had when she came to the bedside to whisper the few words that were allowed. She gratefully remembered, too, that Florence had left the society of her lover, and deprived herself of many amusements, to share with Elizabeth the care of a sick room. Katharine began to hope that her sister really loved her a little, and would love her more in time.

As Katharine grew stronger, this late "autumn-spring" of affection in the hearts of the sisters still withered not, but rather gathered strength. No explanations were given or asked. Such are often very ill-judged, and evil in their effect. The new bud of love will not bear much handling. A silent look now and then, an affectionate smile, were all that marked the reconciliation. Katharine suffered no misgivings or seeming obstacles to hinder her on the path in which she had determined to walk.

One evening the invalid lay resting, half-asleep, in her arm-chair. Elizabeth and Florence were with her; and after a long silence, supposing her asleep, they began to talk in low tones. Their voices broke through Katharine's dream; but they could not see her for the twilight, and it was some time before her roused faculties could distinguish what they talked about.

Elizabeth was saying, "How very beautiful Katharine looked to-day; I thought Owen would never gaze enough at her."

"Yes," said Florence; "and I think her illness has improved her much. She does not look half so proud. Do you know, Elizabeth, that once I thought her anything but handsome, and wondered that Owen could have chosen her after beautiful, gentle Mary Wynn."

"Ah, that was because you did not like Katharine. You were hardly just to her," observed the mild Elizabeth.

"Yet I really had no positive dislike to her: but she had such strange ways, and seemed to think herself so different from us."

"Yet mamma loved her from the first."

"Yes, and so do I now, and you too, and all of us. But she seems so changed, so gentle and affectionate: I begin to think it possible to love one's brother's wife after all," said the gay Florence, giving way to a cheerful laugh, which she immediately checked, lest it should disturb her sister's slumbers.

But Katharine had heard enough A deep and abiding pleasure mingled with the slight pain which Florence's unconscious reminiscences had given her. It is so sweet to be loved, and after a prejudice conquered, that love delayed comes sweeter than ever.

Owen's entrance formed a glad pretext for the termination of Katharine's sleep and Florence's revelations; but the wife kept them closely in her heart.

That night Florence was sent for to return home. Elizabeth, at Katharine's entreaty, remained; but Florence was imperiously demanded by the very patient betrothed, and must depart. So, after a short delay, she was ready, and came to bid adieu to the invalid. It was not for long; but still it was the first time they had been parted since Florence had come, in horror and dismay, to her insensible sister's couch. Katharine rose feebly in her chair, and weeping, threw herself on Florence's bosom.

"Thank you, and bless you, dear girl, for all your care of me," was all she could articulate.

"Nonsense!" cried Florence cheerfully, trying to withstand the unusual moistness in her own eyes. "Do not quite overwhelm me, Katharine; I did nothing but what I ought, and what I liked to do, too."

"And you do love me now, Florence — a little?" whispered Katharine as her sister hung over her.

Florence's warm and kindly nature now entirely predominated. "Yes, indeed I do, with all my heart," she cried with affectionate energy, as she folded both her arms round her brother's wife, and kissed her repeatedly.

"Come, come; all this embracing will be quite too much for Katharine," said the husband, coming forward with a smile, and carrying away his sister to the door, whither Elizabeth followed her. Owen came and sat by his wife's side, and the invalid rested her head on his shoulder, while they talked with full hearts of her happy recovery.

"Florence is a dear girl, is she not?" said Owen after a pause.

This time no feeling of jealousy crossed the young wife's mind. "Indeed she is," Katharine answered; "and I love her very much."

"I thought you would in time, my Katharine."

She did not immediately answer, and then her voice trembled as she said, "Owen, dear, I have not been good; I have been wrong in many things; I have made too much trouble for myself out of slight vexations."

Owen stopped her. "Now, love, I will have no more confessions! Your husband loves you, and you are all good in his eyes now."

"And always will be, if the determination can make me so. And when we are old married people"—a comical twitch came over Owen's mouth as his wife said this — "when we are old married people, we shall be all the wiser, at least I shall, for remembering these minor trials of our youth."

PHILIP ARMYTAGE;

OR,

THE BLIND GIRL'S LOVE.

CHAPTER I.

> "A child most infantine,
> Yet wandering far beyond that innocent age
> In all but its sweet looks and mien divine." — SHELLEY.

IT was morning — beautiful morning — in that fairest season of the year —

> "When April has wept itself to May."

Earth awoke from her winter sleep, fresh and glorious and young, as if it were but a day since she bore on her bosom Adam and Eve, and shed around them the flowers, and breezes, and sunshine of Eden. Beautiful looked the Eternal Mother, in her ever-renewed youth, over which the change, and misery, and crime of six thousand years have passed like a shadow, and left no trace.

There is no glamour like that of the pen; and it has this surpassing spell, that the magic extends also to the one who wields the charm. Let us, therefore, in this wet and gloomy day, when a heavy mist hangs like a shroud over the dreary city — when under our window sound the plashing foot-falls of tired passers by, and the incessant rattle of vehicles — let us, amidst all this, call up to our mind's eye the scene where our story begins, and linger fondly over that beautiful spot, in the delineation of which memory strives with imagination.

It was the breakfast-room of a house that stood alone on a hill side — one of those stately mansions that are found in England, far in the country, where generation after generation of the old families of the gentry are born, live, and die; father, son, and grandson occupying, in their turn, the same abode, and descending to the same ancient stone monument hard by. Cheerfully came the warm morning sun into the room, not stealthily, as in early spring, but with a glad overflow of light and warmth, brightening even the solemn oak furniture, and contending bravely with the tiny fire that was lit through habit, until it fairly put out its puny antagonist, and reigned supreme. The long low windows, on one side, opened on a formal, dainty little flower-garden, and then, winding through a smooth lawn, lay a narrow walk that led into the forest, on whose borders the house lay. In three minutes one might pass into that beautiful wood, wild as if man's foot had never entered it, and alive with the melodies of leaves quivering in the morning breezes. The tender green of the thorn mingled with the dark holly, that here vied even with the oak in size and grandeur; the primroses looking out smiling from the roots of the old trees; and large beds of the wood anemone, or wind-flower, seemed like a white, wavy mantle cast over the long grass, in recesses so thick that not a stray sunbeam could pierce through. The loud songs of the birds reached even to the house, like a flood of aerial music; the ringing carol of the lark, the deep note of the throstle, the silvery warble of the linnet, and the soft coo of the wood-dove, all mingling in sweet harmony.

Listening eagerly, with up-turned face, that did not shrink even from the broad dazzling sunlight, sat a little girl beside the open window. Her soft hair falling in curls, that prettiest fashion for a child, was of that hue which a gleam of sunshine changes into gold; her head was turned aside; but her attitude was full of childish grace, with the little hands crossed on her knee, motionless, in silent thought. Opposite to her was a boy — her twin-brother — a taller and bolder model of herself, sitting carelessly on the floor; he was busily carving the top of a hazel wand. Boy-like, he whistled merrily over his work, and looked so happy and handsome, with his sunny curls, like his sister's, hanging over a face that still preserved the round curves of childhood, his deep blue eyes shaded by dark, heavy lashes, and the perfect classic profile of his mouth and chin, over which smiles were ever dimpling. With these young creatures, as with the earth, it was the spring of life — to them it was beautiful, hopeful, joyous morning.

The mother entered — a sweet, delicate-looking woman, fragile and graceful, in her robe of pure white; and then the father came in, like a shadow after sunshine. He was a tall man, of middle age; but the sharp lines about his mouth, and a crown entirely bald, gave him the appearance of being much older. Yet, not a single gray hair mingled with the thick brown locks at the back of his head, and his form was unbent. His cold, clear, blue eyes gleamed from underhanging brows, and his noble forehead was full of intellect. He looked like a man in whom mind held the pre-eminence over heart. The little ones timidly advanced towards him.

"Why, Edmund — Stella — early this morning?" he said, and stooped mechanically to kiss them, while a smile like winter sunshine just bent his lips. Edmund, the boldest, and the favourite, stayed to show his wonderful wood-carving to his father, with boyish pride; but little Stella crept along by the table, and nestled beside her mother's knee.

"What has my little girl been doing?" said Mrs. Brandreth, twining her fingers in the long silken hair.

"I have been listening to the birds, mamma, and feeling the sunshine, it is so warm and pleasant."

A light sigh heaved the mother's bosom.

"That is well; I like to see my darling happy and gay," she answered, tremulously.

And now came the pleasant breakfast hour — the pleasantest meal of all to country-dwellers and visitants. How cheerful, and fresh, and blithe all look; how welcome is the balmy morning air; nay, to descend to common things, how fragrantly rises up the steam of coffee, and how grateful both to sight and taste are the country viands — snowy new-laid eggs, and golden butter, and cream — rich and luscious as nectar. Commend us to a country breakfast. Who *could* come down with sour looks and bitter speeches, on a sunny morning, and not feel all the hardness and ill-temper melt away from his heart beneath its influence.

Merrily the children laughed and talked, making, at times, even the sedate father look up from his reading, and winning the gentle mother to smiles less pensive than ordinary. At last Mr. Brandreth collected his papers, and laid them carefully aside; he was a learned man, wise in geology and natural philosophy, and always devoted the breakfast-hour to the reperusal and arrangement of his lucubrations. The twins received the signal to retire, and Edmund hastily rose, while Stella moved slowly from her seat. As she passed, her stretched-out arms, by which she guided her steps, came in contact with the heap of papers so carefully arranged, and they fell in confusion on the floor. Mr. Brandreth started up angrily —

"Careless child — always doing some mischief or other," he said, and thrust Stella rudely away. The child fell, and began to weep — not loudly as most children — but with the silent tears of advanced life. The mother took her to her bosom, and soothed her.

"Do take the child away, Marian," said Mr. Brandreth, in a vexed tone, "she annoys one so much."

Mrs. Brandreth looked with meek reproach at her husband. "Hush, hush — you forget," she answered, imploringly, still pressing her little girl closer to her bosom, where the tears at last ceased. Stella walked, or rather crept, to her father's knee, and said, gently —

"Papa, I did not mean to do harm. Forgive poor Stella — she is blind!"

It was so — there was no light in those large, blue, limpid eyes, that were lifted so meekly to the father's face. Six years had the little child looked on the beautiful sky, and seen the flowers, and then a shadow grew over her vision; gradually it darkened and darkened, and the world grew dimmer, until, at last, she saw it no more. Now, all the visible earth was become to her like a scene once beheld in a dream, and then shut out for ever. Yet, but for an uneasy wandering of the eyes, no one could have told that those beautiful blue orbs were sightless. The sweet face wore, at times, that peculiar mournful look which the blind always have, but this was the only outward token of the affliction which had fallen upon her. Affliction it could hardly be called, for the child scarcely felt it as such; her blindness had come on so gradually that Stella had become accustomed to her helpless condition. And, besides, from her very infancy the child had been quiet and thoughtful, caring little for the sports attractive to her age; as if with a fore-shadowing of how soon she was to be deprived of them. Gentle and subdued she was, as became her helpless condition; it seemed as if He who knew how dependent her whole life must be upon the affection of others, had endowed her with that irresistible beauty which wins love, and the meek spirit which preserves it.

But now Stella hardly felt her darkness, so illuminated was

it by the light of a mother's love. More than her own life, more than her handsome frank-hearted boy — nay, more even than the husband of her youth, did Mrs. Brandreth cling to her blind child, with a passionate fervour, an all-absorbing love, that atoned to Stella for the loss of the blessed gift of sight. Perhaps her own delicate health made this love more intense, from the feeling that she would not always be with her darling, to cherish her in her heart's core, and shield her there from all contact with the rough world which the poor stricken one was so ill fitted to brave.

The mother knew well that every year which unfolded, in new beauty, Stella's mind and person drew her own life nearer towards its close. At last, when Stella and Edmund still lingered on the verge of childhood, the mother was called away. Gently, not rudely, came the summons, and yet it was sudden — just as an autumn leaf flutters and flutters until it drops at once and is seen no more.

Thus did Mrs. Brandreth die — even before her husband, who, all-unconscious of danger, was on a journey, could reach his home, the wife whom he had sincerely loved, though hardly with the tenderness meet for her gentle nature, had passed away. So swiftly came the angel of death, that the mother had hardly time to bless her two babes, and commend poor Stella to her brother's care, in a charge that lingered on the boy's memory from youth to old age. Then, worn out with pain, she kept silence, and lay with closed eyes, still holding fast the little hands of her daughter, the thought of whose desolation troubled her spirit, even on the threshold of paradise. It was night, and the wearied child laid her head on the pillow and slept. Mrs. Brandreth's elder sister and tender nurse wished to remove her, but the mother would not suffer it.

"Do not wake her," she whispered, faintly — "let my darling sleep — I have kissed her and said good-night — a long good-night — until comes the eternal morning; let her sleep."

* * * * *

No more words passed through those white lips. Once or twice the eyes opened and rested lovingly, lingeringly on the face of the sleeping child; then they closed for ever! When morning came another spirit had entered the gates of heaven. Silently, and without tears, the sister unclosed Stella's warm fingers from those that stiffened round them, and bore her away, still sleeping.

Wildly and resolutely the child strove to return to her mother. Her darkened eyes could not see the change of death, therefore she did not believe in its reality. An hour before she had heard the voice, had felt the hand; both were the same, though feeble; she could not comprehend that one short sleep had parted her mother from her. So clinging to her twin-brother, Stella came and stood by the dead; she called, but there was no answer.

"Where is she, where is she?" cried the despairing child.

Edmund guided his sister's hand to the fingers that had held hers while life lasted; their marble coldness made her start, and cling, trembling, to her brother's neck.

"Edmund — I cannot see — tell me how she looks," fearfully whispered Stella.

"White — still — with closed eyes and parted lips — oh, mother! mother! it is not you!" and the boy burst into tears.

"No, my children," said the sister of Mrs. Brandreth, who stood behind them. "Edmund — Stella — I will tell you what she is now — a white-robed, glorious angel at the footstool of God's throne — a voice for ever singing His praise — a spirit pure and perfect, though we know not what form she bears in heaven, save that it is in God's image, and must be beautiful."

And in the stillness of the death-chamber that pious and gentle woman drew the orphans of her dead sister to her side and read aloud from the Holy Book the words that speak of the immortality of the soul, and the state of the blessed in heaven; words so simple, that childhood finds in them no mystery hard to be understood — so sublime, that the gray-haired philosopher may feel his heart glow with the consciousness that he bears within his frail mortal frame a spirit that can never know death!

The children listened, standing beside the clay of their mother; yet even then they thought of her no longer as dead on earth, but as rejoicing in heaven.

CHAPTER II.

*"Are we not formed, as notes of music are,
For one another, though dissimilar?
Such difference without discord as can make
Those sweetest sounds in which all spirits shake,
As trembling leaves in a continuous air."* — SHELLEY.

FROM the time of her mother's death Stella drooped and pined. The world had grown all dark to the motherless child. Her wild brother, and her cold, reserved father, alike strove to soften their natures and show tenderness to the helpless one; but man is so different to woman, and all their kindness atoned not for the love of her who was gone. Edmund remembered well his mother's dying injunction, and many a time he left the field sports, of which he was so passionately fond, to come and talk with his sister, and lead her into the beautiful forest, where she could hear the birds' songs and be made glad with the gladness of nature. But nothing could altogether remove the perpetual sadness which now darkened the face of the blind girl. Excluded from the pleasures of childhood, hers passed away like a sorrowful dream. She grew up, living within herself, in a world of her own imagining, over which death hung, like an eternal shadow, a mysterious woe which she could not fathom, and which yet haunted her like a spectre. The remembered touch of that icy hand made her shudder in her dreams; it was all she knew of the great change. Her mind, undiverted from the past by any charms of the present, became dead to all outward impressions, and alive only to imagination, and most of all to memory.

Thus, in this dreamy state of mind, the blind girl insensibly passed from childhood into girlhood. She had attained the age of which poets write as sweetest of all, when the bud is just opening into a flower, and life is in its hopeful spring. How little do these said poets know that this is the saddest age of all. What woman would ever wish to be again "sweet sixteen?" Childhood's life is a never ending present, a contented dwelling on what is best and pleasantest *now*, without memory to sharpen the past, or anxiety to darken the future. But with youth, soon — oh, how soon! comes the thirst for something more — the bitter, unsatisfied yearning after vague happiness, some glorious ideal of human felicity, the same in all, yet varied in form, according to the different minds in which it abides. One dreams of wealth, another of gaiety, another — alas for her! — of love; and so the young creatures go on restlessly seeking to fathom their newly-awakened thoughts and feelings; and, knowing not their own hearts, nor yet life, they wander about blindly dazzled or groping in darkness, until the waking comes from that troubled dream, and they enter on the reality, the true life of heart and soul, for which woman was made.

Stella entered upon girlhood with few or none of the buoyant hopes of most young maidens. She saw not beauty, and love was to her only a name that brought to her the memory of her mother — the sole love she had ever known. Always thoughtful, she lived more than ever within the dark chambers of her own soul — her only world. But that world now became peopled with deeper and wilder fancies; every day new chords were touched in her heart, the mysterious harmonies of which she could scarcely understand. She loved to be alone; in winter she listened to the wind until she almost fancied it talked with her; in summer, she sat for hours in the still, silent sunshine, and thought of heaven, of the time when she should go thither, and see her mother, with eyes no longer darkened. Then a warble — a perfume would bring back the dreaming girl to earth, and she would think how sweet the world must be to others, and droop her head, and weep that she was blind.

One gift atoned to Stella, in some measure, for the loss of sight, and that was, a soul to which music was as its very breath. Her voice had those deep, low tones that thrill from the heart to the heart; not a clear, musical, gladsome warble, but a voice that spoke of mind, of feeling, of passion, such as came from no angel's lips, but from a woman's heart. We once heard, and from one, too, who spoke and thought well, the saying — "One must always love a woman who sings sweetly;" and Stella's was a voice not to be admired, perhaps, but to be loved, as coming from a heart as pure and beautiful and sincere as itself. But now this lovely voice was only to her as the means whereby she poured out that overflowing heart in a river of melody; sitting, Ophelia like, for hours and hours chanting "snatches of old songs," and running her fingers over that sweetest of home friends, the fire-side piano, in harmonious revealings. And when, day by day, the vague sadness of aimless and unsatisfied youth grew upon her, the blind girl still clung to her ever mournful strains, that made her feel less the weight of her solitude.

There are in life crises, distinct and vivid, on which we can look back and feel that they have coloured our whole destiny; can say, but for that one year — one week — one day, how different would all have been. Silently, unconsciously are we swept on towards these moments, which lie like hills, placed here and there, from whose top we can see our whole life, like a panorama, stretched out before us; and know that but for such and such events we should not have felt and been as we are. Chance, fatality, are the words on the lips of the wise proud man, in explanation of this; but the humble, loving spirit looks higher for the unveiling of these marvels which pass worldly wisdom.

Thus, nearer and nearer came the blind girl to the boundary of that golden shadow which overhangs human life, and ever has done so since the time when the first created one wooed the mother of all men, in the twilight of Paradise. Once, and once only, can come this sunny cloud over mortal life. Man may love twice, thrice — nay, even woman's constancy may know the freshness of early fancy or the calm peace of healed affections; but, be it first or last, every man and woman has, or has had, some love supreme to which all others are as nothing. And this is the immortality of love; falsehood, or death, or change may intervene; the wounded heart may be healed, the fickle vow forgotten in other and higher ones, but no other feelings can ever be exactly the same. It is the idealization of love, which happens but once in a lifetime, and which each young life that enters earth renews in itself, thus making an ever fresh eternity of love.

Some inexplicable whim allured the retired and studious Mr. Brandreth from his home; and he set off to travel on the Continent, taking with him his daughter. Wearily did the blind girl ask to be left in peace with her birds and flowers, and heavily and fearfully did she look forward to entering on a world that could bring her nought but pain. Stella did not know that the silken thread of her destiny was insensibly drawing her towards him who was to lighten its burthen, and make all joy and sunshine to her. Thus it was that she met him.

As a man of science and learning, Mr. Brandreth had the

entrée everywhere among the gifted, and the patrons of such. Thither he also carried his blind daughter, perhaps because he thought to please her, for he was a kind father, in the main, and perhaps because he liked to see many eyes resting with admiration on the beautiful English girl, and to hear praises of her glorious voice. Rarely was it that Stella suffered this gift to be shown forth; but, on one night, wearied of herself, of solitude, of society, she gave way to her feelings, and sang, with her whole soul in the music.

"Who is she who sang?" said a clear, low-toned, manly voice, whose pleasant English tones ran through the Babel of French, Italian, and German tongues that filled the saloon, and pierced to the acute ears of the blind girl. The answer was inaudible to her, but then she heard the same pleasant voice again, in tones that were much fainter, and had a mournful emphasis.

"Poor girl — poor girl — I had a sister who was blind."

A deep crimson flushed Stella's cheek, for she was ever sensitive on the subject of her misfortune; but that sweet and compassionate voice healed where it wounded.

As she left the piano, the blind girl felt her hand taken by that of a stranger, and a gentle "suffer me to lead you," fell on her ear, in the same voice to which she had listened before. Ere they could find Mr. Brandreth, the stranger had time to ask and claim pardon, as a countryman, for thus addressing one unknown; and by declaring his name, and speaking of some mutual friends, he won upon even the reserved father. All that evening, Philip Armytage sat by the side of the blind girl, who felt her heart warm to the sound of an English voice in that far land. And his was so sweet, and, when he spoke to her, had such a pitying softness, as if he thought of the sister he had mentioned. No wonder that when sleep came over poor Stella's dimmed eyes, that voice haunted her in her dreams.

Philip Armytage was that darling hero of novelists, that Pariah of real life — a poor gentleman. Heir to an old uncle, who *would* marry and thwart the hopes of the nephew he had educated with all the luxuries and expectations of wealth, young Armytage, at twenty-five, was thrown like a stray seaweed on the ocean of the world, with manners, mind, and education that only made him feel more keenly his changed position. He experienced to the full how differently the world looks on a baronet's heir and a nobleman's secretary; even the fine gentlemanly bearing and richly-gifted mind, which could not be taken away from him, were almost thought to add to the category of his imperfections now.

Under the influence of these changed fortunes, Philip Armytage ought, in order to become a true novel hero, to have grown cold, sarcastic, haughty, misanthropic; but he very wisely did no such thing. A good mother — that guardian angel of a boy's life — had better trained her fatherless and only son. Philip's mind and principles were too well regulated for one blast of misfortune to wither the flowers, and cause ill weeds to spring up rampant in the garden of his heart. That heart was disappointed, but not chilled or soured; he did not scorn or rail at the world, but strove, like a true hero, to brave its frowns, and wait patiently until his own firm will and endurance should earn for him what fortune had denied. Philip Armytage was not perfect — who on earth ever was? but his foibles never amounted to vices; and, young as he was, he had learned wisdom, and bade fair to become, if he were not already, a talented and good man. Thus far we have spoken of the mind of Philip Armytage; reversing the general order, and putting foremost what is indeed the highest. Of his face and person, we may now say, that both were pleasing to a lady's eye; he was certainly not an Apollo, but he was tall, graceful, and looked, moved, spoke like a gentleman. Such was he whom destiny — what can such things be but destiny? — threw in the way of the young, beautiful, blind girl, whose lonely, dreaming heart yearned for an ideal round which to hang, as a garland, all its flowers of love and fancy. And rare as the fact is in the history of most maidens' hearts, in this case the shrine was one worthy to receive that purest and holiest sacrifice, a woman's first love. If this love be so powerful that it is sometimes unchanged — always remembered — to old age, what must be the feelings of those on whom outward impressions can have no influence, whom outward beauty cannot lure to fickleness, — how intense — how all-engrossing must be the love of the blind.

CHAPTER III.

> "Amor che nullo amato amor perdona
> Mi prese, del costui placer sì forte
> Che come vedi, ancor non m'abbandona." — DANTE.
>
> "Love, that to none beloved to love again,
> Remits, seized me with wish to please so strong,
> That as thou seest, even yet it doth remain."

THE wise ones of the earth may ridicule love's mysterious sympathies, as they do the stories of ghosts and apparitions, but there must be some truth in both, or so much pains need not and would not be taken to prove them false. How was it, then, that before Stella and Philip Armytage had met half a dozen times, they began to feel and to talk like old friends? What was that strange sympathy which made the very words he uttered appear to her as if she had heard them before in some dim dream — as if she had thought his thoughts long before? And what was it that caused Philip Armytage, who had basked all his life in the smile of woman, to feel an irresistible charm in gazing on the sweet face of the poor blind girl, who, as yet unconscious of the nature of the invisible tie between them, treated him with the frank regard of a young sister towards a dear brother.

Most welcome is the society of a countryman to those who are travelling abroad; and Stella thought it was this reason that made Philip's presence so grateful to her. Then, too, he was so gentle, and talked to her of his lost sister, blind like herself, until she felt that blindness to be less pain. He read to her, and thus opened a new world to her view; his high and cultivated intellect drawing out the hidden treasures of hers, and his early ripened judgment guiding her, until she awoke from the vague, idle dreams of girlhood unto a better and brighter life. Yet all this while no words of love passed between them.

For weeks, months, their life was a long dream of happiness, so sweet that neither thought of the waking. By slow degrees the truth dawned on Philip Armytage, and he knew that he, over whose heart light fancies before had swept like a summer wind, now loved for the first time, with his whole heart and soul. And who was the object of this passionate love? A blind girl, whose helplessness made her only the dearer, for what is so sweet to proud man as the sense of protection. Often when Philip sat and listened to her voice, or looked on her fragile loveliness, as she clung to his guiding arm, he felt that if he could only take her in his heart's core, and shield her there from every breath of sorrow, what bliss it would be! And then he remembered himself — poor, friendless as he was, how dared he love her! And so his lips were sealed.

Had Philip Armytage guessed that Stella would learn to love him, he would have flown from the spot rather than thus have brought sorrow upon her. He was too honourable, knowing his own poverty, to steal into a girl's heart, whose hand he hoped not to claim. Stella was so different from any woman he had ever met; her manner towards him was so frank, so open, with not a shadow of disguise in her simple, truthful soul, that Philip thought she regarded him only as a friend, and never by one word did he overstep the limits of that friendship. And Stella, in her unworldly and innocent nature, had deceived herself likewise. It was not until he came to tell her that he must soon depart with the noble lord who hired his services, that Stella knew how dearly she loved Philip Armytage.

But with that knowledge came thronging a host of maidenly feelings — not pride, nor yet shame — why should she blush, that in loving him she had loved goodness, and talent, and everything that ennobles man? but painful reserve and sadness, which must now be hidden from sight. How little the poor blind girl knew how to conceal aught! Yet, in a few hours of anguish she learned more than in her whole life, and when Philip came next day to bid her adieu, he was almost startled by the change in her. The wavering colour on her cheek had settled into a deadly paleness; and there was a womanly calmness in her manner, but not the girlish freedom of old.

A wild thought of sweet agony shot through Philip's brain — did she then love him? But no; there was no tremulousness in the lip, no blush, no tear. It could not be.

They talked long and calmly of his proposed journey — of Italy, whither he was going, of the time passed here so pleasantly, of the chances how and where they might again meet.

"I shall hear of you sometimes," said Philip, in that old, old parting sentence, "and you will think of me now and then, Stella?" It was at her own particular wish that he had called her by her sweet Christian name.

"Yes," answered Stella, "I shall not forget how many dull hours you have made pleasant; I shall ever remember your kindness, your pity to one like me."

"You pain me by speaking thus," Philip said, after a pause, during which his heart beat so violently that he vainly tried to make his voice seem calm.

"I am sorry; — then I will say no more about myself, and only thank you very much for all you have been to me," returned Stella, with something of her smile of old.

Philip Armytage rose — he lingered over the last adieu. He held her hand and looked at her as if to imprint every feature of that beautiful face in his memory. Alas, for the blind girl who could not see what a world of love was revealed in his gaze! With a voice whose tremulousness went to Stella's very heart, he said, Farewell! lifted her hand half-way to his lips, and relinquished it without the so-longed-for kiss, and departed.

He had scarcely crossed the threshold when he remembered Mr. Brandreth, whose cold but always courteous welcome had never failed him, and surely merited some adieu. Philip returned; he had not meant to seek Stella again, for her silent farewell had pained him, but he heard a low wailing in the room where he had left her, and came near. There, weeping with a passionate vehemence that shook her slight frame, knelt the blind girl, her head bowed, and her hands tightly clasped together.

"My mother — my Philip — both gone — I am all alone now," she murmured, in accents of thrilling sorrow.

Philip forgot everything except that he loved and was beloved. He darted forward and knelt beside her.

"No, not alone, my Stella — star of my life — my only beloved," he cried, lavishing upon her the passionate epithets that love teaches. "I will never leave you, my heart's darling — my beautiful — more to me than all the world!" he continued, while his arms encircled his treasure, and she, trembling, almost doubting the joyful certainty, could only weep. He asked her why she did so.

"Because I am unworthy of you — I so ignorant — so young, and blind."

"I will be your eyes, my dearest!" cried the lover, kissing

the blue-veined lids that drooped over those poor sightless orbs, as with the most tender and earnest assurances, he told Stella all — how her sweetness and child-like simplicity had awakened his deepest love — how he had struggled against it, and, finally, how he had found out his error, and was resolved, in despite of ill-fortune, pride, poverty, to ask her for his own. And so they plighted their faith one to the other; the blind girl and her lover. One hour — almost one moment — had changed their fate through life.

Philip Armytage went home full of deep thought. His step was firmer, his carriage loftier, for he felt that he was no longer a lonely man — he was the guardian of another's happiness — the object of woman's priceless love. He had not only to think of himself, but of her who trusted him — who placed her fate in his keeping. Since yesterday, his whole thoughts were changed; even his worldly prospects seemed brighter now that Stella loved him, and that his fortunes might one day be linked with hers. Poverty looked dim in the distance; he felt a proud consciousness of his own powers; it seemed that he could brave all things — do all things, if Stella might one day be his wife. The glamour of love overspread all he looked upon; and with these delicious feelings, Philip Armytage, before he slept, sat down and wrote a letter to Mr. Brandreth, asking Stella's hand.

It was refused! The father, though not unkind, was firm. He regretted his own error in not having foreseen the end of such a friendship, and courteously, but resolutely, refused to sanction a marriage, or even betrothal, so wild and imprudent.

The lover read the cold, formal epistle through twice, before he comprehended it clearly; it came like ice upon fire. The sensible, right-minded Philip Armytage was still under the influence of that sweet, bewildering love-dream. Yet, there the words were — freezing and plain — "that a man without riches should never be the husband of Stella Brandreth." His spirit sank within him; he covered his face, and the burning tears, so seldom wrung from manhood, stole through his fingers. How well he loved the poor blind girl!

Night found him still pacing his chamber in utter desolation of heart. Then he yearned once more to look upon the face of her he loved. He longed to tell Stella that he had not forsaken her — that he would never love any but her. Under cover of darkness he stole to her home — crept along the grass to the window of the room where he and Stella had so often sat; the light, through the half-drawn curtains, showed him that she was there, and alone. From the deep sadness of her face and attitude, he guessed that she knew all. Philip touched the window — it was a little way open, and in a moment he stood by her side.

Long and mournful was the conference between the two; but when Philip spoke of his departure for Italy, the girl's sorrow amounted almost to agony.

"Philip — Philip, do not leave me," she cried, imploringly; "I was so desolate before you came; you only brought light and joy to the poor blind girl. No one has loved me but you, since my mother died. Philip, I shall die too, if I lose you. Forsake me not — take me with you; as your wife I shall fear nothing — shall regret nothing."

Poor Stella! she knew so little of the world, and she was so young — hardly more than a child in years, and a child in simplicity. All that she felt was the anguish of losing him who was the only one who made life precious to her. She clung around his neck, and besought him to stay, in spite of her father — of every one.

Bitter, indeed, was the struggle in the young man's bosom; but the right triumphed at last. He would not commit so grievous a sin as to bring sorrow and poverty on the innocent creature who trusted him, by wedding her against her father's will.

"Stella, dearest," he said, "you do not know what you ask — we must part for a while. There never comes a blessing on disobedience; and God forbid that I should be the one to steal a child from her father's arms, even if I loved her as my heart's blood — and thus love I you, my own Stella."

A deep flush of womanly shame crossed the girl's face. She drew herself from her lover's arms, and stood upright.

"I have been wrong, Philip — I have forgotten what I owe to myself, to my father, to you; forgive me — I am very ignorant — you are wiser and better than I. Forget all this, and only remember that I am blind and lonely, with no one to love me but you. Go, you are right; I will strive to be content in thinking how little I deserved to be loved so well by one like you."

Philip used all the sweet language of a lover, to soothe and cheer her. He told her that he would struggle for life and death, to gain that wealth which would enable him to win her — that she was so young — that nothing was impossible to love, and it might only be a few years before he could boldly come and claim his bride.

"I ask no promise, but I trust your love, my Stella; you will not doubt mine?"

"Never, never," murmured the girl. "But I need not say farewell now, you will come once more?" she added, trembling.

Philip promised, for his patron would remain yet a week. He clasped his beloved wildly to his heart, leaped through the window, and was gone. For an hour he haunted the place, until he saw Stella at the window, the lamp showed him her face, pale, sad, but composed; she stayed a moment to breathe the cool night air, and then turned away. It was his last vision of the beautiful blind girl.

When, a few days after, Philip came again to the house where he had been so welcome, it was deserted; the Englishman and his daughter had gone, no one knew whither.

CHAPTER IV.

> "How happy is he born and taught
> That serveth not another's will,
> Whose armour is his honest thought,
> And simple truth his utmost skill.
> This man is freed from servile bands,
> Of hope to rise, or fear to fall,
> Lord of himself, tho' not of lands,
> And having nothing, yet hath all."
> SIR HENRY WOTTON.

PHILIP ARMYTAGE went to Italy, a weary-hearted, disappointed man. He had loved — he loved still; the life of love was over; yet its memory was as a sweet perfume, that would not depart. No true, earnest, pure love can ever be utterly in vain. Such a love is rarely placed on an unworthy object; and the mere act of loving, hallows and elevates the soul. If death takes away the desire of the eyes, who shall repine at having loved, and made life sweet by that love while it lasted? If — more hard to bear still — comes earthly separation from the beloved — nay, even falsehood; still the poor lonely one has not loved in vain. Why do poets rave about unhappy love? There is no unhappiness in love, if it be sinless. The stricken heart has shed its odours like a flower; if they are wasted or cast aside, it is sad; but still they have not been poured out in vain: they have perfumed the air around, and the flower has lived amid the incense it made. Again we say, no man or woman, who loved truly, ever loved in vain.

And Philip's love for Stella was not in vain; it purified his heart; it taught him his own strength; it nerved to energy a spirit that might otherwise have yielded to apathy. In the thorny path of life, even the strong-minded Philip Armytage might have sunk in despair but for that poor little wayside flower which had brightened his way, if only for a time. Love for a virtuous woman is man's best armour against sin, his strongest spur to exertion; and thus, when Philip awoke from his dream of love, he determined resolutely to gain the reality of it.

He saw that to saunter lazily through life, as the dependent of a great man, would not be the way to win him his Stella; that he must strive to enter some profession that might give him wealth and a position in society. Yet how, without means of support, was he to attain this end? How live while he was studying? how bear the expenses of study? Many a time did he ponder over this, until he was nigh unto despair. There was but one chance, and to that he bent his proud spirit. A greater testimony could not be given to the intense love which animated him to exertion, for her sake who had awakened it.

Philip Armytage came to England, and, uninvited, crossed the threshold of the uncle whose delight he had been in boyhood, and from whom he had parted a year before, if not in anger, at least in coolness; the result of suffering on the one hand, and conscious injustice on the other. He did what will at once stamp him as no hero of romance, but yet what was, in itself, the greatest heroism, as it cost him the severest struggle of his life. He asked humbly, and as a favour, that his uncle would, out of his abundant wealth, supply him with a pittance while he studied for the bar, pledging himself, if he lived, to return the loan.

Sir Philip Heathcote was not a man of deep feelings, yet he perceived at once how violently those of his nephew were agitated while making this request. He took his hand kindly, almost deprecatingly, for it seemed to him that his dead sister looked at him out of her son's eyes, reproaching him for the caprice which had brought Philip so low.

"Tell me, first, why you are thus anxious to become a barrister, my dear boy?" said the old man to him.

The endearing expression, and somewhat of the love of former days, melted away all Philip's lingering pride. He told his uncle why he wished advancement in the world, for the sake of one beloved

"It is foolish — very foolish; a girl so young, and blind too! What sort of wife will she make, think you, for a man who must struggle with the world," said the cautious uncle.

Philip's pride once more rose up in his heart. "I only asked if you will show me this kindness; if not, I will depart," he replied coldly.

"I must consider," Sir Philip was about to say, still doubtful, when the rustle of silk announced the old man's young, beautiful, worldly wife, and he hastily grasped his nephew's hand, whispering — "Not a word, Philip, you shall have all you wish!" There was much good in the old baronet after all.

Philip entered on his new career. It was one from which, in his early days of academic honours and literary pleasures, he would have shrunk in disgust as being wearisome and dull; but he had now a great end to gain, and he heeded not how uninviting was the path that led towards it. Month after month he pored over dusty law folios, until his brain grew heated and weary; but then between him and the page would float Stella's face, with the long lashes cast down, and the sweet lips that trembled with every change of feeling, as rose-petals with the breath of the breeze. In the day-time, when mingling with the hurrying scenes of the life he had chosen, that image grew fainter; but when at night he closed his eyes, and his spirit retired within itself deep in his heart's core, did Philip cherish the memory of Stella.

As months, years flew on, and no tidings reached him, this memory became like a dream. He had no clue whereby to trace her, and even if he had, what could it have availed? Still, though hope grew less, it never utterly failed him; he could not but think that he should meet her again one day, and no other love ever came to render him forgetful of that which he bore towards her.

Thus Philip Armytage went on his way, until his brave spirit had conquered all difficulties; and, no longer a dependent on his uncle's kindness, he took his stand among those whose eloquence and talents made them renowned in the land. How was the boyish dreamer changed, and become the thoughtful, high-hearted man, before whose intellect the wisest bowed, and upon whose eloquent tongue the learned and unlearned, the rude and the gentle, hung spell-bound with equal delight! No shallow sophistry, no underhand double-dealing ever sullied the lips or disgraced the actions of Philip Armytage; he ever stood forward for truth and justice. He showed the dignity of the law, and his strong, clear mind was never warped by meanness or prejudice.

And not alone at the bar did his fame make its way; but his fine intellect blossomed anew in the sunshine of good fortune. His darling dream from his boyhood was realized — he became an author. The voice of the poet went forth like a trumpet, sounding aloud for the just and right cause; men listened to it, and woman's lips grew eloquent in praise of the noble spirit that was ever on the side of truth and mercy. His songs went through the length and breadth of the land, to prove what the true poet ought to be — not the idle rhymer, the visionary sentimentalist, but the teacher of all high things, the voice of God to mankind, leading them to a purer life, and himself showing the way. The man of genius stands forth as the high priest of Divinity itself, before whom it befits him to offer up, not only the first-fruits of his intellect, but the continued sweet savour of a life, high and pure, and in accordance with the lore he teaches. He should realize his own ideal, and be what he strives to delineate. And thus, amidst fame and high fortune, was Philip Armytage the eloquent upholder of virtue, the scorner of vice, the earnest, music-breathing poet, the noble man.

CHAPTER V.

*"In the unruffled shelter of thy love,
My bark leaped homewards from a rugged sea,
And furled its sails and dropped right peacefully
Hope's anchor, quiet as a nested dove."* — LOWELL.

AMONG the many whose society was pleasant to Philip Armytage, as his was to them, stood foremost an aged couple, who, united late in life, spent their childless old age in pleasing themselves with all that was good and beautiful around. Mrs. Lyle was one of those few women who know how to "grow old gracefully," and are as winning and lovely in their decay as the twilight of a summer evening fading into the gray of night. None of the sourness and cold-heartedness of age was in her gentle nature; she did not turn away from the young and ardent, but rather clung to them and encouraged them. She loved all that was beautiful; she filled her pretty home with pictures, and statues, and books, so that to enter it was like coming into a sweet garden of fancy, in which the continual perfume of a graceful and elegant mind pervaded all things. And about this pleasant home moved its gentle possessor, with her low voice, her kind manner, and her face still beautiful even in age, from the sweet expression it wore. Hither she welcomed many of those who were rising or risen in art and literature, rejoicing with the fortunate, cheering the doubtful, encouraging the struggling, and sympathizing with all, and with none more than with Philip Armytage.

One day the young barrister came thither, to see Mrs. Lyle. The gentle old lady was in her flower-garden; she loved her flowers so much, as indeed she loved everything in which was a shadow of the beautiful; and Philip was shown into an inner room, where she received her favourite guests. A pleasant, cheerful room it was — with its antique furniture, its crimson walls, from which looked the sweet heads of Raffaelle, and the soft-eyed Madonnas of Guido, beside the pure outlines of Flaxman's marble bas-reliefs, with its painted windows, through which the sunlight struggled quaintly, giving an air of dreaminess and mystery to the whole.

Philip Armytage half entered, but stayed his feet, for the room was not unoccupied. At the further end, a lady sat reading. From her slight but rounded figure she seemed in the meridian of womanhood; her face was turned away, but

Philip looked in admiration at the graceful outline of her cheek, and her Grecian-shaped head, round which soft golden hair was braided, contrasting with the mourning-dress she wore.

Wondering who she could be, he came nearer; she turned round, half bending in acknowledgment to a stranger, and Philip looked upon the face of his early love. Yes! it was indeed Stella, but how changed! the fairy girl was matured in the dignified woman, and those sweet blue eyes, sightless no longer, coldly met his own, without recognising Philip Armytage.

A chill crept over him; he who a day before would have flown to clasp her to his bosom, now stood spell-bound by her presence, as if she had been a vision from the dead.

"Have you forgotten me?" at last burst from his quivering lips.

At the sound of his voice she started, glanced wildly towards him; her cheek grew marble-white and then crimson.

"Have you forgotten me, Stella?—forgotten Philip Armytage?" and he took her hand.

"No — no — no!" cried the girl, as she clasped it in both hers, and looked eagerly in his face. In a moment Philip's arms were round her, and his long-lost, long-beloved one wept joyful tears upon his breast.

"And do you indeed remember me still, Philip?" asked Stella, with a doubtful look in her eyes. "Have all these years brought no change?"

"It is you who are changed, my beloved," Philip answered, gazing earnestly at her.

An expression of rapturous joy irradiated Stella's face.

"Yes! I am not now as when you knew me — I am no longer blind."

They sat down together, hand in hand, and talked of all that had happened since they parted. Stella told her lover how, after their forced separation, months had glided into years, and still she heard no tidings of him; how she and her father at last returned to England, where the skill of an eminent oculist restored to her the light of day, and all the delights of a world so long shut out from her. Thus her girlhood stole into womanhood, and she entered into society, still keeping faithful to the memory of her early dream, dim and hopeless as it had now become. Then Stella spoke of her father — of his increased kindness, which had continued until his death. Her high-spirited brother had gone to India, and she was now all alone, save for the sister of her mother — the gentle-hearted Mrs. Lyle. All this Philip learned, in return for his own tale of faithful love. But Stella, with woman's reserve, did not tell him how entirely the thought of him had engrossed her whole soul; that by night and by day his name was in her heart, his voice in her ear; that she existed but in that one idea, through months and years of absence, during which she knew not if he ever once remembered her. She did not tell him how, when his fame increased, it reached even to her, and her woman's heart swelled with pride at having loved and been loved by one so worthy; how she lived for days on the delight of having read his name, or heard him spoken of by strangers with words of praise; how she hung over his writings, and traced there the ripe harvest of mind which she had known in its early luxuriance; and how at times came the wild yearning to see him once more, and to know if in the memory of the honoured man of genius lingered one thought of the blind girl he had once loved, and who returned that love with such passionate devotion, though it was buried in the depths of her inmost heart.

This sweet communion was broken by the entrance of Mrs. Lyle; but all was soon revealed to her, and she rejoiced with almost a mother's joy over the happiness of the two whom she loved so well. Once more Philip and Stella renewed their early vows; there was now no impediment to their union, save in that lingering pride which made the lover shrink from receiving from his wife those worldly riches with which it would have been his delight to load her. But the young barrister was still poor, and Stella was an heiress.

When Philip spoke of this, she answered with the loving dignity of a woman, who, with her heart, gives her all —

"Do you remember, Philip, years ago, when I was a wild, foolish girl, I besought you to take me as your wife, and you nobly refused to bring sorrow upon me in return for my love. I am now a woman, wiser, I trust, and more worthy of you, though still most humble compared to Philip Armytage. But such as I am, take me, and all that is mine; I count it as nothing when I think of the bliss of being beloved by one like you."

And now the betrothed lovers entered on that sweet time when the doubt and fear of love is over, and the two heart-united ones stand on the threshold of wedded life, and look forward to the future as an endless vista of pleasant paths, to be trodden together. How sweet were the long summer evenings when Philip left weary, dull, dusty London behind him, and came to Mrs. Lyle's cottage at Hampstead, that prettiest of pretty spots, which, but for its metropolitan *prestige*, would be thought a very Arcadia! It was very pleasant to Philip and Stella to stroll along the green lanes between Hampstead and Highgate, and talk of their old favourites who had loved these very spots — the young dreamer, Keats, and Coleridge, the philosopher-poet, and Shelley the gentle-hearted, whose life was a long sunbeam of love and poetry. And when they came home, there was Mrs. Lyle, ever ready to welcome them with her quiet smile; and then there was some book to be read, over which the good-natured, but less ethereally inclined friend dozed in sweet oblivion; or else Stella sang to her lover the dear old songs, of which she had not forgotten one — not even the one which he had first listened to in the gay *soirée*, when sang by the blind English maiden.

Day by day Stella's character unfolded itself more to her betrothed — not as the sweet, innocent girl whose helplessness had entwined her round the heart of the strong man, in spite of her half-formed mind, so inferior to his own, with a tie in which compassion had awakened love; but as the matured, high-souled woman, whose ripened cultivated powers made her a helpmeet for the man of intellect. Philip Armytage did not know how much of this was owing to himself. A woman's character in after-life often, nay, almost always takes its nature from that of her first love — not her first crude girlish fancy, but the one who first unsealed the fountain of woman's feelings. She becomes like him she loves; her thoughts and predilections take their hue from his; if she weds him, their union is thus made sweeter by sympathy; if not, however her lot may be cast, she never entirely ceases to be influenced by those feelings which he first created and guided. Thus had Stella loved one of inferior mind, she would never have become what she was now, her nature would have sank to his, and many of its hidden treasures would have lain dormant for ever.

But though hardly a trace remained of the undeveloped

character of the blind girl, Stella still preserved the pure simplicity and sweetness which had distinguished her then. She was still as humble-minded, as devoted to him she loved, hardly bestowing a thought on her surpassing beauty and her many attractions, except so far as they made her more precious to him and more worthy to be his wife. And such was the bride whom, ere the leaves of autumn had fallen to earth, Philip Armytage took to his home and to his heart, a treasure long wooed, long sighed for, at last won!

CHAPTER VI.

"Their sky was all glory; but a cloud sailed into it; there was lightning in its bosom, and it broke." — BERNARD.

We have seen the blind girl as a child, a young maiden, a woman in the pride of her loveliness; let us now behold her as a wife, no longer the idol of a lover's dream, but the sharer of his life — the joy, the comfort of her husband's home. We would fain describe her, but the words float from our pen, and glide away into poesy — into that sweetest picture of woman that ever dawned on poet's brain. Stella was —

> "A creature not too bright and good
> For human nature's daily food;
> For transient sorrows, simple wiles,
> Praise, blame, love, kisses, tears, and smiles.
> * * * *
> A being breathing thoughtful breath;
> A traveller betwixt life and death;
> A perfect woman nobly planned,
> To warn, to comfort, and command;
> And yet a spirit still and bright,
> And something of an angel light."

After this, what can we say but that Philip Armytage had, in truth, "an angel in the house." Rare, very rare, are such in this world; but we have known some, and others, doubtless, have done the same. Alas! that while they were walking with us we knew them not, until they had spread their invisible wings, and flown to heaven!

The home of Philip Armytage was one in which the world may see that poesy can hallow daily life, and that the glorious light of genius is not incompatible with the subdued, delicious glow of the domestic fire-side. A man of talent is like a beacon set on a hill, exposed to every wind of heaven, and to the gaze of innumerable eyes, eagerly watching lest its light should be extinguished. If it flutter or wane for a moment, like any other common fire, up rises the cry of a hundred voices, and a hundred hands are lifted to quench the unworthy beacon. God help the man of genius! he walks through a road that is full of snares, more, and deeper for him than for men of less exalted minds, and less sensitive natures; and all these set up a rejoicing shout if he only stumble. Yet it is not impossible to tread the path in safety; many strive thus to walk, and all honour to those whose life proves that men may glory at once in a lofty intellect and a blameless and pure heart. Such an one approaches nearest to that ideal of humanity — which all shall, we trust, one day attain — when mind and matter shall no longer strive together, and we become only "a little lower than the angels."

Philip Armytage lived this life, as near as man can do on earth. He brought the treasures of his lofty intellect to brighten his home; he did not relinquish his profession, but he adorned it with the refinements of a gifted mind. He had none of the vagaries of the poet; he did not consider that genius must necessarily be eccentric, and no one would have thought that the clear-headed, sensible man, whose courteous and winning manners were the ornament of the intellectual society which he collected round him in his well-ordered home, or the gentle, affectionate husband, who read and talked cheerfully to his wife during the long winter evenings, was the same high-souled poet, whose brilliant imagination made his writings worshipped by some, and wondered at by others.

When the long, pleasant, summer-days came again, Philip and Stella took "the wings of the dove," and fled away for a time to a home far down in the country, the same where Stella's mournful childhood had been spent, and which was now left half desolate in the absence of its present owner, Edmund Brandreth. The happy wife of Philip Armytage trod, with her husband by her side, all those forest walks where the lonely blind girl had once wandered, and the contrast made her, if possible, happier still. Life was to the young pair an enchanted dream of such deep joy that their hearts trembled under the burthen, like flowers heavy with much dew. Young, rich, with minds gifted to behold and enjoy, to the full, all that was beautiful, and hearts that seemed as one in close and loving union; — what had they more to desire? Sometimes a light shadow of fear would flit over them — a sort of vague doubt that as night comes after day, so grief ever follows happiness. But then love chased the dim phantom away with its angel wings.

It had been a long season of drought, so that the very grass was parched in the meadows, the birds became almost mute, and fled to the deepest shades of the vast forest. Very grateful now was the thick wood, whose verdant recesses formed the only relief from the insupportable heat. Every evening Stella and her husband took their pleasant ramble together, from twilight until the stars came out; the young wife adding to every beautiful sight and sound by her deep sense of enjoyment, while Philip's noble mind invested all things with a halo of poesy, so that to walk with him was to walk with a magician, who unveiled the inner life of nature. One evening they went out together as usual, but did not pass beyond the lawn, for twilight brought with it the tokens of a coming storm. Dark, vapour-fringed cumuli rose up o'er the bed of the departing orb, shutting out all the lovely purple and gold of a September sunset, and growing thicker and blacker, until they reached mid heaven, covering the pale moon, that in her feeble age followed quickly after the fading light. A heavy stillness succeeded — a darkness that might be felt, oppressing both mind and body with a dull weight.

"Let us go in," said Stella, as she leaned wearily upon her husband's arm; "see, the storm is coming nearer; and look! there is a flash."

"It is only summer lightning," Philip answered. "But come, dear, we will go within doors, and watch it from the window, it is so beautiful."

They went in, and stood watching the storm. Stella felt no fear, for her husband was beside her. She rested her head on his shoulder, and felt his arm encircle her, and thus they looked on the gathering clouds, and the brilliant flashes of sheet lightning that momently illumined the whole heavens, and made the dark woods as bright and distinct as in broad daylight. Even when the heavy drops began to fall, and a low rumbling of thunder was heard in the distance, they did not turn away, for the minds of both were of too high an order to experience that weak sorrow which makes the feeble shrink

from that grandest and most beautiful sight — a thunderstorm at night.
"You are not afraid, my dearest?" asked the husband.
"No, Philip," answered Stella. "I like to watch a storm coming on. I feel a kind of awful delight, as though I were drawn nearer to heaven, and heard the voice of God in the thunder. I have no fear, except that I would ever have those I love beside me as now."
Philip pressed his wife nearer to him with a smile. "Now you are quite safe, love."
"Yes, with you. I remember the first storm I ever watched, after my sight was restored. It was here at this very window. I was foolish, my Philip, I know, but I could not turn my thoughts from you. I wondered where you were — if you were safe; and though dreading no danger for myself, I yet felt a shuddering fear lest harm should come to you. Now I have you with me, my own husband."
"For ever — for ever," cried Philip, stooping over her with intense love, "my Stella, my ——"
As he spoke, a dazzling, blinding flash enveloped them in one sheet of lurid flame; then came a burst of thunder, so long and loud, that it seemed as if the heavens were falling. But the husband and wife heard it not. They both lay insensible, Philip's arms still clasping his beloved. Philip Armytage woke to consciousness, and found Stella still lying motionless. Her eyes were fixed and open; her features white and livid, while her arm still twined round his neck, as cold and heavy as stone. He uttered one cry of agonized despair, and then a desperate calmness came over him. He felt her heart; a faint pulse was still beating there. He lifted her hand; it did not fall down again, but remained stiffly extended. She was not dead, but remained in a trance if possible more fearful still than death.
All that night, the next day, and throughout another horrible night, did Philip hang over his insensible wife. No skill could wake her from her terrible repose; she lay immoveable, breathing faintly, but not a tinge of life was on her marble-like face, and the glare of her open eyes was fearful to behold. Philip tried to close them, but the eyelids shrank back again from the dilated pupils. He covered them with a veil, for he could not bear to see the horrible expression they gave to the beautiful face he loved so much.

When the second day was at its meridian, Philip thought he saw her breast heave, a faint hue dyed her white lips — they moved; and with a wild cry, he clasped his wife in his arms, and strove to re-animate those pale lips with kisses.

"Philip," she murmured faintly, "I thought I was dead."

"You are living — here in my arms, my beloved — my heart's treasure," cried the husband, almost weeping with joy.

"Ah, I remember the storm; it is all over now. It is night; but why have you put out the lamp? I cannot see you, love."

Philip shuddered at her words, for the room was flooded with the golden light of noon. He looked at Stella's eyes; their expression revealed the awful truth; the lightning had struck her, and she was once more hopelessly blind.

CHAPTER VII.

> "Go not away! — yet ah, dark shades I see
> Obscure thy brow — thou goest! but give thy hand;
> Must it be so? — Then go — I follow thee;
> Yes! unto death — unto the Silent Land."
> FREDRIKA BREMER.

STELLA awoke from that thunder-stricken trance unto darkness that no human power could henceforth sweep away — those sweet eyes were now blind for ever. Meekly, as became her nature, did she bow beneath the stroke, but Philip writhed under it in insupportable agony. Stella's health slowly recovered, and she rose up from her bed of sickness, and once more wandered about the house, pale, pensive, but still calm. Then burst forth her husband's wild despair. His frantic words sometimes reached almost to imprecations. He wished that the terrible lightning-flash had struck him dead, rather than that he should live to see this wreck of his happiness. His whole nature seemed changed; the gentle, upright, pious-hearted Philip Armytage was all but a maniac in his wild despair.

But Stella seemed to have gained all the firmness which he had lost. Patient, unrepining, she was to him like a guardian angel, soothing and cheering him, as if he had been the stricken one, and she the consoler. He would take her away, to try all that metropolitan skill could effect, and to amuse her, as he thought, with every enjoyment that London could furnish. But Stella knew it was hopeless; and though she submitted, to please her husband, still it was not long before her health failed in the close air of the city, and Philip bore her again to her native home.

There the soft spring breezes once more brought faint roses to the cheek of the blind wife, and hope, almost joy, stole back again to her heart, for she knew that heart would soon throb with the pulses of a mother's love. Again life became sweet to her, and a little of her cheerfulness communicated itself to Philip's melancholy spirit. In his wife's presence he grew more calm, and for her sake he returned to those pursuits which, in the first burst of wild agony, he had vowed to relinquish for ever. He read to her, as of old; he wrote poetry, because it pleased her; he no longer shrank from the pleasant sunshine, because she could behold it no more; but spent whole days in guiding her steps through the forest, describing everything he saw with the eloquence of love.

"Do you remember once when you said, 'I will be your eyes, dearest,'" Stella one day whispered to him, "and now you are so, my Philip! you make me see with your eyes."

Philip groaned, "Hush, hush, I cannot bear it."

"Nay, nay, look at me: I am not sad; indeed, Philip, you do not know how happy I am. If I were now, as I once was — lonely, helpless, with no one to love me — I might indeed lament; but with you for my husband, ever with me, giving up all for me, with the knowledge that my infirmity only proves how strong is your love, how can I murmur? My own Philip; you are the light of my eyes; there is no darkness for me when you are by."

And Philip could only press her to his heart, and weep.

But though when her husband was by, Stella appeared contented and cheerful, and indeed was so, yet there were times when she felt bitterly the deprivation of all those pleasures which had become so dear to her. She longed to behold that beautiful world which had been revealed to her sight, only to be shut out again for ever; and more than all, did she yearn to look once more upon the face of her husband — to watch it kindling into genius, until it became to her, at least, as the face of an angel. She knew, by the tones of his voice when it wore that look, and then her heart sank to think that she must see it no more for ever. At times, too, when in her darkness she was attiring herself, or arranging her long auburn hair, a natural sigh would escape her at the memory of the days in which her unsealed eyes first discovered that she was beautiful; and a throb of pleasure came to her heart at the thought that she was thereby more worthy of the long absent, but well-beloved one. Then, too, Stella would turn from the past to the dim future, and sometimes even weep that she would never behold the face of her child — that the blind mother would not trace, in its opening beauty, a likeness to the features most dear to her. And then, with these mother-thoughts, came memories of her own lost parent, in solemn sweetness leading her from earth to heaven.

Thus the time wore on; Philip's anguish was lulled by happy hopes for the future, and Stella's brow wore a holy calmness. One only, an aged woman, who had nursed her in her infancy, shook her head as she looked mournfully on the changing cheek and transparent hands; she knew well that the mysteries of the coming birth alone kept away the dread phantom, whose shadow already hung over the blind mother.

The hour of trial came; it brought a moment's joy, and then the gloom of despair. In a few days, the faint wailing cry of the young spirit which had entered this world of care was hushed; and silently, slowly, the mother was following her babe to heaven. No earthly power could save her, and Philip knew it. As still and speechless as her whose life was ebbing away on his bosom, the husband waited for death to take his treasure from his arms.

Stella lay in the heavy slumber which a temporary delirium had left behind. She did not even know on whose anguish-riven bosom her head rested. Once only she spoke like one dreaming.

"I see her — there, there with white garments. Mother, I am coming; only let me bid *him* farewell." And her lips closed, murmuring Philip's name.

An hour before death her senses returned. She bade Philip kiss her, then whispered faintly —

"I am content, my husband, my beloved! You will come, too, soon, oh! soon. There is no darkness there."

She felt for his hand, laid it on her heart, and spoke no more. Death stole over that gentle one, not with gloom and sorrow, but with the peaceful shadows of a child's rosy sleep.

* * * * *

Let us pause for a moment to think of death—death, as he comes in the midst of life, and youth, and love, when the world is yet sweet, and the journey has been too short for the limbs to grow weary. Yet, even so; blessed are they who never know the burthen and heat of the day! To them the Dread Presence comes as a white-winged angel, ere they have time to invest him with shadows that are alone the creation of man's fearful heart. He comes smiling, to waft them from earth's pleasures to those which are eternal. It is better to depart while love's roses are blooming than to linger until they fade. Therefore, blessed are the young who die beloved and loving still! And for those, few in years, but many in sorrows, who have already seen the sun of hope set ere noon — who would keep the poor mourning ones from their rest? Thus let us think of thee, O Death; gentle unlooser of life's burthen, who foldest thy calm, still arms round the weary frame, and leavest the immortal spirit to rise rejoicing unto God.

For months after the death of Stella, the world was a blank to Philip Armytage. His noble mind was a wreck, and if at times glimpses of reason and intellect came, like wandering meteors through the ruins, they only showed more plainly the mournful desolation around. One soft woman's voice, and gentle woman's hand had power over him in his wildest moods; they were those of Mrs. Lyle. Many thought that his brain had never recovered from the fearful lightning-stroke, so that any great sorrow was sure to overthrow reason for ever. But the love which had suffered so much, and then been riven by death, was cause sufficient. Rarely do men love to such intensity, but when they do, it is a fearful thing.

After a long season, Philip's mind awoke from its sleep. With declining health came restored reason. He lost that delusion which had constantly haunted him, in which he fancied that the lost one was ever present by his side. It might have been a dream or not; God only knows. If the departed become ministering spirits, as may be, what office would be sweeter to that blessed angel than to watch over and soothe the bewildered mind of him whom she had so fondly loved on earth? Calmly, with a kind of mournful joy, did

Philip Armytage see the world glide from him. Its pleasures were like shadows to him now. He lived near the fatal yet beloved home, whose gloom was now brightened by infant smiles and gay young voices, the children of Edmund Brandreth. These loved to gather round the knees of the pale, but ever-gentle mourner, and hear him talk of her who was gone — of her darkened childhood, her happy youth, her sweetness, and her suffering; and then they would listen with him to the murmuring of the trees in the old churchyard, the more fanciful of them thinking it was her voice whispering to them in the still evening twilight. But when the solitary one had kissed them all, and bade them good night, he would stretch his arms out in the darkness, and cry with a low yearning voice —

"My Stella, my beloved, let me come to thee."

And at length the longing prayer was heard.

ADELAIDE.

BEING FRAGMENTS FROM A YOUNG WIFE'S DIARY.

. . . I have been married seven weeks. . . . I do not rave in girlish fashion about my perfect happiness — I do not even say I love my husband. Such words imply a separate existence — a gift consciously bestowed on one being from another. I feel not thus: my husband is to me as my own soul.

Long, very long, it is since I first knew this. Gradually, not suddenly, the great mystery of love overshadowed me, until at last I found out the truth, that I was my own no more. All the world's beauty I saw through his eyes — all the world's goodness and greatness came to me reflected through his noble heart. In his presence I was as a child; I forgot myself, my own existence, hopes, and aims. Everywhere — at all times and all places — his power was upon me. He seemed to absorb and inhale my whole soul into his, until I became like a cloud melting away in sunshine, and vanishing from the face of heaven.

All this reads very wild and mad; but, oh! Laurence, Laurence! none would marvel at it who had once looked on thee! Not that he is a perfect Apollo — this worshipped husband of mine: you may meet a score far handsomer. But who cares? Not I! All that is grand, all that is beautiful, all that makes a man look godlike through the inward shining of his godlike soul, — I see in my Laurence. His eyes, soft yet proud, his wavy hair, his hand that I sit and clasp, his strong arm that I lean on — all compose an image wherein I see no flaw. Nay, I could scarce believe in any beauty that bore no likeness to Laurence.

Thus is my husband — what am I? His wife — and no more. Everything in me is only a reflection of him. Sometimes I even marvel that he loved me, so unworthy as I seem:

yet, when heaven rained on me the rich blessing of his love, my thirsty soul drank it in, and I felt that had it never come, for lack of it I must have died. I did almost die, for the joy was long in coming. Though, as I know now, he loved me well and dearly; yet for some reason or other he would not tell me so. The veil might never have fallen from our hearts, save for one blessed chance. I will relate it. I love to dream over that brief hour, to which my whole existence can never show a parallel.

We were walking all together, my sisters, Laurence Shelmerdine, and I, when there came on an August thunder-storm. Our danger was great, for we were in the midst of a wood. My sisters fled; but I, being weak and ill; alas! my heart was breaking quietly, though he knew it not — I had no strength to fly. He was too kind to forsake me: so we stayed in an open space of the wood, I clinging to his arm, and thinking, God forgive me! that if I could only die then, close to him, encompassed by his gentle care, it would be so happy — happier far than my life was then. What he thought I knew not. He spoke in hurried, broken words, and turned his face from me all the while.

It grew dark, like night; and there came flash after flash, peal after peal. I could not stand; I leaned against his arm.

At last, there shone all around us a frightful glare, as if the whole wood were in flames — a crash of boughs, a roar above, as though the heavens were falling — then, silence.

Death had passed close by us, and smote us not; and Death was the precursor of Love.

We looked at one another, Laurence and I: then with a great cry, our hearts, long tortured, sprang together. There never can be such a meeting, save that of two parted ones, who meet in heaven. No words were spoken, save a murmur, "Adelaide!" "Laurence!" but we knew that between us two there was but one soul. We stood there — all the while the storm lasted. He sheltered me in his arms, and I felt neither the thunder nor the rain. I feared not life nor death: for I now knew that in either I should never be divided from him.

. . . . . Ours was a brief engagement. Laurence wished it so; and I disputed not — I never disputed with him in anything. Besides, I was not happy at home: my sisters did not understand him. They jested with me because he was grave and reserved, even subject to moody fits sometimes.

They said, "I should have a great deal to put up with; but it was worth while, for Mr. Shelmerdine's grand estate atoned for all." My Laurence! as if I had ever thought whether he were rich or poor! I smiled, too, at my sisters' jests about his melancholy, and the possibility of his being "a bandit in disguise." None truly knew him; none but I. Yet I was half afraid of him at times; but that was only from the intensity of my love. I never asked him of his for me, how it grew, or why he had so long concealed it: enough for me that it was there. Yet he was always calm: he never showed any passionate emotion, save one night, the night before our wedding-day.

I went with him to the gate myself, walking in the moonlight under the holly-trees. I trembled a little; but I was happy, very happy. He held me long in his arms ere he would part with me; the last brief parting ere we would have no need to part any more. I said, looking up from his face unto the stars, "Laurence, in our full joy, let us thank God, and pray Him to bless us!"

His heart seemed bursting: he bowed his proud head, dropped it down upon my shoulder, and cried, "Nay, rather pray Him to *forgive* me. Adelaide, I am not worthy of happiness; I am not worthy of you!"

He to talk in this way! and about me! But I answered him soothingly, so that he might feel how dear was my love, how entire my trust.

He said at last, half mournfully, "You are content to take me then, just as I am: to forgive my past, to bear with my present, to give hope to my future. Will you do this, my love, my Adelaide?"

I answered solemnly, "I will!" Then, for the first time, I dared to lift my arms to his neck; and as he stooped I kissed his forehead. It was the seal of this my promise, which may God give me strength to keep evermore!

We were laughing to-day, Laurence and I, about *first loves*. It was scarcely a subject for mirth; but one of his bachelor friends had been telling us of a new-married couple, who, in some comical fashion, mutually made the discovery of each other's "first loves." I said to my husband, smiling happily, "that *he* need have no such fear." And I repeated, half in sport, the lines —

"'He was her own, her ocean-treasure, cast
Like a rich wreck — her first love and her last.'

So it was with poor Adelaide." Touched by the thought, my gaiety melted almost into tears. But I laughed them off, and added, "Come, Laurence, confess the same! You never, never loved any one but me?"

He looked pained, said coldly, "I believe I have not given cause — —" then stopped. How I trembled; but I went up to him, and whispered, "Laurence, dearest, forgive me." He looked at me a moment, then caught me passionately to his breast. I wept a little — my heart was so full. Yet I could not help again murmuring that question: "You love me? you *do* love me?"

"I love you as I never before loved woman. I swear this in the sight of Heaven. Believe it, my wife!" was his vehement answer. I hated myself for having so tried him. My dear, my noble husband! I was mad to have a moment's doubt of thee.

. . . . . Nearly a year married, and it seems a brief day: yet it seems, also, like a lifetime — as if I had never known any other. My Laurence! daily I grow closer to him — heart to heart. I understand him better — if possible, I love him more: not with the wild worship of my girlhood, but with something dearer, more home-like. I would not have him an "angel," if I could. I know all his little faults and weaknesses quite well; I do not shut my eyes on any of them; but I gaze openly at them, and *love* them down. There is love enough in my heart to fill up all chasms, to remove all stumbling-blocks from our path. Ours is truly a wedded life: not two jarring lives, but an harmonious and complete one.

I have taken a long journey, and am somewhat dreary at being away, even for three days, from my pleasant home. But Laurence was obliged to go, and I would not let him go alone; though, from tender fear, he urged me to stay. So kind and thoughtful he was, too. Because his engagements here would keep him much from me, he made me take likewise my sister Louisa. She is a good girl, and a dear girl; but I miss Laurence; I did especially in my walk to-day, through a lovely wooded country, and a sweet little village.

I was thinking of him all the time; so much so, that I quite started when I heard one of the village children shouted after as "Laurence."

Very foolish it is of me, a loving weakness I have not yet got over — but I never hear the name my husband bears without a pleasant thrill; I never even see it written up in the street without turning again to look at it. So, unconsciously, I turned to the little rosy urchin, whom his grandam honoured by the name of "Laurence."

A pretty, sturdy boy, of five or six years old; a child to glad any mother. I wondered, had he a mother? — stayed, and asked — I always notice children now. Oh, wonderful, solemn mystery sleeping at my heart, my hope, my joy, my prayer! I think, with tears, how I may one day watch the gambols of a boy like this; and how, looking down in his little face, I may see therein my Laurence's eyes. For the sake of this future — which God grant! — I went and kissed the little child who chanced to bear my husband's name. I asked the old woman about the boy's mother. "Dead! dead five years." And his father? A sneer — a muttered curse — bitter words about "poor folk" and "gentlefolk." Alas! alas! I saw it all. Poor, beautiful, unhappy child!

My heart was so pained, that I could not tell the little incident to Laurence. Even when my sister began to talk of it, I asked her to cease. But I pondered over it the more. I think, if I am strong enough, I will go and see the poor little fellow again to-morrow. One might do some good — who knows!

To-morrow has come — to-morrow has gone. What a gulf lies between that yesterday and its to-morrow! . . . . Louisa and I walked to the village — she very much against her will. "It was wrong and foolish," she said; "one should not meddle with vice," and she looked prudent and stern. I tried to speak of the innocent child — of the poor dead mother; and the shadow of motherhood over my own soul taught me compassion towards both. At last, when Louisa was half angry, I said I would go, for I had a secret reason which she did not know. Thank Heaven those words were put into my lips!

So, we went. My little beauty of a boy was not there; and I had the curiosity to approach the cottage where his grandmother lived. It stood in a garden, with a high hedge around. I heard a child's laugh, and could not forbear peeping through. There was my little favourite, held aloft in the arms of a man, who stood half-hidden behind a tree.

"He looks like a gentleman: perhaps it is the wretch of a father!" whispered Louisa. "Sister, we ought to come away." And she walked forward indignantly.

But I still stayed — still looked. Despite my horror of the crime, I felt a sort of attraction: it was some sign of grace in the man that he should at least acknowledge and show kindness to his child. And the miserable mother! I, a happy wife, could have wept to think of her. I wondered, did he think of her, too? He might; for, though the boy laughed and chattered, lavishing on him all those pet diminutives which children make out of the sweet word "father," I did not hear *this* father answer by a single word.

Louisa came to hurry me away. "Hush!" I said: "one moment, and I will go."

The little one had ceased chattering: the father put it down, and came forth from his covert.

O God! it was *my husband!*

. . . . I think I should have then fallen down dead, save for one thing — I turned and met my sister's eyes. They were full of horror — indignation — pity. She, too, had seen.

Like lightning there flashed across me all the future: my father's wrath — the world's mockery — *his* shame.

I said — and I had strength to say it quite calmly — "Louisa, you have guessed our secret; but keep it — promise."

She looked aghast — confounded.

"You see," I went on — and I actually smiled! "you see, I know all about it, and so does Laurence. It is — a friend's child."

May heaven forgive me for that lie I told: it was to save my husband's honour.

Day after day, week after week, goes by, and yet I live — live, and living keep the horrible secret in my soul. It must remain there buried for ever, now.

It so chanced, that after that hour I did not see my husband for some weeks: Louisa and I were hastily summoned home. So I had time to think what I was to do.

I knew all now — all the mystery of his fits of gloom — his secret sufferings. It was remorse, perpetual remorse. No marvel. And for a moment my stern heart said, "Let it be so." I, too, was wronged. Why did he marry me, and hide all this? Oh, vile! Oh, cruel! Then the light broke on me: his long struggle against his love — his terror of winning mine. But he did love me: half-maddening as I was, I grasped at that. Whatever blackness was on the past, he loved me now — he had sworn it — "more than he ever loved woman."

I was yet young: I knew little of the wickedness of the world; but I had heard of that mad passion of a moment, which may seize on a heart not wholly corrupted, and afterwards a whole lifetime of remorse works out the expiation. Six years ago! he must have been then a mere boy. If he had thus erred in youth, I who knew his nature, knew how awful must have been the repentance of his manhood. On any humbled sinner I would have mercy — how much rather must I have mercy on *my husband?*

I *had* mercy. Some, stern in virtue, may condemn me; but God knoweth all.

He is — I believe it in my soul — he is a good man now, and striving more and more after good. I will help him — I will save him. Never shall he know that secret, which out of pride or bitterness might drive him back from virtue, or make him feel shame before me.

I took my resolution — I have fulfilled it. I have met him again, as a faithful wife should meet her husband: no word, no look betrays, or shall betray, what I know. All our outward life goes on as before: his tenderness for me is constant — overflowing. But oh! the agony, worse than death, of knowing my idol fallen — that where I once worshipped, I can only pity, weep, and pray.

He told me yesterday he did not feel like the same man that he was before his marriage. He said I was his good angel: that through me he became calmer, happier, every day. It was true: I read the change in his face. Others read it too. Even his aged mother told me, with tears, how much good I had done to Laurence. For this thank God!

My husband! my husband! At times I could almost think this horror was some delirious dream, cast it all to the winds, and worship him as of old. I do feel, as I ought, deep tenderness — compassion. No, no! let me not deceive myself: I love him; in defiance of all, I love him, and shall do so evermore.

Sometimes his olden sufferings come over him; and then I, knowing the whole truth, feel my very soul moved within me. If he had only told me all: If I could now lay my heart open before him, with all its love and pardon; if he would let me comfort him, and speak of hope, of Heaven's mercy — of atonement, even on earth. But I dare not — I dare not.

Since, from this silence which he has seen fit to keep, I must not share the struggle, but must stay afar off — then, like the prophet who knelt on the rock, supplicating for Israel in the battle, let my hands fall not, nor my prayer cease, until Heaven sendeth the victory.

Nearer and nearer comes the hour which will be to me one of double life, or of death. Sometimes, remembering all I have lately suffered, there comes to me a heavy foreboding. What, if I, so young, to whom, one little year ago, life seemed an opening paradise — what, if I should die — and leave *him*, and he never know how deeply I have loved — how much I have forgiven?

Yes; he might know, and bitterly. Should Louisa tell — but I will prevent that.

In my husband's absence, I have sat up half the night writing; that, in case of my death, he may be made acquainted with the whole truth, and hear it from me alone. I have poured out all my suffering — all my tenderness: I have implored him, for the love of Heaven, for the love of me, that he would in every way atone for the past, and lead for the future a righteous life; that his sin may be forgiven, and that, after death, we may meet in joy evermore.

I have been to church with Laurence — for the last time, as I think. We knelt together, and took the sacrament. His face was grave, but peaceful. When we came home, we sat in our beautiful little rose-garden: he, looking so content —

even happy: so tender over me — so full of hope for the
future. How should this be, if he had on his soul that awful
sin? All seemed a delusion of my own creating: I doubted
even the evidence of my own senses. I longed to throw
myself on his bosom, and tell him all. But then, from some
inexplicable cause, the olden cloud came over him; I read in
his face, or thought I read, the torturing remorse which at
once repels me from him, and yet draws me again, with a
compassion that is almost stronger than love. I thought I
would try to say, in some passing way, words that, should I
die, might afterwards comfort him, by telling him how his
misery had wrung my heart, and how I did not scorn him,
not even for his sin.

"Laurence," I said, very softly, "I wish that you and I
had known one another all our lives — from the time we were
little children."

"Oh, that we had! then I had been a better and a happier
man, my Adelaide!" was his answer.

"We will not talk of that. Please God, we may live a
long and worthy life together; but if not —"

He looked at me with fear. "What is that you say?
Adelaide, you are not going to die? — you, whom I have
made happy, you have no cause to die."

Oh, agony! he thought of the one who *had* cause — to
whose shame and misery death was better than life. Poor
wretch! she, too, might have loved him. Down, wife's jealousy! down, woman's pride! It was long, long ago. She
is dead; and he — Oh, my husband! may God forgive me
according as I pardon you!

I said to him once more, putting my arm round his neck,
leaning so that he could only hear, not see me. "Laurence,
if I should die, remember how happy we have been, and how
dearly we have loved one another. Think of nothing sad or
painful; think only that, living or dying, I loved you as I
have loved none else in the world. And so whatever chances,
be content."

He seemed afraid to speak more lest I should be agitated;
but as he kissed me, I felt on my cheek tears — tears that my
own eyes, long dried up with misery, had no power to shed.

. . . . I have done all I wished to do. I have set
my house in order. Now, whichever way God wills the
event, I am prepared. Life is not to me what it once was:

yet, for Laurence's sake, and for one besides — Ah! now I dimly guess what that poor mother felt, who, dying, left her child to the mercy of the bitter world. But, Heaven's will be done! I shall write here no more — perhaps for ever.

. . . . It is all past and gone. I have been a mother — alas! *have been*; but I never knew it. I woke out of a long, blank dream — a delirium of weeks — to find the blessing had come, and been taken away. ONE only giveth — ONE only taketh. Amen!

For three days, as they tell me, my babe lay by my side — its tiny hands touched mine — it slept at my breast. But I remember nothing — nothing! I was quite mad all the while. And then — it died; and I have no little face to dream of, no memory of the sweetness that has been: it is all to me as if I had never seen my child.

If I had only had my senses for one day — one hour! if I could but have seen Laurence when they gave him his baby-boy! Bitterly he grieves, his mother says, because he has no heir.

. . . . My first waking fear was horrible. Had I betrayed anything during my delirium? I think not. Louisa says I lay all the time silent, dull, and did not even notice my husband, though he bent over me like one distracted. Poor Laurence! I see him but little now: they will not suffer me. It is perhaps well: I could not bear his grief and my own too: I might not be able to keep my secret safe.

I went yesterday to look at the tiny mound — all that is left to me of my dream of motherhood. Such a happy dream as it was, too! How it comforted me, many a time: how I used to sit and think of my darling that was to come: to picture it lying in my arms — playing at my feet — growing in beauty — a boy, a youth, a man! And this, this is all; this little grave!

Perhaps I may never have another child. If so, all the deep love which nature teaches, and which nature has even now awakened in my heart, must find no object, and droop and wither away, or be changed into repining. No! please God, *that* last shall never be: I will not embitter the blessings I have, by mourning over those denied.

But I must love something, in the way that I would have loved my child. I have lost my babe; some babe may have

10*

lost a mother. A thought comes — I shudder — I tremble — yet I follow it. I will pause a little, and then —

In Mr. Shelmerdine's absence I have accomplished my plan. I have contrived to visit the place where lives that hapless child — my husband's child.

I do believe my love to Laurence must be such as never before was borne to man by woman. It draws me even towards this little one: forgetting all wounded pride, I seem to yearn over the boy. But is this strange? In my first girlish dreams, many a time I have taken a book he had touched — a flower he had gathered — hid it from my sisters, kissed it, and wept over it for days. It was folly; but it only showed how precious I held everything belonging to him. And should I not hold precious what is half himself — his own son?

I will go and see the child to-morrow.

Weeks have passed, and yet I have had no strength to tell what that to-morrow brought. Strange book of human fate! each leaf closed until the appointed time, if we could but turn it and read. Yet it is best not.

I went to the cottage — alone, of course. I asked the old woman to let me come in and rest, for I was a stranger, weak and tired. She did so kindly, remembering, perhaps, how I had once noticed the boy. He was her grandchild, she told me; her daughter's child.

Her daughter! — this old creature was a coarse, rough-spoken woman, a labourer's wife — her daughter! Laurence Shelmerdine, the elegant, the refined — what madness could have possessed him?

"She died very young, then, your daughter?" I found courage to say.

"Ay, ay; in a few months after the boy's birth. She was but a weakly thing at best, and she had troubles enow."

Quickly came the blood to my heart — to my cheek, in bitter, bitter shame. Not for myself, but for him. I shrank like a guilty thing before that mother's eye. I dared not ask, what I longed to hear, concerning the poor girl and her sad history.

"Is the child like her?" was all I could say, looking to where the little one was playing, at the far-end of the garden.

I was glad not to see him nearer. "Was his mother as beautiful as he?"

"Ay, a good-looking lass enough; but the little lad's like his father, who was a gentleman born: though Laurence had better ha' been a ploughman's son. A bad business Bess made of it. To this day I dunnot know her right name, nor little Laurence's there; and so I canna make his father own him. He ought; for the lad's growing up as grand a gentleman as himself, and 'll never do to live with poor folk like granny."

"Alas!" I cried, forgetting all but my compassion; "then how will the child bear his lot of shame!"

"Shame!" and the old woman came up fiercely to me. "You'd better mind your own business: my Bess was as good as you."

I trembled violently, but could not speak. The woman went on:—

"I dunnot care if I blab it all out, though Bess begged me not. She was a fool, and the young fellow something worse. His father tried — may-be he wished to try, too — but they couldna undo what had been done. My girl was safe married to him, and the little lad's a gentleman's lawful son."

Oh! joy beyond belief! Oh! bursting, blessed tears! My Laurence! my Laurence!

. . . . I have no clear recollection of anything more, save that I suppose the woman thought me mad, and ran out of the cottage. My first consciousness is of finding myself quite alone, with the door open, and a child looking in at me in wonderment, but with a gentleness such as I have seen my husband wear. No marvel I had loved that childish face: it was just such as might have been his own when he was a boy.

I cried, tremulously, "Laurence! little Laurence!" He came to me, smiling and pleased. One faint struggle I had: forgive me, poor dead girl! and then I took the child in my arms, and kissed him as though I had been his mother. For thy sake, for thy sake, my husband!

I understood all the past now. The boyish passion, making an ideal out of a poor village girl — the unequal union — the dream fading into common day; coarseness creating repulsion, the sting of one folly which had marred a life-time, dread of the world, self-reproach, and shame — all these excuses I could find: and yet Laurence had acted ill. And when the end came: no wonder that remorse pursued him, for he had broken a girl's heart. She might, she must have loved him. I wept for her — I, who so passionately loved him too. He was wrong, also, grievously wrong, in not acknowledging the child. Yet there might have been reasons. His father ruled with an iron hand; and, then, when he died, Laurence had just known me. Alas! I weave all coverings to hide his fault. But surely this strong, faithful love was implanted in my heart for good. It shall not fail him now; it shall encompass him with arms of peace; it shall stand between him and the bitter past: it shall lead him on to a worthy and happy future.

There is one thing which he must do: I will strengthen him to do it. Yet, when I tell him all, how will he meet it? No matter; I must do right. I have walked through this cloud of misery; shall my courage fail me now?

He came home, nor knew that I had been away. Something oppressed him: his old grief, perhaps. My beloved! I have a balm even for that now.

. . . . I told him the story, as it were in a parable, not of myself, but of another, a friend I had. His colour came and went, his hands trembled in my hold. I hid nothing: I told of the wife's first horrible fear of her misery; and the red flush mounted to his very brow. I could have fallen at his feet, and prayed forgiveness; but I dared not yet. At last I spoke of the end, still using the feigned names I had used all along.

He said, hoarsely, "Do you think the wife, a good and pure woman, would forgive her husband all this?"

"Forgive him? oh, Laurence, Laurence!" and I clung to him and wept.

A doubt seemed to strike him. "Adelaide, tell me —"

"I have told. My husband, I know all, and still I love you — I love you!"

I did not say, *I pardon*. I would not let him think that I felt I had need to pardon.

Laurence sank down at my feet, hid his face on my knees, and wept.

. . . . The tale of his youth was as I guessed. He told it me the same night, when we sat in the twilight gloom. I was glad of this, that not even his wife's eyes might scan too closely the pang it cost him to reveal these long-past days. But all the while he spoke my head was on his breast, that he might feel I held my place there still, and that no error, grief, or shame, could change my love for him, nor make me doubt his own, which I had won.

My task is accomplished. I rested not, day or night, until the right was done. Why should he fear the world's sneer, when his wife stands by him — his wife, who most of all might be thought to shrink from this confession that must be made? But I have given him comfort — ay, courage. I have urged him to do his duty, which is one with mine.

My husband has acknowledged his first marriage, and taken home his son. His mother, though shocked and bewildered at first, rejoiced when she saw the beautiful boy — worthy to be the heir of the Shelmerdines. All are delighted that there is such an heir. And I?

I go, but always secretly, to the small daisy-mound. My own lost one! my babe, whose face I never saw! If I have no child on earth, I know there is a little angel awaiting me in heaven.

Let no one say I am not happy, as happy as one can be in this world: never was any woman more blessed than I am in my husband and my son — mine. I adopted him as such: I will fulfil the pledge while I live.

. . . . The other day, our little Laurence did something wrong. He rarely does so — he is his father's own child for gentleness and generosity. But here he was in error: he quarrelled with his aunt Louisa, and refused to be friends. Louisa was not right either: she does not half love the boy.

I took my son on my lap, and tried to show him the holiness and beauty of returning good for evil; of forgetting unkindness, of pardoning sin. He listened, as he always listens to me. After a while, when his heart was softened, I made him kneel down beside me, saying the prayer — "*Forgive us our trespasses, as we forgive them that trespass against us.*"

Little Laurence stole away, repentant and good. I sat thoughtful: I did not notice that behind me had stood *my* Laurence — my husband. He came and knelt where his boy had knelt. Like the child, he laid his head on my shoulder, and blessed me in broken words. The sweetest of all were —

"My wife! my wife, who has saved her husband!"

THE OLD MATHEMATICIAN.

A SKETCH FROM THE LIFE.

I AM about to write of a great man — no ideal, but one who most truly lived, laboured, suffered, died, and "left no sign." You will not find his name in the rolls of the Royal Society; and yet he was a wiser philosopher than nine tenths of that learned body. You will never be asked to subscribe to a testimonial immortalizing his benevolence; and yet he was a philanthropist as sincere — perhaps as great — as Clarkson. You will read no book dilating on his trials; and yet he was a hero — a martyr, too. No painter ever craved permission to transmit his bodily likeness to posterity: the pen shall do it here.

Clement Griffin sprang from that rude mass which is the foundation stone of society, but from whose rough, unformed depths, many a pure marble fragment has been brought to light; and doubtless there might be many more, if some skilful sculptor's hand were found to breathe life and beauty into the shapeless mass. Clement Griffin was one of "the people." He bore in his person the distinctive marks which most commonly descend from one labouring generation to another — the short ungainly stature, the large rough hand, and the ill-formed mouth, in which no curve of beauty was found. But one peculiarity of his face was too striking to be passed over: he had the eye of intellect, gray, piercing, yet at times inexpressibly soft, deeply set under overhanging brows. These eyebrows were so remarkable that even a stranger would have noticed them — thick, bushy, iron-gray even in youth, and meeting in a line over the nose. Had Clement lived in these phrenological days, a Spurzheim or a Gall would have gloried in the strongly-developed head; but at the close of the eighteenth century people only regarded the internal faculties of a man's cranium, and that little enough. Otherwise, Griffin would never have been the poor drudge he was, namely, master of writing and arithmetic in a provincial grammar-school.

Yet this man, who day after day went through the dull round of duty, and might be seen trudging to and from the school in his coarse, threadbare garments, his ribbed worsted stockings, and immense clouted shoes; or in the school-room, carelessly treated by the master, and made game of for his odd old-fashioned ways by youths only a few years his juniors — this man was at once a mathematician, a philosopher, a mechanist of the most ingenious kind, an astronomer, acquainted with nearly all the abstract sciences, and had pursued these various acquirements entirely unaided, save by the force of his own powerful mind. Yet with all this learning, in his manners and habits he was as simple as a child. He would come home from his daily duties, eat his bowl of porridge and milk — for both from poverty and choice Clement Griffin was a Pythagorean — and sit down to pore over mathematical and astronomical lore, which he followed as far as the written science of the times permitted. When he could go no farther on the track of others, he calculated and made discoveries for himself.

I know not how far the wisdom of my hero may be impugned, when I confess that he was a cabalist and astrologer. He was no petty charlatan, no prying sceptic; but his strong, earnest, and withal pious mind, penetrated, or sought to penetrate, into those mysteries of science and nature which the ignorant have ridiculed and the cunning made a tool of, but which many wise — ay, and religious men, too — have in all ages believed. This is not the place to enter into an argument; but while setting forth as a broad principle that no man should scoff at or condemn anything which he has not fathomed to the bottom, let us not think the worse of Clement Griffin because he was an astrologer. He pursued this favourite study, not for gain, but as a lover of science; thus carrying out the astronomical and mathematical principles which are the root of the occult art.

It is not surprising that these pursuits made Clement, even at the early age of thirty, a solitary and prematurely old man. Indeed, no one in the neighbourhood ever remembered his being young. Everybody knew him, thought him an oddity, perhaps slightly mad; but his peculiarities were quite harmless, and no one ever had an ill word to say of "Old Griffin," or "Old Griff," as he had always been called, even when the parish register might have proved him just five-and-twenty. He had none of those home-ties which make the poetry of life — no mother or sister; and as for the young damsels of B—, they would as soon have thought of wedding the grim knight's statue that frowned at the church door, as of laying siege to the heart of Clement Griffin. Moreover, he had risen in mind at least above his own class — that of working artificers — and with the higher ranks he never thought to mingle; so that in every way Clement was essentially a solitary man.

He had no poetry in his composition — probably never read two rhyming lines in his life — had almost a terror of the visible poetry of the world — woman. A fair face alarmed him; the sound of a merry, girlish tongue made him run away. This was not contempt or misogyny, but merely because he understood and felt with the race of womankind even less than he did with his brother men. And he had little sympathy with the latter. There was only one feminine face that Clement ever looked at, and that was the face of a little school-girl, who, day after day, traversed the same road as he did. At first, Griffin thought this very disagreeable, as the chief reason of his choosing that road had been because it was so lonely, and no passers-by ever interrupted his thoughts. But by degrees he grew accustomed to the light step that overtook his, and the passing look of a pair of brown eyes, as fearless and yet shy as those of a young deer.

After a while, instead of hastening off before the little school-girl had passed his door, lest he might meet her, Clement began to go out at the precise hour she came, that he might be close behind her the whole way. He rarely let her see him, but walked on the other side of the road, where the overhanging hedge almost entirely concealed him. There was in the fresh innocence and glad-heartedness of the child, as she went along, dangling her school-basket, sometimes conning her lesson aloud, sometimes singing merrily — something new, and rather pleasant than otherwise, which touched even the philosopher. He often stopped in the middle of some algebraic problem which he was working in his head as he sauntered along, to listen to the little girl's unconscious singing, and wonder whether a baby-sister, the only one he had ever had, whose small grave he passed by every Sunday, had been like her.

This one gentle and humanising feeling was like a golden thread running through the dry and musty web of the mathematician's life; the only spark of involuntary poetry which had ever lighted up the dark caverns of his powerful but rugged mind. The child's daily presence became almost necessary to him; and he was less glad than usual when the holidays came, since she no longer passed his door. But his engrossing pursuits soon diverted Clement's attention; and, released for a time from the torment of instructing noisy, stupid, and headstrong boys in the mysteries of arithmetic, he devoted, as usual, his days to science and his nights to astronomy. When the holidays ended, Clement received a summons to attend a young ladies' school, where the former instructor in writing and arithmetic had absolutely eloped with the eldest pupil! There was no fear of Clement Griffin committing such an enormity, so he was chosen in the room of the transgressor. Woefully repugnant to all Clement's tastes was this situation; but he was so poor — poor even with his simple habits; and there was an astronomical instrument he longed to purchase, and could not, — so he consented to attend Miss Simmons's class.

When Griffin entered on his duties, the first face raised to look inquiringly at the new master was that of the little school-girl. It was smiling and pleasant, almost as if she recognised him, and Clement became less shy and uncomfortable under its influence. From that time the mathematician grew less painfully reserved — less shut up in himself. He had some human thing in which to take an interest; and his heart opened to all the world in proportion as it did to little Agnes Martindale. There was something in common between the philosopher and the child. She was, like himself, essentially solitary; one of among many brothers and sisters: she had no particular qualities to attract notice — little beauty, except those large, soft, brown eyes, and not one showy talent. It was only Clement Griffin's instruction which developed the natural bent of her mind, wherein her whole powers lay — and curious to relate, this strongly resembled his own. The master continually turned from his dull and inattentive boy pupils to this girl, who, by a faculty in general foreign to woman's mind, quickly apprehended as fast as he could teach; so that Clement partly with a vague curiosity to see how far female capacity would go, and partly because these lessons were inexplicably pleasant to him, gradually led her on, far beyond the usual limit of feminine acquirements. When Agnes Martindale had finished her education and left school, Clement still gave her instruction; he could not bear to break the charmed tie.

Oh, how mad — how blind was this man! whose mind had strength to grapple with the deepest mysteries of science and nature, and yet was unlearned as a child in reading the human heart — most of all, his own. He never dreamed for a moment that the secret influence which made life pleasant to him, and lent a new charm even to his dearest pursuits, was the universal spirit which pervades all things; bowing alike the strongest and the weakest; the wise man and the — fool we were about to write — but no! the meanest mind becomes great when it is able to harbour Love.

Clement came in and out as he chose, at Agnes's home. When the mathematical lessons were over, the younger children played with "Aggy's old master," for something in Griffin's nature made him assimilate more with children than with men, perhaps because there was in his own simple character a curious mingling of the child and the sage, without any admixture of the man of the world. Then, by degrees, he got into the habit of establishing himself in one corner, and receiving his bowl of tea from Agnes's hands. No one ever seemed to think it necessary to talk to him or notice him any more than if he were some piece of household furniture, and so he would sit contentedly, hour after hour, in silence, until bed-time came. Then he would quietly shake hands with one or two of the circle with whom he was most at ease, and steal out, unobserved, to his own home. Often when he reached it, he thought how its gloom and darkness contrasted painfully with the cheerful lights and sounds of Farmer Martindale's cosy parlour; and when he looked up at the stars, in whose influence he so firmly believed, he pondered more over the future than he was wont.

It chanced that for some weeks a long and severe illness kept Agnes from his sight, and then Clement Griffin felt and seemed like one from whom the light of day has suddenly been removed. Every morning he crept up to the farm to ask of children or servants the latest tidings, and none were surprised at his anxious face; it was "only Aggy's old master, who made such a pet of her still." When the invalid came down stairs, the first greeting that met her was his. Agnes was almost startled when she gave him her hand, to feel a hot tear drop upon it.

"You have been very kind in asking after me, Mr. Griffin. I assure you I am really better," said the unconscious girl. "I shall soon be able to go on with the lesson. Pray, be content about me."

He did not answer, but went quietly to his own corner. This illness of hers had made him restless. No longer satisfied with the present, he began to think of chances that might put an end to his happiness. Following, too, the natural inclination of his character, he one day asked Agnes to tell him the day and hour of her birth, that he might cast her horoscope, and know her future fate.

Agnes looked at him eagerly, for he had half made her a convert to his own belief. Then a sudden thought appeared to strike her. She blushed deeply, and answered in a hurried tone — "No; I had rather not know more — more than I do already — it might make me unhappy, and I am now so —"

The door opened quickly, and the girl's blush deepened to the brightest crimson, as it admitted one who had of late been as frequent a visitor as Clement himself. Griffin was never quite pleased at this, for Rupert Nicol's entrance always put a stop to the mathematical studies, and, moreover, having been one of the refractory boys at the grammar-school, the young man had hardly learned to treat his former teacher with consideration. Many a whisper and look from Agnes was necessary to quell his propensity for quizzing "old Griff," even now.

Clement went home early that night, wondering why Agnes had blushed at the thought of her future fate; feeling vexed at Nicol's sudden entrance, and oppressed by a vague sense of restless disquietude, which made him seize the next half-holiday to walk to the farm. When he came there, the family were all out in the hay-harvest, the maid said, all but Miss Agnes. Clement was rather glad of this. They would have the lesson in peace and quietness. He went to the little parlour, and looked through the half-open door.

The room was very still; so still that it might have had no

occupants; but there were two — Agnes, and Rupert Nicol. They sat together; her right hand lay on his shoulder, and above it rested her sweet, young face, not lifted up, but drooping and blushing with deep happiness. Her left hand was held in both of his; he was trying on the third finger a gold circlet — the wedding-ring.

That terrible moment discovered to Clement Griffin his love and its doom. The quiet, cold, dreaming philosopher found out that he was a man, with all the long-slumbering passions and emotions of man roused up within him. He knew likewise that they were all in vain; for a love more baseless, mad, and utterly hopeless, never tortured human breast than now racked that of Clement Griffin.

The young betrothed, as she sat in her quiet chamber, preparing for her bridal, or laid her head on her pillow, but to be haunted by dreams of her beloved, his last tender words, his dearest of all dear smiles, knew not that there was another who paced night after night beneath her window, in agony so deep, so wild, that had the girl seen it, her emotions would have been less of pity than of terror — who spent whole hours in lying on the stone steps of the threshold, which her light happy footfall had just crossed. Clement was no sighing dreamer, indulging in delicious sorrow and sentimental woe; he was not young, and the one great feeling of love had never been frittered away into smaller fancies; it was no boyish ideal, but a terrible reality. He was not a poet to make an idol of the past; the future suddenly and for ever became a blank; and Love itself was changed into Despair.

Agnes married Rupert, and went with him to the far-off home which he had made for her. After she was gone, a few of the neighbours observed that the "Old Mathematician" — they had cause to call him old now, for his hair was quite grey — that Clement Griffin seemed lost without his pupil; that he shut himself up much at home, and was more eccentric than ever when abroad. No tongue whispered, no heart guessed, the real truth. When, a short time afterwards, Clement threw up his situation, with the excuse that he was going elsewhere to bring out a new invention of his own, the only observation made was that "mad folk always get madder the older they grow." In another year, when Agnes came home on a visit, and inquired after her old teacher, the people at B— seemed almost to have forgotten his name.

Twenty years from the last epoch in my story, a lady in widow's weeds, accompanied by two children, entered the shop of a working mathematician, in one of the large provincial towns. She wanted to have a little casket repaired; it was made of ebony, and the lock, of very curious workmanship, had been broken. The spruce shopman, whose profusely-scented hair and aquiline nose, under which grew a delicate moustache, bespoke him that most disagreeable of modern anomalies, an Adonised Jew, examined it with a puzzled air.

"I never saw anything like this before, madam. We have nothing of the sort in our shop," he said.

"Very likely not; I did not buy it; it was made for me many years ago. I believe the lock is quite original of its kind. Do you think it possible to repair it?"

The shopman shook his head. "I don't know, ma'am; there is something very odd about it: but we have a clever workman here. I will send for him, if you will wait a moment."

The lady sat down: her two boys amused themselves with peering at the curiosities of the shop, but the mother drew down her veil, and seemed rather thinking of the past than alive to the present. The shopman still pored over the casket with much curiosity.

"It must have been a skilful workman who made this, madam. Ebony will turn the edge of our hardest tools."

The lady did not reply to his evident curiosity, except by a bend of the head; and in a few minutes the person who had been sent for came. He was a little old man, nearly bald, with gray bushy eyebrows, and wonderfully keen eyes; as these fell upon the casket, he started and trembled visibly.

"Do you think you can mend this, old fellow?" said the young Jew, carelessly.

The person addressed took the casket in his hand, and walked to the light. He never looked at the customer; he saw nothing but the casket; and did not notice how the lady had risen, and was watching him in extreme surprise.

"I know this well. I can easily mend it. Where did you get it, Mr. Salomans?" anxiously inquired he.

"It is mine," answered a sweet voice under the widow's veil, and a hand was stretched out to the old man. "Do you not know me, Mr. Griffin? I remembered you at once."

The casket fell from his hand.

"Miss Agnes, is it you, Miss Agnes!" He glanced at her dress. "I beg pardon, Mrs. —. I am old, and cannot remember your name now."

"Never mind, call me anything you like; I am so glad to have found you out at last. Many a time, Rupert and I — ah! poor Rupert," — the widow's voice faltered, and her tears fell fast. A strange dimness had gathered over the eyes of Clement Griffin too. It was well that the young Jew was busy with some new customer at the other end of the shop.

"And are these children yours, Miss Agnes?" said the Old Mathematician, trying with instinctive delicacy to divert her from her grief, though his whole frame trembled with agitation, and his voice was almost inaudible.

"Yes: Robert and Charles, go and shake hands with Mr. Griffin; you have often heard about him. They know you quite well, indeed, dear old friend. Robert has learned all the definitions you wrote out for me, long, long ago."

"And did you keep those definitions, Miss Agnes? How good of you!" said Clement, taking her hand with a sudden impulse, and then dropping it again in alarm, as he saw the eyes of his superior bent on him with astonishment. "We cannot talk here: may I come and see you?"

Mrs. Nicol told him where she lived, shook his hand again warmly, and departed.

"So you can mend this, Griffin, I suppose," said Salomans, with a sneer.

"Mend what?" Clement repeated, dreamily.

"The casket, you old idiot."

"Yes, I ought; for I made it myself."

"And that lady, pray do you know her?"

"A friend, an old friend — yes, I think I may say that," muttered the old man.

"Umph! I did not know you had a friend in the world. Come, off with you! nobody wants an old goose like you in the shop."

Patiently, without answering a word, the poor old man stole back to his workshop. Strange, that with his commanding intellect, he should have been the slave and butt of a petty fop like this! But, throughout his life, Clement Griffin, in all worldly things, was as ignorant as a child. Agnes Nicol felt this, with a compassion almost amounting to pain, when he told her, as they sat in her little parlour, the outward story of his life since they had last met. She discovered how more than one curious mechanical invention of his, now making a noise in the world, had brought wealth to others, while the deceived inventor toiled on for very bread by the labour of his hands; how his talents and skill had been traded upon — and were so even now — while he himself was treated as a poor drudge. Not that he told all this, for he hardly perceived it himself; but Agnes found it out from his simple and undisguised tale.

It was to them both a strange return of old times. When the children were gone to bed, Griffin sat in the fire-side corner. Agnes had made ready for him the supper he always liked — bread-and-milk: when he took the basin from her hand, the old man put it down on the chair beside him, and burst into tears.

"You are very good to me, Miss Agnes, very! I beg your pardon; I am but a foolish old man, and you make me think of past times."

Agnes herself was much moved; the more so since she had her own story to relate — not a happy one. The girlish dream had hardly been fulfilled. Alas! when is it? But the widow's sorrow sufficiently testified to the wife's abiding love. A mother's cares were added too, for her boys were growing up; and Mrs. Nicol was poor, very poor. Clement had as yet seen nothing but herself; now he glanced at the meanly furnished room, and though he understood little of such things, he felt that it was hardly meet for an inhabitant like Agnes. How he longed for every coin which he had cast away, or been robbed of, that he might pour all at her feet, and then go and work for his own daily bread all his life long!

If ever an earnest, noble, disinterested love abided in human heart, it was in that of Clement Griffin. Strangely distorted though his nature was — a compound of strength and weakness — of wisdom and madness — of unworldliness that amounted to ignorance — warped through circumstances, and yet intrinsically noble – most surely there was in it one spot, an altar, that might have been a resting-place for angels' feet. Time had quenched the burning fire which once consumed him, and he could now look on Agnes' still fair face, and feel no pain. He felt thankful that she had never known his madness, or she would have despised him. It *was* madness; but Agnes was too much of a woman to have despised any true and earnest love, however presumptuous and hopeless it might have been. It was over — the wildest imagination could not rekindle its ashes now.

It was a pleasure to Agnes in her widowed and poverty-haunted solitude to have the occasional presence of the kind old man, whom in her childhood and youth she had sincerely regarded. He taught the boys, too, all that lay in his power; and it revived his old enthusiasm to take young Robert on his knee, and instruct him in pursuits to which the boy had already an ardent inclination.

"He will make a great man — a first-rate mathematician," Clement would say, while his eyes brightened, and he looked from his young scholar to the mother who had once been his pupil too, while Agnes would smile, half pensively, and only hope that her boy's life might not resemble that of the hapless enthusiast before her. Sometimes she tried to reason with him; but the old man was quite contented with his present home.

"Salomans gives me food and clothes, almost as much as I want," he argued. "What more can I desire? He only requires me to work in the day, and then I have the night for study. I am really quite content. Besides, he took me in when I had not a penny, and saved me from going to the parish perhaps," said the old man smiling sadly. "I ought to stay with him out of gratitude; and every now and then he gives me some money too: so that in time I shall have bought back all the books I lost."

Poor simple philosopher! — simple, yet wise; for all the sages in Christendom could not have boasted that truest, purest wisdom, which is before all things in the sight of the All-wise.

Agnes Nicol had to struggle hard to bring up her boys as she desired. As Robert's talents developed themselves, she longed to give him every advantage; but it was a hard thing even to provide him with books. Clement Griffin found out this, and soon the needful volumes were brought by him. He said they were his own — a loving and generous fiction. The old man, conquering his natural shyness, had sought for stray pieces of work from the other opticians of the town, and devoted his nights to their completion, to gain the payment which his skill readily commanded. Thus it was that his pupil's little library grew. Clement Griffin, in his simplicity, could imagine no other need but that of books, or else his whole nights would have been spent in thus working to supply comforts to Agnes Nicol and her children.

At last Robert had a chance of obtaining advancement in the branch of science to which his taste inclined. A distant cousin of his father's, who was a mathematical-instrument maker in London, offered to take the boy for a small premium. But all the mother's contrivances could not procure the sum. Clement Griffin's sorrow was equal to hers, for he loved Robert, and was proud of his talents. Night after night, as he traced his way homeward, the old man pondered over every possible expedient to get over this difficulty, and find the necessary money. Sometimes in his simplicity he thought of walking to London — only a hundred miles — and offering to work six months in old Nicol's shop, if he would but remit the premium for Robert. But then iron fetters could not be stronger than those self-forged chains which bound Clement, as he thought out of gratitude, to Salomans. Likewise, with instinctive delicacy, he felt that Mrs. Nicol must not be acquainted with any sacrifice for her sake, or her refusal would at once make it vain. The old man was floating in a sea of doubt and perplexity. To him, coining twenty gold guineas would have seemed far less difficult than earning them in the ordinary old-world fashion like any other man.

At last, as the Old Mathematician sat one night among his books, a bright idea flashed across him. Those beloved volumes suddenly assumed a value, not like that he had so long set upon them, but a marketable value. They might be sold! Had he himself been starving, the thought would never have entered Clement's mind; but for Robert — for *her* child — yes! he would sell them! The dusty old tomes seemed transformed into bright shining coins already, all whispering in his ear, "Do it, Clement; what good are we to an old fellow like you? Use us to make a great man of this boy, who will grow up to be famous, when you are no more." Clement turned over their leaves that he might come to some conclusion as to the definite value of these his treasures. It seemed almost like a man anatomising the bodies of his own children;

11*

so dear, so sacred were they to the old philosopher. But stronger feelings than even these were at work within. The man's noble heart triumphed over his devotion to knowledge. He sold the books.

Then, even when the struggle was over, the twenty gold coins sat like a weight of lead upon Clement's heart. Day after day he carried them with him to Mrs. Nicol's, and yet he could not tell how to give them so as to prevent her knowing through whom the gift came, and the sacrifice by which it had been purchased. At length chance opened a way. Agnes, in despair at her boy's melancholy, proposed writing to a rich relative, and entreating, not as a gift but as a loan, that he would provide the means for Robert's outset in life.

"Strangers are sometimes kinder than friends," the mother tried to moralize; "and he is almost a stranger, though connected by blood, for I never saw his face or had a letter from him in my life. Yet people say he is a good man. I will try him."

It chanced that Clement Griffin, in the course of his chequered life, had known this man; and known, too, that the outward character he bore was false. But he did not undeceive the sanguine mother; for, with a quickness and loving stratagem, most unwonted to him, he conceived a plan of doing what the rich man would never have done. He assented eagerly, almost tremblingly, to Agnes's proposition.

"I knew him once. I will take the letter myself," cried Clement.

He took it, and returned next day with a kind message and twenty pounds, "as a gift," he said, though the eccentric but generous donor refused any acknowledgment, either personal or written. Agnes, almost wild in her joy, did not notice the quivering lips, the tremulous voice of her old friend, nor the hasty confusion with which he retreated home. He had suffered far more from the contrivance of this *ruse* than even from the noble self-denial which had prompted it. His truthful conscience reproached him even for the generous lie, and it was long before he could meet the eye of Agnes Nicol.

As Clement grew older, he plunged the deeper into his dreamy pursuits. While Mrs. Nicol and her children lived in his neighbourhood, there was still one tie that connected him with the outer world. But ere long, a small accession of fortune came to the long-enduring widow, and she went to establish herself near her prosperous boy Robert. Before she left, she entreated her old master to come and settle in London, where Robert would be able to requite the care which had mainly contributed to his success. But the old man only shook his head, with the smile of quiet melancholy that had become habitual to him.

"No, no, Miss Agnes. What should such as I do in London? People would only laugh at my odd ways — perhaps you yourself might be ashamed of me."

"Never — dear, good friend," cried Agnes. She felt it at the time; but afterwards she thought the gray ribbed stockings and clumsy shoes would look rather strange in the pretty drawing-room of which Robert wrote. "And is there nothing I can do to show how much I value you?" she asked.

Clement's eyes looked dim, and the muscles about his mouth twitched convulsively. "You are very kind, Miss Agnes; — then, will you think of me now and then, and perhaps write to me? Direct to the post-office, because I rather imagine Salomans reads all my letters when any come for me."

"And yet you stay with him?"

"Oh, yes. It does me no harm. I have no secrets. God bless you, Miss Agnes — and good-bye!"

"But Robert, who owes you so much: can he do nothing?"

"Why, yes," said the old man, hesitating; "I have heard of a new achromatic object-glass for a telescope. I should like to see it, because I thought of inventing one myself. Perhaps Robert would send me down one, if not too much trouble. And tell him I am very glad he is growing a rich man — only he must keep to mathematics — a head-full of geometry is worth a house-full of gold. Good-bye, and God bless you once more. Miss Agnes — you have been very kind to me, you and your boys. Good-bye."

Agnes watched him down the street. A quaint figure he looked, in the long gray coat and broad-brimmed hat. She noticed how slow and trembling was his gait, and how he stooped more than ever over his thick stick, which had of late become indispensable to him. A few tears rose to her eyes, but they were more to the remembrance of past days than to him.

"Poor old Griffin — he is a good soul, though he is so odd. I wish Robert could have done something for him; but then he seems quite content, and has so few wants. Well, well, I suppose he is quite happy in his own way." And she turned away to think of the cheerful home which Robert had prepared for her.

Mrs. Nicol was a good woman, — thoughtful, kind, — ay, grateful. For a long season, the strange, long, rambling letters of Clement Griffin were regularly answered; and many times a gift of the kind most likely to please him — a new scientific book of curious invention — found its way to the garret at Salomans'. At last Clement wrote that perhaps Robert had better not send again, for Mr. Salomans generally took them in his own care, and he himself had little use of them.

"How tiresome that he will stay with those wretches," said Robert Nicol; "there is no doing anything for him while he is at Salomans'."

Mrs. Nicol wrote to the same effect — begging him to come at once and make his home with them. But there was no reply for many weeks. Then Agnes received one letter, which follows here, in all its quaint mournfulness: —

"MRS. AGNES NICOL.

"DEAR FRIEND. — Not having received any answer to my last three letters, I am afraid you have forgotten me. It is not surprising; for I believe London is a strange place. I write these few lines to say farewell, as I may never be able to write to you, or see you again on earth. I have been very ill. Indeed, I think, from the appearance of the stars, and Saturn being in opposition to my *Hyleg* — that I shall not get better. Mr. Salomans says I am a great expense to him, and I believe I must be, as I can work little now. So he has told me to leave him next week. I hope he will give me a little money: but I am afraid he will not; and then I shall have to go to my parish, if I can walk there. So, dear Miss Agnes, if you should not hear any more of me, this comes to bid you farewell, and may God bless you and yours, and may He take my soul to Himself when the time comes! I wish you had let me cast your nativity, as my horoscope has come so true — of which I am rather glad. I hope you are well in health — should have liked to have heard from you once again, but suppose you had other and better things to think about. My hand shakes, but I hope you will make out this. I pray God to bless you all your life, as He has me, in spite of all my troubles. And so no more until we meet with Him. From your sincere friend,

"CLEMENT GRIFFIN."

Agnes was painfully startled, and almost conscience-stricken by this letter. She was in weak health, or she would have gone immediately to the succour of her old master. "However, Robert shall go down to-morrow, and bring him safe back," was her first thought.

But Robert was just then very busy, constructing a curious machine for a scientific nobleman, and could not be spared. "Next week will do, mother; you know it is not the first time those wretches have threatened to turn him away — it may be only his fancies. He must be quite an old man now, and perhaps his mind wanders. The letter bears no date, you see, and is written very unconnectedly."

Mrs. Nicol agreed that it was, and perhaps matters were not so bad as old Mr. Griffin thought. She was over-persuaded by her son to wait a day or two; and it was no use writing. She put the letter — a soiled, crumpled, rough sheet of paper it was — in her gay work-box, thought of it many a time that day, until her many household interests slowly blotted it out. The thing was not unnatural or unkind.

On the morrow, Mrs. Nicol received another letter — a formal missive from a parish doctor. It stated "how an old man, found dying in the road, had been brought into the workhouse at H——. There he had died, and been buried at the parish expense. The only thing that was found upon the deceased — a book, on whose cover was written the name and address of Mrs. Nicol — the workhouse-master begged to enclose."

It was a Bible, inscribed in a cramped, childish hand, to "Clement Griffin, from his pupil, Agnes Martindale, 2nd May, 17—."

When she saw it, Mrs. Nicol bowed her head upon its torn, worm-eaten cover, and wept bitter tears of remembrance, not unmingled with self-reproach. They were the only ones which ever fell to the memory of Clement Griffin. Had that gentle, humble spirit beheld them, he would have thought them more than his due.

No admiring disciple has ever raised a stone above this unknown philosopher. He foretold, half a century ago, that men would journey by steam; now, the lightning-like railway passes within sight of his grave. He spent years in perfecting a mechanical invention: its wheels now whirl and roar in a manufactory not two hundred yards from the green pillow where the brain which first conceived their uses is peacefully mingling with the dust. He first declared that the human mind and character were faithfully portrayed in the human head as in a map: not long since, in the little town where his wanderings ended for ever, a phrenologist — a learned man too — lectured to crowded audiences on the new science. The sage — the philosopher — the devoted follower of science — has passed away and left no memory — no, not even a poor name written on a churchyard stone. Yet what matters it? The great men of earth are those who have done most good to that world which may never know or utter their names. But —

> "The seeds of truth they sow are sacred seeds,
> And bear their righteous fruits for general weal
> When sleeps the husbandman."

THE HALF-CASTE.

AN OLD GOVERNESS' TALE, FOUNDED ON FACT.

"We know what we are, but we know not what we may be," as my quaintly clever niece and name-child, Cassia, a great reader and quoter of Shakspeare, would say. And truly who could have thought that I, a plain governess, should in my old age have become a writer. Yet I cannot invent a plot — I must write nothing but truth. Here I pause, recollecting painfully that in my first sentence I have sinned against truth by entitling Cassia my "niece and name-child," when, strictly speaking, she is neither the one nor the other. She is no blood-relation at all, and my own name happens to be Cassandra. I always disliked it heartily until Mr. Sutherland called me ——. But I forget that I must explain a little.

Mr. Sutherland was — no, thank Heaven! — is, a very good man; a friend of my late father, and of the same business — an Indian merchant. When in my twenty-fifth year my dear father died, and we were ruined — a quiet way of expressing this, but in time one learns to speak so quietly of every pang — Mr. Sutherland was very kind to my mother and to me. I remember, as though it were yesterday, one day, when he sat with us in our little parlour, and hearing my mother calling me "Cassie," said, laughingly, that I always put him in mind of a certain Indian spice. "In fact," he added, looking affectionately at my dear, gentle, little mother, and approvingly — yes, it was approvingly, at me — "in fact, I think we three sitting thus, with myself in the centre, might be likened to myrrh, aloes, and cassia." One similitude was untrue; for he was not bitter, but "sweet as summer." However, from that time he always called me Cassia. I rather like the name; and latterly it was very kind of him to ——. There, I am forestalling my history again!

When I was twenty-five, as I said, I first went out as a

governess. This plan was the result of many consultations between my mother and myself. A hard thing was my leaving home; but I found I could thereby earn a larger and more regular salary, part of which being put by would some time enable me to live altogether with my mother. Such were her plannings and hopes for the future. As for my own ——. But it is idle to dwell upon things so long past. God knew best, and it all comes to the same at the end of life.

It was through Mr. Sutherland that I got my first situation. He wrote my mother a hurried letter, saying he had arranged for me to enter a family concerning whom he would explain before my departure. But something hindered his coming: it was a public meeting, I remember; for, though still a young man, he was held in much honour among the city merchants, and knew the affairs of India well, from early residence there. Of course, having these duties to fulfil, it was natural he should not recollect my departure; so I started without seeing him, and without knowing more of my future abode than its name, and that of my employer. It was a Yorkshire village, and the gentleman whose family I was going to was a Mr. Le Poer.

My long journey was dreary — God knows how dreary! in youth one suffers so much; and parting from my mother was any time a sufficient grief. In those days railways were not numerous, and I had to journey a good way by coach. About eleven at night I found myself at my destination. At the door a maid-servant appeared; no one else: it was scarcely to be expected by "the governess." This was a new and sad "coming home" to me. I was shown to my bedroom, hearing, as I passed the landing, much rustling of dresses and "squittling" away of little feet. (1 ought to apologize for that odd expression, which I think I learned when I was quite a child, and used to go angling with my father and Mr. Sutherland. It means a scampering off in all directions, as a shoal of minnows do when you throw a pebble among them.) I asked if the family were gone to bed, and was informed, "No;" so I arranged my dress and went down-stairs, unconsciously reassured by the fact that the house was neither so large nor so aristocratic as my very liberal salary had inclined me to expect.

"Who shall I say, miss?" asked the rather untidy servant,

meeting me in the lobby, and staring with all her eyes, as if a stranger were some rare sight.

"Miss Pryor," I said, thinking regretfully that I should be henceforth that, and not "Cassia;" and seeing the maid still stared, I added with an effort: "I am the new governess."

So under that double announcement I appeared at the parlour-door. The room was rather dark: there were two candles; but one had been extinguished, and was being hurriedly relighted as I entered. At first I saw nothing clearly; then I perceived a little pale lady sitting at one end of the table, and two half-grown-up girls, dressed in "going-out-to-tea" costume, seated primly together on the sofa. There was a third; but she vanished out of one door as I entered the other.

"Miss Pryor, I believe?" said a timid voice — so timid that I could hardly believe that it was a lady addressing her governess. I glanced at her: she was a little woman, with pale hair and light eyes — frightened-looking eyes — that just rose, and fell in a minute. I said "I was Miss Pryor, and concluded I addressed Mrs. Le Poer." She answered, "Yes, yes;" and held out hesitatingly a thin, cold, bird-like hand, which I took rather warmly than otherwise; for I felt really sorry for her evident nervousness. It seemed so strange for anybody to be afraid of *me*. "My daughters, Miss Pryor," she then said in a louder tone. Whereupon the two girls rose, courtesied, blushed — seemingly more from awkwardness than modesty — and sat down again. I shook hands with both, trying to take the initiative, and make myself sociable and at home — a difficult matter, my position feeling much like that of a fly in an ice-house.

"These are my pupils, then?" said I, cheerfully. "Which is Miss Zillah?" — for I remembered Mr. Sutherland had mentioned that name in his letter, and its peculiarity naturally struck me.

The mother and daughters looked rather blankly at each other, and the former said: "This is Miss Le Poer and Miss Matilda — Zillah is not in the room at present."

"Oh, a third sister?" I observed.

"No," rather pertly answered Miss Le Poer; "Zill is not our sister at all, but only a sort of a distant relation of pa's, whom he is very kind to and maintains at his own expense, and who mends our stockings and brushes our hair of nights, and whom we are very kind to also."

"Oh, indeed!" was all I said in reply to this running stream of very provincially-spoken and unpunctuated English. I was rather puzzled too; for if my memory was correct — and I generally remembered Mr. Sutherland's letters very clearly, probably because they were themselves so clear — he had particularly mentioned my future pupil Zillah Le Poer, and no Miss Le Poer besides. I waited with some curiosity for the girl's reappearance; at last I ventured to say — "I should like to see Miss Zillah. I understood" here I hesitated, but thought afterwards that plain speech was best — "I understood from Mr. Sutherland that she was to be my pupil."

"Of course, of course," hastily said the lady, and I fancied she coloured slightly. "Caroline, fetch your cousin."

Caroline sulkily went out, and shortly returned, followed by a girl older than herself, though clad in childish, or rather servant fashion, with short petticoats, short sleeves, and a big brown-holland pinafore. "Zill wouldn't stay to be dressed," explained Caroline in a loud whisper to her mother; at which Mrs. Le Poer looked more nervous and uncomfortable than ever.

Meanwhile I observed my pupil. I had fancied the Zillah so carefully entrusted to my care by Mr. Sutherland to be a grown young lady, who only wanted "finishing." I even thought she might be a beauty. With some surprise I found her a half-caste girl — with an olive complexion, full Hindoo lips, and eyes very black and bright. She was untidily dressed: which looked the worse, since she was almost a woman grown; though her dull, heavy face had the stupidity of an ultra-stupid child. I saw all this; for somehow — probably because I had heard of her before — I examined the girl rather closely. Zillah herself stared at me much as if I had been a wild animal, and then put her finger in her mouth with a babyish air.

"How do you do, my dear?" said I, desperately, feeling that all four pair of family eyes were upon me. "I hope we shall be good friends soon." And I put out my hand.

At first the girl seemed not to understand that I meant to shake hands with her. Then she resolutely poked out her brown fingers, having first taken the precaution to wipe them on her pinafore. I made another remark or two about my being her governess, and her studying with her cousins; at which she opened her large eyes with a dull amaze, but I never heard the sound of her voice.

It must have been now near twelve o'clock. I thought it odd the girls should be kept up so late; and began at last to speculate whether I was to see Mr. Le Poer. My conjectures were soon set at rest by a loud pull at the door-bell, which made Mrs. Le Poer spring up from her chair, and Zillah vanish like lightning. The two others sat cowed, with their hands before them, and I myself felt none of the bravest. So upon this frightened group the master of the house walked in.

"Hallo, Mrs. Le Poer! Cary! Zill, you fool! Confound it, where's the supper?" (*I* might have asked that too, being very hungry.) "What the deuce are you all about?"

"My dear!" whispered the wife beseechingly, as she met him at the door, and seemed pointing to me.

Certainly I could not have believed that the voice just heard belonged to the gentleman who now entered. The *gentleman*, I repeat; for I never saw one who more thoroughly looked the character. He was about fifty, very handsome, very well dressed — his whole mien bespeaking that stately, gracious courtliness which now, except in rare instances, belongs to a past age. Bowing, he examined me curiously, with a look that somehow or other made me uncomfortable. He seemed viewing over my feminine attractions as a horse-dealer does the points of a new bargain. But soon the interest of the look died away. I knew he considered me as all others did — a very plain and shy young woman, perhaps lady-like (I believe I was that, for I heard of some one saying so), but nothing more.

"I have the pleasure of meeting Miss Pryor?" said he, in an ultra-bland tone, which, after his first coarse manner, would have positively startled me, had I not always noticed that the two are often combined in the same individual. (I always distrust a man who speaks in a very mild, measured, womanish voice.)

I mentioned the name of his friend Mr. Sutherland.

"Oh, I recollect," said he, stiffly; "Mr. Sutherland informed you that - that ——." He evidently wished to find out exactly what I knew of himself and his family.

Now, it being always my habit to speak the plain truth, I saw no reason why I should not gratify him; so I stated the simple facts of our friend's letter to my mother — that he had found for me a situation in the family of a Mr. Le Poer, and had particularly charged me with completing the education of Miss Zillah Le Poer.

"Oh!" said Mr. Le Poer. "Were those all your instructions, my dear Miss Pryor?" he added, insinuatingly.

I answered that I knew no more, having missed seeing Mr. Sutherland before I came away.

"Then you come quite a stranger into my family. I hope you have received the hearty welcome a stranger should receive, and I trust you will soon cease to merit that name." So saying, he graciously touched the tips of my fingers, and in mellifluous tones ordered supper, gently reproaching his wife for having delayed that meal. "You know, my dear, it was a pity to wait for me; and Miss Pryor must be needing refreshment."

Indeed, I was being literally famished. The meal was ordinary enough — mere bread, butter, and cheese; but Mr. Le Poer did the honours with most gentlemanly courtesy. I thought, never did a poor governess meet with such attention! The girls did not sup with us; they had taken the earliest opportunity of disappearing; nor was the half-caste cousin again visible. We had soon done eating — that is, Mrs. Le Poer and I; for the gentleman seemed so indifferent to the very moderate attractions of his table, that from this fact, and from a certain redness of his eyes, I could not help suspecting he had well supped before. Still, that did not prevent his asking for wine; and having politely drunk with me, he composed himself to have a little confidential talk while he finished the decanter.

"Miss Pryor, do you correspond with Mr. Sutherland?"

The abruptness of his question startled me. I felt my cheeks tingling as I answered most truthfully — "No."

"Still, you are a dear and valued friend of his, he tells me?"

I felt glad, so glad that I forgot to make the due answer about Mr. Sutherland's being "very kind."

My host had probably gained the information he wanted, and became communicative on his part. "I ought, my dear young lady, to explain a few things concerning your pupils, which have been thus accidentally omitted by my friend Mr. Sutherland, who could not better have acceded to my request than by sending a lady like yourself to instruct my family." Here he bowed, and I bowed. We did a great deal in that way of dumb civility, as it saved him trouble and me words. "My daughters you have seen. They are, I believe, tolerably well-informed for such mere children." I wondered if I had rightly judged them at thirteen and fourteen. "My only trouble, Miss Pryor, is concerning my niece." Here I looked surprised, not suspecting Zillah to be so near a relative. "I call her niece through habit, and for the sake of her father, my poor deceased brother," continued Mr. Le Poer, with a lengthened and martyr-like visage; "but in truth she has no legal claim to belong to my family. My brother — sad fellow always — Indian life not over-scrupulous — ties between natives and Europeans: in fact, my dear Miss Pryor, Zillah's mother —. You understand?"

Ignorant as I was, I did dimly understand, coloured deeply, and was silent. In the unpleasant pause which ensued, I noticed that Mrs. Le Poer had let her knitting fall, and sat gazing on her husband with a blank, horrified look, until he called her to order by an impressive "A little more wine, my dear!" Her head sank with an alarmed gesture, and her lord and master continued addressing me — "Of course this explanation is in strict confidence. Regard for my brother's memory induces me to keep the secret, and to bring up this girl exactly as my own — except," he added, recollecting himself, "with a slight, indeed a necessary difference. Therefore you will educate them all alike; at least so far as Zillah's small capacity allows. I believe," and he smiled sarcastically, "her modicum of intellect is not greater than generally belongs to her mother's race. She would make an excellent *ayah*, and that is all."

"Poor thing!" I thought, not inclined to despise her even after this painful information: how could I, when — Now that fairly nonplussed me! What made the girl an object of interest to Mr. Sutherland? and why did he mention her as Miss Zillah Le Poer when she could legally have no right to the name? I should, in my straightforward way, have asked the question, but Mr. Le Poer's manner showed that he wished no more conversation. He hinted something about my fatigue, and the advisability of retiring; nay, even lighted my candle for me, and dismissed his wife and myself with an air so pleasant and gracious, that I thought I had scarcely ever seen such a perfect gentleman.

Mrs. Le Poer preceded me up-stairs to my room, bade me

good-night, asked timidly, but kindly, if all was to my liking, and if I would take anything more — seemed half inclined to say something else, and then, hearing her husband's voice, instantaneously disappeared.

I was at last alone. I sat thinking over this strange evening — so strange, that it kept my thoughts from immediately flying were I had supposed they were sure to fly. During my cogitations there came a knock to the door, and on my answering it, a voice spoke without, in a dull, sullen tone, and an accent slightly foreign and broken — "Please, do you want to be called to-morrow, and will you have any hot water?"

I opened the door at once to Zillah. "Is it you, dear? Come in and say good-night to me."

The girl entered with the air and manner of a servant except for a certain desperate sullenness. I took her hand, and thanked her for coming to see after my comforts. She looked thoroughly astonished; but as I went on talking, began to watch me with more interest. Once she even smiled, which threw a soft expression over her mouth. I cannot tell what reason I had — whether from a mere impulse of kindness, with which my own state of desolation had something to do, or whether I compelled myself from a sense of duty to take all means of making a good first impression on the girl's feelings — but when I bade Zillah good-night, I leaned forward, and just touched her brown cheek with mine — French fashion; for I could not really *kiss* anybody except for love.

I never saw a creature so utterly amazed! She might never have received that token of affection since her birth. She muttered a few unintelligible words — I fancy they were in Hindostanee — flung herself before me, Eastern fashion, and my poor hand was kissed passionately, weepingly, as the beloved ladies' hands are in novels and romances. Ah! my hand was never kissed save by this poor child!

All passed in a moment, and I had hardly recovered my first surprise when Zillah was gone. I sat a little while, feeling as strange as if I had suddenly become the heroine of a fairy tale; then caught a vision of my own known self, with my pale, tired face, and sad-coloured gown. It soon brought me back to the realities of life, and to the fact that I was now two hundred miles away from my mother and from — London.

I had not been three weeks resident in the Le Poer family, before I discovered that if out of the domestic mysteries into which I became gradually initiated I could create any fairy tale, it would certainly be that of "Cinderella;" but my poor Cinderella had all the troubles of her prototype without any of the graces either of mind or person. It is a great mistake to suppose that every victim of tyranny must of necessity be an angel. On most minds oppression has exactly the opposite effect. It dulls the faculties, stupifies the instinctive sense of right, and makes the most awful havoc among the natural affections. I was often forced to doubt whether Mr. Le Poer was very far wrong when he called Zillah by his favourite name of the "ugly little devil." There was something quite demoniac in her black eyes at times. She was lazy too — full of the languor of her native clime. Neither threats nor punishments could rouse her into the slightest activity. The only person to whom she paid the least attention was Mrs. Le Poer, who alone never ill-used her. Poor lady! she was too broken-spirited to ill-use anybody; but she never praised. I do not think Zillah had heard the common civility, "Thank you," until I came into the house; since, when I uttered it, she seemed scarcely to believe her ears. When she joined us in the schoolroom I found the girl was very ignorant. Her youngest cousin was far before her even in the commonest knowledge; and, as in all cases of deadened intellect, it cost her incalculable trouble to learn the simplest things. I took infinite pains with her, ay, and felt in her a strong interest — ten times stronger than in the other two; yet for weeks she seemed scarcely to have advanced at all. However, it must be taken into account that she was rarely suffered to remain with me half the school-hours without being summoned to some menial duty or other; and the one maidservant bestowed on me many black looks, as being the cause why she herself had sometimes to do a morning's household work alone.

Often I puzzled myself in seeing how strangely incompatible was Zillah's position with Mr. Sutherland's expressed desire concerning her. Sometimes I thought I would write and explain all to him; but I did not like. Nor did I tell my mother half the *désagréments* and odd things belonging to this family — considering that such reticence even towards her nearest kindred is every governess' duty. In all domestic circles there must be a little Eleusinia, the secrets of which chance observers should strictly keep.

More than once I determined to take advantage of the very polite and sociable terms which Mr. Le Poer and myself were on, to speak to him on the subject, and argue that his benevolence in adopting his brother's unfortunate child might not suffer by being testified in a more complete and gracious form. But he was so little at home — and no wonder; for the miserably dull, secluded, and painfully-economical way in which they lived could have little charms for a man of fashion and talent, or at least the remains of such, which he evidently was. And so agreeable as he could be! His conversation at meals — the only time I ever saw him — was a positive relief from the dull blank, broken only by the girls' squabbles and their mother's faint remonstrances and complaints. But whenever, by dint of great courage, I contrived to bring Zillah's name on the *tapis*, he always so adroitly crept out of the subject, without pointedly changing it, that afterwards I used to wonder how I had contrived to forget my purpose, and leave matters as they were.

The next scheme I tried was one which, in many family jars and family bitternesses among which my calling has placed me, I have found to answer amazingly well. It is my maxim that "a wrong is seldom a one-sided wrong;" and when you cannot amend one party, the next best thing is to try the other. Likewise, I always had a doctrine that it is only those who have the instinct and the sins of servitude who will remain hopelessly oppressed. I determined to try if there was anything in Zillah's mind or disposition that could be awakened, so as to render her worthy of a higher position than that she held. And as my firm belief is, that everything and everybody in time rise or sink to their own proper level, so I felt convinced that if there were any natural superiority in Zillah, all the tyranny in the world would not keep her the pitiable Cinderella of such ordinary people as the Le Poers.

I began my system by teaching her, not in public, where she was exposed to the silent but not less apparent contempt of her cousins, but at night in my own room after all the house had retired. I made this hour as little like lessons as possible, by letting her sit and work with me, or brush my hair, instructing her orally the while. As much as her reserve permitted, I lured her into conversation on every indifferent subject. All I wanted was to get at the girl's heart.

One day I was lecturing her in a quiet way on the subject concerning which she was the first young woman I ever knew that needed lecturing — care over her personal appearance. She certainly was the most slovenly girl I ever saw. Poor thing! she had many excuses; for, though the whole family dressed shabbily, and, worse — tawdrily, her clothes were the meanest of all. Still, nothing but positive rags can excuse a woman for neglecting womanly neatness. I often urged despairingly upon poor Zillah that the coarsest frock was no apology for untidy hair; that the most unpleasant work did not exclude the possibility of making face and hands clean after it was over.

"Look at yours, my dear," said I once, taking the reluctant fingers and spreading them out on mine. Then I saw what I have often noticed in the Hindoo race, how delicate was the shape of her hands, even despite her hard servant's-work. I told her so; for in a creature so crushed there was little fear of exciting vanity, and I made it a point to praise her every good quality, personal or mental.

Zillah looked pleased. "My hands are like my mother's, who was very handsome, and a Parsee."

"Do you remember her?"

"A little, not much; and chiefly her hands, which were covered with rings. One, a great diamond, was worth, she told me, ever so many hundred rupees. It was lost once, and my mother cried. I saw it, a good while after, on my father's finger when he was dying," continued she carelessly; and afterwards added mysteriously, "I think he stole it."

"Hush, child! hush! It is wrong to speak so of a dead father," cried I, much shocked.

"Is it? Well, I'll not do it, if it vexes you, Miss Pryor."

This seemed her only consciousness of right and wrong — pleasing or displeasing me. It argued well for her power of being guided by the affections. I asked again about her father: somehow, with a feminine prejudice, natural though scarcely right, I felt a delicacy in mentioning the mother; but she was the only parent of whom Zillah would speak. "I hardly know," "I can't remember," "I don't care," were all the answers my questions won.

"You saw your father when he was dying," I persisted; "what did he say to you?"

"I don't remember, except that I was like my mother. All the rest was mere swearing, as uncle swears at me now. But uncle did not do it then."

"So Mr. Le Poer was present?"

"Yes; and the ugly, horrible-looking man they said was my father talked to him in whispers, and uncle took me on his knee, and called me 'My dear.' He never did so afterwards."

I asked her one more question — "How long was this ago?" and she said, "Several years; she did not recollect how many."

I talked to her no more that night, but bade her go to rest. In fact my mind was so full of her that I was glad to get her visible self out of the way. She went, lazily and stupidly as ever. Only at the door she paused. "You won't tell what I have been saying, Miss Pryor? — You'll not mention my mother before them? I did once, and they laughed and made game of her, uncle and all. They did — they —." She stopped, literally foaming at the mouth with rage.

"Come in again; do, my poor child," said I, gently approaching. But she shut the door hurriedly, and ran down-stairs to the kitchen, where she slept with her dire enemy, yet sole companion, the servant-maid.

Six months after coming to the Le Poers I began heartily to wish for some of my salary; not that I had any doubt of it — Mr. Sutherland had said it was safe and sure — but I wanted some replenishment of my wardrobe, and besides it was near my mother's birthday, when I always took care she had some nice useful gift. It quite puzzled me to think what little luxury she wanted, for she wrote me word Mr. Sutherland brought her so many. "He was just like a son to her," she said. — Ah me!

One day, when disconsolately examining my last pair of boots — the "wee boots" that, for a foolish reason I had, were one of my few feminine vanities — I took courage to go down-stairs and ask Mr. Le Poer "if he could make it convenient," &c. &c.

"My dear Miss Pryor," said he, with most gentlemanly *empressement*, "if I had thought — indeed you should have asked me before. Let me see, you have been here six months, and our stipulated sum was —."

I thought he hesitated on account of the delicacy some gentlemen feel in business-dealings with a lady; indeed I supposed it was from that cause he had never spoken to me about money-matters. However, I felt no such delicacy, but answered plainly: "My salary, Mr. Sutherland said, was to be one hundred guineas a year."

"Exactly so; and payable yearly, I believe?" Mr. Le Poer added, carelessly.

Now, I had not remembered that; but of course he knew. However, I looked and felt disappointed. At last, as Mr. Le Poer spoke with the greatest politeness, I confessed the fact that I wanted the money for habiliments.

"Oh, is that all? Then pray, my excellent young lady, go with Caroline to H— at once. Order anything you like of my trades-people. Bid them put all to my account: we can settle afterwards. No excuses; indeed you must." He bowed me away with the air of a benefactor disdaining gratitude, and set off immediately on one of his frequent jaunts. There was no help for it; so I accepted his plan, and went to H— with Caroline and Matilda.

It seemed a long time since I had been in any town, and the girls might never have been there in their lives, so eagerly did they linger at shop-windows, admiring and longing after finery. The younger consoled the elder, saying that they would have all these sort of grand things some time. "It's only four years," whispered she, "just four years, and then that stupid Zill —." Here Caroline pushed her away with an angry "hush!" and walked up to my side with a prim smile. I thought it strange, but took no notice, always disliking to play the governess out of school hours.

Another odd thing happened the same week. There came a letter to Mr. Le Poer from Mr. Sutherland. I could not help noticing this, as it lay on the mantel-shelf two days before the former returned, and I used to see it always when I sat at meals. His — Mr. Sutherland's I mean — was a fair, large hand, which would have caught any one's eye: besides, it was like old times to see it again.

I happened to be by when Mr. Le Poer opened the letter. He was so anxious over it that he did not notice my presence. Perhaps it was wrong of me to glance toward him, but yet natural, considering it was the letter of a friend of mine. I saw a little note enclosed, the address of which, I was almost sure, bore my own name. I waited, thinking he would give it to me. I even made some slight movement to attract his attention. He looked up — he actually started — but next moment smiled, as only Mr. Le Poer could smile.

"News from our friend, you see!" said he, showing me the outside envelope. "He is quite well, and — let me consider," — glancing over his own letter — "he sends his kindest remembrances to you. A most worthy man is Mr. Sutherland."

So saying he folded the epistle, and placed it in his desk. The little note, which he had turned seal uppermost he quietly put, unopened, into his pocket. It must have been my own delusion then. Yet I was disappointed.

At the expiration of my first year as a governess, just as I was looking with untold eagerness to my midsummer holidays, when I was at length to go home to my mother — for the journey to London was too expensive to admit of that happiness more than once a year — there happened a great disaster to the Le Poer family: no less than that terrible scourge, typhus fever. Matilda took it first, then Caroline, then the mother. These three were scarcely convalescent when Zillah caught the fever in her turn, and had it more dangerously than any of the rest. Her life was in danger for many days, during which I had the sole anxiety and responsibility; for Mr. Le Poer, on the first tidings of the fever, had taken flight, and been visible at home no more. True, he wrote every other day most touching letters, and I in return kept him constantly informed as to the progress of his wife and children. When Zillah was taken ill, however, I did not think it necessary to send him word concerning her, feeling that the poor orphan's life was precious to no one. I never was more surprised than when on Mr. Le Poer's venturing back and finding Zillah in the crisis of her disease, his terror and anxiety appeared uncontrollable.

"Good God!" he cried, "Zillah ill? Zillah going to die? Impossible! Why was I not informed before? Confound you, madam!" — and he turned furiously to his still ailing wife — "did you not think? Are you mad — quite mad?"

I declare I thought *he* was. Mrs. Le Poer only sobbed in silence. Meanwhile the outcries of the delirious girl were heard in the very parlour. I had given her my room; I thought, poor soul, she should not die in her damp kitchen-closet.

Mr. Le Poer turned absolutely white with terror — he who had expressed only mild concern when his wife and daughters were in peril. "Miss Pryor," said he, hoarsely, "something must be done. That girl *must* be saved; I'd snatch her from the very fiend himself! Send for advice, physicians, nurses; send to Leeds, Liverpool — to London even. Only, by —, she must not die!"

Poor Zillah did not die. She was saved, for Heaven's strange purposes; though I, in my then blindness, often and often, while sitting by her bedside, thought it would be better did she slip quietly out of the bitter world in which she seemed to be only an unsightly and trampled weed. Mr. Le Poer's unwonted anxiety did not end with her convalescence, which was very slow. "She may die yet!" I heard him muttering to himself, the first day after he saw his niece. "Miss Pryor, my wife is a foo —, I mean a rather undecided person. Tell me what *you* think ought to be done for Zillah's recovery?" I prescribed, but with little hope that my advice would be followed — immediate change to sea air. "It shall be done!" at once said he. "Mrs. Le Poer and the girls can take care of her; or stay — she likes you best. Miss Pryor, are you willing to go?"

This question perfectly confounded me. I had been so longingly anticipating my going home — delayed, as in common charity I could not but delay it, on account of the fever. Now this trouble was over I had quite counted on my departure. That very week I had been preparing my small wardrobe, so as to look as nice as possible in my mother's eyes. She had given me a hint to do so, since she and I were to spend the vacation together at Mr. Sutherland's country-house, and old Mrs. Sutherland was so very particular.

"Why do you hesitate?" said Mr. Le Poer, rather sharply. "Are you thinking of the money? You shall have any additional salary — 50*l.* more if you choose. Upon my soul, madam, you shall! only I entreat you to go."

I would not have minded *his* entreaties, but I was touched by those of Zillah, who seemed terrified at the idea of going to a strange place without me. Then, too, the additional money, not unneeded; for Mr. Sutherland, so kindly generous in other things, had the still rarer generosity never to offer us *that*. I determined to write and tell my mother the position of affairs. Her good judgment would decide; or if hers failed, she would be sure to appeal to Mr. Sutherland, her trusty and only adviser since my father died; and I was content to abide by his decision.

He did decide. He told my mother that it was his earnest wish I should stay a little longer with Zillah Le Poer, whom he called "his ward." Her history, he said, he would inform me when we met; which must be soon, as he was contemplating returning to India for some years, and had something to communicate to me before he went away.

Mr. Sutherland returning to India! And before his departure he must see me — *me!* It was a very simple and natural thing, as I felt afterwards, but not then. I did what he desired — as indeed I had long been in the habit of doing — and accompanied Zillah.

I had supposed that we should go to some near watering-place, or at all events to the Liverpool shore. Indeed I had pointedly recommended Tranmere, where, as I stated to Mr. Le Poer, there was living an aunt of Mr. Sutherland's, who would have taken lodgings or done anything in her power for her nephew's ward. To my surprise he objected to this plan. After staying a night in Liverpool, instead of crossing to the opposite shore, as I expected, he put us all — that is, Zillah, the two other girls, and myself — on board the Belfast boat, and there we found ourselves floating across the Irish Channel!

The two Misses Le Poer were considerably frightened; Zillah looked most happy. She said it reminded her of her voyage to England when she was a little child. She had never seen the sea since. Long after we got out of sight of land she and I sat together on the deck in the calm summer evening, talking of this Indian voyage, and what it was like, and what people did during the long four months from land to land. She gave me much information, to which I listened with strange interest. I well remember, fool that I was! sitting on the deck of that Belfast boat, with the sun dipping into the sea before us, and the moon rising on the other side — sitting and thinking what it would be to feel one's self on the deck of some India-bound ship, alone, or else in companionship that might make the word still correct, according to its original reading — *all one*. An etymological notion worthy of a poor governess!

The only remarkable event of our voyage was my sudden introduction by Mr. Le Poer to a personage whom I had not thought existed. "My son, Miss Pryor; my eldest and only son, Lieutenant Augustus Le Poer."

I was very considerably surprised, as I had never heard of the young gentleman. I could only conjecture, what I afterwards found to be the truth, that this was the son of a former marriage, and that there had been some family quarrel, lately healed. The lieutenant bowed to me, and I to him. Zillah, who sat by me, had no share in the introduction, until the young man, sticking his glass in his eye, stared at her energetically, muttering to his father some question, in which I just detected the words, "odd fish."

"Only Zillah," answered Mr. Le Poer, carelessly. "Child, this is your cousin Augustus, lately returned from foreign service. Shake hands with him."

Zillah listlessly obeyed; but her "cousin" seemed not at all to relish the title. He cast his eyes superciliously over her. I must confess my poor child's appearance was not very attractive. I did not wonder that Lieutenant Augustus merely nodded his head, twirled his moustache, and walked away. Zillah just looked lazily after him, and then her eyes declined upon the beautiful expanse of sea.

For my part I watched our new friend with some curiosity and amusement, especially when Caroline and Matilda appeared, trying to do the agreeable. The lieutenant was to them evidently the *beau idéal* of a brother. For myself, I did not admire him at all. Unluckily, if I have three positive aversions in the world, it is for dandies, men with moustaches, and soldiers — and he was a compound of all three. Also, he was a small man; and I, like most little women, have a great reverence for height in the other sex. Not universally, for some of my truest friends have been diminutive men — excellent, noble, admirable Zaccheuses. Still, from an ancient prejudice, acquired — no matter how — my first impression of any man is usually in proportion to his inches: therefore Lieutenant Le Poer did not stand very high in my estimation.

Little notice did he condescend to take of us, which was rather a satisfaction than otherwise; but he soon became very fraternal and confidential with his two sisters. I saw them all chattering together until it grew dusk; and long after that, the night being fine, I watched their dark figures walking up and down the other side of the deck. More than once I heard their laughter, and detected in their talk the name of Zillah; so I supposed the girls were ridiculing her to their brother. Poor child! she was fast asleep, with her head on my shoulder, wrapped closely up, so that the mild night could do her no harm. She looked almost pretty — the light of the August moon so spiritualized her face. I felt thankful she had not died, but that, under Heaven, my care had saved her — for what? Ay, and for whom? If, as I kissed the child, I had then known —. But no, I should have kissed her and loved her still!

Our brief voyage ended, we reached Belfast and proceeded to Holywood — a small sea-bathing village a few miles down the coast. To this day I have never found out why Mr. Le Poer took the trouble to bring us all over the water and settle us there; where, to all intents and purposes, we might as well have been buried in the solitudes of the Desert of Sahara. But perhaps that was exactly what he wanted.

I think that never in her life, at least since childhood, could Zillah have been so happy as she was during the first week or two of our sojourn at Holywood. To me, who in my youth, when we were rich and could travel, had seen much beautiful scenery, the place was rather uninteresting; to her it was perfection! As she grew stronger, life seemed to return to her again under quite a new aspect. Certainly, it was a great change in her existence to have no one over her but me — for her uncle and cousin Augustus had of course speedily vanished from this quiet spot — to be able to do just what she liked, which was usually nothing at all. She was not made for activity; she would lie whole days on the beach, or on the grassy walk which came down to the very edge of high-water mark — covering her eyes with her poke-bonnet, or gazing sleepily from under her black lashes at the smooth Lough, and the wavy line of hills on the opposite shore. Matilda and Caroline ran very wild also: since we had no lessons I found it hard work to make them obey me; indeed it was always a great pain for a quiet soul like me to have to assume authority. I should have got on better even with Mrs. Le Poer to assist me; but she, poor little woman, terrified at change, had preferred staying quietly at home in Yorkshire. I was not quite sure but that she had the best of it after all.

In the course of a week, my cares were somewhat lightened. The lieutenant re-appeared, and from that time forward I had very little of the girls' company. He was certainly a kind brother; I could not but acknowledge that. He took them about a great deal, or else stayed at Holywood, leaving us by the late evening train, as he said, to go to his lodgings at Belfast. I, the temporary mistress of the establishment, was of course duly polite to my pupils' brother, and he was really very civil to me, though he treated me with the distance due to an ancient duenna. This amused me sometimes, seeing I was only twenty-six — probably his own age; but I was always used to be regarded as an old maid.

Of Zillah the lieutenant hardly ever took any notice at all, and she seemed to keep out of his way as much as possible. When he left us in the evening — and there was always a tolerable confusion at that time, his two sisters wanting to see him off by the train, which he never by any chance allowed — then came the quietest and pleasantest half-hour of the day. The Misses Le Poer disliked twilight rambles, so Zillah and I always set off together; though oftentimes we parted company, and I was left sitting on the beach, while she strolled on to a pleasant walk she said she had found — a deserted house, whose grounds sloped down to the very shore. But I, not very strong then, and weighed down by many anxious thoughts, loved better to sit and stupify myself with the murmur of the sea — a habit not good for me, but pleasant. No fear had I of Zillah's losing herself, or coming to any harm; and the girl seemed so happy in her solitary rambles that I had not the desire to stop them, knowing how a habit of self-dependence is the greatest comfort to a woman, especially to one in her desolate position. But as the frost of her nature broke up, and her dulness was melting away, Zillah seemed more *self-contained*, so to speak; more reserved, and relying on her own thoughts for occupation and amusement: — still she had never been so attentive or affectionate to me.

It was a curious and interesting study — this young mind's unfolding; though I shame to say that just then I did not think about Zillah as much as I ought to have done. Often I reproached myself for this afterwards; but as things have turned out, I now feel, with a quiet self-compassion, that my error was pardonable.

I mind one evening — that "*I mind*" is not quite English, but I learned it with other phrases, in my young days, so let it stand! — I mind one evening, that, being not quite in a mood for solitude, I went out walking with Zillah. Somehow the murmur of the sea wearied me; I turned through the village and along the high road — almost like an English road, so beautiful with overhanging trees. I did not talk much, and Zillah walked quite silently, which indeed was nothing new. I think I see her now, floating along with her thin but lithe figure, and limp, clinging dress — the very antipodes of fashion — nothing about her that would really be called beautiful except her great eyes, which were perfect oceans of light. When we came to a gateway — which, like most things in poor Ireland, seemed either broken down or left half finished — she looked round rather anxiously.

"Do you know this place, my dear?"

"It is an old mansion — where I often like to stroll."

"What! have you been there alone?"

"Of course I have," said she quickly, and slightly colouring. "You knew it: or I thought you did."

She appeared apprehensive of reproof; which struck me as odd, in so inoffensive a matter as her adventuring a solitary stroll; especially as I was anything but a cross governess. To please and reassure her I said: "Well, never mind, my dear; you shall show me your pet paradise. It will be quite a treat."

"I don't think so, Miss Pryor. It's all weeds and disorder, and you can't endure that. And the ground is very wet, here and there. I am sure you'll not like it at all."

"Oh, but I will, if only to please you, Zillah," said I, determined to be at once firm and pacific; for I saw a trace of her old sullen look troubling my pupil's face, as if she did not like her haunts to be intruded upon even by me. However, she made no more open opposition, and we entered the grounds, which were almost English in their aspect, except in one thing — their entire desolation. The house might not have been inhabited, or the grounds cultivated, for twenty years. The rose-beds grew wild — great patches of white clover overspread the lawn and flower-garden, and all the underwood was one mass of tall fern.

I had not gone far in and out of the tangled walks of the shrubbery when I found that Zillah had slipped away. I saw her at a distance standing under a tall Portugal laurel, seemingly doing nothing but meditate — a new occupation for her; so I left her to it, and penetrated deeper into what my old French governess would have called the *bocage*. My feet sunk deep in fern, amidst which I plunged, trying to gather a great armful of that and of wild flowers; for I had, and have still, the babyish propensity of wishing to pluck everything I see, and never can conquer the delight I feel in losing myself in a wilderness of vegetation. In that oblivion of childlike content I was happy — happier than I had been for a long time. The ferns nearly hid me, when I heard a stirring in the bushes behind, which I took for some harmless animal that I had disturbed. However, hares, foxes, or even squirrels, do not usually give a loud "Ahem!" in the perfectly human tone which followed. At first I had terrors of some stray keeper, who might possibly shoot me for a rabbit or a poacher, till I recollected that I was not in England but in Ireland, where unjust landlords are regarded as the more convenient game.

"Ahem!" reiterated the mysterious voice; "ahem! Is it you, my angel?"

Never could any poor governess be more thoroughly dumbfounded! Of course the adjective was not meant for me. Impossible! Still it was unpleasant to come into such near contact with a case of philandering. Mere philandering it must be, for this was no honest village-tryste, the man's accent being refined and quite English. Besides, little as I knew of love-making, it struck me that in any serious attachment people would never address one another by the silly title of "my angel." It must be some idle flirtation going on among the strolling visitants whom we occasionally met on the beach, and who had probably wandered up through the gate which led to these grounds.

To put an end to any more confidential disclosures from this unseen gentleman, I likewise said "Ahem!" as loudly as I could, and immediately called aloud for Zillah. Whereupon there was a hasty rustling in the bushes; which, however, soon subsided, and the place became quite still again, without my ever having caught sight of the very complimentary individual who had in this extempore manner addressed me as his "angel." "Certainly," I thought, "I must have been as invisible to him as he to me, or he never would have done it."

Zillah joined me quickly. She looked half frightened, and said she feared something was the matter. "Had I seen anything?"

At first I was on the point of telling her all, but somehow it now appeared a rather ridiculous position for a governess to be placed in — to have shouted for assistance on being addressed by mistake by an unknown admirer; and besides I did not wish to put any love-notions into the girl's head: they come quite soon enough of their own accord. So I merely said I had been startled by hearing voices in the bushes — that perhaps we were intruders on the domain, and had better not stay longer.

"Yet the place seems retired and desolate," said I, as we walked down the tangled walk that led to the beach, Zillah evidently rather unwilling to go home. "Do you ever meet any strangers about here?"

She answered briefly, "No."

"Did you see any one to-night?"

"Yes." Given with a slight hesitation.

"Who was it?"

"A man, I think — at a distance."

"Did he speak to you?"

"No."

I give these questions and answers verbatim, to show — what I believed then, and believe now — that, so far as I questioned, Zillah answered me truthfully. I should be sorry to think that either at that time or any other she had told me a wilful lie.

But this adventure left an uncomfortable sensation on my mind — not from any doubt of Zillah herself, for she appeared still too much of a child, and too awkward and unattractive, for me to fear her engaging in love-affairs, clandestine or otherwise, for some time to come. Nevertheless, after this evening, I always contrived that we should take our twilight strolls in company, and that I should never lose sight of her for more than a few minutes together. Yet even with this precaution I proved to be a very simple and short-sighted governess after all.

We had been at Holywood a whole month, and I began to wonder when we should return home, as Zillah was quite well, indeed more blooming than I had ever seen her. Mr. Le Poer made himself visible once or twice, at rare intervals: he had always "business in Dublin," or "country visits to pay." His son acted as regent in his absence — I always supposed by his desire; nevertheless I often noticed that these two lights of the family never shone together, and the father's expected arrival was the signal of Mr. Augustus's non-appearance for some days. Nor did the girls ever allude to their brother. I thought family quarrels might perhaps have lessoned them in this, and so was not surprised.

It was certainly a relief to all when the head of the family again departed. We usually kept his letters for him, he not being very anxious about them; for which indifference, as I afterwards comprehended, he might have good reasons. Once there came a letter — I knew from whom — marked in the corner, "*If absent, to be opened by Miss Pryor.*" Greatly surprised was I to find it contained a bank-note, apparently hurriedly enclosed, with this brief line: —

"If Zillah requires more let me know at once. She must have every luxury needful for her health. — A. S."

The initials certainly meant his name — Andrew Sutherland — nor could I be mistaken in the hand. Yet it seemed very odd, as I had no idea that he held over her more than a nominal guardianship, just undertaken out of charity to the orphan, and from his having slightly known her father. At least so Mr. Le Poer told me. The only solution I could find for his sending Zillah the money was the simple one of its being a gift, springing from the generosity of a heart whose goodness I knew but too well.

However, to be quite sure, I called Caroline into counsel; thinking, silly as she was, she might know something of the matter. But she only tittered, looked mysteriously important, and would speak clearly on no point, except "that we had a perfect right to use the money — Pa always did; and that she wanted a new bonnet very badly indeed."

A day or two after, Mr. Le Poer, returning unexpectedly,

took the note into his own possession, saying, smilingly, "that it was all right;" and I heard no more.

But if I had not been the very simplest woman in the world I should certainly have suspected that things were not "all right." Nevertheless, I do not now wonder at my blindness. How could I think otherwise than well of a man whom I innocently supposed to be a friend of Mr. Sutherland?

So matters went on at Holywood for a little time longer.

"Zillah, my dear, do not look so disappointed. There is no help for it. Your uncle told me before he left us that we must go home next week."

So said I one day, trying to say it gently, and not marvelling that the girl was unhappy at the near prospect of returning to her old miserable life. It was a future so bitter that I almost blamed myself for not having urged our longer stay. Still human nature is weak, and I did so thirst for home — my own home. But it was hard that my pleasure should be the poor child's pain.

"Don't cry, my love," I went on, seeing her eyes brimming, and the colour coming and going in her face: — strange changes which latterly, on the most trifling occasions, had disturbed the apparent stolidity of her countenance. "Don't be unhappy: things may be smoother now; and I am sure your cousins behave better and kinder to you than they did: even the lieutenant is very civil to you."

A sparkle, which was either pleasure or pride, flashed from the girl's eyes, and then they drooped, unable to meet mine.

"Be content, dear child; all may be happier for you than you expect. You must write to me regularly — you can write pretty well now, you know: you must tell me all that happens to you, and remember that in everything you can trust me entirely."

Here I was astonished by Zillah's casting herself at my knees as I sat, and bursting into a storm of tears. Anxiously I asked her what was the matter.

"Nothing — everything! I am so happy — so wretched! Ah! what must I do?"

These words bubbled up brokenly from her lips, but just at that unlucky moment her three cousins came in. She sprang up like a frightened deer, and was off to her own room. I did not see her again all the afternoon, for Lieutenant Augustus kept me in the parlour on one excuse or another until I was heartily vexed at him and myself. When I went up stairs to put on my bonnet — we were all going to walk that evening — Zillah slipped away almost as soon as I appeared. I noticed that she was quite composed now, and had resumed her usual manner. I called after her to tell the two other girls to get ready, thinking it wisest to make no remarks concerning her excitement of the morning.

I never take long in dressing, and soon went down, rather quietly perhaps; for I was meditating with pain on how much this passionate child might yet have to suffer in the world. I believe I have rather a light step; at all events I was once told so. Certainly I did not intend to come into the parlour stealthily or pryingly; in fact, I never thought of its occupants at all. On entering, what was my amazement to see standing at the window — Lieutenant Augustus and — my Zillah! He was embracing — in plain English, kissing her.

Now, I am no prude in such things; I have oftentimes known a harmless father-like or brother-like embrace between two, who, quite certain of each other's feelings, gave and received the same in all frank affection and simplicity. But generally I am very particular: more so than most women. I often used to think that, were I a man, I would wish, in the sweet day of my betrothal, to know for certain that mine was the first *lover's* kiss ever pressed on the dear lips which I then sealed as wholly my own.

But in this case, at one glance, even if I had not caught the silly phrase, "My angel!" — the same I heard in the wood (ah, that wood!) — I or any one would have detected the truth. It came upon me like a thunderbolt; but knowing Zillah's disposition, I had just wit enough to glide back unseen, and re-enter, talking loudly at the door. Upon which I found the lieutenant tapping his boots carelessly, and Zillah shrinking into a corner like a frightened hare. He went off very soon — he said, to an engagement at Belfast; and we started for our ramble. I noticed that Zillah walked alongside of Caroline, as if she could not approach or look at me.

I know not whether I was most shocked at my poor girl, or puzzled to think what possible attraction this young man could find in such a mere child — so plain and awkward-looking too. That he could be "in love" with her, even in the lowest sense of that phrase, seemed all but an impossibility; and if not in love, what possible purpose could he have in wooing or wanting to marry her? — for I was simple enough to suppose that all wooing must necessarily be in earnest.

Half-bewildered with conjectures, fears, and doubts as to what course I must pursue, did I walk on beside Matilda, who, having quarrelled with her sister, kept close to me. She went chattering on about some misdoings of Caroline. At last my attention was caught by Zillah's name.

"I won't bear it always," said the angry child; "I'll only bear it till Zillah comes of age."

"Bear what?"

"Why, that Carry should always have two new frocks to my one. It's a shame!"

"But what has that to say to Zillah's coming of age?"

"Don't you know, Miss Pryor? — oh, of course you don't, for Carry wouldn't let me tell you; but I will!" she added, maliciously.

I hardly knew whether I was right or wrong in not stopping the girl's tongue, but I could not do it.

"Do you know," she added, in a sly whisper, "Carry says we shall all be very rich when Zillah comes of age. Pa and ma kept it very secret; but Carry found it out, and told it to brother Augustus and to me."

"Told what?" said I, forgetful that I was prying into a family secret, and stung into curiosity by the mention of Augustus.

"That Zillah will then be very rich, as her father left her all he had; and uncle Henry was a great nabob, because he married an Indian princess, and got all her money. Now, you see," she continued with a cunning smile, shocking on that young face, "we must be very civil to Zillah, and of course she will give us all her money. Eh, you understand?"

I stood aghast. In a moment all came clear upon me; the secret of Mr. Sutherland's guardianship — of his letter to me intercepted — of the money lately sent — of Mr. Le Poer's anxiety concerning his niece's life, and his desire to keep her hidden from the world, lest she might come to a knowledge of her position. The whole was a tissue of crimes. And, deepest crime of all! I now guessed why Lieutenant Augustus wished, unknown to his father, to entrap her still childish affections, marry her, and secure all to himself.

I never knew much of the world and its wickedness; I believed all men were like my father or Mr. Sutherland. This discovery for the time quite dizzied my faculties. I have not the slightest recollection of anything more that passed on that sea-side walk, except that, coming in at the door of the cottage, I heard Zillah say in anxious tones, "What ails Miss Pryor, I wonder?" I had wisdom enough to answer, "Nothing, my dears!" and sent them all to bed.

"Shall you be long after us?" asked Zillah, who, as I said, was my chamber-companion.

"An hour or two," I replied, turning away.

I went and sat alone in the little parlour, trying to collect my thoughts. To any governess the discovery of a clandestine and unworthy love-affair among her pupils would be most painful, but my discoveries were all horror together. The more I thought it over, the more my agonised pity for Zillah overcame my grief at her deceitfulness. Love is always so weak, and girlish love at fifteen such a fascinating dream. Whatever I thought of the lieutenant, he was very attractive to most people. He was, besides, the first young man Zillah had ever made acquaintance with, and the first human being except myself who had treated her with kindness. But what opportunities could they have had to become lovers? I recollected Zillah's wanderings, evening after evening, in the grounds of the deserted estate. She must have met him there. Poor girl! I could well imagine what it must be to be wooed under the glamour of summer twilight and beautiful solitude. No wonder Zillah's heart was stolen away!— Thinking of this now, I feel I am wrong in saying "heart" of what at best could have been mere "fancy." Women's natures are different; but some women have been gravely, mournfully, fatally in earnest, even at sixteen.

However, in earnest or not, she must be snatched from this marriage at all risks. There could be no doubt of that. But to whom should I apply for aid? Not to Mr. Le Poer certainly. The poor orphan seemed trembling between the grasp of either villain, father and son. Whatever must be done for her I must do myself of my own judgment, and on my own responsibility.

It was a very hard strait for me. In my necessity I instinctively turned to my best friend in the world, and — as I suddenly remembered — Zillah's too: I determined to write and explain all to Mr. Sutherland.

How well I remember that hour! The little parlour quite still and quiet, except for the faint sound of the waves rolling in; for it was rather a wild night, and our small one-storied cottage stood by itself in a solitary part of the beach. How well I remember myself! sitting with the pen in my hand, uncertain how to begin; for I felt awkward, never having written to him since I was a child.

At first I almost forgot what I had to write about. While musing, I was startled by a noise like the opening of a window. Now, as I explained, our house was all on one flat, and we could easily step from any window to the beach. In considerable alarm, I hurried into Zillah's room. There, by the dim night-light, I saw her bed was empty. She had apparently dressed herself, — for I saw none of her clothes — and crept out at the window. Terrified inexpressibly, I was about to follow her, when I saw the flutter of a shawl outside, and heard her voice speaking.

"No, cousin — no, dear cousin! Don't ask me. I can't go away with you to-night. It would be very wrong when Miss Pryor knows nothing about it. If she had found us out, or threatened, and we were obliged to run away ——." (Immediately I saw that, with a girl of Zillah's fierce obstinacy, discovery would be most dangerous. I put out the light and kept quite still.)

"I can't, indeed I can't," pursued Zillah's voice, in answer to some urging which was inaudible; adding, with a childish laugh, "You know, Cousin Augustus, it would never do for me to go and be married in a cotton dressing-gown; and Miss Pryor keeps all my best clothes. Dear Miss Pryor! I would much rather have told her, only you say she would be so much the more surprised and pleased when I came back married. And you are quite sure that she shall always live with us, and never return to Yorkshire again?"

Her words, so childish, so unconscious of the wrong she was doing, perfectly startled me. All my romantic notions of girlish passion following its own wild will were put to flight. Here was a mere child led away by the dazzle of a new toy to the brink of a precipice. She evidently knew no more of love and marriage than a baby!

For a little time longer, the wicked — lover I cannot call him — suitor, urged his suit, playing with her simplicity in a manner that he must have inwardly laughed at all the time. He lured her to matrimony by puerile pet names, such as "My angel"— by idle rhapsodies, and promises of fine houses and clothes.

"I don't mind these things at all," said poor Zillah, innocently; "I would not go with you, only you say that when I am married I shall have nothing to do, and you will never scold me, and I shall have Miss Pryor always near me. Promise!"

Here was a pause, until the child's simple voice was heard again: "I don't like that, cousin. I won't kiss you again. Miss Pryor once said we ought never to kiss anybody unless we love them very much."

"And don't you love me, my adorable creature?"

"I — I'm not quite sure: sometimes I love you and sometimes not; but I suppose I shall always, when we are married."

"That blissful day must be very soon," said the lieutenant; and I thought I heard him trying to suppress a yawn. "Let us settle it at once, my dear, for it grows late. If you will not come to night, let me have the happiness, the entire felicity, of fetching you to-morrow."

"No, no," Zillah answered; "Miss Pryor will want me to help her to pack. We leave this day week: let me stay still the night before; then come for me, and I'll have my best frock on, and we can be married in time to meet them all before the boat sails the next day."

In other circumstances I should have smiled at this child's idea of marriage: but now the crisis was far too real and awful: and the more her ignorance lightened her own error, the more it increased the crime of that bad man who was about to ruin her peace for ever. A little he tried to reverse her plan and make the marriage earlier; but Zillah was too steady. In the obstinacy of her character — in the little influence which, lover as he was, he seemed to have over her — I found her safeguard, past and present. It would just allow me time to save her in the only way she could be saved.

I listened till I heard her say good-bye to her cousin, creep back into the dark room through the open window, and fasten it securely as before. Then I stole away to the parlour, and, supported by the strong excitement of the moment, wrote my letter to Mr. Sutherland.

There would be in the six days just time for the arrival of an answer, or — himself. I left everything to him, merely stating the facts, knowing he would do right. At midnight I went to bed. Zillah was fast asleep. As I lay awake, hour after hour, I thanked Heaven that the poor child, deluded as she had been, knew nothing of what love was in its reality. She was at least spared that sorrow.

During all the week I contrived to keep Zillah as near me as was possible, consistent with the necessity of not awaking her suspicions. This was the more practicable, as she seemed to cling to me with an unwonted and even painful tenderness. The other girls grumbled sadly at our departure; but luckily all had been definitively arranged by their father, who had even, strange to say, given me money for the journey. He had likewise gracefully apologised for being obliged to let us women-kind travel alone, as he had himself some business engagements, while his son had lately rejoined his regiment. I really think the deceiving and deceived father fully credited the latter fact. Certainly they were a worthy pair!

I made all my plans secure, and screwed up my courage as well as I could; but I own on the evening previous to our journey — the evening which, from several attesting proofs, I knew was still fixed for the elopement — I began to feel a good deal alarmed. Of Mr. Sutherland was no tidings. At twilight I saw plainly that the sole hope must lie in my own presence of mind, my influence over Zillah, and my appeal to her sense of honour and affection. I sent the children early to bed, saying I had letters to write, and prepared myself for whatever was to happen.

Now many may think me foolish, and at times I thought myself so likewise, for not going to Zillah and telling her all I had discovered; but I knew her character better than that. The idea of being betrayed, waylaid, controlled, would drive her fierce Eastern nature into the very commission of the madness she contemplated. In everything I must trust to the impulse of the moment, and to the result of her suddenly discovering her own position and the villanous plans laid against her.

Never in my life do I remember a more anxious hour than that I spent sitting in the dark by the parlour window, whence, myself unseen, I could see all that passed without the house; for it was a lovely night — the moon high up over the Lough, and making visible the Antrim hills. I think in all moments of great peril one grows quiet: so did I.

At eleven there was a sound of wheels on the beach, and the shadow of a man passed the window. I looked out. It was the most unromantic and common-place elopement with an heiress: he was merely going to take her away on an outside car. There was no one with him but the carman, who was left whistling contentedly on the shore.

The moment had come; with the energy of desperation, I put off the shawl in which I had wrapped myself in case I had to follow the child; for follow her I had determined to do, were it necessary. Quietly, and with as ordinary a manner as I could assume, I walked into Zillah's room.

She was just stepping from the window on the beach. She had on her best frock and shawl, poor innocent! with her favourite white bonnet, that I had lately trimmed for her, carefully tied up in a kerchief.

I touched her shoulder. "Zillah, where are you going?"

She started and screamed.

"Tell me: I must know!" I repeated, holding her fast by the arm, while Augustus rather roughly pulled her by the other.

"Cousin, you hurt me!" she cried; and instinctively drew back. Then for the first time the lieutenant saw me.

I have often noticed that cunning and deceitful people — small villains, not great ones — are always cowards. Mr. Augustus drew back as if he had been shot. I took no notice of him, but still appealed to Zillah.

"Tell me, my child, the plain truth, as you always do — where were you going?"

She stammered out: "I was going to — to Belfast — to be married."

"Married to your cousin?"

She hung her head and murmured: "Yes."

At this frank confession the bridegroom interposed. He perhaps was all the braver for reflecting that he had only women to deal with. He leaped in at the chamber-window, and angrily asked me by what right I interfered.

"I will tell you," said I, "if you have enough gentlemanly

feeling to leave my apartment, and will speak with me in the open air."

He retreated, I bolted the window, and still keeping a firm hold on the trembling girl, met him outside the front door. It certainly was the oddest place for such a scene; but I did not wish to admit him inside the house.

"Now, Miss Pryor," said he imperatively, but still politely, — a Le Poer could not be otherwise — "will you be so kind as to relinquish that young lady, who has confided herself to *my* care, and intends honouring me with her hand?"

"Is that true, Zillah? Do you love this man, and voluntarily intend to marry him?"

"Yes, if you will let me, Miss Pryor. He told me you would be so pleased. He promises always to be kind to me, and never let me work. Please don't be angry with me, dear Miss Pryor! Oh, do let me marry my cousin!"

"Listen to me a few minutes, Zillah," said I, "and you shall choose." And then I told her, in as few words as I could, what her position was — how that it had been concealed from her that she was an heiress, and how by marrying her, her cousin Augustus would be master over all her wealth. So unworldly was she, that I think the girl herself hardly understood me; but the lieutenant was furious.

"It is all a lie — an infamous cheat!" he cried. "Don't believe it, Zillah! Don't be frightened, little fool! I promised to marry you, and, by Heaven! marry you I will!"

"Lieutenant Le Poer," said I, very quietly, "that may not be quite so easy as you think. However, I do not prevent you, as indeed I have no right; I only ask my dear child Zillah here to grant me one favour, as for the sake of my love to her " — (here Zillah sobbed) — "I doubt not she will: namely, that she should do as every other young woman of common sense and delicacy would do, and wait until to-morrow to ask the consent of one who will then probably be here, if he is not already arrived — her guardian — Mr. Andrew Sutherland."

Lieutenant Augustus burst out with an oath, probably very mild in the mess-room, but very shocking here to two women's ears. Zillah crept farther from him, and nearer to me.

"I'll not be cheated so!" stormed he. "Come, child, you'll trust your cousin? You'll come away to-night?" — and he tried to lift her on the car, which had approached — the Irish driver evidently much enjoying the scene.

"No, cousin; not to-night," said the girl, resisting. "I'd rather wait and have Miss Pryor with me, and proper bridesmaids, and a wedding-dress, and all that — that is, if I marry you at all, which I won't unless Miss Pryor thinks you will be kind to me. So good-bye till to-morrow, cousin."

He was so enraged by this time that he tried forcibly to drag her on the car. But I wound my arms round my dear child's waist, and shrieked for help.

"Faith, sir," said the sturdy Irishman, interfering, half in amusement, half in indignation, "ye'd betther lave the women alone. I'd rather not meddle with an abduction."

So Zillah was set free from the lieutenant's grasp, for, as I said before, a scoundrel is often a great coward. I drew the trembling and terrified girl into the house — he following with a storm of oaths and threatenings. At last I forcibly shut the door upon him, and bolted him out. Whether this indignity was too much for the valorous soldier, or whether he felt sure that all chance was over, I know not; but when I looked out ten minutes after, the coast was clear. I took my erring, wronged, yet still more wronged than erring, child into my bosom, and thanked Heaven she was saved.

The next morning Mr. Sutherland arrived.

After this night's events I have little to say, or rather I prefer to say but little of what passed during the remainder of that summer. We all travelled to England together, going round by Yorkshire in order to leave Mr. Le Poer's daughters at their own home. This was Mr. Sutherland's kind plan, that the two girls might be kept in ignorance of the whole affair, and especially of their father's ill-deeds. What they suspected I know not: they were merely told that it was the desire of Zillah's guardian to take her and her governess home with him.

So we parted at Halifax, and I never saw any of the family again. I had no scruples about thus quitting them, as I found out from Mr. Sutherland that I had been engaged solely as governess to his ward, and that he had himself paid my salary in advance; the whole of which, in some way or other, had been intercepted by Mr. Le Poer. The money of course was gone; but he had written to me with each remittance, and thus I had lost his letters. That was hard!

I also found out, with great joy and comfort, that my Zillah was truly Zillah Le Poer — her father's legitimate daughter and heiress. All I had been led to believe was a cruel and wicked lie. The whole history of her father and mother was one of those family tragedies, only too frequent, which, the actors in them being dead, are best forgotten. I shall not revive the tale.

In late autumn Mr. Sutherland sailed for India. Before he quitted England, he made me sole guardian in his stead over Zillah Le Poer, assigning for her a handsome maintenance. He said he hoped we should all live happily together — she, my mother, and I — until he came back. He spent a short time with us all at his country-seat — a time which, looking back upon, seems in its eight days like eight separate years.

I ought to speak of Zillah, the unmoved centre of so many convolving fates. She remained still and silent as ever — dull, grieved, humiliated. I told her gradually and gently the whole truth, and explained from how much she had been saved. She seemed grateful and penitent: it was clear that her heart had never been touched by love; she was yet a mere child. The only evidence of womanly shame she gave was in keeping entirely out of her guardian's way: nor did he take much notice of her except in reproaching himself to me with being neglectful of his charge; but he had so thoroughly trusted in the girl's uncle as being her best protector.

The only remark he ever made on Zillah's personal self was that she had beautiful eyes, adding, with a half sigh, "that he liked dark Oriental eyes." One day his mother told me something which explained this. She said he had been engaged to a young lady in India, who on the eve of their marriage had died. He had never cared much for women's society since, and his mother thought would probably never marry. After his departure I learned the whole story. My heart bled over every pang that he had suffered: he was so good and noble a man. And when I knew about his indifference to all women, I felt the more grateful for the trust he showed in me, by making me Zillah's guardian in his absence, and wishing me to write to him regularly of her welfare. The last words he said were asking me to go and see his mother often; and then he bade God bless me, and called me "his dear friend." He was very kind always!

We had a quiet winter, for my health was not good — I

being often delicate in winter time. My mother and Zillah took care of me, and I was very grateful for their love. I got well at last, as the spring time advanced, and went on in my old ways.

There are sometimes long pauses in one's life — deep rests or sleeps of years — in which month after month, and season after season, float on each the same; during which the soul lies either quiet or torpid, as may be. Thus, without any trouble, joy, or change, we lived for several years — my mother, Zillah Le Poer, and I. One morning I found with a curious surprise, but without any of the horror which most women are supposed to feel at that fact, that I was thirty years old!

We discovered by the same reckoning that Zillah was just nineteen. I remember she put her laughing face beside mine in the glass. There was a great difference truly. I do not mean the difference in her from me, for I never compared that, but in her from her former self. She had grown up into a woman, and, as that glass told her, and my own eyes told me, a very striking woman too. I was little of a judge in beauty myself; still, I knew well that everybody we met thought her handsome. Likewise, she had grown up beautiful in mind as well as in body. I was very proud of my dear child.

I well remember this day, when she was nineteen and I thirty. I remember it, I say, because our kind friend in India had remembered it likewise, and sent us each a magnificent shawl; far too magnificent it was for a little body like me, but it became Zillah splendidly. She tucked me under her arm as if I had been a little girl, and walked me up and down the room; for she was of a cheerful, gay temper now — just the one to make an old heart young again, to flash upon a worn spirit with the brightness of its own long-past morning.

I recollect thinking thus at the time — I wish I had thought so oftener! But it matters little: I only chronicle this day, as being the first when Zillah unconsciously put herself on a level with me, becoming thenceforward a woman, and my equal — no longer a mere pet and a child.

About this time — I may as well just state the fact to comfort other maidens of thirty years' standing — I received an offer of marriage, the first I had ever had. He who asked me was a gentleman of my own age, an old acquaintance, though never a very intimate friend. I examined myself well, with great humility and regret, for he was an excellent man; but I found I could not marry him. It was very strange that he should ask me, I thought. My mother, proud and pleased — first, because I had the honour of a proposal; secondly, that it was refused, and she kept her child still — would have it that the circumstance was not strange at all. She said many women were handsomer and more attractive at thirty than they had ever been in their lives. My poor, fond, deluded and deluding mother, in whose sight even I was fair! That night I was foolish enough to look long into the glass, at my quiet little face, and my pale, gray-blue eyes — not dark, like Zillah's — foolish enough to count narrowly the white threads that were coming one by one into my hair. This trouble — I mean the offer of marriage — I did not quite get over for many weeks, even months.

The following year of my life there befell me a great pang. Of this, a grief never to be forgotten, a loss never to be restored — I cannot even now say more than is implied in three words — *my mother died!* After that Zillah and I lived together alone for twelve months or more.

There are some scenes in our life — landscape scenes, I mean — that we remember very clearly: one strikes me now. A quiet, soft May day; the hedges just in their first green, the horse-chestnuts white with flowers: the long, silent country lanes swept through by a travelling carriage, in which two women, equally silent, sat — Zillah Le Poer and I.

It was the month before her coming of age, and she was going to meet her guardian, who had just returned from India.

Mrs. Sutherland had received a letter from Southampton, and immediately sent for us into the country to meet her son, her "beloved Andrew." I merely repeat the words as I remember Zillah's doing, while she laughed at the ugly name. I never thought it ugly.

When we had really started, however, Zillah ceased laughing, and became grave, probably at the recollection of that humiliating circumstance which first brought her acquainted with her guardian. But despite this ill-omened beginning, her youth had blossomed into great perfection. As she sat there before me, fair in person, well cultured in mind, and pure and virgin in heart — for I had so kept her out of harm's way that, though nearly twenty-one, I knew she had never been "in love" with any man — as she sat thus, I felt proud and glad in her, feeling sure that Mr. Sutherland would say I had well fulfilled the charge he gave.

We drove to the lodge gates. An English country-house is always fair to see: this was very beautiful — I remembered it seven years ago, only then it was autumn, and now spring. Zillah remembered it likewise: she drew back, and I heard her whisper uneasily: "Now we shall soon see Mr. Sutherland."

I did not answer her a word.

We rolled up the avenue under the large chestnut-trees. I saw some one standing at the portico; then I think the motion of the carriage must have made me dizzy, for all grew indistinct, except a firm, kind hand holding me as I stepped down, and the words, "Take care, my dear Cassia!" It was Mr. Sutherland!

He scarcely observed Zillah, till in the hall I introduced her to him. He seemed surprised, startled, pleased. Talking of her to me that evening he said, he had not thought she would have grown up thus; and I noticed him look at her at times with a pensive kindness. Mrs. Sutherland whispered me that the lady he had been engaged to was a half-caste like Zillah, which accounted for it. — His mother's prophecy had been right: he had come back as he went out — unmarried.

When Zillah went to bed she was full of admiration for her guardian. He was so tall, so stately. Then his thick, curling fair hair — just like a young man's, with scarcely a shadow of gray. She would not believe that he was over forty — ten years older than myself — until by some pertinacity I had impressed this fact upon her. And then she said it did not signify, as she liked such "dear old souls" as him and me much better than any young people. Her fervour of admiration made me smile; but after this night I observed that the expression of it gradually ceased.

Though I was not so demonstrative as Zillah, it will not be supposed but that I was truly glad to see my old friend Mr. Sutherland. He was very kind, talked to me long of past things, and as he cast a glance on my black dress, I saw his lips quiver; he took my hand and pressed it like a brother. God bless him for that!

But one thing struck me — a thing I had not calculated on

— the alteration seven years had made in us both. When he took me down to dinner, I accidentally caught sight of our two figures in the large pier-glass. Age tells so differently on man and woman: I remember the time when he was a grown man and I a mere girl; now he looked a stately gentleman in the prime of life, and I a middle-aged, old-maidish woman. Perhaps something more than years had done this; yet it was quite natural, only I had never thought of it before.

So, when that first meeting was over, with the excitement, pleasurable or otherwise, which as a matter of course it brought to us all — when we had severally bidden each other good-night, and Mr. Sutherland had said smilingly that he was glad it was only good-night, not good-bye — when the whole house was quiet and asleep — to use the psalmist's solemn words, "*At night on my bed I communed with my own heart in my chamber, and was still.*"

"Cassia, I want to speak to you particularly," said Mr. Sutherland to me one morning, as after breakfast he was about to go into his study. Zillah placed herself in the doorway with the pretty obstinacy, half womanish, half girlish, that she sometimes used with her guardian — much to my surprise. Zillah was on excellent terms with him, considering their brief acquaintance of three weeks. In that time she had treated him as I in my whole lifetime had never ventured to do — wilfully, jestingly, even crossly, yet he seemed to like it. They were very social and merry, for his disposition had apparently grown more cheerful as he advanced in life. Their relation was scarcely like guardian and ward, but that of perfect equality – pleasant and confidential, which somewhat surprised me, until I recollected what opportunities they had of intercourse, and what strong friendships are sometimes formed even in a single week or fortnight when people are shut up together in a rather lonely country-house. This was the state of things among us all on the morning when Mr. Sutherland called me to his study. Zillah wanted to go likewise.

"Not to-day," he answered her, very gently and smilingly. "I have business to talk over with Miss Pryor." (I knew he said "Miss Pryor" out of respect, yet it hurt me — I had been "Cassia" with him so many years. Perhaps he thought I was outgrowing my baby name now.)

The business he wished to speak of was about Zillah's

coming of age next week, and what was to be done on the occasion. "Should he, ought he, to give a ball, a dinner, anything of that sort? Would Zillah like it?"

This was a great concession, for in old times he always disliked society. I answered that I did not think such display necessary, but I would try to find out Zillah's mind.

I did so. It was an innocent, girlish mind, keenly alive to pleasure, and new to everything. The consequences were natural — the ball must be. A little she hesitated when I hinted at her guardian's peculiarities, and then she offered cheerfully to renounce her delight. But he, his eyes beaming with a deeper delight still, would not consent. So the thing was settled.

It was a very brilliant affair, for Mr. Sutherland spared no expense. He seemed to show a restless eagerness in providing for his young favourite everything she could desire. Nay, in answer to her wayward entreaties, he even consented to open the ball with her, though saying "he was sure he should make an old simpleton of himself." That was not likely!

I watched them walk down the room together, and heard many people say with a smile what a handsome pair they were, notwithstanding the considerable difference of age.

It was a very quiet evening to me. Being strange to almost every one there, I sat near old Mrs. Sutherland in a corner. Mr. Sutherland asked me to dance once, but I did not feel strong, and indeed for the last few years I had almost given up dancing. He laughed, and said, merrily: "It was not fair for him to be beginning life just when I ended it." A true word spoken in jest! But I only smiled.

The ball produced results not unlikely, when one considered that it was meant for the introduction into society of a young woman, handsome, attractive, and an heiress. A week or two after Zillah's birthday, Mr. Sutherland called me once more into his study.

I noticed he looked rather paler and less composed than usual. He forgot even to ask me to sit down, and we stood together by the fire-place, which I remember was filled with a great vase of lilacs that Zillah had insisted on placing there. It filled the room with a strong, rich scent, which now I never perceive without its bringing back to my mind that room and that day.

He said: "I have had a letter to-day on which I wish to consult with you before showing it to Miss Le Poer." (I was rather startled by the formal words, since he usually called her "Zillah," as was natural.)

"It is a letter — scarcely surprising — in fact to be expected after what I noticed at the dinner-party yesterday; in fact —. But you had better read it yourself."

He took the letter from his desk, and gave it to me. It was an earnest and apparently sincere application for the hand of his ward. The suitor, the Honourable Henry French, was of good family and moderate prospects. I had noticed he was very attentive to Zillah at the ball, and on some occasions since; still I was a good deal surprised, more so even than was Mr. Sutherland, who had evidently watched her far closer than I. I gave him back the letter in silence, and avoided looking at his face.

"Well, Cassia," he said, after a pause, and with an appearance of gaiety, "what is to be done? You women are the best counsellors in these matters."

I smiled, but both he and I very soon became grave once more.

"It is a thing to be expected," continued he, in a voice rather formal and hard. "With Zillah's personal attractions and large fortune she was sure to receive many offers. Still it is early to begin these affairs."

I reminded him that she was twenty-one.

"True, true. She might, under other circumstances, have been married long before this. Do you think that she —?"

I suppose he was going to ask me whether I thought she was likely to accept Mr. French, or had hitherto formed any attachment. But probably delicacy withheld him, for he suddenly stopped and omitted the question. Soon he went on in the same steady tone: —

"I think Zillah ought to be made acquainted with this circumstance. Mr. French states that this letter to me is the first confession of his feelings. That was honourable on his part. He is a gentleman of good standing, though far her inferior in fortune. People might say that he wanted her property to patch up the decayed estates at Weston-Brook."

This was spoken bitterly, very bitterly for a man of such kind nature as Andrew Sutherland. He seemed conscious of it, and added: "I may wrong him, and if so, I regret it. But do you not think, Cassia, that of all things it must be most despicable, most mean, most galling to a man of any pride or honest feeling, the thought of the world's saying that he married his wife for money, as a prop to his falling fortunes, or a shield to his crumbling honour? I would die a thousand deaths first!"

In the passion of the moment the red colour rushed violently to his cheek, and then he became more pallid than ever. I watched him; my eyes were opened now. I held fast by the marble chimney-piece, so that I could stand quite upright, firm, and quiet. He walked hurriedly to the window, and flung it open, saying the scent of the lilacs was too strong. When he came back, we were both ready to talk again. I believe I spoke first — to save him the pain of doing so.

"I have no idea," said I, and I said truly, "what answer Zillah will give to this letter. Hitherto I have known all her feelings, and am confident that while she stayed with me her heart was untouched."

Here I waited for him to speak, but he did not. I went on: —

"Mr. French is very agreeable, and she seems to like him; but a girl's heart, if of any value at all, is rarely won in three meetings. I think, however, that Zillah ought to be made acquainted with this letter. Will you tell her, or shall I?"

"Go you and do it — a woman can best deal with a woman in these cases. And," he added, rising slowly and looking down upon me with that grave and self-possessed smile which was likewise as sweet as any woman's, "tell Zillah from me, that though I wish her to marry in her own rank and with near equality of fortune, to save her from all those dangers of mercenary offers to which an heiress is so cruelly exposed, still, both now and at all times, I leave her to the dictates of her own affections, and her happiness will ever be my chief consideration in life."

He spoke with formal serenity until the latter words, when his voice faltered a little. Then he led me to the door, and I went out.

Zillah lay on a sofa reading a love-story. Her crisped black hair was tossed about the crimson cushions, and her whole figure was that of rich Eastern luxuriance. She had always rather a fantastic way of dress, and now she looked almost like a princess out of the Arabian Nights. Even though her skin was that of a half-caste, and her little hands were not white, but brown, there was no denying that she was a very beautiful woman. I felt it — saw it — knew it!

After a minute's pause I went to her side; she jumped up and kissed me, as she was rather fond of doing. I half shrank back — her kisses were very painful to me just then. I came as quickly as possible to my errand, and gave her the letter to read.

As she glanced through it her cheeks flushed, and her lips began to curl. She threw the letter on my lap, and said, abruptly, "Well, and what of that?"

I began a few necessary explanations. Zillah stopped me —

"Oh, I heard something of the sort from Mr. French last night. I did not believe him, nor do I now. He is only making a jest of me."

I answered that this was impossible. In my own mind I was surprised at Zillah's having known the matter before, and having kept it so quietly. Mr. French's statement about his honourable reticence towards the lady of his devotions must have been untrue. Still this was not so remarkable as Zillah's own secresy about her having a lover.

"Why did you not tell me, my dear?" said I: "you know your happiness is of the first importance to me as well as to your guardian." And, rather hesitating, I repeated, word by word, as near as I could, Mr. Sutherland's message.

While I spoke, Zillah hid her face among the cushions, and then drew it out burning red.

"He thinks I am going to accept the creature then? He would have me marry a conceited, chattering, mean-looking foolish boy!" (Now Mr. French was certainly twenty-five.) "One, too, that only wants me for my fortune and nothing else. It is very wrong, cruel, and heartless of him, and you may go and tell him so."

"Tell who?" said I, bewildered by this outburst of indignation, and great confusion of personal pronouns.

"Mr. Sutherland, of course! Who else would I tell? Whose opinion else do I care for? Go and say to him — — No," she added, abruptly: "no; you needn't trouble him with anything about me. Just say I shall not marry Mr. French, and will he be so kind as to give him his answer, and bid him let me alone."

Here, quite exhausted with her wrath, Zillah sank back and took her book, turning her head from me. But I saw that she did not read one line, that her motionless eyes were fixed and full of a strange deep expression. I began to cease wondering what the future would bring.

Very soon afterwards I went back to Mr. Sutherland, and told him all that had passed; just the plain facts without any comments of my own.

He apparently required none. I found him sitting composedly with some papers before him — he had for the last few days been immersed in business which seemed rather to trouble him: he started a little as I entered, but immediately came forward and listened with a quiet aspect to the message I had to bring. I could not tell whether it made him happy or the contrary; his countenance could be at times so totally impassive that no friend, dearest or nearest, could ever find out from it anything he did not wish to betray.

"The matter is settled then," said he, gravely: "I will write to Mr. French to-day, and perhaps it would be as well if we never alluded to what has passed. I, at least, shall not do it; tell Zillah so. But, in the future, say that I entreat she keeps no secret back from you. Remember this, my dear Cassia; watch over her as you love her — and you do love her?" continued he, grasping my hand.

I answered that I did; and God knows, even then I told no lie. She was a very dear child to me always!

Mr. Sutherland seemed quite satisfied and at rest. He bade me a cheerful good-bye, which I knew meant that I should go away, so accordingly I went.

Passing the drawing-room door, I saw Zillah lying in her old position on the sofa; so I would not disturb her, but went and walked up and down under a clump of fir-trees in the garden. They made a shadow dark and grave and still; it was more natural than being on the lawn, among the flowers, the sunshine, and the bees. I did not come in for some hours.

At dinner there were fortunately only ourselves, just a family party. — Mr. Sutherland did not join us until we reached the dining-room door. I noticed that Zillah's colour changed as he approached, and that all dinner-time she hardly spoke to him; but he behaved to her as usual. He was rather thoughtful, for, as he told me privately, he had some trifling business-anxieties burdening him just then; otherwise he seemed the same. Nevertheless, whether it was his fault or Zillah's, in a few days the fact grew apparent to me that they were not quite such good friends as heretofore. A restraint, a discomfort, a shadow scarcely tangible, yet still real, was felt between them. Such a cloud often rises — a mist that comes just before the day-dawn; or, as happens sometimes, before the night.

For many days — how many I do not recollect, since about this time all in the house and in the world without seemed to go on so strangely — for many days afterwards nothing happened of any consequence, except that one Sunday afternoon I made a faint struggle of politeness in some remark about "going home" and "encroaching on their hospitality," which was met with such evident pain and alarm by all parties, that I was silent; so we stayed yet longer.

One morning — it was high summer now — we were sitting at breakfast; we three only, as Mrs. Sutherland never rose early. I was making tea, Zillah near me, and Mr. Sutherland at the foot of the table. He looked anxious, and did not talk much, though I remember he rose up once to throw a handful of crumbs to a half-tame thrush that had built in a laurel-bush on the lawn — he was always so kind to every living thing.

"There, my fine bird, take some food home to your wife and weans!" said he, pleasantly; but at the words became grave, even sad, once more. He had his letters beside him, and opened them successively until he came to *one* — a momentous one, I knew; for though he never moved, but read quietly on, every ray of colour faded out of his face. He dropped his head upon his hand, and sat so long in that attitude that we were both frightened.

"Is anything the matter?" I said gently, for Zillah was dumb.

"Did you speak?" he answered, with a bewildered stare. "Forgive me; I — I have had bad news!" — and he tried to resume the duties of the meal; but it was impossible: he was evidently crushed, as even the strongest and bravest men will be for the moment under some great and unexpected shock.

We said to him — I repeat *we*, because, though Zillah spoke not, her look was enough, had he seen it — we said to him those few soothing things that women can, and ought to say in such a time.

"Ay," he answered, quite unmanned — "ay, you are very kind. I think it would do me good if I could speak to some one — Cassia, will you come?"

He rose slowly, and held out his hand to me. *To me!* That proof of his confidence, his tenderness, his friendship, I have ever after remembered, and thought, with thankful heart, that, though not made to give him happiness, I have sometimes done him a little good when he was in trouble.

We walked together from the room. I heard a low sob behind us, but had no power to stay; besides a momentary pang mattered little to the child — her sobs would be hushed ere long.

Standing behind the chair where he sat, I heard the story of Mr. Sutherland's misfortunes — misfortunes neither strange nor rare in the mercantile world. In one brief word, he was ruined; that is, so far as a man can be considered ruined who has enough left to pay all his creditors, and start in the world afresh as a penniless honest man. He told me this — an everyday story; nay, it had been my own father's — told it me with great composure, and I listened with the same. I was acquainted with all these kind of business-matters of old. It was very strange, but I felt no grief, no pity for his losses; I only felt, on my own account, a burning, avaricious thirst for gold; a frantic envy — a mad longing to have for a single day, a single hour, wealth in millions.

"Yes, it must be so," said he, when, after talking to me a little more, I saw the hard muscles of his face relax, and he grew patient, ready to bear his troubles like a man — like Andrew Sutherland. "Yes, I must give up this house, and all my pleasant life here; but I can do it, since I shall be alone." And then he added in a low tone: "I am glad, Cassia, very glad of two things: my mother's safe settlement, and the winding-up last month of all my affairs with — Miss Le Poer."

"When," said I, after a pause — "when do you intend to tell Zillah what has happened?" I felt feverishly anxious that she should know all, and that I should learn how she would act.

"Tell Zillah? Ay," he repeated, "tell her at once — tell her at once." — And then he sunk back into his chair muttering something about "its signifying little now."

I left him, and with my heart nerved as it were to anything, went back to the room where Zillah was. Her eyes met me with a bitter, fierce, jealous look — jealous of me, the foolish child! — until I told her what had happened to our friend. Then she wept, but only for a moment, until a light broke upon her.

"What does it signify?" cried she, echoing, curiously enough, his own words. "I am of age — I can do just what I like: I will give my guardian all my money. Go back and tell him so!"

I hesitated.

"Go — quick, quick! — all I have in the world is not too good for him. Everything belonging to me is his, and — —" Here she stopped, and catching my fixed look, became covered with confusion. Still the generous heart did not waver. "And when he has my fortune, you and I will go and live together, and be governesses."

I felt the girl was in earnest, nor wished to deceive me; and though I let her deceive herself a little longer, it was with joy — ay, with joy, that in the heart I clasped to mine was such unselfishness, such true nobility, not unworthy even of the bliss it was about to win.

I went once more through the hall — the long, cool, silent hall, which I trod so dizzily, daring not to pause — into Mr. Sutherland's presence.

"Well!" said he, looking up.

I told — in what words I cannot now remember, but solemnly, faithfully, as if I were answering my account before Heaven — the truth, and the whole truth.

He listened, pressing his hands upon his eyes, and then gave vent to one heavy sigh like a woman's sob. At last he rose, and walked feebly to the door. There he paused, as though to excuse his going.

"I ought to thank her, you know. It must not be — not by any means: still I ought to go and thank her — the — dear child!"

His voice ceased, broken by emotion. Once more he held out his hand: I grasped it, and said, "Go!"

At the parlour-door he stopped, apparently for me to precede him in entering there; but, as if accidentally, I passed on and let him enter alone. Whether he knew it or not, I knew clear as light what would happen then and there.

The door shut — they two being within, and I without.

In an hour I came back towards the house.

I had been wandering somewhere, I think under the firwood. It was broad noon, but I felt very cold; it was always cold under those trees. I had no way to pass but near the parlour-window; and some insane attraction made me look up as I went by.

They were standing — they two — close together, as lovers stand. His arm folded her round; his face all radiant, yet trembling with tenderness, was pressed upon hers — Oh, my God!

I am half inclined to blot out the last sentence, as, growing older, one feels the more how rarely and how solemnly the Holy Name ought to be mingled with any mere burst of human emotion. But I think the All-merciful One would pardon it then. — Of course no reader will marvel at my showing emotion over the union of these my two dearest objects on earth.

From that union I can now truly say I have derived the greatest comfort of my life. They were married quickly, as I urged; Mr. Sutherland settling his wife's whole property upon herself. This was the only balm his manly pride could know; and no greater proof could he give of his passionate love for her, than that he humbled himself to marry an heiress. As to what the world thought, no one could ever suspect the shadow of mercenary feeling in Andrew Sutherland. All was as it should be — and so best.

After Zillah's marriage, I took a situation abroad. Mr. Sutherland was very angry when he knew; but I told him I longed for the soft Italian air, and could not live an idle life on any account. So they let me go, knowing, as he smilingly said, "That Cassia could be obstinate when she chose — that her will, like her heart, was as firm as a rock." — Ah me!

When I came back, it was to a calm, contented, and cheerful middle age; to the home of a dear brother and sister; to the love of a new generation; to a life filled with peace of heart and thankfulness towards God; to —.

Hey-day! writing is this moment become quite impossible; for there peeps in a face at my bedroom door, and, while I live, not for worlds shall my young folk know that Aunt Cassia is an authoress. Therefore good-bye, pen! — And now come in, my namesake, my darling, my fair-haired Cassia, with her mother's smile, and her father's eyes and brow — I may kiss both now. Ah, God in heaven bless thee, my dear, dear child!

MISS LETTY'S EXPERIENCES.

I. — FIRST QUARRELS.

A SKETCH FROM LIFE.

I am one of the many from whom Heaven has seen fit to take away the individual interests of life, that perchance they might become universal. Sometimes I could almost liken myself to a mirror, which receives on its silent, solitary breast the fleeting images that pass it by, and so takes them, for the time being, as companions to its own void heart, while it makes of them life-pictures to be reflected abroad. These passing interests I create for myself continually. They seem, too, to meet me voluntarily on every side, not merely in society, but in chance rencounters along the waysides of life. I rarely journey five miles from my home without discovering — or, if you will, manufacturing — some pleasant and useful passage in human life, which makes me feel one with my fellow-creatures, as though the world stretched out lovingly its hand to the solitary one, and called her "Sister!"

The other day I took my way homeward. Reader, I may as well tell the truth, that I am an old maid, living in London, and working hard that I may live at all; also that, in order to add a small mite to my slender modicum of health, I had abided for a brief space at that paradise of Cockneys — Southend. A very respectable paradise it is too, with its lovely green lanes extending close to the shore of what is all but the sea; its pleasant cliffs feathered with rich underwood, which the tide almost kisses at high-water; making the whole neighbourhood as pretty a compound of seaside and rural scenery as the lovers of both would wish. When my "fairie barque" (the London steamboat *Dryad*, please, reader) wafted me from thence, I felt a slight pain at my heart. One suffers many such on quitting earth's pleasant nooks. "I ought to have got used to 'good-bye' by this time," thought I to myself, half patiently, half sadly, and began to divert my attention by noticing the various groups on deck. I always do so on principle, and it is hard if I do not find some bit of human nature to study, or some form of outward beauty in man, woman, or child, to fall in love with. Travelling alone (as I ever do travel — what should I fear, with my quiet face and my forty years) I had plenty of opportunity to look around, and soon my eye fell on two persons, meet subjects to awaken interest.

They were a young couple who sat opposite to me — so close, that I could hear every word above a whisper. But whispering with them seemed pleasantest, at least for a long time. I should have taken them for lovers, save for a certain air of cheerful unreserve which lovers never have, and an occasional undisguised "my dear," falling from both their lips. At last, keeping a watch over the girl's left hand, I saw it ungloved, and thereon the wedding-ring! It rested with a sort of new importance, as though the hand were unused to its weight. Unconsciously she played and fidgeted with its shining circlet, and then recollected herself with a smile and a blush. It was quite clear my new pets were a bridegroom and bride.

Here then, was a page in human life open before me: I tried to read it, line by line, romancing where I could not read. Full opportunity I had, for they took no notice of me: they saw nothing in the world but their own two selves. Happy blindness! I believe much in physiognomy, so I amused myself with deciphering theirs. The girl's face was strikingly pretty. There was the high brow, showing little talent, but much sense; the candid, loving, yet half-wicked dark eyes; the straight nose; and short, curled upper lip; but there the face changed, as faces sometimes do, from beauty into positive ugliness. The lower lip was full — pouting — showing that it *could* look both sulky and sensual; and the chin retreated — in fact, positively "ran away!" I said to myself, "If the under half of the character matches the under half of the face, the young husband there will find a few more difficulties with the wife he has married than with the 'lassie' he wooed."

So I turned to his countenance, and speculated thereon. It was decidedly handsome — Greek in its outline; in expression so sweet as to be almost feeble; — at least so I thought at first, when he was smiling, as he ever did when he looked at her. But in a few minutes of silence I saw the mouth settle into firm horizontal lines, indicating that with its gentleness was united that resolute decision without which no man can be the worthy head of a household — respected, loved, and obeyed. For in all households *one* must rule; and woe be to that family wherein its proper head is either a petty tyrant, or, through his own weakness, a dethroned and contemned slave!

Therefore, when I noticed the pretty, wilful ways, and sometimes half-silly remarks of the bride, I felt that this young, thoughtless creature might yet have cause to thank Heaven that she had married a man who knew how to rule as well as to cherish her.

Until now, I had not speculated on their station or calling: it was enough for me that they belonged to the wide family of humanity. But as my musings wandered idly on into their future life, I took this also into consideration. Both had a certain grace and ease in mien and speech, though, through the wife's tones, I distinguished the vague drawl which infects most classes of Londoners. But the husband looked and spoke like a gentleman. I felt sure he was such, even though he might stand behind a counter. A third individual broke their *tête-à-tête* — a middle-aged Cockney *père de famille* — evidently some beach acquaintance made at Southend. His chance questions produced an answer to my inward wondering.

"Oh," said the bride, "we could only stay at Southend a few days, because of my —." She paused a moment, and then changed the word *husband* into "Mr. Goodriche. He cannot be longer away from business."

The young bridegroom, then, was "in business" — one of those worthy labouring bees who furnish the community with honey. I thought how hard he must have toiled, in office or shop, to have gained so early in life a home and a wife. I respected him accordingly.

My "interesting couple" began a lively chat with their new companion: at least the wife did. She put forth all her smiles, all that battery of fascination with which she had probably before her marriage won her spurs in the field of conquest, and been dubbed "a most shocking flirt." And in the shadow that gathered over the quiet husband's face, I saw the reflection of that which must often have bitterly troubled the peace of the still more retiring lover. True, the girl was doing nothing wrong — her new friend was old enough to have been her father, so no jealousy could be aroused; but still she was taking her attention and conversation from her husband to give it to a perfect stranger. She would not have done so had he been only her lover still. Alas, that women should take so much pains to win love, and so little to keep it!

Each minute the young husband spoke less, and his countenance grew darker. She only laughed, and chattered the more. Foolish, foolish one! There came on a heavy shower, and there was a rush below. "Come with us to the further end; I will find a place for you," kindly said the blithe young wife, turning back to the little old maid. I thanked her, but declined. For the world, I would not have prevented the chance that, in the solitude of a crowd, some word or look might pass between husband and wife to take away his gloom. Yet when I left the cabin, I saw her sitting — bonnetless, and laughing with a childish gaiety — between her silent, grave husband and the disagreeable old man.

I went to my quiet place at the stern of the boat, and turned away, so that I could see only the turbid river and the dull gray sky. It was as complete a solitude as though I had been on Robinson Crusoe's raft in the midst of the Pacific. I pondered over life and its mysteries, as one does who is used to loneliness — who is accustomed to dwell, as it were, on a mountain-top, seeing the world and its inhabitants move below like puppets in a show. And herein does fate half atone for ties riven, and ties never formed — that in such a life one learns to forget self; and all individual joys and griefs, loves and hatreds, are swallowed up in universal sympathies.

I pondered much on the two young creatures I had left below; and, woman-like, I thought chiefly of the woman. She seemed to me like a child toying with a precious jewel, little knowing what a fearful thing it is to throw away love, or to play lightly, mockingly, with those feelings on which must rest the joy or woe of two human souls for a lifetime. And passing from this individual case, I thought solemnly, almost painfully, of the strange mysteries of human life, which seem often to bestow the priceless boon of love where it is unvalued and cast away. Unconsciously I repeated the well known words, "*To him that hath shall be given, and from him that hath not shall be taken away.*" But my soul answered meekly, "Only on earth; and life is not long — not long!"

And turning once more to the group of my fellow-voyagers, I saw the two in whom I took such an interest. They were standing together a little apart, leaning on the vessel's side. He was talking to her, not angrily, but very earnestly. In the expression of his face I scarce recognised the young man who had borne smilingly all her idle jests, contradictions, and caprices, an hour ago. She tried them again for a few minutes, but in vain.

Then she hung her head, and pouted. Soon quick, wilful answers came, — I heard them not; but I was sure of the fact, from her flushed cheek and sparkling eye, as she disengaged her arm from his. Man's patience is never very great, not even in the honeymoon; he spoke to her firmly, while his face darkened into positive anger. Then a sullen silence fell over them.

The time passed, and still they remained in the same position — close together; but oh, what a sea of anger was between them! Neither saw the other's face; but I saw both. He stood gazing up into the leaden clouds, his mouth firmly set, yet twitching every now and then with suppressed feeling. Was it, perchance, the bitter disappointment of the man who has with pain and toil built for himself a household temple, and finds it trodden into ruins by the very idol whom he hoped to place there for ever? Foolish girl! wishing to try your power, and keep the honoured husband a tyrannized lover still, — do you think what it is you do, when you suffer your own hands to tear down the fair adornments of idolatry with which his passion has decked you, and appear before him, not as an angelic ideal, but a selfish, sullen, or vain woman. Little know you that it may take years of devotion to efface the bitterness produced by that one hour — the first when he sees you *as you are!*

The young husband glanced once only at his wife; but that was enough. The lower lip — that odious lower lip, which had at first awakened my doubt! — was the very image of weak, pouting ill-humour. But its weakness was its safeguard against continued obstinacy; and I saw — though the husband did not see — that as she bent over the side, tear after tear dropped silently into the river. There was hope still!

She was leaning over the gangway door, an attitude scarcely dangerous, save to the watchful anxiety of affection. However, the possibility seemed to strike her husband; for he suddenly drew her away, though formally, and without any sign of wishing for reconciliation. But this one slight act showed the thoughtfulness, the love — oh, if she had only answered it by one kind look, one word of atonement! But no; there she stood — immovable; neither would yield. I would have given anything to have whispered in the wife's ear, "For the love of Heaven — for the love of him — for the peace of your whole life, be the first to ask forgiveness! Right or wrong, never mind. Whichever has erred, it is your place, as weakest and most loving, to yield first. Oh, did you but know the joy, the blessedness of creeping close to your husband's wounded, perchance angry heart, and saying — 'Take me in there again; let us not be divided more!' And he would take you, ay, at once; and love you the more for the forbearance which never even asked of his pride the concession that he also was wrong!"

Perhaps this long speech was partly written in my eyes; for when by chance, they met the young wife's, she turned away, colouring crimson: and at that moment up came the enemy once more, in the shape of the intrusive elderly gentleman. But the husband's lecture, whatever it was, had its effect in the girl's demeanour. She drew back with a quiet, womanly reserve, strongly contrasted with her former coquettish forwardness, and left "Mr. Goodriche" in possession of the field. And I liked the husband ten times better for the gentlemanly dignity with which he shook off all trace of ill-humour, and conversed with the intruder. The boyish lover seemed changed into the firm, self-dependent man. And when the wife timidly crept up, and put her arm through his, he turned round and smiled upon her. How gladly, yet how shyly, she answered the slight token of peace! And I said to myself, "That man will have a just, and firm, yet tender sway: he will make a first-rate head of a family!"

I saw little more of them until near the journey's end. They were then sitting in the half empty cabin alone together; for to my delight, and perhaps theirs, the obnoxious individual of middle age had landed at Blackwall. Very quiet they seemed: all the exuberant happiness which at first had found vent in almost childish frolic, was over. The girl no longer laughed and jested with her young husband; but she drew close to his side, her head bending toward his shoulder, as though but for the presence of a stranger it would fain droop there, heavy with its weight of penitence and love. Yet, as I watched the restless look in her eyes, and the faint shadow that still lingered on the young man's brow, I thought how much had been perilled, and how happy — ay, ten times happier — would both have felt had the *first quarrel* never been!

In the confusion of departure I lost my young friends, as I thought, for ever; but on penetrating the mysterious depths of an omnibus, I heard a pleasant voice addressing me — "So you are again our fellow-passenger to —."

But I will not say where, lest the young couple should "speer" for me, and demand why I dared to put them "in print." And yet they would scarce be wroth did they know the many chords they touched, and the warm interests they awakened in a heart which had so few.

It was the dreariest of wet nights in London — Heaven knows how dreary that is! — but they did not seem to feel it at all. They were quite happy — quite gay. I wondered whether for them was prepared what always seemed to my imagination the deepest bliss of earth — the first "coming home." I felt almost sure of it when the husband called out to the conductor, "Set us down at —;" naming a quiet, unobtrusive, new-built square. He said it with the half-conscious importance of one who gives a new address, thinking the world must notice what is of so much interest to himself; and then the young people looked at one another, and smiled.

I said to the wife — drawing the bow at a venture — "What a miserable night this is! — Is it not pleasant coming home?"

She looked first at her husband, and then turned to me, her whole face beaming and glowing with happiness, "Oh, it is — it is!"

They bade me good-night, and disappeared. I leaned back in my dark corner, my heart very full: it had just strength to give them a silent blessing, and no more. I remembered only that I had been young once, and that I was now an old maid of forty years.

II. — MY OPPOSITE NEIGHBOURS.

I AM at home now: I call it *home* because I have lived in these my lodgings for some years. My street has grown beneath my eyes; passing from its infancy of three new-built houses and a brick-field, through a comical, one-sided, half-paved youth, to the dignified maturity of a respectable suburban thoroughfare. The time when my sketch begins was between the first and second era — when there rose up before my gaze, instead of the brick-field, one solitary house — and its inhabitants became, *par excellence*, my "opposite neighbours."

It was really quite an event in my life when they came into possession, and I had something to look at and somebody to watch from my window. Now, reader, misjudge me not; I am no prying old maid — though of necessity I sit at my window the greater part of the day: — the secret is, I am a wood-engraver. Oh, the weariness of labouring from breakfast-time till dusk — hearing nothing but the scoop — scoop — scoop of the tool against the wood, save when listening with nervous eagerness to the boom of the near church-clock, that marks the passing of another hour, every moment of which is to me worth so much precious coin! Oh, the relief of lifting one's head for a brief space to drink in light and air, and to gain a few passing interests of life without, that may drive away the throng of memories which such a dull, mechanical occupation cannot fail to bring! Surely "my opposite neighbours," if ever so retiring, would not have grudged me this innocent recreation.

They *were* very retiring indeed. They came into their new abode at dusk, and for several days I saw no specimens of living humanity except the small servant, a tidy, little, rosy-cheeked country-girl, who enlivened her dreary existence each morning by cleaning the steps, which, during the succeeding day, were never defiled by any footmarks save her own. Moreover, if there were no visible inhabitants, it also seemed as if there was no visible furniture, for the drawing-room shutters were kept closed, and the parlour-blinds half-drawn down.

However, ere the week ended, I saw, placed within the wire-blind, one of those framed advertisements which are used by "genteel" professions. It bore the inscription, "Miss Waters, *Milliner*." I saw, too, the hand that was placing it there — one evidently belonging to a young woman round, pretty, and rosy. And on the very next day — Sunday — I beheld its owner.

At church-time two persons walked out of the house, one a girl, apparently just gliding out of her teens into maturer womanhood; the other a tall, thin stripling of a boy. They were very like one another — brother and sister apparently — and both wore that fresh simplicity which we designate "a country look." Moreover, as the boy took his elder sister's prayer-book, and gave her his arm to lean on, it was with an air of independent dignity, as much as to say, "I'm a man at last."

For months I never saw anybody in the house but these two. I supposed they lived there all alone, a desolate, perhaps orphaned pair, of the number of those who are early doomed to merge youth's pleasures in age's carking cares — to spend their life's tender spring in self-dependent but bitter toil, and so grow old long ere winter comes.

I pictured to myself a cold, half-furnished house, and the brother and sister — forced misers! — sitting with pale, early-wrinkled brows, counting up their little store. Little it must be, for there came no customers to "Miss Waters, Milliner." And as for the boy, I saw him pass in and out daily, not with the quick, active, self-important step of one who "must be at his office at nine," but with the dull lounge of one who has no occupation, no aim in life. He grew taller and thinner every day, his long limbs shaming the boy's jacket — a shabby one too — which he still wore. At last, from taking his walks in the broad noon, he never went out until dusk. Poor lad! I well guessed why. Moreover his sister now went to church alone. I marvelled not that it was with a drooping head, and a veil scarcely ever raised — but still she went.

"God help her!" I said to myself. "One-half her fellow-

Domestic Stories. 15

worshippers will never know, and never heed, how solemnly to her sounds the prayer, "Give us this day our daily bread."

One morning I was surprised to notice on the window a second framed inscription — "MR. ALFRED WATERS, *Artist*." And then I penetrated into a little mystery which had puzzled me for weeks — namely, that the lower half of the second-floor window was almost always kept darkened. At once I pictured to myself the poor young artist's studio — the home-made easel — the common colour-box, and all the adjuncts of that wretched struggle of genius against poverty.

"Simpleton that I am!" I sometimes said to myself, "how do I know that the lad's a genius? May he not be one of those lazy drones who take to art because daubing canvas and lounging about sketch-book in hand seems easier than learning a trade?"

But I watched the boy's face as he sat one evening at his attic window, gazing out on the sunset, and I knew that he *was* a genius. — By no means one of the romantic, interesting sort — nor handsome either — not a bit of it! — But what a steadfast, noble, earnest, and withal tender face it was. I felt in a minute what a man the boy would grow to. And, if so, what miserable heart-burnings he must have felt — what shame in being obliged to make money out of the crude pro-ductions which in years to come he would wish consigned to oblivion — what self-degradation in writing up after his name the word "artist," just as he might have written "brick-layer!" Poor fellow! I had better have read in his face the assurance of conceited puppyism than of such genius.

My young friends — for so I called them in my heart — had interested me for at least six months. One day, a little before Christmas-time, I sat speculating rather drearily on my own Christmas and on theirs — how lonely both would be spent, and what a pity it was that I had not riches at command to send them in anonymously a capital Christmas dinner, and invite myself to dine with them!

As I looked, there seemed to be a slight confusion in the house; and through the open folding-doors I distinguished the pretty, slight figure of Miss Waters flitting to and fro, clearly visible between the windows. She moved cheerily, as one does in pleasant expectation, now stirring the fire, now arranging the table, and anon pressing her cheek close to the frosty pane, and looking anxiously down the street. She was evidently waiting for some person or persons unknown.

I thought to myself pensively, how happy it was to have some one to wait for — to arrange all little things — to watch and keep the fire bright and blazing — to wheel the easy-chair, and have the pet footstool ready — to listen eagerly, yet trembling, for the striking of the appointed hour — and then to sit down and try to "play patience" — perhaps indifference, talk of common things, and look quite calm and careless — as though the heart within were not leaping wildly at every sound. Ah, fool! — fool! to call up such visions when thou sittest silent, looking down the murky street, along which no foot will come! or gazing with dull, vacant stare upon the winter fire, that will shine upon no face save that pale, tear-blinded one — thine own! But patience, patience! if hope may come no more to thy lonely hearth, there sits there ever one whom no chance or change can now take from thee — the solemn, meek-browed angel, Memory!

I could gaze no longer on my opposite neighbour. So, remembering that I had a block to take home, I put on my bonnet and walked out. As I opened the street-door, a trunk-laden, railway-cab drove up, and there was an inquiry for the name of "Waters." Just then a stream of light darted on the wet pavement from an opened door on the opposite side, and the tall, thin boy came bounding across the narrow street.

"Father — mother — here's the house. Lucy, hold the light! they're come at last!"

So my young people were not orphans. It took away from the romance, but it added to the joy. Ah, they at least would keep a happy Christmas-day!

I knew they did. I saw them all go to church together, the boy supporting his mother, and Lucy leaning on her bluff old father's arm. Then, judging from their appearance, I added to my romance that of a ruined country farmer, whose duteous children had tried to make for their broken-down parents a London home. Well, poor as it was, there was great joy within its walls this day.

The little family had a visitor, too, a tall young man, who, in mien and bearing, was superior to any of them. At dusk, when, thanks to the firelight and the undrawn blind, I had a complete Dutch picture of the whole circle, I noticed how the guest sat between old Mrs. Waters and her daughter. And once, when a clear bright gleam flashed on her face, I saw Lucy regarding him with a look of such intense pride — such deep tenderness! "Ah," thought I, "it is the old tale once more."

After that time I did not wonder to see the stranger knocking certainly thrice a week at the Waterses' door. Smiling, I sometimes repeated Hood's rhyme —

> "There is a young man very fond of calling
> Over the way."

He always came at the same hour, and I generally guessed the time by seeing Lucy sit working at the parlour-window, her eyes glancing every five minutes down the street. And when the door was opened to him, it was ten to one that the janitor was no other than Lucy's own smiling self.

Thus matters went on for several months. There was apparently a decided improvement in their circumstances, though whether through the increase of Miss Waters's business I could not tell. But I rather thought not, especially as there appeared in addition to the millinery advertisement one which informed the public in general that within there was "wax-flower-making taught on moderate terms." Also, shortly after, I noticed a "Times" advertisement, stating that "A respectable person would be glad to have entrusted to his charge bookkeeping, the collecting of accounts, &c.;" also that there were "Unfurnished apartments to be let in a quiet family." The address of all these was no other than that of my friends the Waterses.

Truly, if ever there was a hard-working, struggling family, it was my Opposite Neighbours.

They were to me an infinite blessing. It did me good to have such sweet heart-warming interests — although secret. And little harm my watching did them. The old mother, coming in blithely from her small marketings, knew not of a hidden eye which, gazing, wished that tenfold plenty might come to her basket and her store; the boy-artist was none the worse for the sympathy that penetrated his half-closed shutters understanding well the life he led within: and when Lucy and her lover — as of course I thought he was — walked out together in the gloaming, were they less happy because of the silent blessing that followed their footsteps from the heart which felt the more what such wealth of love must be, because itself through life had been so poor?

One evening they took a shorter walk than usual, and when they re-entered the house, I saw Lucy's handkerchief to her eyes. It made me quite unhappy; I thought of it constantly, as I sat at my engraving till late at night. When I went up-stairs at last, I looked mechanically over the way; there was still a lamp burning in the Waterses' little parlour. Then I saw the door open, and Lucy, holding a light, stood in the passage. Beside her was their usual guest — her supposed lover. They stood talking for many minutes, he clasping her hand all the while. At last he moved to depart; she put down the light, and throwing her arms round his neck, hung there in such utter abandonment of woe, that I felt the parting was not for a day, a week, but one of those farewells that wring the very heartstrings of youth.

He went away — the door closed — and there was darkness. What darkness must then have fallen on that poor girl's soul, I knew!

After that night I never saw the lover again — Lucy took her evening walks alone. For a time I fancied that her step was slow, and her head bent; but these tokens of grief changed. Youth can bear so much, and for so long. In spite of her trouble, Lucy Waters looked well and pretty, and I was glad to see her so. Moreover, the family fortunes seemed still improving, for ere summer ended, the drawing-room shutters were at last taken down, furniture came, and, I supposed, an inhabitant — for there appeared on the door a goodly brass-plate with "Mr. Gambier, *Surgeon.*"

I saw this said individual in due time. He was rather small — and I, like most little women, have an aversion to little men; he wore green spectacles, which I hate; he was slightly bald; and might have been any age from thirty to fifty. I did not take any interest in him at all. I only noticed that he seemed on good terms with the Waterses, and went to church with them every Sunday.

"Pray can you tell me anything about your opposite neighbours?" said to me one of those few benignant friends who take compassion on my loneliness, and now and then enliven my engraving by chatting to me the while.

I did not like to reveal what was only a romance founded on guess-work, so I answered, "Why do you ask?"

"Because I saw in passing that they taught wax-flower-making, and I wanted my Rosa to learn—just for amusement. So I went in there to-day, and saw the nicest family. Such a mild-looking old woman is the mother — and the daughter, Miss Lucy Waters, so very pretty and ladylike! I was quite charmed. Positively Rosa shall learn of her."

This was accomplished; and consequently Rosa — the most blithe, good-natured lassie that ever sported through her teens — was continually putting her merry face in at my parlour-door, with various anecdotes of my opposite neighbours; anecdotes, too, always of the most favourable kind. Never was there such a charming old lady as Mrs. Waters, such a clever youth as Mr. Alfred, and such a complete angel in every way as Miss Lucy!

One day my friend Rosa sprang into my room with such a burst of joyance that I was quite overpowered.

"Oh, Letty!" — (Reader, do you know the sort of people whom everybody calls by their Christian names? Well, of such am I!) — "Oh, Letty, I've found it out now. I thought I should. I know why they've all been smiling, and whispering, and dressmaking, and putting off my lessons now and then: and ——."

"Well, my lassie — why?"

"Because she's going to be married: sweet, darling Lucy Waters is going to be married. They're all so glad; and so am I, even though I wish it had been somebody younger and handsomer than that quiet Mr. Gambier."

"Mr. Gambier!" My block fell to the floor. "Impossible, child! Don't tell me so — don't let me think that pretty, quiet creature, such a ——."

I stopped. I would not for worlds have revealed what I knew. I pressed down the indignation, the scorn which rose up in my bosom. I listened to Rosa's story of the merry wedding that was to be next week, the bride's good luck, the bridegroom's excellent property.

"Ay, there it is!" I said to myself, when my young favourite was gone. "One more added to the list of weak-minded, unstable women: faithless, heartless; changing their lovers as easily as their gloves; ready to marry anybody, so that they are married at last. Oh, Lucy, pretty Lucy! to think that you should be one of these!"

When, next day, I saw her walk down the street, leaning on Mr. Gambier's arm, looking so quietly happy, as a betrothed bride should, I positively hated the girl. I would have gone from home on the wedding-day, so as not to see the atrocious sacrifice of broken faith; but that naughty, bewitching Miss Rosa came with her coaxing ways, to beg she might see the wedding from my windows. I never can refuse that lassie anything — so I stayed. But I would not go near the window.

"Tell me all you see, Rosa dear." And so she did, and a great deal more, too; for her little tongue ran on unceasingly about the "people over the way," especially Mr. Gambier.

"Don't, child — I hate to hear about him," said I, snappishly. "The disagreeable, ugly, old man!"

"Old man! Why, he is only just past thirty. Lucy told me so; and she loves him very much, and says he is the best man in all the world."

"The wretch!" I muttered, thinking of that night — the wild embrace — the mournful parting. How dared she stand where they two stood — cross the same threshold which he crossed — he to his eternal exile, she to her marriage altar!

"Rosa, my dear child!" And I went up, intending to read my young friend a homily against faithlessness, when I saw, standing by the Waterses' parlour-window, a young man — he with whom Lucy had so often walked. "Tell me, Rosa, do you know who is that gentleman?" I cried.

"Who? — he with the curly brown hair — so handsome? Why, 'tis Lucy's brother — her elder brother, and her favourite. He is a tutor in a gentleman's family. He helped to maintain them all, and used to come and see them very often, till he went abroad travelling. Lucy almost broke her heart at parting with him, she loved him so much."

"Bless Lucy — God bless sweet Lucy!" I muttered, feeling half ready to cry. What an idiot I had been! And yet the mistake was quite natural. Only I erred in one thing — I should have trusted that innocent, loving face. I should have guessed that it was the sure token of a true woman's heart.

"But yet," said I, smiling to Rosa, when I had told her of my blunder, and she had quizzed me heartily for it, "I don't see why Lucy should marry such a man as Mr. Gambier."

"There you are, Letty, judging by appearances again. Why, that is the most noble part of Lucy Waters' story. She knew him from her childhood, and he was so good and generous! He saved her mother's life in a long, weary illness; and then, just before he came to lodge with them, he was very near dying himself too — dying of a broken heart because he thought Lucy could not care for an old-looking ugly man, and was too proud to ask her to marry him from gratitude. And she does not; she marries him from love. Look at her now!"

Lucy came to the door with Mr. Gambier — the worthy, noble man! Even with his small stature and his green spectacles, he looked a perfect Apollo in my eyes, and so he would in those of his happy wife — evermore!

I have been a year absent from my little home — not from pleasure, but from duty — what duty I may tell some time, not now. I returned hither last week, to live my lonely, peaceful life of old. My first look was to my opposite neighbours.

"Mr. Gambier, surgeon," still flourished on the hall-door; but there were no other professional inscriptions indicating the rest of the family. However, I heard that the old people came there every day, and must consequently live very near. And accidentally taking up a catalogue of the Water-Colour Exhibition, I saw among the W.'s, *Alfred Waters*. Bravo, my boy of genius! my dear boy, whom I shall always love, though I may never speak to him in my life. I shall go and see his picture to-morrow.

To-night, as I sit writing, somewhere near twelve o'clock, I am greatly disturbed by the sound of music and dancing "over the way." The Gambiers are quite right to be merry if they choose; but really — Ah, I remember now! this very morning I saw a cab at the door, and old Mrs. Waters handed therein, together with a bundle of white lace and muslin.

Oh, the wretches! They are absolutely giving a christening party!

III. — LAST CHRISTMAS EVE.

CERTAINLY it was the most original, exciting, serio-comical Christmas-eve that ever was spent! Shall I tell you the story, reader? You can extract from it, if not a moral, at least a wholesome warning; one that, if you be a provincial, will make you fasten your shutters, and draw round the fire, and declare "that you would not live in such a place as London on any account whatever."

"Well, it is not such a bad world after all, is it, Pussy?" said I, musingly, to my sole interlocutor, the one point into which my "family circle" has now dwindled. And a faithful and loving companion is my cat Cid. Well, Cid, my dear, creep to my heart, nestling there almost like a bairn.

"Foolish Miss Letty! if you have no bairns of your own, not even nephews and nieces, you have plenty of other people's." That's what you would say, Cid — and you're right. It is something to be a universal aunt. And I flatter myself that in the coming generation there will be half-a-score of little Letitias to spread gladness over society in general, and to prove that, after all, my poor old name was not a misnomer.

"It is, indeed, a very good, kindly world," I pursued, as Cid and I kept our Christmas-eve together by the fire: "Only to think — I have had five invitations for to-morrow, and three for to-night. Now, if I had been a beauty, a woman of property, a 'charming person,' a 'dear, sweet girl,' this would not have been marvellous; but to be just plain Miss Letty, whom nobody can get anything out of, except thankfulness — well! it is a good world, and a kind world, and I am very much obliged to it."

The clock struck seven. "Come, Cid, you must go down, and keep Christmas-eve by yourself," said I, as I prepared to depart for the one which I had accepted from my triad of invitations. I had made my choice, as the novelists say, solely from "the dictates of the heart." Rejecting all other delights, I had said to myself firmly, "I will spend this evening with Jemima."

Here the question arises, "Who is Jemima?" She is a lassie in her teens: one of those cruelly-christened ones who have struggled through life under an ill name, which at length, despite godfathers and godmothers, has become so thoroughly love-sanctified that everybody thinks it pretty, and its owner would not change it for the world. So it is with Jemima. She isn't a genius — she isn't a beauty — nor is she an angel; she has her little weaknesses, all of which I know quite well, though I am not going to speak of them. Yet I will defy any one to help admiring and loving Jemima: I can't, I confess it. But one thing I never could understand — how it is that Jemima loves me! We are as different as a young ash-tree and an old crooked thorn. Moreover she has seen my soul in *deshabille* — a hard test for any friendship; she has wept with me, laughed with me, teased me, lectured me; I am sure I have given her as much trouble as I ever gave anybody in the world; and yet — Jemima loves me! It is very odd, very odd indeed; but I take it calmly upon *primâ facie* evidence, believing in it as we are taught to do in our own existence, which nobody ever can prove.

I started for Jemima's home — for she has a home, rich, happy girl! rich in every possible tie, save that of sisterhood — which little omission is perhaps the better for me. I walked quickly through the damp, raw night, passing out of the region of Christmas shops into the dark quiet streets of private houses, which in London always look desolate, especially after dusk. Down them I sauntered, all alone, save for the ghosts of many a past Christmas-eve and Christmas-day that came behind and plucked at my heart, or voices nearer — perhaps better — that kept singing in the silent air life's ever-recurring dirge — "*It might have been — it might have been.*"

"But, Miss Letty," whispered my conscience, "is this a frame of mind in which to go out visiting?" So I took the warning, put off my blues with my bonnet, and entered the drawing-room with a perfect Christmas face.

"I hope you understand what sort of an evening you have come to spend," said Miss Jemima, rising from the shadowy solitudes of the room, one corner of which was inhabited by her brother Frank, his desk, and a solitary candle. "There's nobody asked to meet you, Miss Letty, and you won't even get a mince-pie." And she looked as if she meant to insinuate that I should feel this last as the climax of my woes. Wicked Jemima!

"I can keep Christmas-eve quite well with only you and Frank; and I don't care about mince-pies; and I'm determined to be comfortable," said I, resolutely settling myself in a fireside corner; quite prepared for what evidently seemed "the pursuit of pleasure under difficulties."

For we certainly were not the merriest party in the world, nor the largest. Frank's pen went on scratching away — I suppose it was poetry — I *hope* it was; but that is not my affair. There seemed, too, a shadow over me and Mimie. I ought to explain that she answers to that name likewise: in fact, she is a compound of two characters, the woman and the child; when she appears as the former, I dignify her as Jemima, when she sinks into the sweet loveableness of the latter, I call her Mimie. My dreariness, if such it was, nobody had any business with but myself: Mimie had no reason to give for hers, except the purely young ladyish one of having lost all her little ornaments.

"Look," said she, in a child-like piteousness, putting forth her bonnie bare arm, where bracelets always looked so pretty, "I can't find one of them in my room, and I don't feel happy without them — especially the one that Letty gave me." (Bless her! thought I; I wish I could coin my love into one great diamond fetter, and hang it on her arm!) "I am sure," pursued poor Mimie, "it is that mischievous boy, who has been playing me some trick. Confess, Frank."

"Ay, confess!" echoed I, putting on tragedy airs, and trying to make myself young with these young folk. But Frank is the queerest fellow in the world: you never know whether he is in jest or earnest; so, though he denied the deed, during the whole evening he lay under the imputation of having spirited away his sister's little treasures.

It certainly *was* a quiet evening. I tried to diversify its "intense inane" by producing a pomegranate, the eating of which disposed of half-an-hour tolerably well, and moreover created a little conversation. We floated over to the East, with the old patriarchs, who are sometimes described, "sitting under a pomegranate-tree;" then spoke of "the juice of spiced wine of my pomegranate," which the Beloved in Solomon's Song is made to drink; and at last landed in modern days amidst Browning's "Bells and Pomegranates." But the gods have not made Jemima very poetical, though, perhaps, she is all the better for that. So, ere long, our conversation and the pomegranate were finished together.

A pause — Frank's pen growls on — the firelight shadows dance silently over Mimie and me. We begin talking in a low tone and in the dark, conjuring back our last Christmas-eve, a year ago, passed in the same room.

"What fun we had! and how we played at forfeits! and what admirable jokes Bob made at 'What-is-my-thought-like?' and how we all fretted and scolded for want of May, who afterwards burst in at nine o'clock, like a flash of lightning! And didn't we drink our elder wine, and wait till twelve o'clock, and then wish one another infinitudes of merry Christmases — ah, well!"

And we paused, counting over all the names of our little party, and wondering about them now. It was a change, greater than is often brought by one little year. Some were scattered wide, in this our England and elsewhere. One was at this moment probably hunting kangaroos for a Christmas dinner, or, for Christmas-carols, listening to the screaming of parrots under the noon-day sun of an Australian summer. Another, too, had gone from among us, though no further than to the little burying-place down the road, where, through the thin railings which part the ever-flowing tide of life from the stillness and silence of death, we, coming home from evening parties, often saw the white gravestones glimmering, and thought how soon even the best of us are forgotten.

These and other thoughts we spoke of — Mimie and I. Some, perhaps heavier than all, were unspoken; but none can lift the veil from his brother's heart. We all live, like the poor hypochondriac, with some shape haunting us, which to our neighbour is invisible as air. He may walk beside it, cross its path, or even stand in its place; but there we see it, grinning over his shoulder still.

Well, we talked ourselves grave, and then talked ourselves merry again; especially when on us fell the influence of parental mirth — for Mimie boasts the most popular of papas, and most majestic of mammas. At last I was persuaded into the acknowledgment that there was no positive necessity for my going home that night, and that Christmas morning shining on a solitary breakfast-table was not the pleasantest thing in the world. So we grew "crouse and canty," and nothing broke our cosy cheer save an occasional pathetic reminder from the incredulous and disconsolate Mimie: —

"Oh, Frank! what did you do with my poor little ornaments?"

We waited for Old Christmas — drinking our elder-wine — regretting faintly that there were fewer glasses to fill than last year, but still drinking, when our peace was broken by another domestic attack upon the unfortunate Frank: —

"Please, Master Frank, what have you been doing with your mamma's jewel box? It is carried up to the top of the house, and all the things scattered about!"

Here Frank, being well abused on all sides, denied the

deed with such seriousness that a little surprise arose among our circle.

"How very extraordinary!" said one. "It looks as if some evil agency had been at work in the house." A very unpleasant suggestion, by the by, though a curious instance of "superstition in the nineteenth century." However, it was deemed expedient that the head of the household — who was not, and need not be, afraid of elf, ghost, or devil, — should go up-stairs, and investigate. Meanwhile, Mimie and I remained quietly below, drank "a merry Christmas" aloud to each other, and then, perhaps, drank one more, in silence. In this world how many blessings, how many prayers go forth dove-winged, and finding no welcome, no rest, flutter back wearily over the sorrowful waters!

This last dolorous sentiment, reader, you may ascribe to whomsoever you like, but don't lay it to the charge of my young, innocent, merry Jemima.

"Well, Mimie, shall we go and look after the ghost up-stairs?" I said; and lo! there greeted us a domestic hurricane of voices and trampling feet.

"The house has been robbed! Thieves in the house! Thieves!" A pretty amusement that for Christmas-eve!

I don't think any one of us could lucidly describe the events of the next ten minutes. There was a rush to pokers and shovels, dim ghastly suspicions of "a man in the house," — which man, in time, was multiplied into two or three. Some awful, omnipresent burglar was hunted for in dark corners, and in clothes-closets, and under sofas; and there were heard various agonized thanksgivings "that we had not all been murdered in our beds." Frantic cries of "Police-man!" at last produced one of that redoubtable body; then two, three, four, until we were surrounded within and without by those perambulating letters of the alphabet.

The extent of the robbery was ascertained, also the time of its perpetration — which was probably some hours before. The formidable "they" dwindled into one small thief, who must have crept over the roofs of houses, and in at an attic window.

"There's the footmarks of the young villain, sir," observed the astute B 3; and behold a track of Indian perfection — five toes and a heel — imprinted blackly on the spotless floor, thence descending to Jemima's chamber. In the missing ornaments there was no mystery now.

"What! all my pretty things gone?" cried Mimie, in a burst of natural and child-like regret; she has not ceased to be a child so very long, the innocent lassie! "I wonder the wretch could have had the heart to come in here!" And certainly, if a thief's heart could be moved by the sanctity pervading the prettiest of pretty bedrooms, decorated all over with holly and ivy, — poor Mimie had not lost her treasures! But so it was: the house had been rifled completely of jewellery, while its inmates were comfortably at dinner below.

"A nice Christmas-eve we're keeping," observed the much-maligned Frank, as, rubbing his hands, he scampered here, there, and everywhere, in the delicious excitement of "the robbery." And, truly, it was an original celebration of Yule-tide. Policemen tramping up-stairs and down-stairs, in the house and out again, clambering over roofs, and searching in cellars; little anecdotes pouring in of neighbours wakened up in terror — I believe we thought it our duty to be robbed as publicly as possible: some of us women-kind becoming "agitated," and requiring consolation and elder-wine; everybody at last growing voluble, all talking at once and nobody listening: such were the eccentric elements of our Christmas-eve.

At length the alarm subsided a little, the door closed on the last policeman, the troop of imaginary burglars subsided into the probable "little vulgar boy," who, six hours since, had made his exit by the attic window. Of him and his depredations no trace remained save the dirty foot-marks on the floor. We sat over the fire speculating concerning him.

"I wish he had tumbled off the parapet," said one, rather unchristianly inclined.

"Perhaps he wanted a Christmas dinner: well! he'll get one now," observed another; who, having lost nothing, was calmly philanthropic.

"I don't care what becomes of him, if I could only get back my pretty things!" was Mimie's wail — neither a vain nor a selfish one. Dear child! may she never learn that there are bitterer things to lose than ornaments!

We gathered once more round the fire to enjoy that inexpressible satisfaction after every adventure — "talking it over." We all felt very heroic now the alarm was past; in fact, some of us regretted openly that we could not find the thief, whether with any contemplation of Lynch-law, it is impossible to say. On the whole, we took the losses quietly, and congratulated ourselves that things were no worse. Though still the prevailing opinion ran that we had miraculously escaped some awful catastrophe — and that it was a marvel we were then and there alive to tell the tale to admiring neighbours. And perhaps some of us thought with harmless pride, of our coming notoriety — as "the family that was robbed."

"Bless my life," cried Frank, taking out his watch, "it's Christmas morning!"

And so it was! No going to the hall-door to open it and let in Christmas: the worthy Old Fellow had come in of his own accord — after the policemen. So we drank his health, and one another's, and decided that though he came under somewhat troublous and eccentric circumstances, he was very welcome after all. Losses were forgotten, and blessings counted over — as should be at Christmas time. And in remembering our own good things, and wishing the like to all our brethren, perhaps some of us thought that if there was no poverty there would be no thieves; and our hearts softened even towards the juvenile monster of iniquity whose footprints yet defiled the attic floors.

Ere long the holly-decorated chamber received Mimie and me.

"Oh! how could the wretch profane this pretty little room, and steal the poor little ornaments?" was our conjoint lament. But it was Christmas morn; we looked out on the winter stars and grew comforted. She, probably, thought of her human treasures — I of mine, laid up, still safer, "where thieves do not break through nor steal."

Ere we went to sleep we heard the waits playing in the distance. Unlike all other seems this music — coming year by year, solemn, strange, and sweet; at least, it is so unto me. One after the other rose its waves of sound, eddying over my heart, washing away all things that should not be there; each swelled, laden with some memory, or ebbed, bearing away some pain. And over the great peaceful tide came well-known forms, walking like angels, some human, as I see them now, some exalted into the image that I see not yet — but shall see.

My heart melted; and to each and all I stretched out my arms with a Christmas blessing, which they could not hear, but ministering spirits may.

"Mistress Letty," hints my Cid, as she puts her velvet paw on the paper in mute remonstrance, "don't you think you have made fool enough of yourself for once? Have you not said sufficient about that Christmas-eve?"

Cid! you're right. Farewell.

IV. — OUR OLD DRESSMAKER.

"This will never do, my dear," said my aunt ruefully, as she pondered over a long account just come in, being the sum expended in the making of my first "evening dress." (When I say, "my *first* evening dress," the reader will understand that this "experience" of mine happened a good many years ago.) "Sixteen shillings!" repeated my aunt, "and only for making up the materials. These London dress-makers are ruinous. We must find some one to work in the house, as did Lydia Jones."

And my worthy aunt, newly imported from the country, sighed while she fastened my new dress — called frock now no more; for it marked my passing into the charmed regions of young ladyhood. I loved it, the pretty pale silk, of simple yet graceful fashion, which did duty as a "best dress" for more time than richer maidens would care to confess. The poor old thing! I found a fragment of it the other day, and sighed, remembering the scenes where it had been, and the girlish bosom which beneath its folds had learned to throb with deeper pulses than those of pleasure at a new silk dress.

My aunt's lamentations that night brought forth their fruits. "Letty," said she, on our next investment in costume, "I have found a dressmaker, to work as Lydia did, for eighteen-pence a day. You can help her, my dear, as you used to help Lydia. Women can never learn too much of the use of their fingers."

I acquiesced, for I had a fancy, indeed quite a genius, that way; only I always wished to make the dresses on artistic rather than fashionable principles, and I began to fear the London workwoman would not coincide with my vagaries so readily as quiet Lydia in the country. So I rather dreaded the advent of the new dressmaker.

"Who is she, and when does she come, aunt?"
"Her name is Miss Hilton, and she comes to-morrow. Now, my dear, go to your practising."

I obeyed — but, with the curiosity of fifteen, I did not cease to speculate on the young workwoman. In fact I confess to having bestirred my lazy self half an hour earlier on the following morning, in honour of her coming, which, in our monotonous life, was quite an event.

It was, I remember, one of the wettest of all wet September days. Still, at half-past eight A. M., there faithfully appeared "our dressmaker." Little cause had I to be alarmed at *her* — a poor, pale thing, who, when she had taken off her damp shawl — I recollect inwardly wondering at her folly in putting on such a thin one — sat down very quiet and demure, and ate her breakfast in silent respect.

I was a shy girl, a *very* shy girl; but I believe my good feeling so far conquered my timidity as to make me inquire if Miss Hilton would not take off her wet shoes, and have a pair of slippers; and then meeting my aunt's eye, I subsided in fearful blushes, lest I had taken too much notice of "the dressmaker."

We got on very well together, Miss Hilton and I, when the work began. She took the patterns skilfully, and yielded to all my little peculiarities about grace and beauty in costume. Moreover, she did not treat me as a child, but as a "young lady;" and when, with great dignity, I sat down to assist her in making the skirt of my aunt's new dress, Miss Hilton still kept a respectful silence, which soothed my pride, and won my favour amazingly.

Now I was a most romantic young damsel, and knew nothing of the world except from books, of which I had read an infinity, good, bad, and indifferent. So, watching my companion — with her small neat figure, her face of that sort not properly termed good-looking, but yet decidedly *looking good* — I began to take a liking for her very soon, and ventured a few questions.

"Had she come far that wet morning?"
"Only about two miles."
"She must have risen early then?"
"Yes, about five: she had had to finish a dress before she came."

What a life! To rise at five, work till eight, walk two

miles through those muddy lanes (we lived a short distance out of London), and then begin and work again! I said nothing, but I thought much; and I remember the next time Miss Hilton stood cutting out, I had the sense to place a chair for her. This she acknowledged with a faint blush, which made me think of the sweetest ideal of all young dressmakers — Miss Mitford's "Olive Hathaway."

My dressmaker was no ideal — I do not mean to set her up as one. She was merely a gentle, modest, quiet young woman, who worked slowly, though carefully, and who for the first day did not seem to have an idea beyond her needle and thread. The next, I found she had.

I, always an odd sort of girl, happened just then to be wild about a new hobby — phrenology. Now Miss Hilton had a remarkably-shaped forehead, and I never rested until I brought the plaster mapped-out head, and compared her bumps therewith; upon which she smiled, and becoming conversational, seemed to wish to learn something about the new science. So I, forgetting alike my shyness and my pride of caste, began seriously to inform the mind of our new dressmaker.

I found she *had* a mind, and some graceful taste withal, whereupon I valorously undertook my "mission." I indulged her with my juvenile notions on art and literature, and while she developed the skill of my fingers, I tried to arouse her dormant intellect. Poor, simple soul! I do believe she enjoyed it all, sitting working at my open window, with the vine-leaves peeping in, I dilating the while upon innumerable subjects, which doubtless had never before entered her mind. Among these were the country and its beauties. One day some fortunate chance had brought me a nosegay of honeysuckles, and showing them to her, I found, to my intense pity, that my young Londoner did not even know their name!

"What! Had she never seen wild flowers? Had she never been in the country?"

"Oh, yes, she had once lived for six months in a guardship off Woolwich, where she had seen the country on the river banks, and her little sisters had sometimes brought home handfuls of daisies from the fields. But for herself she had worked ever since she could remember; and except those six months in the ship, had never lived anywhere but at Chelsea."

To me, how dreary seemed such an existence! To stitch — stitch — stitch one's days away; never to read a book, or walk in a country field, or even to know the name of a wild flower! Perhaps, in my deep pity, I overlooked the fact that one rarely misses pleasures never known; yet still my feelings were strongly excited for poor Mary Hilton. I did not like her the less for learning that her Christian name was that sweet one — Mary. And when all the work was done, and I began to wear the new dresses we had together fabricated, I often thought of the pale, quiet, little thing, and hoped that wherever she was "working out," it was with no harder taskmistresses than my good aunt and myself.

When we sent for Miss Hilton again it was a sudden call — to make mourning. The lost relative was one too aged and too distant to occasion me much grief, yet I remember the very fact of our sitting sewing black dresses caused our talk to be rather grave. The dressmaker told me of a brother — the only one she ever had — who died of consumption; and how she used to sit by him at night, and go out working in the day — towards the last, hurrying home very fast, lest "anything might have happened" (that disguise we shrinkingly cast over the word *death*) while she was away. How, at the end, it was as she feared. She was working with a lady, who kept her late to finish — just to sew on a few trimmings and hooks-and-eyes — a mere half-hour's work. But she was that one half-hour *too late*, and never again saw her living brother!

"It was a chance — a mere chance," she said; "the lady was not to blame." And sighing, though without tears — she seemed too quiet for that — the little dressmaker went on with her work again.

We could not finish the mourning in time: it was my fault, I fear, inasmuch as I had invented a fantastic trimming which cost a world of trouble to make, to which poor Miss Hilton submitted with infinite patience. She only asked if she might bring her sister to help her, to which my aunt graciously assented. But I — always shy of strangers — found great discomfort in the plan. Moreover, the sister's name was Caroline, and I had a girlish prejudice — I have it still — against all Carolines. Miss Caroline Hilton was the exact

16*

image of my abhorrence — pretty, vain, talkative — the very type of the worst class of London dressmakers. My aristocratic pride rebelled against her forwardness: I ceased to work in the room; in fact, from the moment she came, I — to travestie irreverently a line from almost the grandest modern poet —

"Shrank into myself, and was missing ever after."

Only I made my aunt promise that never again should Miss Caroline darken our doors.

It seems to me, jotting down this sketch at random, that there are in it many lines and touches which belong not alone to the portrait of our dressmaker. Well, let it be so.

When Mary Hilton came to us again it was in the wintertime. She looked, as ever, pale, and was still prone to silence; but there was a greater air of content about her, which spoke of improved fortunes. And in making our engagements with her, it came out accidentally that her hands were full of profitable occupation. Among her "new ladies," I remember, were the juvenile scions of a ducal household, where she used to be employed for weeks together. Now I was a simpleton in those days: I had a romantic reverence for rank — not vulgar curiosity, but an ideal homage — and greatly did I delight in hearing about the little noblewomen; and Mary Hilton seemed to like telling — not pompously, very simply — how Lady Alice was a beautiful child, Lady Gertrude rather cross, but baby Lady Blanche was the sweetest little fairy in the world, and would come and talk and play with "the dressmaker" as much as ever she was allowed. Many visions I mentally had of the lordly household, where the chief filial duty was the privilege of entering carefully dressed with the dessert, and where mamma was not mamma at all, but "the duchess." How time passes! The other day I saw in the paper the marriage of the "beautiful and accomplished Lady Blanche H—." I thought of "baby Lady Blanche," then of poor Mary Hilton and sighed.

Our dressmaker worked blithely through the short winterday, and even when night closed she seemed in no hurry to go home. About nine o'clock there came up to our workroom a message that some one had called to fetch Miss Hilton: "A young — man," explained the domestic, hesitating, I suppose, whether she should or should not say "gentleman."

"I am really quite glad. I did not like your walking through those dark lanes alone," said I, with infinite relief; and then added, in extreme simplicity, "I thought you had no brother now?"

"It is — not my brother," murmured our dressmaker, blushing, but faintly, for even the quick blood of youth seemed to creep languidly beneath her constant pallor. I was a child — a very child then. I don't believe I had ever thought of love or lovers — that is, in real life; but some instinct made me cease to question the young woman. Likewise, instead of descending with her, I stayed up-stairs; so that she met her friend alone. But I remember opening the blind a little way, and watching two dark figures passing down the snowy lane — watching them, and thinking strange thoughts. It seemed as if a new page were half-opening in life's book.

It *had* opened; and with eyes light-blinded I had begun to read for myself, and not for another — before I again saw my little dressmaker.

My aunt and I had changed our abode to the very heart of London, and Mary Hilton had to come to us through four miles of weary streets. I think she would scarcely have done it for gain: it must have been from positive regard for her old customers. She looked much as usual — a little paler perhaps; and she had a slight cough, which I was sorry to hear had lasted some time. But she worked just as well, and just as patiently; and when at nine o'clock came the knock at the hall-door, her smile, though half-concealed, was quite pleasant to see.

I am getting an old woman now, but to this day I incline to love two people who love one another. I do not mind what their rank in life may be: true love is the same in all ranks; and I honestly believe there was true love between my little dressmaker and her Daniel Ray. A respectable, worthy young man was Daniel, as my good and prudent aunt took care to discover. I, in my simple, girlish way, discovered much more. Little did Mary Hilton talk about it; but from her disjointed words I learned that theirs was a long engagement — that Daniel was assistant in a chinashop; that they were waiting, perhaps might have to wait for years, until he could afford to rent a little shop of his own, where she would carry on the dressmaking in the floor above. Meanwhile she at least was quite content; for he came to tea to her father's every Sunday, and in the week-day, wherever she worked, he always fetched her home — saw her safe to Chelsea, and walked back to the City again. Honest, unselfish, faithful lover! Poor Mary Hilton, in her humble way, had great happiness — the only happiness which suffices to a woman's heart.

But one night she had to go home without Daniel Ray. He was in the Potteries, she said, on business; and the poor little thing seemed grieved and trembling when she set out to walk home alone and at night. She scarce minded the bright, cheerful streets, she said; but she did not like to pass through the lonely squares. The next evening she begged permission to leave by daylight; and at last, with much hesitation, confessed that she had been spoken to by some rude man, and had hurried on past her strength, until, reaching home, she fainted. And then, in my inmost heart, I drew a parallel between myself — a young *lady*, tenderly guarded, never suffered to cross the threshold alone — and this young *person*, exposed, without consideration, to any annoyance or danger. The lesson was not lost upon me. All my life, as far as my power went, I have taken care that, whatever her station, a woman should be treated *as* a woman.

For a week Mary Hilton worked for us, coming and returning each night, walking the whole way, I believe — though I never thought about it then, I have since; and the heedlessness of girlhood has risen up before me as the veriest hard-heartedness. My aunt, too — but she had many things to occupy her mind, and to her Mary Hilton was only "the dressmaker." Doubtless we did but as others did, and the young woman expected no more. For I remember, the last night, she looked so pale and wearied that my aunt gave her at supper a glass of wine, and putting into her hand two shillings, instead of the usual eighteenpence, told her to have an omnibus ride home. And then Mary Hilton blushed and resisted, but finally took the sixpence with a look of such thankfulness! Poor thing!

The next time we wrote for our dressmaker, there came, not gentle little Mary Hilton, but the obnoxious Caroline. Her sister was in ill health, she said, and had been obliged to give up working out, but would make the dress at home, if we liked. It was settled so, only we premised that Mary must come to us to try it on. She came one evening, accompanied by Daniel Ray. For this she faintly apologized, saying, "he never would let her go out alone now." Whereat my aunt looked pleased; and when she quitted the room, I heard her go into the hall and speak in her own kindly tones to honest Daniel.

Mary Hilton tried on my dress, but seemed scarcely able to stand the while. I remembered this afterwards, not then, for I was thinking of my pretty dress, and whether I would look well in it. At that time how I longed to make myself fair! Poor fool! but it was not vanity, God knows!

I did not forget to put my usual question to Mary — how she was prospering in the world? and whether there was any near chance of the little china-shop, with "Mrs. Ray, Dressmaker," on the first floor? She smiled hopefully, and said something about "the spring," and "when her health was better;" and in a very shy and timid way she hinted that, if we wanted bonnets or millinery, there was a sister of Daniel's lately established in the next street — a sister always dependent on him till now. Faithfully I promised to give our small custom to Miss Ray: and so, looking quite happy, our little dressmaker descended. I am glad I saw that happy look — I am glad I noticed the perfect content with which the little delicate thing walked away slowly, leaning on her faithful Daniel. Otherwise, in my deep pity, I might have thought life's burden heavy, and its fates unequal. But it is not so.

Soon after, my aunt wanted a winter bonnet, and I proposed to visit Miss Ray. "Certainly, my dear Letty," was the contented acquiescence. So we went, and found there a sharp-featured, Frenchified young milliner, not at all like Daniel. During the trying on I inquired after Miss Hilton.

"Very ill, miss — confined to the house — consumption, I think. — But wouldn't a paler blue suit your complexion best?"

I laid down my ribbons, startled and distressed.

"Poor Miss Hilton!" said my compassionate aunt. "I thought she would die of consumption — so many dressmakers do. But how does your brother bear it?"

"As well as he can, ma'am. It was a foolish thing from

the beginning," added the milliner, sharply, her natural manner getting the better of her politeness. "The Hiltons are all consumptive, and Daniel knew it. But I beg your pardon, ma'am; perhaps you will try on this shape?"

I turned away, feeling very sorrowful. My first intent was to ask my aunt to let me go and see poor Mary Hilton; but when one is so young, one sometimes feels ashamed even of a good impulse which might be termed romantic; and I was so mocked for my romance already. I planned various schemes to fulfil and yet disguise my purpose; but somehow they all faded away. And then my own life was so tremblingly full, so rich in youth's dreams, that out of it the remembrance of the poor dressmaker soon melted like a cloud.

Late in April I wanted a new bonnet. It must be a pretty and becoming one — I was wildly anxious about that — one that hid the faults of my poor face, and set off to advantage any solitary beauty that Heaven had given it. At Miss Ray's I tried on bonnet after bonnet, examined myself eagerly yet tremblingly in all, tried to gain a clear, unbiassed notion of what my poor self was like, and at each look felt my cheek changing and my heart throbbing.

"Letty, my dear! —."

My aunt coming forward after a confabulation with Miss Ray, roused me from what might have seemed a reverie of girlish vanity; and was — no matter what it was.

"Letty, you will be sorry to hear that poor Mary Hilton —."

Mary Hilton! For weeks she had not crossed my thoughts: nay! not even now, so full was I of anxiety about my new bonnet.

"Poor Mary Hilton died last week!"

It came upon me like a shock — a pang — a sense of the end that must come to life, and all life's dreams. I — walking in the dazzling light of mine — felt a coldness creep over me; a sting, too, of self-reproach and shame.

I laid down the pretty bonnet, and thought, almost with tears, of the poor little dressmaker, who would never work for me any more — of her hard toils ended, her humble love-dream closed, her life's brief story told, and all passed into silence!

Then I thought of the poor faithful lover; I could not ask after him — but my aunt did.

"Daniel bears it pretty well," answered the sister, looking grave and shedding one little tear. It must be a hard woman indeed who does not show some feeling when brought into immediate contact with death. "He was with her to the last — she died holding his hand."

"Poor thing — poor thing!" murmured my tender-hearted aunt.

"Yes; she was a good creature, was Mary Hilton; but as for the rest of the family, they were nothing over-good — not fit for my brother Daniel," said the young woman, rather proudly. "Perhaps all was for the best. He will get over it in time."

So doubtless he did: possibly the humble little creature who loved him, and died thus loving, might even have wished it so. Every unselfish woman would. But I never heard what became of Daniel Ray, for my aunt and I soon after vanished from London; and when we returned, our milliner had vanished too. Mary Hilton, and all memories belonging to her, were thus swept utterly away into the chambers of the past — my girlish past.

But the other day, finding an old, many years' old dress, one whose veriest fragments I could kiss and weep over, I remembered, among other things, who it was that had then fashioned it; and looking on the careful stitches, thought of the poor fingers, now only dust. And a great sense came over me of the nothingness of all things, and of our need to do good in the daytime, because of the quick-coming night "wherein no man can work."

My lady readers — my "lilies that neither toil nor spin" — show womanly tenderness to those who do toil and spin for your pleasure or profit; and if you are disposed to be harsh, thoughtless, or exacting, think of this simple sketch from actual life of Our Old Dressmaker.

V. — SKETCHES (FROM NATURE) IN A RAILWAY CARRIAGE.

"'From nature!' Is that quite right?" whispers, or would whisper, a grave young voice, to which, despite its youth, I listen oftener than the world in general or its owner herself imagines. "Yes, my dear, quite right: since I shall paint nothing ill of my unknown sisters, and as no one precisely knows his own likeness, possibly none of them may ever recognise theirs."

I took a journey. When, where, or under what circumstances, is of no moment to the reader; and I shall explain just as much as I choose, and no more. It was a journey that lasted "from morn to dewy eve," even in the swift-winged express of one of our rapidest railway lines. How I glory in an express train! It is, of all things on earth, likest to a soul's travelling. The "horse with wings," of Imogen's fond longing, was surely a foreshadowing of it. How delicious to feel ourselves borne almost like thought to our desire! to see the bridges and trim stations dash by! to cease counting the quick coming milestones, and idly watch the brownish line of the rocky cuttings, or the poppy-beds on the embankments gleaming past in a flash of crimson, while the distant landscape keeps changing like a panorama, and county melts in county, each one bringing us nearer to our hope and our delight! So much for a happy travelling! On the other hand, with what a sense of blessed exhaustion do we lean back, on some weary journeys, shut our eyes, and hear nothing but the dull whiz of the engine as it goes flying on, whirling us, we care little whither, even if it were —

"Anywhere — anywhere, out of the world."

Of either of these pictures the reader may make me the heroine as he pleases.

For myself, I commenced the journey with nothing heroic about me at all. Fancy a quiet little woman lying dreamily in a corner of the carriage, and never looking up for at least one hundred miles, and you have my likeness complete. I had one only fellow-traveller, a gentleman. Now, though too old and ordinary to have any prudish alarms, I own I dislike a railway *tête-à-tête*. It generally produces either a stupid silence, or conversation which is often wearisome, because felt to be a necessary courtesy. But on this journey, for many hours no such reflections crossed my dull thoughts; I just saw there was a "thing" in a coat near me, and no more.

After a while I opened my eyes, looked out of the window mechanically, and saw that the long cool morning shadows had melted into the brightness of noon. Turning back, "I was ware" (as the knights expressed it in my beloved Mort d'Arthur) of two kindly, but rather curious hazel eyes fixed on me.

"Would you like a newspaper?" The voice was half polite, half blunt, and the quick blush of boyish shyness rose to the brown cheek of my travelling companion, who, I now noticed, was, or seemed to be, a "sailor laddie" of about eighteen. Despite the careless dress, and the rough, though not coarsely-formed hands, there was an unmistakeable air of a "gentleman's son" about the boy. I looked at the fair hair curling under the tarpaulin hat; the merry, tanned face; the neck-tie, sailor fashion, and my heart warmed to the laddie. It was no wonder *that day*, God knows! The sailor little thought how, regarding him with dimmed eyes, I saw sitting there, not him, but one whose face to me is now and will be ever young, as it was when I ceased to see it any more on earth.

This and many another feeling made me still rather silent towards my companion, who, after exchanging with me various *courtesies de voyage*, subsided into a boyish restlessness, and alternately peered out of the windows at the risk of his neck, held colloquies with guards and porters on every possible opportunity, or beguiled the time in consuming the most Titanic sandwiches that ever allayed a nautical appetite. Occasionally, my young friend settled himself to a quiet doze in the corner, and then I amused myself with contemplating his face, for I must confess that all the world is to me an animated picture-gallery.

He was a handsome lad — very! Above all, he had one of those rarely-shaped mouths wherein the olden Greek model seems revived; and I have such a weakness for a beautiful mouth! This was to me a perfect study. In fancy I saw it, baby-like, on the maternal breast; boy-like, dimpling with fun, or compressed in passion, for there was a high spirit about the lad, too; and then I speculated how it would look when the youth grew a man, and learned to smile upon other faces than his mother's. It would smile many a heart away, I knew!

Thus I filled my thoughts, most thankful that they could be so filled, with interest about this boy. I wove round him a perfect romance; and when he told me his destination — the same as my own — I, tender-hearted simpleton, feeling sure that he was a young sailor coming home, bestowed on him an imaginary mother and sisters; and putting myself in their place, fairly wept (aside, of course) when I looked at the laddie, and conjured up the meeting that would be that night at —.

We had speeded across shire after shire, and morning had become afternoon, when our quiet railway carriage was invaded by a host of fellow-voyagers. First were lifted in, staring about with frightened looks, two little children, boys apparently, though at that anomalous age when sex is almost indistinguishable. After them came a stalwart nurse, with a Scotch tongue, and a handsome, rather Highland-looking face. Last, after having first carefully noted that the children were safe, and then bidden a hasty good-bye to an elderly dame and an awkward young man, there entered a lady. I thought at first that she was the mother of the young fry, so anxious did she appear about them; but on a second glance, her face, though not exactly young, and rather worn, had not about it the indescribable look of matronhood, which can never be mistaken. Also, as she took the younger boy on her knee, and tried to hush him to rest, there was an out-looking, half-sorrowful restlessness in her eyes — such as one never sees in those of any mother when watching her slumbering child. The very consciousness of motherhood gives a sense of content and rest.

No, she was not the mother; I felt that even before I saw her ringless left hand. She must be an elder sister — governess — or most likely an aunt. Yes, she was the aunt. — Why was it that, hearing the little ones call her so, a sudden pain smote my heart, and once, but for very shame, I could have turned away my face and wept? Reader, you cannot guess the reason, and you need not be told. You know at least as much of me as you do of your next neighbour at a dinner party, or your pleasant companion on a journey, in whose breast some unconscious word or look of yours may call up a tide of thought or memory, while you both are as little aware of one another's real natures, or feelings, or histories, as if you belonged to two separate worlds. Each man living is to himself a world, moving on in his own orbit, intermingling with, yet distinct from, all his fellows, and able to draw light alone from the One unchanging Sun.

Pshaw! I am "at my old lunes" again. I must be rational

not sentimental. Well, it took a long time to dispose of our new fellow-travellers, for your infantocracy is the most absolute government under the sun. Behold us now — the children, aunt, and nurse, filling one seat, while I sat fronting them, having on either side my friend the young sailor, and another new-comer, a dark, bilious-looking gentleman of forty, who eyed our opposite neighbours with dislike and suspicion. So we travelled on for another hundred miles (we count by hundreds in this express), none of us making any efforts at acquaintanceship. But I — who ever walk through the world with my eyes open, thinking decidedly that "the noblest study of mankind is man" — did not fail to make a few sketches for my mental commonplace-book.

I watched the children with delight, drinking in large draughts of infantile beauty, for they were at the age when every motion is grace. The elder was a boy of five or six, delicate-featured, with a precocious gravity, even sadness, in his look. It was the sort of face that makes one instinctively turn round to gaze once more, and gazing, to speculate on the child's future; not knowing but in the mysteries of those thoughtful baby-eyes lies dawning the spirit of a poet, painter, or philosopher. This child was apparently the aunt's pet. He sat on her lap, and looked about gravely, though with some slight hesitation, till he apparently became satisfied with his novel position. But the younger one still cowered in the centre seat, with a half-frightened, half-pouting air, which made me think him not nearly so pretty as his brother, until the Highland nurse took him in her arms. Then he looked up to her with such a smile! The fat, rosy cheeks dimpled all over; the brown eyes literally seemed to float in radiance; I never saw a child's face so waken into almost angelic beauty. From that moment the "wee thing" was my darling!

I watched him both in his sleeping and waking moods for another half-hour, my glance taking in also the nurse's face, which bent over him full of tenderness and pride. She was a good study too. Looking at her, there came into my mind many a tale of Highland fidelity lasting a whole lifetime I could understand it as I beheld these two. I felt a strange, half-envious sensation to see how the "bonnie bairn" nestled in her breast, where probably he had rested night and day ever since his birth; how she bent her hard features into comical grimaces to amuse her pet of three years' old, and patted his little fat knees with her great brown hands. It was no use — I could not resist any longer. I took the plump rosy fingers in mine, and began to talk to the child; but I could not gain from the shy little elf any more information than that his name was Johnnie, and his brother's Willie: after which communication, which the nurse civilly but coldly confirmed, my wee sweetheart subsided again behind his "mammie's" plaid, and silence once more spread itself over our railway carriage.

Heaven only knows how long it might have lasted, and we fellow-travellers have gone on eating our hearts out in most uncomfortable and uncourteous dumbness, had it not been for the blessed interposition of a storm of rain, which came dripping in a tiny cascade from the top of the carriage.

"Bless my soul!" cried the bilious gentleman; "this is unpleasant — very! It must be looked to. Hollo, there!" But shouting to the guard of an express train, then going sixty miles an hour, and with no hope of a stoppage within a county or two at least, is rather a work of supererogation. So the irascible gentleman found it easier to stop the leak himself, which he tried to do with most heterogeneous articles selected from his pocket, such as lucifer-matches, cigar-ends, fragments of torn letters, &c.; but in vain. The water-spout continued, though less than before, and it would drip upon wee Johnnie however he was placed. So I took off my plaid, and wrapped the child doubly and trebly, from which safe shelter he contemplated the waterfall with infinite satisfaction. And somehow, in our combined efforts against our watery foe, we all grew sociable together.

My dark-looking neighbour began to converse with me most affably and confidentially; and the phrase introduced within five minutes, and repeated every other five, "When I was in India," enlightened me as to his character and standing in the world. Afterwards, becoming more explicit, he gave me his whole history from the cradle upwards, with sketches of his present life, and portraits of his family, including what seemed the great man among them, "My cousin, Sir —, the —." But hold! for the baronet is known far and wide in Indian story, and I must not trespass on the sanctities of private life.

While we talked, my black-bearded neighbour and I, the young aunt opposite sat quiet and grave, occasionally putting in a word when addressed by the Indian officer, who did not seem to take her fancy any more than he did mine, though I responded to his courtesy as was due. But there was a certain coarseness in his aspect, and a selfish military dogmatism — (ah, I hate soldiers!) — in all he said. And he had scowled so on the poor innocent children when first they entered the carriage and were made of such importance by aunt and nurse, that I had somehow taken a dislike to him. However, it was apparently not mutual, so I did the agreeable to the best of my power.

Now, too, woke up the dormant powers of my sailor laddie. I discovered him in the act of making friends with wee Johnnie by means of various baby-tricks — the sure road to a child's favour. Johnnie, after looking deliciously shy — the darling! — for a minute or two, began to respond to the young sailor's attention, and very soon the whole carriage was amused by a game of play between the two. I do love to see a boy or a young man fond of children: it argues a simple innocence of mind, and a kindly gentleness, which in manhood is so beautiful. My sailor laddie rose ten degrees in my estimation. I thought his face looked handsomer than ever, especially his exquisite mouth, while leaning over smiling to the child, or coaxing wee Johnnie to his arms, in which he at last triumphantly succeeded.

"You seem to understand amusing children: have you brothers and sisters of your own?" I asked.

"Oh, yes; plenty!" and he laughed merrily, and suffered Johnnie, now transformed into a most boisterous little king, to take all sorts of liberties with his hair and his neckerchief. He seemed quite in his element, bless him! I felt sure he was as good as he was handsome — my sailor laddie!

All the while the Indian looked on, sometimes condescending to a grim smile. The aunt smiled too, but rather pensively; and when Johnnie wished to draw his delicate-looking elder brother into his rather rough play, she came to the rescue of the gentle, half-reluctant Willie.

"He likes to be quiet — he is soon tired," she said to me. "They are neither of them very strong."

"Yet Johnnie at least appears a sturdy little fellow — a thorough Scotch laddie: is he not so?"

"His father was Scotch."
"And his mother?"
"She was an Englishwoman."

Was! — I could not help repeating the word she had twice used, with, I suppose, a look of inquiry, for she answered — "The children are orphans: both their father and mother have been dead these two years and more."

More than two years. Then the youngest must have been a mere babe. What a picture of life was opened up to me! With what different eyes did I now look on the two children, and on the youthful aunt — for she *was* young. I found that out when, in talking, her grave face began to soften. She was even pretty, especially when her loving eyes rested on her *protégés*. I felt sure that here was another of those stories of female self-devotion of which the world never hears, and never will, until the day when peals the divine sentence — "Inasmuch as thou hast done it unto the least of all these little ones, thou hast done it unto Me."

And when, tired with play, the two children crept to the arms of aunt and nurse, I began to frame for them a whole history both of past and future. I thought of the lost parents: of the mother especially, probably dying that saddest of all deaths — that which, in giving a new life, resigns her own. How keen must have been the pang in leaving those two babes to the bitter world! Then I turned and looked at the young creature who had assumed a mother's place and a mother's duties, and it seemed to me that her face was one of those in which one can read a story. She might be of the number of "old maids," made such by their own will, governed by some sad fate; and if so, blessed was she who had so many holy cares to occupy her solitary youth — so many hopes of even filial gratitude to comfort her declining years.

"Rain still — how very annoying!" grumbled the military gentleman, breaking upon my musings in his anxiety to point out the scenery of a most lauded lake-country, which, however, is to this day to me a blank picture of mist, and cold, and down-pouring rain. And then my polite companion hinted, with a covert, self-satisfied smile, that when he came next to this region, in a few weeks more, it would be a happier excursion than the present — in fact a bridal trip.

A comical communication this! But as I think we should travel by railway as we ought to do through life, making

ourselves as agreeable as possible, and creating as many
interests as we can by the way, I repressed my inclination
to laugh, or to condemn the bridegroom's rather too great
unreserve, and congratulated heartily this illustrious member
of the H. E. I. C.'s service. Upon which he told me the
whole course of his wooing, and how he and his new wife
were shortly to proceed to India, where I suppose they both
are by this time; and if this page should ever meet his eye, I
hope my fellow-traveller will accept the good wishes of his
friend the unsuspected author.

Hours went on, dragging heavily enough. Towards night-
fall the children grew very weary and restless, and then it was
beautiful to see the unity that had grown among us fellow-
travellers, and how we all combined to amuse the little creatures whom fate had given to our care for a day. I made my
little basket of dainties — owed to kindness too deeply felt to
be named here — into a general feast, wherein Johnnie especially gloried; the young sailor spent his time in contriving
an infinitude of cats'-cradles, and even the Indian jumped out
in the pouring rain to purchase gingerbread cakes, which, I
suppose, were his panacea for all infantile woes. Yet he turned
out not such an ogre after all, worthy man! and as his journey
drew near its close — it was some hours shorter than the rest
of us had to traverse — his sallow face lighted up into a positively benevolent expression. These lovely, loveable children
were creeping into even his hard heart. And when, in perfect
despair of amusement, Johnnie had gone the round of every
knee in the carriage except his, I heard to my amazement the
grim officer say, in the most mellifluous tone he could assume
— "Wouldn't the little fellow come to me?"

And the little fellow, being now of most adventurous mood,
did come. At first our dark-visaged friend looked as uncomfortable and awkward as if he had got a young tiger on his
knee; but soon Johnnie's winning ways conquered all. The
fat baby hand began pulling his stiff grizzled hair, where probably a child's hand had never played before; the innocent
eyes looking up and laughing, brought into his harsh-lined,
worldly face a softness that it probably had not known for
years. I never saw such a transformation!

At last our East Indian neared his destination. Lingeringly he put down wee Johnnie, and began to search for his
carpet-bag. He bade us all a cordial adieu, then took the child

again and looked at him wistfully for a minute. Perhaps — for there is a warm, tender corner in every man's heart — perhaps some softened feeling came across the mind of the bridegroom expectant, and he thought of the time when he, too, might have a "bonnie bairn" on his knee, and his rough life might merge into the gentle charities of home. However that was, I saw — yes, indeed I did — a tear on his eyelash: he kissed the child, once, twice, hastily jumped out of the carriage, and we saw him no more.

Night soon fell upon us now wearied fellow-travellers. We ceased trying to entertain one another, or looking out at the country, and the carriage windows were closed lest the damp evening air might harm the sleeping children. "We are always obliged to take such care of them," the young aunt said. Even she at last dozed, and so did the sailor laddie in the corner. I only was wakeful; for alas! the temporary interests of the journey ceasing, I had forgotten my companions, and was sinking back into myself — a dreary thing always.

We had come now into a region I knew: sharp and clear against the fading sunset rose the outline of the —— Hills, with the young moon floating above their peaks, just as it had done one evening a year ago. A year! — say rather a life — for it seemed thus long. I steadily turned my eyes away, and looked back into the carriage, where beside me Johnnie lay asleep. I cannot — or else I will not — tell the feeling that came over me as I looked at his dimpled face, his thickly-curling hair of the colour I love, and the heavy lashes that hid his sweet brown eyes, which oftentimes during the journey had made me almost start with their strange, clear, un-childlike gaze. If, as I kissed him, a tear dropped over him, it would not harm him — my bonnie boy! *Mine!* — truly I must have been dreaming; and it was well the train stopped, to bring the little old woman to her right mind.

I shall never see Willie nor Johnnie more — never! They may grow up to be men — great and honoured perhaps — if, as in wee Johnnie at least, one may read the soul of genius even in a child's eyes. But I shall never know it: to me they are only Willie and Johnnie, for I did not bear their surname. Or, it may be — though Heaven forefend! that the young aunt's anxious guardianship was half prophetic — that they may never grow old in the harsh world, but remain eternally children in the family above. However, and wherever their fate be, God bless them!

VI. — THE PLACE WHERE I WAS BORN.

I ought to premise that, in spite of the assumption of the aforesaid title, I, Miss Letitia N——, am not, on the whole, a very conceited person. Nor, though scarcely quite unknown, do I pretend to cast lustre on the spot which gave me to an admiring world! I know full well, that if I were to die to-morrow, one year would suffice to blot out all I was, or did, or said, or wrote, from the memory of every human being. Except perhaps, an occasional thought given by one or two that loved me, or who, after my death, might remember me for my loving.

Still, truth is truth — and every individual reality convolving in its circle, will now and then touch the orbit of some other individual reality. So, whether I myself be noticeable or obscure — it may be worth while to tell the tale of my revisiting "the place where I was born."

It was after a lapse of years, during which from a mere child I had grown into a person of — say an uncertain age; but having to all intents and purposes attained the middle of a somewhat "well-foughten" life. I came — not to sentimentalize — there was little opportunity for that; nor yet affectionately to lament — I, like many more, had grown to love other places twenty times dearer than the place where I was born. My visit, so far as the topographical interests were concerned, was one of pure curiosity — a wish to see the familiar regions, and compare old impressions daguerreotyped, some firmly, some faintly, on a childish memory, with the vivid realities as they would appear, life-size, to a matured mind.

The place itself, I shall, for various reasons, not attempt to particularize, merely stating that it is anything but a romantic region, though one of much commercial importance, and that it lies — somewhere between Cornwall and Northumberland.

It was on a winter evening, long after dusk, that I found myself whirling thither by a branch-line of rail. In my time no such thing was thought of, and people used to have to join the one northern and southern route by a very inconvenient coach transit. Entirely nonplussed as to what course we were taking across the country, and likewise as to what length of time the journey would occupy, I determined to address my only fellow-traveller, a burly, comfortable-looking soul (or rather body, for matter had decidedly the predominance over mind).

He answered me very civilly, in the broad drawl which all classes have more or less in this my native county, and which, after all these years, I sometimes detect in my own speech. If ever I get in a passion I always storm in a —— shire accent.

"Ay, here we are," observed my fellow-traveller, apparently politely desirous to inform my ignorance as to our locality. "Look out o' th' window; there you may see th' fires. It's a rather cur'ous sight to a stranger."

I looked out at that sight — once unnoticed because so familiar to my childish eyes, but which now seemed strangely, awfully beautiful. It was the great furnace-fires that are seen everywhere in this district, blazing in near intervals, some lighting up one part of the sky, and some another, while the country between lies buried in a blackness the deeper for the contrast with such a vivid glow. I had not the least idea that my native place would appear so picturesque. But my unknown friend did not seem to perceive it any more than I had done in my childhood. To him these Dantesque, Rembrandtesque visions, were simply "th' fires," and nothing more.

We stopped at a small station, and I heard the guard bellowing from carriage to carriage, "E——! E——!" It quite made me start — it was such a familiar name. Many a time, in frosty winter days, the grand boundary of our childish walks used to be this place — first the mere nucleus of a manufacture — then growing into a small town. I remembered too, being greatly astonished to find its quaintly-given name in my Roman History, and reading Sir William Gell with a strange confusion between ancient E—— and modern E——. And to hear this and other names — long unheard and quite forgotten — shouted out at railway stations! It seemed so strange.

I reached my destination, a very quiet, sleepy, dirty town — which as a child I never much liked — there was no interest, no amusement, nothing stirring in it. — Surely, I must have made some mistake! Here is a large, bustling, handsome railway-station. "Porter, porter, can this be S—— ?"

It certainly is; though how they have evolved such a dazzling erection out of the little dirty town I knew, quite passes my comprehension. Aladdin's palace, or Sir Joseph Paxton's — an equal marvel — are harmlessly rivalled by my compatriots here.

"Do you want a cab? I'll get one from the hotel," says my friend, "the proud young porter."

I assent — dumb with astonishment — and start off.

So, I am really here at last? I am jolting in a carriage along the very streets once so familiar to my juvenile feet. If I looked out I should see the same familiar objects. It is a cold bitter night, but I pull down the glass, and gaze.

I have not the least recollection of anything I see. Lights, houses, shops, and streets, but all is quite strange. Then I recollect that, not knowing at what side of the town they have built that wondrous station, my puzzle is quite natural. Besides, it is night — there may be slight changes in the town, many things may be in fault, but — not my memory. I am very tenacious indeed of that.

A world of pains do I give myself in staring from each window, trying to make out where I am, and whither I am being driven. Surely we shall get to the high-road in time, and I *must* recognise that! I try to calculate which would be the direct way from S—— to the house whither I am bound. But I find that, though clear about the two places in themselves, I have so dim a recollection of the intermediate district, that were I on foot, I doubt if I could find my way. Nor do I even call to mind the precise distance of the road I have to traverse. A good deal humiliated at the faintness of childish memory, and the vagueness of childish topography, I throw myself back, giving the reins to destiny and my driver; and try to keep to those solemn thoughts which befit me — thus coming back alone to my old home, the last and only one of my household who will ever come back more.

Ah! — there's a church clock striking nine! It must be — yes, it is! — the very old clock I knew! It belongs to the church where we were christened, and where we used to go, across the fields, Sunday after Sunday, year after year — through the successive seasons of primroses, hawthorn, hedge-roses, blackberries, and frost. That was the way we then counted our cycles. Clang! clang! — it sounds just as clear and sharp as ever, like an old friend calling from another world. Or rather, it is I who seem the ghost from another world, coming back in the night-time and finding all things the same, except its own wandering airy sprite, which alone has no business there.

The pretty church and its steeple! I wish I could see them — but it is too dark. There are railings; perhaps we are passing the churchyard or the rectory-gates. A thought strikes me! Possibly they have built the railway station not in the town itself, but in those beautiful meadows behind the rectory, where the narrow river — afterwards growing one of the great rivers of England — ran so safely, and where we children used to be allowed to go a-fishing, being afterwards admitted to lunch at the rectory-house — an honour at which we were a great deal more frightened than pleased. If so, surely I know where I am.

In vain — street upon street, and town upon town, all converging upon and into one another, as they do here, glide past me, as I drive on. About every half-mile, as it seems, I am roused from my meditations by an imperative cry of "Toll!" which bewilders me more and more. I had no idea my native place was such a region of turnpike-gates — it certainly could not be so in *my* time. But then I recollect that in those days — and I thank Heaven for the same — I was not used to ride in carriages.

So I let myself be whirled on, occasionally looking out, just as if I were in a strange country, for I have long lost all clue to my whereabouts. The general likeness of things is familiar; the narrow streets, the tall warehouses, floor above floor; also the aspect of the people, rather peculiar in their way. I notice as with the observant eye of a stranger, the workmen with their linen sleeves and aprons, and pale faces, giving one a general notion of *whiteyness;* the work-girls, too, who in this district are remarkable for extraordinarily fair complexions, I watch them standing in groups, and think with a sort of patriotic satisfaction that I never saw anywhere a more respectable good-looking set of working people, earnestly wishing that despite low wages and Chartism they may always continue the same!

The towns fade behind me in darkness — we have reached a solitary road, banked on either side by *débris* of manufacture. Now again the lurid furnace fires appear glowing in every direction. The gas-lamps studding the road are quite pale beside them. It would be a region not unworthy the studies of a great painter or novelist, if such could ever come out of ———, this anonymous place, which I offer to my reader as a geographical puzzle.

There are two people talking earnestly under that lamp — a young workman and one of those neat-looking, fair-skinned girls, which, as I said, are, as a class, the prettiest working-girls I know of in England. They are surely "love-making," those two!

"Toll!" again! Insufferable! Still it must be paid, as surely and inevitably as the last toll of life, grimly exacted by the great turnpike-keeper of the universe. And I am now beyond all grumbling — fairly tired out. I even humble myself to ask of the tollman, meekly, and like an ordinary stranger, "How far is it to ———?"

"You're there," gruffly replies the man.

So I had reached the very gate — the well-known gate — the dear old gate — without recognising it. I felt half ashamed of myself, but had small time to think of myself at all. Then came the sweep of the gravel-walk — the great tree with its drooping branches — the hall-door open, casting out into the frosty night its glowing welcome ———. But the public in general has nothing to do with *that*.

The next day I went for a drive to revisit the old familiar spots. It was a thorough winter-day, such a day as I do not remember for years. I know not if the theory is borne out by meteorological evidence, but it seems to me that in my childish days the winters were much colder than they are now. Such long, keen, hard-bound frosts, lasting for weeks. Such snows, not falling in tiny showers, but snowing for days together, and leaving drifts under the hedges which lasted until April rains. Those were something like winters, indeed!

And it so happened — as if the more vividly to revive the memory of those days — that a sharp frost lay over the country. When I passed out of the railway region little change was visible. It might have been but yesterday since I had walked up the road, and seen the fields white with rime, and the shivering cows crawling about by hedge-sides. All came back as minutely as a Dutch picture, unlike every other landscape. Only, all seemed so very small. I seemed to view the scenery as with two distinct visions; one, that of my childhood, when a few narrow miles constituted the whole world; the other that of a stranger, seeing with matured eye, able to judge and compare. Once there flashed across me another picture — rivers, mountains, lakes, glorious scenes of nature, into which my spirit had plunged and bathed itself, as if in its pre-existent native element. My poor birth-place, with its quiet roads, smooth undulating meadows, and innocent cows! Not for worlds would I have droned out a lifetime there.

We neared a village that was always a favourite walk with me, my attraction being the parish church, so wondrously old, and its spire, so wondrously high. It tapered right into the sky, and was visible for miles. On its apex sat a gilded cock, for which I had a great reverence. I always associated something of the supernatural with this strange bird, sitting continually on his perch among the clouds, and turning round according as the wind blew. I had in secret mysterious doubts as to whether the wind controlled the bird, or the bird the wind — an awful idea! It was years before I got to look upon this quaint gilded ornithological pun as a mere weather-cock.

What a mystery to me hung over that ancient village temple! How, for years, I longed to go to church there, and sit among the old brasses and tombs! But I never did go — except creeping in stealthily one week-day, and peering often at the great east windows that looked so black and awful at night. I used to take good care we passed it very quickly, with a full conviction that inside the church, perhaps glowering out from the dusky window-panes, were — *what*, I did not dare to think.

There, too, in that quiet churchyard, I first heard the burial service. We were playing among the graves one sunny afternoon, and there entered a funeral — of some villager, probably. We were told to come away, but I stayed behind — near enough to hear the words, then new — alas! how familiar now!

I thought of that funeral as I passed by the old church this day.

The village held another object of attraction — a wondrous marsh, or rather, a common of marshy ground, studded with large water-holes. Very safe ponds they were; broad, shallow, magnificent for sliding and skating. So like old times the marsh looked — all in a frosty haze, with the red sun setting over the road before us, and on either hand boys clustering like bees on the various ponds, which were black and smooth as glass, the very perfection of skaters' ice.

So vivid was the delusion that for the moment I said to myself, "What a grand day for skating this will be for —— and —— and ——," naming boyish names that are now nearly all written upon grave-stones. I will speak of it no more.

On the Sunday I resolved on going to morning service at the church whose clock I had heard booming out near the railway-station — in fact the church where, strange to say, I quite well remembered being christened, circumstances having deferred that momentous ceremony till I was fully seven years old. I could to this day conjure up myself and the rest — wee toddling creatures — dressed (rather inappropriately), in braided frocks of crimson, of the which we were mightily proud. I could call up the desolate week-day-looking church, the silent chancel, the clergyman's cold wet finger signing my forehead. I remember I impiously rubbed it off — and went unblamed, no one in those lax days dreaming of the Gorham controversy.

The "New Church" it used to be called then — now, what a black-looking building! begrimed with the smoke of myriad chimneys. Another change, too, I discern: the churchyard, once studded here and there with solitary mounds, has become thickly populated with many years of dead. While the service-bell rings I stroll idly on along the path leading to the rectory gate. Here is no change; I could almost walk in and ask for one — whose name I know I shall find inscribed in the church-chancel, though, for all other memory, like many another virtuous name, "writ in water." But not so written — O thou long-suffering and much afflicted woman! — in the eternal Book of Life.

Coming back I overtake a long line of Sunday-school children — once my terror and aversion. But I forget that those my old enemies have long grown up, married, or died, and that these are a new generation, who instead of staring and mocking at the child, will drop innocent curtsies to the "stranger" lady as they pass.

I enter the church. All looks as it used to look. The great painted window with its sixteen Apostles, which furnished me with a perpetual puzzle during sermon-time, in trying to find out which was which, and in accounting for the four overplus, which I at last decided must be meant for a reduplication of Matthew, Mark, Luke, and John. The chancel, with its urns and monumental inscriptions, and marble figures, once white, new, and beautiful, but now wearing a grayish hue, the dust lying inches thick upon some of them.

I would fain have sat in our own old pew, but am placed in one opposite. Before service commences, I pause, and try to fill the church as it used to be filled. First, the rectory-pew, large, grand, and — desolate. Then the square, aristocratic pews, well cushioned, well lined, that occupied the middle aisle, where footmen usually walked up with prayer-books, and elderly ladies lounged through the service in sedate devotion. In great awe did I hold the occupants of those three or four pews.

Then, our own: it was just under the pulpit — a terrible fact! for both priest and clerk could easily see whether we were reading our prayer-books or not; and with infantile importance we fully believed that they *did* keep an eye upon our proceedings! In front was a large pew, called the "strangers' seat," and variously occupied. But close by was another whose occupants never changed. I see them now, the four old maiden sisters, sitting one in each of the four corners, dressed alike, yet with a slight difference of two and two. That is, two would wear bonnets trimmed with a mixture of gray and lilac, the two others gray and green; but the bonnets themselves — I could remember the identical ones — were precisely of the same make. Winter and summer their attire was of this dual fashion; they walked in church and out of church like automaton images; I never knew their names, or where they lived, or saw them anywhere else but there. At last, there used to come but three, then two — the odd two — who still kept up the slight variety in costume, and refused to amalgamate. Whether the others had married or died, I cannot tell, but the vision of the four sisters remains vividly fixed in my memory, a perpetual problem never to be solved.

The church rapidly fills — but strange faces are in every

pew. Of the whole congregation I do not recognise a single person. Half sighing, I go on mustering the spectral congregation of old times.

There was one pew, just in the shadow, whither a lame invalid lady used to crawl up the aisle, every fine Sunday, leaning on the arm of a servant; while her daughter — her only daughter — a pretty young lady, ultra-fashionable, walked on carelessly before. I remember I thought that strange, and did not like it at all. Doubtless, the invalid mother is long at rest — the daughter too, for all I know, unless that matronly lady sitting in the pew be she. But I do not care to look. The condemnatory prejudice of childhood affects me still.

There was another family in the pew to our left hand. The old lady was a grandmamma, dutifully cared for by daughter and son-in-law. How regularly they came to church, first, second, and third generation; and of what a wondrous deal of childish self-conceit on my part was that worthy old lady the cause, when she once patted my head after service, and praised me for my singing! If I did chant at the top of my juvenile voice for months after, who was to be blamed but she, for whose approbation I did it? Also a little — a very little, for the approbation (I fear never won!) of her grandson, a very tall, lanky boy, with an awkward stoop, but a most gentle face, who appeared at church at Midsummer and Christmas, and whom, in spite of all this my secret interest — which in its precocious fidelity lasted for several years — I never spoke to in my life!

I turn away, for the organ has commenced — the same organ that I in baby-fashion used to sing to. When I look again, the pew is filled. There is, sitting in the corner, where the old lady's son-in-law always sat, a tall, bending middle-aged man, his hair seamed with gray. It is a good face, very thoughtful, benevolent, sweet. Gradually there dawns in it a half-familiar likeness. Ha! I recognise it now. It is my old favourite, the tall, stooping boy! And there, sitting where his gentle old grandmamma used to sit, is his equally gentle-looking wife. In his sisters' place are those little girls, doubtless his children. They seem a happy family. But where are the rest? Swept away, probably, I know not how or where! But I look with a pensive yet pleasant interest on the pew, and think myself growing a very old person, since I have seen four generations successively sitting there.

The clerk mounts his desk — the same old clerk, but how much older! The stranger clergyman begins reading the service from the known desk; the winter sunshine gleams as ever through the painted Apostles of the gorgeous chancel window, throwing glittering hues of all shades and shapes on the chancel floor. These dancing tints, watched so often, fall on the very spots where they were wont to fall; the marble tablets, in gradations of black, grey, and white, which I spelled over during lapses of dimly-understood sermons; the monumental figures, especially one female, eternally weeping, with her arm thrown over an urn, in an attitude which I long puzzled over, and privately imitated, finally deciding that it was utterly impracticable to human limbs in anything but stone.

At length, the prism of rainbow-colours flits to a new and very lovely monument, which until now I have scarcely noticed. The pulpit partly hides it, but I can just see an upraised hand, and two half-expanded wings. It is an angel — life size — pointing upwards. How mysterious it looks, its pure white marble tinged with this many-hued glory, shed one sees not whence or how!

They commence the hymn after prayers. I read it out of the old "Collection," which I find lying here, every page of which is familiar. Hymn and tune too, were my favourites as a child; the Advent hymn, "Lo! He comes" — for this is Advent Sunday. I do not sing, somehow I cannot; but I listen, my lips moving to the tune, my eyes fixed on the glittering wings and upward-pointed hand of the marble angel.

"Oh, come quickly!
Hallelujah! Come, Lord, come."

As the hymn thus ceases, the prismatic tints fade from the angel's wings. A snow-cloud is sweeping past the church windows. I shut my eyes, and think less of what was, or what is, than of *what will be*. Amen!

* * * *

The next morning, very early, I go away, scarce regretting though it should be for ever, from "the place where I was born."

A BRIDE'S TRAGEDY.

PART I.

It was Alice Wynyard's wedding-day. I had had a weary two months, for our household atmosphere was full of storms. My good cousin John Wynyard long withstood all my arguments and his daughter's tears, before he would take Mr. Sylvester for his son-in-law. I could never clearly understand how Alice learned to love her betrothed, but love him she did; and I saw it was breaking the heart of the child to part her from him; so I threw all my influence into the scale, until at last we gained the point. And yet I did it more for the sake of my Alice — the motherless child who had been my darling for seventeen years — than from regard towards her chosen. I could not teach myself to like that wayward, fitful, gloomy Arthur Sylvester; yet perhaps it was only a vague jealousy — and one feeling more.

I knew that my nephew Everard — my treasure next to Alice — loved her with every pulse of his true and noble heart. She never guessed it, — no one in the world did, save me. I only understood him — since for twenty years all the shut-up tenderness of my soul had centred themselves in that boy.

I went into Alice's room late on the night before her wedding. She had been reading in the Bible — her dead mother's Bible — her forehead rested on the open page, and her hands were clasped together. I stayed at the door, — I could not choose but look at her, — so beautiful was she in her attitude of graceful *abandon*, her white drapery, and her long, loose-falling hair. I heard her lips murmur — she was praying for *him*.

"Bless my Arthur — my own — my husband!"

"Amen!" said I, softly, as I touched her shoulder, and she started from her seat. Her eyes sought mine with a doubtful look, as if they would pierce into my soul.

"You think he has need of blessing," cried she, suddenly. "Ah! I know, there is no one here who loves him but me."

"I said not so, Alice."

"No! but you thought it, Aunt Susan," — she always called me aunt, though we were only second cousins. "Well, I care not, my love shall make amends to him for all. My Arthur, my noble Arthur! How dare they doubt him?" said Alice, proudly, as she drew herself up, and her head was thrown back, and her lips curled, while from her eyes beamed ineffable love. How perfect was the young heart's faith in its idol! My eyes swam in tears; I shrank abashed before that gentle child, so strong in her loving trust. I would, at that moment, have staked my life for the worth of a man who could inspire an attachment so fervent and faithful.

In my thoughts that night Alice's bridegroom seemed to me nearer perfection than I had ever deemed him. But I had no time for dreaming — the wedding-day was come! O ye romantic damsels! know that a wedding-day brings other thoughts than those of trembling happy love, and cupids, and rose-fetters. Scorn not the old-maid housekeeper if she confesses, that while her first thought was of sweet Alice, her second was of the wedding-breakfast, lest aught should mar the effect of the whole, and change to wintry storms the passing autumn-sunshine which we had brought to Mr. Wynyard's countenance.

I did not go with them to church — I could not.

"Miss Susan never thinks about such things; her time for lovers and weddings is past, if it ever existed," I heard one of the bridesmaids whisper. "She never cared for any one, or any one for her."

O heart, be still! what is the babble of foolish tongues to thee? Thou hast throbbed and grown calm; let the days of thy youth be like a troubled dream. With thee the night is passing — it is near morning! Be still — be still!

When Alice *Sylvester* entered her father's doors, I was there waiting for her. I took her in my arms and kissed her; she wept a little, but it was only a summer shower; her whole face trembled and dimpled with happiness. I unfastened her white bonnet, and smoothed her hair; but she said she would come with me until breakfast was ready, and unlinked her arm from her bridegroom's. He looked restless and uneasy, his wild black eyes wandering from one to the other with a troubled gaze.

"You will not go, Alice?" he said, holding her hand fast "I must not lose you."

"Only for a few moments, dear Arthur," she answered; and then, seeing how agitated he appeared, she laid her hand on his with a soothing smile, and whispered, "No more parting: no one can part us now, my *husband*."

He took her in his arms, kissed her, and ere she was out of sight I saw him dash into the garden, leaving the wedding-party to think of it as they would. "Truly, a strange bridegroom!" muttered some of them; and the father's face grew so dark that I trembled for the consequences.

"Thank Heaven, Alice is right: no one can part them now," I thought to myself, as I followed the bride up-stairs.

She was very quiet and composed, thoughtful for me and for all in the house; leaving messages and tokens for friends and dependents, and forgetting no one.

"I should have been less sorry to go, Aunt Susan, if my father had not been so kind latterly. He will learn to know and appreciate my Arthur in time, I think. I am glad that our wedding has been with his consent; it is much happier. But," she added, while her cheek flushed, and her eye dilated, "had it not been so, no power on earth should have parted Arthur from me; I would have married him, and followed him to the world's end. I dare say it now, for I am his wife, and God only knows how I love my husband!"

How fondly the girl's lips lingered over those new, sweet words, "*my husband!*" I could only press her to my heart, and inly pray that such a love might know no cloud.

"There is Arthur, walking in the shrubbery!" cried the bride, as her quick eye caught a sight of his figure. "He is weary of waiting for me, — I have kept him too long alone. Forgive me, dear Aunt Susan," she continued, hesitating, and slightly blushing, "it is not that I love you less — but — but —."

"Go to your husband, my Alice," said I, trying to smile through my tears; I felt a light kiss on my forehead, and in a few moments more I saw a white dress fluttering through the trees leading to the little summer-house. Ah, well! I ought to have known before now, that a maiden regards all the world as nothing in comparison with him she loves.

"Where are the bride and bridegroom? We want to cut the cake over their heads," said the sportive damsels who had attended their late playfellow to the altar.

"Ay — where is Alice? she might think of her old father a little," grumbled Mr. Wynyard.

"She is walking in the garden — I sent her," I hastily apologized.

"You, cousin! — What business had you to do any such thing! Go and fetch her directly." And I hurried away.

The summer-house was at the end of a pleasant shady walk. I knew I should find the young lovers there, for it was a place they both loved — the place where their hearts had first broken the spell of silence, and poured out their secret, each to each. There was something sacred in the spot ever after. I trod softly, and lingered on my way; but ere I reached the summer-house, there arose from it a woman's cry — long, shrill, terrible. O horror! I hardly knew my Alice's voice. I rushed forward — the door was fastened — I burst it open with superhuman strength.

There, on the floor, crouched the bride; her eyes starting with fear, her face frozen into an expression of the wildest terror. Blood was flowing from her arm — drop by drop falling on her white dress. Over her stood the bridegroom, glaring upon her with his frenzied eyes, while in his uplifted hand sparkled a knife. I sprang in — he let it fall — and dashed, with a yell like that of a wild beast, across the fields.

Arthur Sylvester had gone mad on his wedding-day!

* * * * *

It was not until many weeks after that fearful bridal, that my Alice lifted up her head from the pillow to which I had borne her like an infant. She had received no wound except the slight one in her arm which had probably intercepted the first blow of the maniac, and thereby saved her life. But this we could only conjecture, for she refused to reveal to human being what passed in that fatal summer-house. When she became convalescent, Alice never uttered her husband's name, nor, by word or look, gave any sign that she remembered the past. Only once, when she lay regarding her wasted fingers, a sudden thought seemed to flash across her mind — the wedding-ring was not there. I had taken it away by the physician's order, that during her illness there should be no connecting link to awaken thoughts so terrible. Alice looked at me earnestly and pointed to her third finger. I would not understand her.

"Another time, my child, when you are better," I whispered. "You must not think now. Try to sleep, my Alice." But still she kept her hand stretched out, with her imploring eyes fixed on mine. It was impossible to resist. I took the fatal circlet and placed it on her finger: she seized it as a child would its toy-treasure; kissed it, and then folding the wedded left hand in the other, laid it in her bosom, and turned her head away. God knows what vague thoughts passed through the weak and still confused brain of that young creature. I watched her as she lay, and fancied I saw tears starting from under the closed eyelids; but she seemed calm, and soon fell asleep through feebleness.

From that time Alice gradually improved. Her shattered mind and body gathered strength together, and, by slow degrees, she became almost herself again. In the early days of her convalescence, we had taken her far away from the home which had witnessed so terrible a scene; and had made our abode in a quiet, lonely, sea-side village — Alice, her old father, and I. We would not let the world's curiosity torture the desolate bride.

My cousin Wynyard was almost as much to be pitied as his child. At first he had been nigh frantic with anguish, not unmixed with anger; had cursed his own folly in ever consenting to the marriage, and poured terrible anathemas on the head of him whom a higher power had so fearfully stricken. Many were the causes assigned for the sudden paroxysm which had left the admired Arthur Sylvester that awful spectacle, a living body without a reasoning soul. Many whispered of the power of conscience, and of some mysterious sin, thus justly punished. True, the world said Arthur Sylvester had lived, in his early youth a gay, thoughtless life — but the world is a harsh judge over the unfortunate. It could not be that my pure Alice had loved one who was a sinner of so deep a dye, that his own conscience had been to him as the thunderbolt of Heaven's vengeance. It was a mystery too deep to penetrate. My very soul shuddered when I thought of the proud and handsome bridegroom — a howling maniac in his cell; the noble form degraded — the lofty mind, which Alice had so worshipped, shattered and sunk into idiotic weakness. Oh, poor Alice! had she but heard what I heard of that unfortunate! — nay, even stern John Wynyard, whose heart was so full of bitterness against the destroyer of his peace, even he would have melted into tears, had he listened to the tale.

It was my nephew, Everard Brooke, whom I charged to bring me tidings of Alice's husband. He did so — he sought out the maniac, who had fled wildly over the country — watched over him, and guarded him from doing injury to himself or to others, until he was restored to his friends. When Everard told me how he had left Arthur Sylvester, idly playing with straws, talking to his own shadow and calling it Alice Wynyard, while his aged mother sat weeping over him, I felt thankful that his name had never been uttered by Alice, so that I could still keep her in ignorance of his mournful state.

With Everard only could I talk calmly over what had passed, and what was to be done for the future. My cousin Wynyard would bear no allusion to the unhappy man; the moment I mentioned Arthur's name he would burst out into invectives and imprecations that made my blood run cold.

"God's curse is upon him, and mine; therefore it is that he bears the burden of his sin," John Wynyard would cry. "His name is hateful in my ears — utter it no more!"

"But Alice loved him — he is her husband."

"It is a lie! — I madly gave her to him — and I reclaim her: I made the bond, and I will break it." Thus raved Alice's father; and, at the time, I did not heed his words, but I soon found out their purport.

One day, when he came to pay his daily visit to Alice's chamber, she, in talking to him, laid her left hand on his arm. The wedding-ring shone brightly on the thin white finger. It caught his eye; and immediately his whole countenance darkened. He put the hand aside, and walked out of the room. Immediately I was summoned to his presence.

"Cousin Susan, how dare you let Alice wear that accursed ring? Did not Dr. Egerton take it from her finger, and say she was never to see it?"

"But the poor child entreated. Oh, cousin, if you had seen her look! I could not keep it from her; I cannot take it away."

"But I say you shall. Take it off, Susan; hide it — steal it — or I shall hate my own child."

"It is cruelty to take from a wife her wedding-ring."

"I tell you, she is no wife. Marriage with a madman is no marriage at all. I can free her; and I will." And the storm of passion began to rise so violently that it was a joyful escape for me, when Alice's maid summoned me to her mistress.

She was weeping — my poor child! "Why did my father go away — is he angry? Ask him to come back again, Aunt Susan. What have I done to offend him? Do not deceive me — tell me the truth; *you* always do." And her eyes were fixed so earnestly on mine that for my life's worth I could not have framed an excuse.

"You must not feel pained, my dearest," I whispered; "your father will get over it in time — but now he does not like to see — this;" and I touched the ring.

I expected Alice would have wept more than ever; but not so. Her tears ceased, and the low complaining tone of sickness became firm and composed.

"What does my father desire, Aunt Susan?"

"That you would take it off — and not wear it for a little."

I started to see the sick girl rise from her pillowed chair, and stand upright on her feet, in an attitude of almost fierce defiance.

"How dares my father ask this? Can he expect me — a wife — to give up the symbol of my marriage? I will not do it. I am a wife without a husband — a wife only in name; but I will keep that name while I live. Go and tell my father so!"

She sank back in her chair, and I saw she trembled like an aspen leaf, though her words were so firm. I laid her head on my bosom, and soothed her like a child. Then her feelings burst forth in one long, mournful cry.

"Oh, aunt, you knew my heart was broken — why did you torture it thus?"

A wretch that had committed murder could not have felt more guilty than I did then.

After a time Alice's words became more calm. "It is well, perhaps, that I dare now speak of what lies day and night upon my heart like a leaden weight. Aunt Susan, answer me truly. Where is Arthur? where is my husband?"

"He is safe at home — but he is —."

"I know it — you need not utter the horrible word. Oh, my Arthur — my own! Why did I live to see this day?"

She said no more, but lay back in her chair. For hours she remained motionless, with folded hands and closed eyes, looking like a marble statue. I sat beside her, pondering mournfully over the long, dark future which lay before that young creature of just eighteen: widowhood, without its patient hopelessness — without the calm and holy shadow of death, which in time brings peace to the most bruised heart. I thought of her, and then of *him*, and I knew not which seemed the most bitter lot — that of the maniac husband, or the worse than widowed wife.

After this painful scene, Alice became so much worse that her father was considerably alarmed. I told him what had passed between us, every word; and he did not make a single reply. I led him where Alice lay, in a heavy slumber, approaching to insensibility, and I saw that he was touched. He wished to send for Dr. Egerton; but I told him it was useless, that calmness of mind alone was necessary for Alice's recovery. He could not understand how any mental agitation could have made her so much worse — men never can. The wise ones! they can feel for the agony of a broken limb, but they have no sympathy for a broken heart. Well! I am an old maid — I have a right to speak of the other sex as I list; and I can truly affirm that I never knew but one man living who had a really feeling heart.

Yes — I except one more; and that was my dear good Everard. He was a comforter and a strengthener to me in all this sad time. To an almost womanlike tenderness he united clear sense and firmness such as few men can boast. In Mr. Wynyard's first paroxysm of anger and despair, Everard's influence over him was marvellous. My own, alas! was considerably weakened; for it was hardly surprising that, in the blindness of his wrath and sorrow, my cousin reproached me for this marriage, which I had urged through love towards my sweet child. Perhaps I was wrong; and yet, were the time to come over again, I think I should do the same. Everard stood manfully between me and the torrent of wrath; he was an angel of peace and consolation. Yet this was he whose heart the arrow had pierced; and I knew it was there still, and must remain for ever. Noble, self-denying Everard! When, as Alice recovered, I saw him watching her like a brother (poor girl! in her unsuspicious nature she considered him as such), striving to divert her thoughts, soothing the conflicting passions of father and daughter, and never by word or look giving sign of what I knew was in his heart, — then I felt rejoiced that there was one man in the world who loved truly and unselfishly. It restored my faith in the whole sex.

After the little episode of the wedding-ring, John Wynyard's anger seemed to lull. He said no more on the subject; and, after a time, Everard persuaded him to visit his daughter again. What innumerable feminine contrivances did I use lest the obnoxious ring should again catch his eye! such as hiding the poor erring left hand in my own affectionate clasp, or finding out the prettiest pair of gloves in the world, to keep the thin, pale fingers warm during winter-time. Whether he yielded to Alice's determination or not, I cannot tell; but he said nothing. However, by degrees, his manner grew harsh and bitter; he would sit for whole hours in silence, and spend morning after morning in consultations with his lawyer. Somehow or another that man's entrance always boded evil; he was a bird of ill-omen — the creature! with his wiry voice, his hooked nose, and his sharp black eyes. I disliked him heartily, for I knew there was some fresh vagary dawning in John Wynyard's brain. At last the storm burst.

We — that is, Everard, my cousin, and I — were sitting round the fire, after Alice had retired; poor thing! she always crept away early, and said often and often that during sleep was her only happy time. How sad it was, this longing for even a temporary oblivion! I wondered not at those who seek repose in another and a deeper sleep.

"Susan," said Mr. Wynyard, suddenly breaking a dead, uncomfortable silence which had fallen upon us, "has Alice given up that foolish notion about the ring?"

I hardly knew what to answer, but Everard spoke for me.

"Surely, sir, you will not revive a subject so painful. Let it rest, for Alice's sake."

"It is exactly for her sake that I will not let it rest. And now, cousin Susan, and Everard, I will tell you what I have been long thinking about, and what I intend to do. My girl shall not be tied for life to a villain — a madman."

"Hush, hush, cousin!" I entreated, "speak not thus of him; remember, he is Alice's husband in the sight of God and man."

"But the marriage can be dissolved — and it shall; my child shall not bear the name of a wretch, an assassin. The law shall make her free. If it costs me half my fortune, by Heaven it shall!" and he struck the table violently, uttering a stronger asseveration than I dare write.

"My poor Alice! it will break her heart," was all I could say.

"Pooh, pooh! girls' hearts are not so easily broken. Five years hence she will thank me for this. At eighteen to be bound for life to a maniac — a widow, without a widow's freedom — no, cousin; neither law, common-sense, nor justice, can sanction that."

There was reason in what he said — I could not deny it. Alice was only a girl; and girlhood's love, warm and gushing as it is, will change sometimes. If the time should come when she might find the nominal tie to which her riven soul now clung so fondly, a burden and a galling chain — if she should love again, or another should love her — — I turned to look at Everard; his face was ashen, his lips were compressed, as if in a spasm of acute pain. A hope — wild, mad, as passing as a meteor, but yet a distinct hope — had entered his soul; and a reaction from despair to even a glimmer of joy was such that it became positive suffering. He was like a man brought suddenly from freezing cold to light and warmth, to whom the change gives sharp but momentary pain through the entire frame.

God forgive me, if, when I looked at him, I forgot even Alice's sorrow! If she could be free — if she could be brought in time to love him — so noble as he was — so faithful — so true-hearted; superior to Arthur Sylvester in all things save in outward appearance. Nay, to me he seemed as handsome as Alice's chosen. But then it was not young Everard alone that I saw in the clear brown eyes, the soft curling hair, so dear and well known of old!

"Have neither of you a word to say?" cried John Wynyard, impatiently, after a long silence. "But perhaps it is as well; for I tell you my mind is made up — this very day I have taken the first legal steps in the affair. Everard Brooke, you are a man of sense, though you are but young; tell me, am I not right? — Alice must consent."

Everard lifted up his head like one roused from a dream.

"It is so sudden — I can hardly say — you must consider this well before you act, Mr. Wynyard."

"I tell you I have considered, and fully: you are a man, and will at once see the justice of the case; but as for cousin Susan there, with her womanish nonsense about feelings and broken hearts, why, she must e'en get over them as fast as she can, and persuade Alice to do so too. A fine thing to have a madman for a son-in-law! and my pretty Alice pining her life away in her father's house, neither old maid, wife, nor widow, when she might have the best men in England at her feet. I will endure no such thing: Arthur Sylvester is hateful to me; I will not suffer my child even to bear his name. I tell you I will have the marriage annulled!"

Louder and louder grew John Wynyard's tones; his vehement gestures and excited looks engrossed the attention of us both, so that neither Everard nor I observed that the door opened, and a fourth person stood among us.

It was Alice; and she had heard all!

If a ghost from the dead had risen up in the midst, we could not have looked more aghast. And, truly, the girl's own appearance was like that of the dead rather than the living. She walked up to her father's chair, caught his arm convulsively, and looked into his face with her stony eyes until he seemed absolutely to quail beneath them. At last there came from between her white lips words terribly calm: —

"Father, you say my husband is mad — I know it — but I am his wife still. You never shall annul our marriage with my will. If you can do it without — try. And I will curse you to your face, and die."

When she had said this, her whole frame seemed to collapse, like that of a corpse suddenly animated, and then sinking down again, cold, still, and dead, as before. Her arms fell, her eyes closed, and Everard carried her out totally insensible.

My cousin Wynyard was not on the whole a harsh man, still less an unkind father; but he had vehement antipathies, and was obstinacy itself when he once determined on a project; nay, such are the ins and outs of human nature, that generally the worse the scheme, the more he was bent upon it. His hatred for poor Arthur Sylvester outweighed even his love for Alice. In his determination there might have been some lingering of care for her future, as he had stated, but I verily believe he thought of himself first and his child second. He would have moved the whole world, have sacrificed everything he loved, rather than that the blot of Sylvester's name should ever darken the family pedigree of the Wynyards. Scarcely had Alice recovered, when he began the attack again. This time, however, he put me entirely out of the question, regarding mo as an ally on the other side, and tried to enlist my nephew in his cause.

Now came the struggle in Everard's breast. Day after day he listened to Mr. Wynyard's arguments, until hope — vague as it was — whispered to him that there was reason in them, and that the cold-hearted father might be right after all. Then, on the other hand, when he saw the face of the broken-spirited girl, he hated himself for conceiving this wild hope, the fulfilment of which must be purchased by such torture to her. Poor Alice grew paler and paler every day, but neither threats nor arguments could induce her to give her consent, and without it Mr. Wynyard knew the divorce could not be legally accomplished. He entreated Everard to try and persuade her.

"You were children together," he said one day, when in Alice's absence he was discussing the usual agonizing subject with Everard, while I sat in a corner, my lips closed, but my ears open. "Everard, Alice would always listen to you — she was so fond of you — you two were like brother and sister, as one may say. If you would persuade her she might consent. The lawyer comes to-morrow, and I want to do things quietly. We might soon get the formalities over, and Alice would be free."

"Alice free! Alice free!" muttered Everard; and his whole countenance brightened. But in a moment it fell again. "Mr. Wynyard, this is cruel! — I cannot — dare not urge her. Do not ask me!"

"You are a fool, Everard Brooke," angrily returned Mr. Wynyard. "Don't you see it is for Alice's good? — A woman is no use in the world at all, unless she has half-a-dozen children and a house to be mistress of. I want to see my girl really married to some one I like — some on who will make her happy — in short, just such a fellow as yourself, Everard! — Who knows but she might marry you?"

Everard grew very pale, and his lips trembled; but he

drew himself up, and said, proudly — "Mr. Wynyard, I do not understand this jesting."

"Pshaw, you foolish boy, you are standing in your own light! Do you think that I cannot see as far through a stone wall as most people? You and Alice used to play at husband and wife when she was a baby; and you, at least, would have kept up the game now, but for that man — I wish he had been dead before Alice saw him! But, to speak plainly, Everard Brooke, I see you would be well content to have Alice for a wife; and you may take her with my good-will and blessing."

Everard covered his face with his hands. Oh, how bitter was the strife! Love fighting against love — the earthly passion which desires its own bliss, against the holy, pure, divine essence, in which self is absorbed and annihilated, which seeks only the happiness of the beloved one! Everard! — dear Everard! — how my heart clung to thee in that struggle!

Mr. Wynyard's coarse voice broke the dead silence: "Well, my dear boy, you see I am right now; you will help me — and gain the best little wife in England in the bargain. See, there she is, walking in the garden. Go and persuade her, and we will have all right directly."

Everard lifted up his head, and saw Alice as she slowly passed the window. Her gait, her attitude, showed utter dejection; there was neither life, nor hope, in the marble-like face that drooped upon her bosom. Her eyes had no expression save that of vague apathy — she looked the picture of stricken despair. Everard started to his feet in a burst of indignation: —

"Mr. Wynyard, if you have any feeling, see there! Is that the girl you would make an object of barter — a bribe — regarding her own free choice as little as if it were your horse, instead of your child, that you were disposing of? Sir — I will not be a party to such cruelty."

"Then you scorn my daughter — you despise her?" muttered Mr. Wynyard between his set teeth.

"Scorn Alice! — despise Alice!" repeated Everard.

"Yes; you came here with your pining and puling, and it was all false! *You* love her, indeed!"

Every muscle of Everard's face quivered, and yet he tried to speak calmly.

"Mr. Wynyard, I will tell you what I never breathed before, because I knew it was in vain — that I do love Alice — that I have loved her from boyhood — that I would give my life and soul for her. And because I loved her, I never told her this, lest it should cause her a moment's pain. Can I torture her poor broken spirit now? No; it would be cowardly — dishonourable. To win Alice, I would sacrifice everything, save her peace and my own honour."

How the spirit of true love — the earnest, the self-denying — shone out in every lineament of young Everard's face as he spoke! Surely the good angel which had triumphed in his soul stood behind him invisibly, and shed upon him brightness and glory. How strange that Alice had not loved my Everard!

My cousin Wynyard stood a few moments, confounded; he was unprepared to meet such firmness. It incensed him beyond endurance. In a burst of anger, such as I had rarely witnessed even in him, he rushed to his own study, locking the door with violence.

Then I crept out from my corner, where Mr. Wynyard's commands had sealed my tongue, and went up to my dear nephew. I laid my hand on his shoulder: —

"Everard, my own, good, noble Everard, take comfort!"

He seized my hands, pressed his forehead upon them, and wept like a child.

My life has been lonely; it was my destiny. No child has ever nestled in my bosom, and called me "mother" — the yearnings, the mysteries of maternity, were not for me to know — and yet, had it been otherwise, there is love in my heart's depths that would, I feel it would, have answered to the call. But, if ever I experienced the faint shadowings of what mother-love must be, it was when I bent over Everard Brooke, and tried to pour comfort into his bruised spirit. In that hour I could have shed the dearest blood of my own heart to bring peace to his.

Everard went away, and Alice was not told of the cause of his departure; even John Wynyard had sufficient delicacy and good feeling to agree with this; but not the less did he persevere in his constant endeavours to win over Alice to his will. And I — my heart was torn by conflicting feelings: on one side Alice and her sorrows — on the other, Everard; why, oh! why was it that these two had not loved one another and been happy? At times I was almost ready to acknowledge that my cousin Wynyard had the right on his side after all, and that his persecution was only the rough but kindly ministering of the leech, who wounds for a time in order to heal at last.

The wisest of all wise men says, "A continual dropping weareth away the stone," and so it was in the case of my poor Alice. Yet, perchance, her consent might never have been gained to the act which parted her from a husband so passionately loved, had not fate overruled matters so as to win from grief and filial duty the concession which would never have been yielded to threats and harshness. Mr. Wynyard fairly stormed and argued himself into a severe illness; and then, like most men, he grew alarmed, felt sure that his doom was come, and took most touching farewells of all the household. My poor Alice, struck with terror and remorse by what she believed the result of her own opposition to her father, promised solemnly to fulfil his dying injunction (I must say this for my good cousin, that he really thought himself *in articulo mortis*), and consent to the legal process, easily attainable under the tragical circumstances, which declared her marriage with Arthur Sylvester to be null and void.

The deed was done — that evil genius, Lawyer Doubletongue, effected it without delay — and Alice was free. I shall never forget the day when that hateful Double-tongue first addressed Alice as *Miss Wynyard*.

She had moved about the whole morning, pale, dreamy, and silent, only seeming conscious of herself when beside her invalid father. But the instant that name struck on her ear — the signal that all was over — that she was Arthur's wife no longer — it had the effect of a thunder-clap. She drew up her tall stature with icy haughtiness, and looked at the mean shrinking fellow before her as though she could have trodden him under foot.

"'This to me, sir! you forget yourself!" And then her tone changed — she glanced wildly round, pressed her hand to her brow, "No, no! it is I who forget. Ah me! ah me! all is over!" She fled from the room, and I found her lying ... floor of her own chamber in strong convul-

...t fearful struggle, and the last. Alice and
e parted. Alas! this was of little moment
...ac, who was doomed to spend his life in

darkness — the most awful darkness, the darkness of the soul. But with all my pity for the unhappy Sylvester, I felt a vague relief in knowing, that whether he recovered or not, Alice could be no more to him than the stranger in the street: they were husband and wife no longer — not even in name.

PART II.

Who would wish that the days of youth should last for ever? or even that their memory should be eternal? No — let them go: let their stormy joys and aching sorrows be alike blotted out; let the after-growth of calmer feelings shut them from sight; even as when you wound a young tree, the bark grows over it in time until the cleft is seen no more. So it is with the griefs of youth. Life is continually changing, or we could not endure the fourscore years that make up our longest span. There is in the Infinite ordering of the world no blessing greater than that of mutability.

Alice Wynyard at seven-and-twenty was no more like the grief-stricken bride of seventeen, than I in my gray hairs am like a blithesome child, a dreamy maiden, of whom I can dimly remember; — in my prayers I lift up a thankful heart that those days are now more dim than a dream at morning. But it is not of myself that I write; it is of Alice. A broken heart was not her doom: I ought, when I prophesied this, to have known better. Who should know more than I, how much one can endure and live? Alice left her girlhood behind, and grew up into placid, patient, thoughtful womanhood; a womanhood bearing the goodlier fruit because the stern hand of affliction had torn off a few of its early blossoms. The soul, like a tree, needs much pruning to make its fruit perfect and abundant.

Alice was an heiress, and independent; for her father had died not many years after he had gained his heart's wish, and seen her free. He had not attained one desire, though; for his daughter firmly refused all offers of marriage. Once or twice he gently and tenderly murmured against this, but Alice's answer was conclusive: —

"Father, I have done your will — I can do no more."

And he soon ceased to urge her. Indeed, so penetrated

was John Wynyard by the patient obedience which had renounced so much, that from the time of the divorce until his death I never knew him give Alice an unkind look or an angry word. His whole soul seemed bound up in her; he lived but to anticipate her every wish; and his character became so utterly changed, from sternness to gentleness and forbearance, that when at last he died no man was more fervently mourned by his whole household than was Mr. Wynyard. But he passed away, and I remained, the last of my generation, honoured and beloved in the home of which Alice was mistress. Now more than ever, did wooers come to lure her from that home, but in vain. I was glad of it: there was no man living to whom I could have cheerfully given my Alice, save to Everard Brooke.

It was not until after Mr. Wynyard's death that my dear nephew returned from abroad, and sought us out. One of my cousin's latest charges had been that Everard should be told how much their angry parting had grieved him, and how sincerely he had honoured to the last that noble spirit which he then offended. Another charge he also privately left to my discretion, that if, when Everard and Alice met again, my nephew still loved her, they were both to be told that the wish for such a union had lain nearest the dying father's heart. They did meet, and I saw how true Everard had kept to his early dream. After one little month spent in her constant society, he loved Alice the woman ten thousand times more passionately than Alice the sweet childlike idol of his boyhood. And she — how did she feel towards him? This was a secret that with all my skill I could not penetrate. She was frank, sincere, affectionate, seemed to delight in his presence, was dull without him, and openly said so; but there were none of those tremulous tones, those fitful blushes, that mark a maiden's dawn of love. She was as serene as a summer sky at noon.

At last Everard's suspense grew to agony, and mine was not much less. I urged him to learn the whole truth from her lips — she could not but requite a love so true. He mentioned with visible tremor the name, not breathed for years, of Arthur Sylvester. I told him what I had lately learned by chance, and had communicated to no living soul, that the maniac had, after his mother's death, partially recovered his reason, and left the country, to go no one knew whither, nor had he since been heard of. Everard drew a long sigh of relief, and his face glowed with emotion, hope, and love. I looked at him as he stood before me with his noble manly port, and his whole bearing replete with the conscious dignity of one who had won and held a position of honour in the world.

"My dear Everard," I whispered, fondly, "there is no woman living who would not be proud of your love."

He smiled, but faintly; I urged him the more.

"I cannot speak to her, Aunt Susan," he said, "my heart would burst; but I will write, then I can tell all, and you shall give her the letter with your own hands."

He left us that night, and the day afterwards his letter came. I watched her while she read it. Her face wore at first a surprised, almost frightened look; but as she went on, I could see how deeply she was touched by the earnest outbreathings of that noble heart whose whole life's love was thus at last poured out at her feet. The tears gathered to her eyes, and she became very pale.

"Aunt," she said, coming towards me with the letter in her hand, "I never dreamed of this; poor Everard! Why did he never tell me before?"

"Because he would have died rather than have given you pain, my Alice!" And then, with an earnestness that came from my inmost heart, I told Alice the true reason of Mr. Wynyard's quarrel with Everard, and ended by informing her of her father's last wish, that such faithfulness might be requited at last.

"My dear father — my kind father!" she murmured, tremulously. "And you wish it too, Aunt Susan; I see you do."

I could not deny it. With tears I prayed her to try and give Everard the love he sought.

"I — to love! I — to marry! it sounds strange!" and she shuddered visibly all over. At last, speaking with a strong effort, she said, "Aunt Susan, I never told you — I could not; but three years ago, just before the fever I had, I heard that *he died* in the West Indies. I could not learn how; but — but — *he died.*" And she wept. I saw by their calmness that they were a widow's quiet tears. She had outlived her agony.

Was it a sin that there rose up in my heart a thanksgiving

— that the clouded soul of the poor maniac was gone where He who gave could restore it to its original glory?

"Aunt Susan," Alice continued, after a pause, "you must give me time — time: I must search my own heart, for I feel bewildered. I know Everard's worth — he is very dear to me — you may tell him so — but to love him as he asks — as a wife, I never dreamed of that; to-morrow — no — the day after, I will decide."

She kissed me, and moved, with an agitated step, to her own apartments. I saw her no more, alone, until the morning of the second day; then she approached me with a calm, sweet look, and said —

"To-day, in an hour, let Everard come to me."

They were together a long time — an age it seemed to me, as I sat in my own chamber, my heart fluttering like that of a girl. How well I loved those two! how earnestly I prayed that they might love one another! At last Everard came and pressed his lips to my cheek. I felt his tears, tears for which no man need blush; but they were the overflow of joy. Alice had accepted him!

Now all the friends that surrounded our quiet country home were full of curiosity and congratulations. The affianced lovers were courted, admired, envied. During the time which intervened between the engagement and the appointed wedding, I was perfectly bewildered with dinner parties abroad and at home. I sometimes thought that Alice would better have shrunk from this gaiety, and hid herself in her own happiness, as maiden-love would fain ever do. But hers was not that love; I felt it was not. Warmly, affectionately, as she regarded her betrothed, it was not the one true love of woman's life, compared to which all on earth is not once weighed in the balance. But Everard, thinking of himself so little, and of her so much, never saw this; and I trusted to the might of his love — love is so strong to win a return! — they might be happy when once united.

It was not one week before the marriage-day that, Everard having quitted us, Alice and I went to dine with some acquaintances whom we both liked — friends we could not have called any of our society, for not one among them knew us as otherwise than what we appeared to the world — Miss Wynyard and her maiden aunt. In that quiet spot where we settled, we took care that the history of the past should not follow us, to be a bye-word and a mark for intrusive pity or insolent curiosity.

I thought, as we drove to our destination, that Alice had not for years looked so cheerful, or so calmly happy. In that beautiful face there was not a trace of girlhood's sufferings, save in a chastened thoughtfulness which lent additional sweetness to its expression. I could not restrain my admiration.

"Beautiful, am I?" answered Alice, with a quiet smile; "but then, I am getting ancient, dear aunt; who can think me beautiful at seven-and-twenty?"

"Everard does, my dearest," said I, rather mischievously. I would have given anything to see on that fair cheek a deeper blush than the faint hue which crept there and passed away.

"Ah, you and Everard think of me thus, because you love me so well. But here we are at our journey's end."

"Miss Wynyard, have you seen our new neighbour at the Priory?" inquired one of the young ladies, who vied with each other in paying Alice attention — it might be under the influence of foreshadowings of bride-cake and flowers.

"No, truly," was the reply; "who is he?"

"We scarcely know, but that he is a rich, unmarried man — always a treasure in dull country places, you know — a Mr. *Something* L'Estrange; I forget the first surname; he assumed the second when some friend abroad left him a fortune. We asked him to-night, thinking you would like to see him."

"Thank you. Oh yes, certainly," said Alice, cheerfully, and turned to talk to some one else.

A short time after, I saw a tall, foreign looking man approach Alice. "Mr. L'Estrange, Miss Wynyard," said his introducer.

He started at the name; Alice turned round, lifted up her quiet eyes — they fell on the face of Arthur Sylvester!

Rumour had lied — it was the dead alive! I flew to my Alice — she clutched my hand tight — but no motion or word escaped her. She seemed as paralysed as if she really beheld the dead — the wronged, forgotten, unforgiving dead. She did not approach him by one step, though with wild eyes she stood gazing — gazing.

And her husband? — He bowed, fixed upon her his piercing

glance of complete recognition, and a strange look passed over his face; it was a look neither of love nor sorrow, but of cold aversion. His reason had returned, and with it had come a great change — so incomprehensible is the human mind — he now hated Alice as he had once apparently loved her.

She saw it all, and gave no sign. Only, when a few moments after I bent over her in the crowd, she murmured in a low hollow tone, "Aunt, take me home, take me home."

I feigned illness — and we came away. All the miserable drive, Alice lay moaning on my breast, "Arthur, my husband, my only husband, my own still!"

Everard, poor Everard! I saw there was no hope for thee. Oh, the eternity of love! "Many waters cannot quench love, neither can the floods drown it." In Arthur Sylvester, Alice saw not the madman who had well-nigh been a murderer — the blight of her youth — the one agonizing memory of long widowed years; but only the beloved of her girlhood, whom she had set up as an idol in her heart. He hated her with a pitiless, unforgiving, maddened hatred — she knew it, she felt it — yet she loved him, and all thought of her betrothed vanished instantaneously from her mind.

Unhappy Everard! when he returned to us — what a welcome — what a bride! And I had to unfold all! I had to pierce the dagger into his heart. He reeled and fell down insensible. When he recovered, all that he uttered was, "Alice — I must see Alice."

Alice came, and was smitten with fear at the look he wore; it was indeed hardly that of a living man. She fell on her knees before him, she took his hands, she wept over them, and yet Everard never moved.

"And this is my doing!" Alice cried. "Oh, Everard, good, generous Everard! forgive me!"

"Alice," he said at last, "is this all true? will you forsake me?"

She wept in silence.

"Alice, you are a free woman. No law, human or divine, gives *him* any right over you. By the memory of your dead father, who gave you to me, will you let this part us? will you break all your vows?"

"Oh, pity me! How wretched am I! Everard, you love me — I feel it — then think how I love *him*. Let your own heart speak for mine. I cannot, I dare not marry. My Arthur

Domestic Stories. 19

lives; and I am his wife still, in heart and soul. To wed another would be a sin — a fearful sin. Everard, I dare not!"

There was a long silence, and then Everard said —

"I saw you his wife once, and I did not murmur. Even now I would give my life for your happiness; but that is impossible. They tell me that after what has passed, he hates you with a deadly hatred? Can you love him still?"

She looked piercingly into his face: "Everard, ask yourself, is love always given for love? — can it not live unreturned?"

They were bitter, cruel words to say to him. He understood them, and sank under their keen arrows.

"O Heaven! I feel that — I have felt it all my life. Alice, say no more — you are free!"

And thus they parted; the two to whom destiny had made love not a blessing but a curse; in whose hearts it had been planted so early, and had grown up through life not as a beautiful flower, but as a poison-tree, whose leaves blighted wherever they touched, whose fruit was ashes to the taste. And yet, how different it might have been! Truly there are mysteries in life that no human power can solve. But we shall read the dark page clearly one day, and then all will be plain that now seems so strangely tortuous. Poor insects that we are! how shall we dare to unravel the mystic web of human fate, until the time comes when we shall see clearly with our spirit-eyes, and "know even as we are known."

Everard's severe illness formed a temporary pretext to the little world around us for the delay of the marriage. After a time the talk and the wonder grew again, but we heeded it not. What was the opinion of the idle world to Alice and to me! I would fain have taken her out of its power, and hidden ourselves once more in some blessed solitude, but Alice would not go. That man seemed to have the influence of an evil spirit over her: she lived but in the track of Arthur Sylvester L'Estrange; she roamed over the country only to gain a passing glimpse of him in his rides; she went into society that she might watch him from some secluded corner and listen for his voice. Yet he never looked at her, or spoke to her: if they met in the open country roads he turned his horse another way; if they passed in the street he acknowledged her with the bow that common courtesy exacted, and passed on. At all times, in all places, I saw that her presence made his face darken, until its lofty beauty was like that of a fallen angel. All the world spoke well of him, and it seemed that the only remnant of his past madness was in this terrible hatred of her, who loved him so that she would have laid herself down for his feet to trample on, and thought it a joyful death. A coldness, almost an estrangement sprang up between Alice and me. There was something in my eyes repulsive, unfeminine, in this passionate and hopeless love. At times I ventured to utter what I thought, but then the deep sorrow, the entreating looks, of that poor girl melted the frost from my heart.

"Aunt Susan," she would say, "is it wrong or unworthy for a wife to love her husband?"

And I could not answer her another word. There is something so ennobling in a woman's true and earnest love, that it elevates the meaner object on which it at times wastes itself. Thus, even while I marvelled at Alice's blind devotion to her former lover; while in my heart I condemned it as unworthy of her; while every feeling of reason and affection clung to the forsaken Everard, now a wanderer once more; still I could not but regard with a strange emotion, almost akin to reverence, the workings of that faithful woman-heart, and Arthur Sylvester himself rose to be at once an object of wonder and of fear. He shot across our quiet heaven of peace like an evil star, and yet he himself moved on, seemingly unconscious of, or unheeding, the terrible effects he had caused, and was still causing.

Whether Alice in her wildest imagination ever dreamed that his love would return, I cannot tell. At times, with all my dislike and horror of the man, I almost wished that it might be so; for I saw her day by day fading before my eyes, and knew that her heart was breaking. He must have seen it, too; he must have heard the world's chatter concerning her engagement with Everard Brooke, and its breaking off — the cause of which one who had once read the depths of that loving heart, as Arthur had done, could never doubt. It was a strange monomania that turned his mind against her, I thought; and more than once, in my overweening love for Alice, I considered whether I ought not myself to go and tell Mr. L'Estrange the whole truth, imploring him to end a story which seemed as romantic as a fairy tale and as fearful as the old Greek tragedies of doom, by again wooing and wedding his long-parted bride. I might have done so, but that the web of destiny was drawing closer and closer round us all.

It chanced that in our garden, overlooking the high road, there was a shady walk, leading to a summer-house, which in its form and embowerings had often, strangely enough, reminded me of the spot which had witnessed that terrible scene on Alice's wedding-day; so much so, that I framed all manner of reasons to have it pulled down, lest the similarity should strike her painfully. Whether it was so or not, I cannot say; I never hinted the real cause of my dislike; but Alice steadily resisted the plan of having her bower destroyed. She had always loved it, she said; and after Arthur Sylvester's reappearance had changed the current of her whole life, habits, and thoughts, a curious fatality seemed to make her cling more than ever to this solitary spot. There she remained, ostensibly with her books, her music, or her work; but often and often I found thick dust lying on her favourite volumes, her harp untuned, her embroidery scattered, and I knew that she had been spending those hours of loneliness in vague and mournful reveries.

One day, when Alice had left me as usual, I sat idly looking out from my window down the road, watching three horsemen descending the hill: I soon saw that one of them was Arthur Sylvester L'Estrange. This surprised me, for hitherto he had carefully avoided passing our house. But I supposed his two friends had led him on unwitting, for they seemed all conversing merrily together. The world said there was not a gayer or wittier companion than Mr. Sylvester L'Estrange, he was so blithe — so lighthearted! How the world lies sometimes! Yet one would not have thought so now, when through the open window came the ringing of his laughter borne upon the clear, still country air. I heard its every tone, and I felt that another had heard it too. Poor Alice! a chance sight of that man always made her like a marble image of woe for many hours.

Suddenly at a bend in the road he came in sight of the summer-house. At its door stood Alice. She wore that day a white dress, and, with her long falling hair, her appearance curiously resembled what it had been on her marriage morning. The sudden sight and recollection struck Sylvester's yet diseased brain; he uttered a loud heart-piercing cry, which made the horse he rode unmanageable with terror. A mist came before my eyes; I heard another cry, of "Arthur, Arthur!" and then the clanking hoofs of the riderless steed galloping madly away.

When I looked again, Alice was supporting on her bosom the death-like form of him who had once been her bridegroom. I flew to her side with all the speed my aged feet could exert. She was weeping over him, calling him "her Arthur, her beloved, her *husband*."

We bore him into the house, and the husband and wife were again under one roof. But of little moment was this either to the heart that hated, or the heart that loved; for Arthur Sylvester had in his fall been struck on the head, and lay perfectly insensible for many days. Then came a season of terrific ravings, which drove even the devoted Alice from the presence of the maniac. Strange words did the unfortunate man utter — Alice's name, and another, a woman's too; but the latter was breathed in low tender murmurings, while Alice's came mingled with curses and bursts of passionate remorse. I closed the chamber to all intruders — even Alice; I would not that those fearful revealings of an unquiet conscience should be known to her or to the world. Thus much I gathered from his delirious words, that never, no, not in those early days, had Arthur Sylvester really loved my Alice. I guessed — wrongly or rightly — that his much-protested love was only for the rich Miss Wynyard.

It was with a calmness akin to thankfulness that I saw life ebbing from that wretched man. The physicians had told us that no earthly power could ever restore the shattered mind, and that death would come in mercy. I knew this, and Alice knew it too. She also had heard — but only once — that strange name mingled with her own on the lips of the maniac. It had frozen her into stone; yet she did not leave him, but ministered day and night with unwearied care. The physicians said that no hand but death's would still those ravings; that no glimpse of light would gild the passing of the bewildered soul; but it was not so. Just as the spirit parted he saw Alice, and knew her. There was no hatred in those dying eyes, nor was there love; only contrition and trembling entreaty.

"Alice Wynyard," breathed the white lips, "forgive! I deceived — both — both — you most. *That* drove me mad. Poor angel, forgive!"

She clasped his hand, she would have drawn the dying head to her bosom, with the last kiss of peace and wife-like affection; but on his lips came that other name, not Alice's, murmured in tones of deepest love. And with its utterance the spirit fled.

There was none to lay the stranger in his grave, save Alice and I. She had called him her husband, and none doubted the fact. He had no relatives living, and when a will was found, leaving all his wealth to a charity, there was little chance of any claimant springing up to deny our right in arranging the affairs of the departed. I say "our," because in all things Alice took the direction. I had thought she would have been utterly overwhelmed; but no! When all was over, a superhuman strength seemed to possess her. "My husband!" was ever on her lips, and with a wife's duty she acted towards his memory. When I brought her mourning, she would have none other than widow's weeds, and on my remonstrating, she turned round with a dignity and solemnity that made me marvel:—

"Be silent, Aunt: I rule here! God and my own heart made me Arthur's wife — the world and a wicked law broke the outward bond, but the holiest tie remains. I am his widow now."

When we examined the papers of the departed, not even from that mournful task did Alice shrink. I sat by her, but she would not let me see any record of his dark and stormy life. Only once, when she opened a packet of letters, I saw her cheek blanch. As she read, her hands grew rigid, and her eyes glassy. I drew near, and she repulsed me not. The letters, outpourings of tenderest love, were addressed to Arthur Sylvester; they were signed with the name which he had uttered in his ravings; — each ended with, "*Your wife, Isabel.*" Aghast, almost stupified, I gazed on the date of the last — it was the eve of Alice's wedding-day!

I had lived to bless the terrible stroke which had saved my darling from a fate more terrible still. I fell on my knees beside her — I clasped my aged arms about her neck, and murmured —

"Alice, let us thank God for all."

"Amen!" was her answer. May I never while I live hear another tone like that in which she uttered the word!

With the letters was a lock of hair, and one line, in his own handwriting, "Isabel Sylvester L'Estrange, died —," the date two years since. The sin of two broken hearts lay upon that man's conscience. His madness was no marvel now.

Alice pointed out the line. "You see this!" she gasped — "now let all the past be as if it had never been."

With her own hands she laid all the papers upon the red embers, and the flame rose up, — it was the funeral pyre of her dead love of old. From Alice's lips the name of Arthur Sylvester was never heard more.

* * * *

In this world no sorrow is eternal. Life can never be utterly dark: to the pure, the earnest, the God-fearing, there is still a future — a future on earth — besides the glorious one beyond. Even in the lightning-blasted tree there are always some boughs that will grow green again, and show that life is not utterly dead within it. And so it was with Alice. When that wild passionate love had been consumed in the furnace of affliction, so that not even its ashes remained; when the ideal image which she had so worshipped was shattered to pieces in her sight, and she knew it was only a dumb idol, not a life-breathing form; then her pure soul drew back into itself, and grew strong. She did not die, but lived; lived to be a yet nobler creature than she had ever been, and in the earnest charities and high aspirings of a pure and holy nature she found peace.

And Everard?

In my extreme old age, with one foot on the threshold of that dark gate which leads to the land of light, I have seen my dear, my noble Everard, happy at last. I have done what I never dreamed I should, I have lived to see his marriage. What though youth and youth's comeliness had long passed away from the two who bent before the altar, there is much of life yet before them. Everard is happy, for the true heart and the tried has won at last — he has Alice for his wife. Who should rejoice so much as I, for has she not been my treasure, the light of my eyes? And he? — his mother was my only sister; and his father — there was a time when I did not think to have called Henry Brooke my *brother*. Hush, vain heart! the fault was all thine own; none else was to blame.

Reader! believe the word of one who has passed through the world's ordeal, has seen its hollowness, has endured its griefs: the greatest, the only truth of life — next to the fear of God — is *love*.

'T IS USELESS TRYING.

"You will never succeed — 'tis useless trying," was the answer we received one day when talking of something quite unimportant to you, dear reader, but very near our own heart. The voice was one we always listen to, and not seldom follow; but this time its discouraging arguments were unheeded. We *did* try, and we *did* succeed.

The fact set us moralizing on the good or evil tendency of these three words — "'tis useless trying." And the conclusion we came to was this, that for one vain idea dispelled, one wild project overturned by their prudent influence, these chilling words have rung the knell of a hundred brilliant and life-sustaining hopes, and paralyzed into apathy a thousand active and ardent minds, who might otherwise have elevated themselves, and helped the world on in its progress. What would America have been if that strong-hearted Columbus had been discouraged by sneers and arguments about the uselessness of his attempt to discover a new world? Or where would have been Newton's stupendous theory, if, at the commencement of his researches, some meddling friend at his ear had whispered, "Don't try; you will be sure to fail!" In aid of the "Never try" doctrine comes vanity, with its potent arguments that no attempt at all is better than a failure. We deny the fact *in toto*. Should a man fail in a project too high for him, he at least becomes acquainted with the extent of his own powers; he loses that inflated self-exaltation which is the greatest bane to real merit; and in finding his own level he may yet do well. And better, far better, that all the false pretenders in the world should sink back into deserved obscurity, than that one spark of real talent should be extinguished by the cold-hearted check — "'Tis useless trying!" Now, having prosed enough, let us enlighten our arguments by a story.

Between ten and twenty years ago — the precise date is immaterial — there was in the city of New York a barber's apprentice, a young boy named Reuben Vandrest. His Dutch lineage was indicated by his surname, which, in course of years and generations, had been corrupted from Van der Dest to Vandrest, while for his scriptural Christian name he was indebted to a worthy Quaker, his maternal grandfather who had come over with William Penn. These names were, in truth, all the boy owed to his progenitors, as from his cradle he had been an orphan, cast on the charity of the wide world. But the excellent sect to which Reuben's mother had belonged, is one of the few who never cast the lambs from their bosom, and the orphan child was not deserted. The Friends took care of him; and when he was able to earn a livelihood one of their number received him as an apprentice. Such was the short and simple story of the barber's boy.

Every human being has some inner life which the outside world knows nothing of. Thus from his earliest childhood the passion of Reuben Vandrest had been music. He would follow the itinerant minstrels of the city through one street after another, often thus losing his meals, his rest, everything except his schooling, which precious benefit he was too wise to throw away even for music. He made friendships with blind pipers, Italian hurdygurdyists, and, above all, with wandering fiddlers; for, with an intuitive perception, the violin — the prince of stringed instruments — was his chief favourite. From all and each of these wandering musicians Reuben was intent on gaining something: they were won by his childish manners and his earnest admiration — for love of praise is the same in a blind fiddler as in an opera-singer — and by degrees Reuben not only listened, but learned to play. No instrument came amiss to him; but his sole private property was an old fife: and with this simplest of all orchestral varieties the poor barber's boy used to creep to his garret, and there strive, with his acute ear and retentive memory, to make out the tunes he had heard in the streets, or invent others.

But the grand era in the boy's life was coming. One day as he stood wistfully looking at a violin which he held in his arms fondly and lingeringly, prior to returning it to its right owner, a poor street musician, the idea of its construction first entered Reuben's mind. He had been accustomed to regard a violin as a mysterious thing — a self-creating, sound-producing being; and never once had he considered of what it was made, or how. Now he began to peer into its mysteries;

and to find out that it was only wood and catgut after all. He questioned his friend the fiddler, but the man had scraped away during a lifetime without once casting a thought on the mechanism of his instrument. True, he could replace a broken string, and at times even manufacture a bridge with his penknife, but that was all. When Reuben inquisitively wanted to learn how violins were made, the fiddler shook his head, and said he did not know.

"Do you think I could make one?" pursued the anxious boy.

A burst of laughter, so cuttingly derisive that Reuben's face grew crimson, was the only answer. "Why, you little simpleton," cried the fiddler, when his mirth had subsided, "surely you'll not be so silly as to try? You could as soon build a house as make a violin."

"But violins must be made by somebody?"

"Yes, by people who know all about it; not by a lad like you. Take my advice, and don't try."

Reuben said no more; but he could not get the idea from his mind. Every violin that he saw he begged to look at: he examined the varieties of construction, the sort of wood used, the thickness and fashion of the strings: and, after weeks of consideration, he at last determined to try and make one for himself. During the long, light summer nights he worked hour after hour in his garret, or on the roof of the house; his natural mechanical skill was aided by patience and ardour; and with the few tools which he borrowed from the good-natured carpenters who had given him the wood, he succeeded in forming the body of the violin. But here a long cessation took place in Reuben's toil; for he had not even the few pence necessary to purchase strings; and the bow, which he could not make, it was utterly out of his power to buy. He sat looking in despair at the half-finished instrument — a body without a soul — and even his fife could not console him.

But one day a kind-hearted customer noticed the slight, pale-looking boy who had arranged his locks so gently and carefully, and Reuben became the glad recipient of a dollar. He flew to buy catgut and an old bow, and with trembling hands stringed his instrument. Who can describe the important moment? Leverrier's crowning calculation for the new planet, Lord Rosse's first peep through his giant telescope, are little compared to poor Reuben's first attempt to draw sounds from his violin. The sounds came; string after string was tuned; the bow was applied, and the violin had a soul! Feeble and thin the notes were, but still they were distinct musical tones; and the boy hugged his self-made treasure to his beating heart, actually sobbing with joy.

He played tune after tune; he never noticed that evening darkened into night; he forgot his supper; and forgot too — what but for his musical enthusiasm would long since have come into his mind — that though the childish fife might pass muster in the house of his master, a violin never would. The good Quaker, one of the strictest of his sect, thought music was useless, sinful, heathenish; and a fiddler, in his eyes, was as bad as a thief. Therefore who can picture Reuben's consternation when his garret-door opened, and his master stood before him? Reuben bore all Ephraim's wrath in silence, only he took care to keep his darling violin safe from the storm, by pressing it closely in his arms.

"Thee hast been neglecting thy work and stealing fiddles," cried the angry man.

"I have not neglected my work," timidly answered the boy, "and I have not stolen the violin — indeed I have not."

"How didst thee get it?"

"I made it myself."

Old Ephraim looked surprised. All the music in the world was nothing to him, but he had a fancy for mechanical employments, and the idea of making a violin struck him as ingenious. He examined it and became less angry. "Will it play?" asked he.

Reuben, delighted, began one of his most touching airs; but his master stopped him. "That will do," said he; "I only want to see if it sounds — all tunes are the same. And I suppose thou wilt turn musician?"

Reuben hung his head and said nothing.

"Well, that thou canst never do, so I would advise thee not to try. Forget the fiddle, and be a good barber. However, I will say no more; only thou must play out of doors next time."

But all the discouragements of the old Quaker could not repress Reuben's love for music. He cut, and curled, and shaved, as in duty bound, and then fled away to his violin. From the roof of the house his music went forth; and in this most original concert-room, with the open sky above him, and the pert city sparrows, now used to his melody, hopping by his side, did the boy gradually acquire the first secrets of his science. It is needless to enumerate the contrivances he resorted to for instruction — how he wandered through the streets with his violin at night, to gain a few cents wherewith to purchase old music; and how he gradually acquired skill, so as to be admitted as a sort of supernumerary into a wandering band.

One night, when this primitive orchestra was engaged for a ball at a private house in the city, the first violin mysteriously disappeared. In this dilemma, young Reuben found courage to offer himself as a substitute. It was a daring thing. The other musicians first laughed at him; then heard him play the part which no one else could take; and finally suffered him to try. For the first time in his life the barber's boy witnessed a ball; and it was a brilliant New York ball. It seemed to him a fairy scene: he was dazzled, bewildered, excited, and in his enthusiasm he played excellently. The night wore away; the dancers seemed never weary; not so the aching fingers of the musicians. Reuben, especially, to whom the excitement was new, grew more and more exhausted, and at last, just as he had finished playing a waltz, fell fainting from his chair. Most of the gay couples passed on — it was only a poor musician; but one young girl, in whom the compassionate and simple nature of a child had not been swept away by the formalities of young ladyhood, held a glass of water to the young man's lips.

"Cora Dacres bringing to life a fainting fiddler!" said a tittering voice. "Oh, what a nice story when we go back to school!"

The girl turned round indignantly, saying, "Cora Dacres is never ashamed of doing what is right. Are you better, now?" she added gently to poor Reuben, who had opened his eyes.

The youth recovered, and she disappeared again among the dancers; but many a time did the auburn curls, and soft, brown, sympathizing eyes of the little school-girl float before the vision of Reuben Vandrest; and the young musician often caught himself repeating to his sole confidant — his violin — the pretty name he had heard on his waking, and dimly recognised as hers — Cora Dacres.

Long before he was twenty-one, Reuben had entirely de-

voted himself to the musical profession. The turning point in
his career was given by a curious incident. One moonlight
night, as he was playing on the roof, as usual, he saw a head
peep out from the uppermost window of the opposite house.
This head was drawn in when he ceased playing, and again
put forward as soon as he recommenced. A natural feeling of
gratified vanity prevented the young man from yielding to his
first shy impulse of retiring; and besides, sympathy in anything relating to his art was so new to Reuben, that it gave him
pleasure to be attentively listened to, even by an unknown
neighbour over the way. He threw all his soul into his violin,
and played until midnight.

Next day, while at his duties in his master's shop, the apprentice was sent for to the house opposite. Reuben went,
bearing the insignia of his lowly trade; but instead of a
patient customer, he saw a gentleman who only smiled at his
array of brushes.

"I did not send for you to act as barber," said the stranger
in English, which was strongly tinctured with a foreign accent,
"but to speak to you about the violin-playing which I heard
last night. Am I rightly informed that the performer was
yourself?"

"It was, sir," answered Reuben, trembling with eagerness.

"Who taught you?"

"I myself."

"Then you love music?"

"With my whole heart and soul!" cried the young man,
enthusiastically.

The stranger skilfully drew from Reuben the little history
of himself and his violin, and talked to him long and earnestly.
"You have a true feeling for that noble art to which I, too,
belong," he said. "You may have many difficulties to en-
counter; but never be discouraged — you will surmount them
all. You have had many hindrances; but listen, and I will
tell you what I went through at your age. I once came, a
poor boy like you, to the greatest capital in Europe, my heart
full of music, but utterly without means. My only wealth was
my violin. I left it one day in my poor chamber, while I went
out to buy a loaf with my last coin. When I came back, my
violin was gone! It had been stolen. May God forgive me
for the crime I contemplated in my mad despair! I rushed to
the river; I plunged in: but I was saved from the death I

sought—saved to live for better things. My friend," continued the musician after a long silence, during which his face was hidden by his hands, "in all the trials of your career remember this of mine, and take warning."

"I will — I will!" cried Reuben, much moved.

"And now, after having told you this terrible secret in my life, it is as well that I should not reveal my name; and besides, it could do you no good, as I set out for Europe to-morrow. But should you ever be in Paris, come to this address, leaving this writing, and you will hear of me."

The gentleman wrote some lines in a foreign language, which Reuben could not make out, though among his musical acquaintance he had gained a little knowledge of both French and Italian. He then gave Vandrest the address, and bade him adieu. The young man long pondered over this adventure, and it was the final crisis which made him relinquish a trade so unpleasing to him, for the practice of his beloved art.

It is a mistake to suppose that the profession of music is an easy careless life, to which any one may turn who has a distaste for more solid pursuits. In no calling is intellectual activity and arduous study more imperatively required. He who would attain to even moderate eminence in it, must devote years of daily patient toil to dry and uninteresting branches of study. A poet may be one by nature: it is utterly impossible that a musician can be great without as deep science as ever puzzled a mathematical brain. He must work — work every inch of his way — must dig the foundation, and enrich the soil, before he can form his garden and plant his flowers. Thus did our young ex-barber of New York: he studied scientifically what he had first learned through the instinct of genius, and rose slowly and gradually in his profession. Sometimes his slight and ordinary appearance, which made him look more boyish than he really was — his quaint old-world name — and, above all, a simplicity and Quaker-like peculiarity in his dress and manner, aroused the ridicule of his companions, who followed music more for show than through real love of the art. But the story of his early perseverance always disarmed them; and it was a common saying, with reference to young Vandrest, that he who, untaught, could make a violin, would surely learn to play it.

By degrees the young violinist rose into note, and became received into society where he could hardly have dreamed that he should ever set his foot. Many a rich citizen was pleased to welcome to his house Mr. Vandrest, the young and unassuming musician, whose gentle manners and acknowledged talent were equally prized. The barber's apprentice of New York was utterly forgotten, or only thought of as a proof of how much a man's fortune lies in his own hands, if he will only try.

In one of those elegant reunions which were established when worthy Brother Jonathan was first beginning to show his soul and mind — when Bryant's songs, and Allston's pictures, and Channing's lectures, first gave evidence of transatlantic genius — Vandrest again heard the name which had never utterly gone from his memory through all his vicissitudes — Cora Dacres. He turned round, and saw the altered likeness of the girl who had held the water to his lips on the night of the ball. She had grown into womanly beauty; but he remembered the face still. She had not the faintest memory of him — how could it be so? Light and darkness were not more different than the pleasing, intellectual, gentlemanlike man who was introduced to her, and the pale, angular, ill-clad boy whom she had pitied and aided. Sometimes Vandrest thought he would remind her of the circumstance; but then a vague feeling of sensitiveness and shame, not entirely the result of the memory of those poverty-stricken days, prevented him. He went home, and again his old violin might have heard breathed over it the name of Cora Dacres; but this time not in boyish enthusiasm for whatever was pleasing and beautiful, but in the first strong, all-absorbing love of manhood, awakened in a nature which was in every way calculated to receive and retain that sentiment in its highest, purest, and most enduring form.

Reuben Vandrest, who had hitherto cared for nothing on earth but his violin, soon learned to love: and with the enthusiastic attachment of an earnest and upright nature. For with all the allurements of a musical career, Reuben continued as simple-minded and guileless in character as the primitive sect from which he sprung. And Cora was worthy to inspire the love of such a man: whether she returned it or not Reuben did not consider — he was too utterly absorbed in the new delight of loving, and of loving her, to think of asking himself the question. He visited at her house, and became a favourite with her father — a would-be amateur, who took pleasure in filling his drawing-rooms with musicians, and treating them as costly and not disagreeable playthings.

But at last Mr. Dacres was roused from his apathy by the evident regard subsisting between his daughter and young Vandrest. Though he liked the violinist well enough, the hint of Reuben's marrying Cora sounded ill in the ears of the prudent man, especially when given by one of those odious, good-natured friends with whom the world abounds. The result was a conversation between himself and Vandrest, in which, utterly bewildered and despairing, poor Reuben declared his hidden and treasured love, first with the shrinking timidity of a man who sees his inmost heart rudely laid bare, and then with a firmness given by a consciousness that there is in that heart nothing for which an honest man need blush.

"I am sorry for you, Mr. Vandrest," said the blunt yet not ill-meaning citizen. "But it is impossible that you can ever hope for Cora's hand."

"Why impossible?" said the young man, recovering all his just pride and self-possession. "I am not rich; but I have an unspotted name, and the world is all before me. Do you object to my profession?"

"By no means; a musician is an honourable man, just as much so as a storekeeper."

At any other time the very complimentary comparison would have made Reuben smile; but now he only answered, while the colour deepened on his cheek, "Is it because of my early life? My father was of good family; but it may be, you would blush to remember that your daughter's husband once served in a barber's shop?"

"My dear sir," said Mr. Dacres, "you forget we are Americans, and talent and wealth are our only aristocracy. The first you undoubtedly possess; but without the second, you cannot marry Cora; and there is no chance of your ever becoming a rich man."

"Will you let me try?" eagerly cried Vandrest.

"It would be of no use; you could not succeed."

"I could — I could!" exclaimed the young man, impetuously. "Only let me hope. I would try anything to win Cora!"

And in this earnestness of love did Reuben pursue his almost hopeless way. He had pledged his word that he would not speak of his love to Cora, that he would not try to win hers — this her father imperatively demanded; but Mr. Dacres also promised that he would leave his daughter free, nor urge her to accept any other husband during the three years of absence that he required of Reuben Vandrest.

They parted — Reuben and Cora — with the outward seeming of ordinary acquaintance; but was it likely that a love so deep and absorbed as that of the young musician should have been entirely suppressed by him, and unappreciated by her who was its object? They parted without any open confession; but did not Cora's heart follow the wanderer as he sailed towards Europe? — did she not call up his image, and repeat his unmusical name, as though it had contained a world of melody in itself? — and did she not feel as certain in her heart of hearts that he loved her, as if he had told her so a hundred times?

When Vandrest was preparing for the voyage, he accidentally found the long-forgotten note of the stranger musician. It directed him to Paris; and to Paris he determined to proceed, as all Europe was alike to one who knew not a single soul on the wide expanse of the old world. He arrived there; and found in his unknown friend the kind-hearted and talented Swede, who, on the death of Paganini, had become the first violinist in the world — Ole Bull.

The success of the young American was now made sure. The great violinist had too much true genius to fear competitors, and no mean jealousy kept him from advancing the fortunes of Vandrest by every means in his power. Reuben traversed Europe, going from capital to capital, everywhere making friends, and, what was still more important to him, money. He allowed himself no pleasures, only the necessaries of life; and laid up all his gains for the one grand object of his care — the acquiring a fortune for Cora. He rarely heard of her; he knew not but that her love might change; and sometimes a sense of the utter wildness of his project came upon him with freezing reality. But intense love like his, in an otherwise calm and unimpassioned nature, acquires a strength unknown to those who are stirred by every passing impulse; and Reuben's love —

"By its own energy, fulfilled itself."

Ere the three years had expired, he returned to America, having realized a competence. With a beating heart the young musician stood before his mistress, told her all his love, and knew that she loved him. It was very sweet to hear Cora reveal, in the frankness of her true heart, which felt no shame for having loved one so worthy, how her thoughts had continually followed his wanderings, and how every success of his had been doubly sweet to her. But human happiness is never unmixed with pain; and when Cora looked at the altered form of her betrothed, his sunken and colourless face, and his large bright eyes, a dreadful fear took possession of her, and she felt that joy itself might be bought with too dear a price. It was so indeed. Reuben's energy had sustained him until came the reaction of hope fulfilled, and then his health failed. A long illness followed. But he had one blessing; his affianced wife was near him; and amidst all her anguish Cora felt thankful that he had come home first, and that it was her hand and her voice which now brought comfort to her beloved, and that she could pray he might live for her.

And Reuben did live. Love struggled with death, and won the victory. In the next year, in the lovely season of an American spring, the musician wedded his betrothed, and took her to a sweet country home, such as he had often dreamed of when he used to sit on summer evenings on the house-top in New York looking at the blue sky, and luring sweet music from his rude violin. And in Reuben's pleasant home was there no relic more treasured than this same violin, which had first taught him how much can be done with a brave heart.

Reader, the whole of Reuben Vandrest's life was influenced by his acting up to that little word — "try!" Two old proverbs — and there is much sterling wisdom in old proverbs — say, "Everything must have a beginning," and "No man knows what he can do until he tries." Now, kind reader, keep this in mind; and never, while you live, damp the energies of yourself or of any other person by the heartless and dangerous sentence, "'Tis useless trying."

THE ONLY SON.

THE Rev. Cyril Danvers was about to ascend his village pulpit to preach his first sermon. A formidable effort was this to the young curate, for he was hardly six-and-twenty, and of a studious and retiring disposition. He stood in the little vestry, while the old man who fulfilled the combined lay and clerical duties of gardener to the rector, verger, and sexton, arranged his gown with ceremonious care. The tiny cracked looking glass over the fireplace reflected the young clergyman's face — fair, and pleasant to look upon, but changing from red to pale, like that of a timid girl. The last verse of the simple, but sweet and solemn hymn, resounded from within, warning the curate that he must muster up all his courage. A respectful "God be with you, sir!" from the old man, turned his thoughts from his own natural timidity to the high and holy duty he had to perform; and the young curate walked from the vestry to the pulpit, with a pale face, indeed, and a beating heart, but with a quiet and religious feeling that befitted the time and place.

As Cyril Danvers began, his voice trembled, for he thought how much depended on this his first sermon; for on his talents and success hung the hopes, almost the means of subsistence, of a widowed mother and two young sisters; but as he proceeded, the sacredness of his task drove away all worldly thoughts, and he spoke with an earnest enthusiasm that went to the hearts of his simple hearers. Perhaps Cyril felt relieved that they were chiefly of the humbler class, and that his own good, but somewhat cold and stern superior, was absent from his pew, whose only occupant was the rector's daughter, Lucy Morton. We fancy all *Lucies* must be fair, and gentle, and good; and Lucy Morton did not belie her name, so that the young curate need not have feared harsh criticism from her. He was too lately arrived in the village even to know her by sight; but a passing glance at the rector's pew showed him a sweet face, lifted up with such pious and earnest attention, that it gave him courage; and Cyril Danvers ended his first sermon, feeling that the great effort of his life was over, and over well.

He walked to his lonely lodgings through the quiet meadows, that lay sleeping in the Sabbath sunshine of June, with feelings of calm and thankful gladness, and thought of his future life with less doubt and hopelessness than he had done since the day when the young collegian had been called home to his dying father, to have intrusted to his care the three helpless women, whose sole stay and succour in this world was the only brother and only son. What a charm there is often in the words "only son!" Sometimes it conjures up visions of petted childhood, unrestrained youth, heirship to broad lands, and everything that undivided love and fortune can bestow. But Cyril Danvers had to prove the darkness of the other side of the subject, when family cares, heavy enough for ripe manhood, overwhelm the youth of an only son, who has so many dependent on him, and him alone, until nothing but love can lighten the burden.

However, the young man had borne and triumphed over many cares; and when at last, a few weeks after the Sunday with which our tale begins, he brought his mother and sisters to a small but pretty cottage within a short walk of his new curacy, Cyril felt the content of a man who has done his duty so far, and has reason to look forward to a season of tranquillity and happiness. Most joyful was he in having secured a home for his aged mother, and the two young and beautiful creatures who called him brother. But for him, these would have been thrown on the bitter world, in utter helplessness; for, fifty years ago — the date of our tale — women were but imperfectly educated, nor held the same position in society which they now justly sustain, and it was almost impossible for a young female, plunged from affluence into poverty, to gain a livelihood by any of the many ways through which unmarried and unprotected women may in our days honourably and successfully struggle against hard fortune. For this reason, the high-principled and affectionate brother murmured not for a moment at his burden, but was thankful that his own hardly-earned salary, and the poor remnant of his mother's dowry, would suffice to keep Frances and Jessie from suffering the bitterness of want.

The summer passed lightly and pleasantly over the curate's little family. There had been time enough to remove the shadow of death which had overwhelmed them when their father was taken away. The sisters and brother were all young, and in youth life is so easily made pleasant! even the void which death leaves is not eternal; and now the sole token of him who was gone, remained in the mourning garb of the widowed mother, which she would never lay aside, save for the garments of eternal rest. Light-hearted Jessie sang like a bird once more; was wild with joy at living in the beautiful country; and enticed Cyril from his books, and Frances from her charities in the village, where she and the rector's daughter were the good angels of the poor and needy. Lucy Morton had at first sight liked the curate's eldest sister, and the liking soon became love. Not that they were similar in disposition, for that friendship does not always require. Lucy's nature was joyous as a sunny summer's day, while Frances was like the same day — calm, serene, but sunless. Hers was the temperament over which sorrow never passes lightly, and she had had one bitterness which her brother and sister were spared: Frances had been loved and had loved, deeply and truly, as those only can, who have been tried by the fiery ordeal of resigning. She did not sink under the loss; but her smiles were less frequent; and many of her companions used to say that Frances Danvers, at four-and-twenty, looked like one certain to be an old maid.

Nevertheless, every one loved Miss Danvers, from the village children, whom she taught to sing — to the wonder and annoyance of the rural Orpheus, a blacksmith, who was wont to lead the church-music, showing forth his six-feet height and stentorian lungs in front of the gallery — even to the grave rector himself, who invariably seemed pleased to see the gentle and ladylike Frances as his daughter's companion. Together they visited the poor and sick, often meeting in their rounds with the curate himself, on whom devolved much of the pastoral duties of the parish, and whose gentle manners, and earnest but unobtrusive zeal, endeared him every month more and more to the simple people among whom his lot was cast. In this primitive region there were few above the rank of farmers, so that the rector's daughter, while too gentle to despise her more uncultured neighbours, felt and expressed herself very happy in having found associates of her own age, similar in station, education, and pursuits.

The frank-hearted and unsophisticated Lucy did not disguise her love for Frances, nor the sincere pleasure she felt in the society of Cyril. Her laugh was gayest, her sweet face brightest, when he was by; until the student ceased to shut himself up with his books, and his countenance wore a look of continual happiness, which gladdened his mother's heart. All the winter, the four young people met almost every day; and it was only when the spring brought to the rectory a visitor, who took away a slight share of Lucy's society from them, that the curate and his sisters began to think how dull their little parlour was without the bright smile and cheerful voice of the rector's daughter.

Miss Hester Dimsdale, Lucy's guest, was one of those plain but attractive girls who make tact, good sense, and good nature, atone for the want of beauty. She was very lively and open-hearted: too much so, perhaps, for she had a way of telling unpleasant truths, and of making cutting remarks, which she called "speaking her mind," but which was often anything but agreeable to the feelings of others. Her penetration discovered at once the state of things between her friend Lucy and the Danverses and a few pointed words at once tore the veil from Cyril's eyes: he beheld his own heart, and while he saw, he trembled.

"Why are you so thoughtful, Cyril?" asked Frances one evening, after she had for some minutes watched her brother, who sat with a book on his knee, though evidently not reading.

Jessie started up, and looked over his shoulder. "Why, he has been sitting here an hour, and has not even turned over the second page! A pretty student is my clever brother becoming!" said the laughing girl, shaking her curls in his face.

Cyril looked confused. "I fear I am getting lazy, Jessie, but I have so many things to think about and to do."

"And is that the reason you have been so grave lately? Why, Cyril, I have hardly seen a smile on your face since — yes, ever since Hester Dimsdale came."

"Is that the grand era, then?" said her brother, forcing the long absent smile to his lips.

Jessie looked very wise. "Ah, I see how it is!" she answered, in a sedate whisper. "I know what has come over the grave Cyril Danvers — he is in love."

"Yes, with my mother, and you, little torment!" interrupted the young man quickly, as he stooped over his kneeling sister, and kissed her cheek, so that his face was hidden from her view.

"What! and not Frances, too?" archly said the merry Jessie.

Cyril turned towards the elder sister a look which needed no words: it was evident he loved her even more than he did the gay damsel of eighteen, who was ever the pet of the family. Then he took up his book, and went silently into his own room.

The gay girl had touched a chord that vibrated fearfully in her brother's heart. Cyril did love, and love passionately; and he knew it was all in vain; for how could he hope to marry? Even had Lucy loved him — he never thought she did; but even had it been so, how could he tear from his heart and home those dear ties, without which cruel severance he could not hope to take a wife? The strife was very bitter in the young man's bosom. He had been so happy with his mother and sisters; and now it seemed that they stood between him and the girl he loved, so that, without sacrificing them, he could never hope to marry her. Sometimes he felt thankful that Lucy seemed not to love him, or the struggle would have been harder still. But then she regarded him kindly — he might soon have gained her love, had he dared; and her father was a kind, good man, who would not oppose his child's happiness. Then poor Cyril fell at once from his dream: he thought of his deserted sisters, alone and unprotected by the shelter of a brother's love, knowing that his income and his home were now the right of another, and they were desolate. He could not be the cause of this — not even to win Lucy.

No wonder was it that such an agonizing strife in his heart made Cyril's face mournful, much as he strove to hide his feelings from every eye. But it was terrible to have at times to struggle with the bitter thoughts that would rise up against the innocent ones who knew not how much he sacrificed for their sakes; and to be in the presence of her who had awakened this passionate and fatal love, was almost more than the young man could bear. He would have sunk under the conflict, but that it did not last long.

One day, Hester Dimsdale came to announce her sudden departure, and Lucy was to return with her for a twelvemonth's visit to London; and the two girls had come to bid an abrupt adieu at the cottage. Frances was rather pained to see that her sweet friend Lucy so little regretted the parting. She might have been more sad; but then she was so young and gay, and was going to so many anticipated pleasures! When Lucy kissed Mrs. Danvers with a tearful adieu, Frances forgave her at once for looking so happy. Cyril saw nothing, felt nothing, except that Lucy was going, that his heart was riven with despairing love, and that he must conceal it.

Frances and her brother walked home with them, in the twilight, across the still meadows. Cyril felt as if dreaming. He only knew that Lucy's hand trembled on his arm, and that her downcast face was sad as she spoke of her departure.

"Are you sorry to leave us?" asked Cyril, in earnest tones, that mocked his attempts to conceal his feelings.

Lucy did not speak, but one large tear fell on the handful of bright flowers which Mrs. Danvers had, for the last time, gathered for her favourite.

Another moment, and Cyril would have forgotten all his resolves, and poured forth his impassioned love; but Frances unconsciously turned round. He saw her pale, languid face, and the weakness was gone. The son and brother would not forsake his duty.

When, after a passing silence, Lucy's voice beside him sounded cheerful as ever, Cyril thought with a stern joy that his love was unreturned, and became calm once more. As they parted, he looked with one fixed gaze in her face, half raised her hand to his lips, then relinquished it without any kiss, drew his sister's arm within his own, and turned homeward.

For many weeks after Lucy had departed the village seemed desolate indeed. So the curate's sisters felt and said; and Frances, with a quick-sighted earnestness, given by her own olden love, watched her brother's every look. But he seemed calmer than usual, spoke of Lucy in his usual tone, read her frequent letters, and even sent some few kind messages in answer to hers. The anxious sister was deceived. Concealment was impossible to her own nature; she felt satisfied that she had been mistaken, for Cyril never could thus have hidden his feelings. She knew not the extent to which love can give strength of purpose.

It happened, too, that before very long another subject engrossed the thoughts of the tender sister. The gay and beautiful Jessie gained a lover; one who had seen her at the village church wooed, and won her; for he was comparatively rich, handsome, and withal worthy to be trusted with the youngest darling of the family. So in a few months Jessie Danvers became a bride.

There is always a vague sadness attendant on the first wedding in a family. It is the first tie broken, the first bird that leaves the nest to venture, on half-fledged wings, in a world untried. Mrs. Danvers wept almost as much at her daughter's wedding as at her husband's death. Frances, too, was sad: it brought back her own sorrows — unspoken, but still unhealed. Cyril only seemed cheerful; he was sorry to part with his sister, his pretty plaything from boyhood. But then Jessie was so happy; she loved and was beloved: and the brother acknowledged to himself, without feeling it to be a sinful thought, that thus one bar had been removed from between himself and Lucy Morton. Cyril knew that she was still free, for she wrote unreservedly to Frances; and the delicious dream would come oftener and oftener to his heart, that sweet Lucy might be his wife after all. The young curate was always delicate in health; but now renewed hope lent a colour to his cheek, and a firmness to his step, so that when Frances left the village to pay a visit to the bride. she only quitted one happy home for another. As the affectionate sister looked upon Jessie's beaming face, and remembered Cyril's cheerful adieu, she felt glad that there was still happiness in the world; though, in her own bitter loneliness, she thought of the past and wept.

This time did not pass wearily with Cyril and his mother, even though the visit of Frances extended from weeks to months. Her letters, too, had a cheerful, hopeful tone, which cheered them both; and Cyril, who knew not how deeply that sad first-love had entwined itself with every fibre of his sister's heart, thought with pleasure — in which it surely was hardly wrong if one selfish idea combined — that there might come a time when Frances too would be a happy wife, and his own reward for all he had sacrificed might be Lucy Morton's love. Thus Cyril would dream, as he sat by his winter fireside, and thought how that fireside would look with his aged mother in her arm-chair, and a young wife in the other, who wore the sweet face of Lucy Morton, until Mrs. Danvers would rouse her son from his reverie, to ask him what he was thinking about to make him look so happy.

When winter was stealing into spring, Frances suddenly returned. They had not known of her coming, and both mother and brother gazed with wondering delight on her face. She was still pale, but there was a soft light in her blue eyes, and a tremulous smile playing about her mouth, that told of some happy secret. After a few hours, Frances said, with a deep blush, that made the transparent cheek glow, until the once sedate Frances looked as beautiful as Jessie, "Dear mamma! shall you be glad to see an old friend? Charles — that is, Mr. Wilmington — said he should be passing Elmdale to-morrow; and — and —."

Frances could say no more; her arms were thrown round her mother's neck, and the blush and the smile ended in tears more delicious still. The secret was told: the two, long parted for conscience sake and filial duty, had again met — free. Nothing could part them now. So the gentle Frances was not destined to be an old maid, but a happy wife, and that ere long.

"Why did you not write to us of this, my most mysterious sister?" asked Cyril, when he had given his warm brotherly congratulations.

"Because — because I thought I would rather tell you; and you know good news will bear delay," said Frances, laughing and blushing.

"Then I had better delay mine. But no; I must tell you: Old Mr. Calvert died last month, and I was this morning greeted as rector of Charlewood."

"What! the pretty village close by? I am so glad! My dear, dear Cyril, how happy you will be!" cried Frances, joyfully.

"How happy I am!" answered her brother; and no one who looked on his radiant face could doubt it.

The brother and sister took their old twilight walk together through the green meadows that led to Elmdale. They were too happy to talk much; but they breathed the soft evening air, and looked at the tinted clouds, and thought — as hundreds of young hearts have done, are doing, and ever will do — how pleasant is the coming of spring, and how sweet it is to love! Suddenly, from the old church of Elmdale came the cheerful sound of marriage-bells; Cyril and Frances glanced at one another with that beaming, half-conscious smile, the free-masonry of love.

"Who are those bells ringing for?" asked Cyril of the old sexton, who was hastily crossing the field.

"Don't you know, sir? But master went away, and told nobody, I think. It is Miss Lucy: she was married to a grand London gentleman yesterday morning."

"Then that is the reason she has not written to me for so long," said Frances, as the old man walked quickly away.—But "Cyril—oh, Cyril!" the sister almost shrieked, as she turned and saw her brother's face. In a moment Frances read there the tale of hidden, self-denying, and now hopeless love. Without a word she led him to a bank, for he could not stand; and there, with his sister's hand in his, Cyril gave way to all the passion of his love—all its unutterable despair. Merrily the wedding-bells rang on: they sounded now like a funeral knell to the two, who went home through the gathering darkness. The gloom without was nothing to that within the hearts of both. How all things had changed in one little hour!

Charles Wilmington came, but his affianced bride met him with a welcome in which there was more of sadness than joy. Frances wished to defer her marriage; but Cyril would not suffer it. He gave his sister away to her long faithful lover, and tried to congratulate them, and to smile cheerfully; but it was a mournful wedding. Frances felt that her presence gave Cyril an additional pang; her own happy love was too strong a contrast to his desolate sorrow. The sister saw that it was best she should go; yet, as the carriage whirled her away, ever and anon that pale, agonized face floated between her and the husband so dearly loved; and, amidst her bridal happiness, Frances mourned for her brother.

Cyril and his mother were now left alone together. He had exacted a promise from Frances, that neither this fond mother, nor Jessie, should ever be pained by the knowledge of his fatal secret; and so Mrs. Danvers came to live at Charlewood Rectory with a feeling of unmixed pleasure and hope. Sometimes she thought her son looked sadder and paler than he had done for some months; but then Cyril was always grave, and never very strong. His new duties also took him much away from her; for he was none of those idle shepherds, who think one day's tending in the week enough for the flock. And Cyril, however weary he came in, had always a smile and a cheerful word for his mother. He was too gentle and good to make her suffer for the deadly gloom which had fallen over his whole life: it was not her fault, nor that of his innocent sisters, that he had lost sweet Lucy Morton.

That name now was never breathed, save by Cyril himself, in the lonely hours of suffering, of which no one knew. She did not revisit Elmdale, but went abroad with her husband. Change of abode happily removed Cyril from many haunting memories of his lost love; and to every one else it seemed as though she had never been. After some years many began to wonder why the young rector of Charlewood never married; but then he was so devoted to his aged mother, that it might be there was no room in his heart for any other love. Jessie's troop of children sported round their quiet, pale-faced uncle; and Mrs. Wilmington, too, came with her little Cyril — so like his namesake, even in childhood. Frances saw that her brother was calm and content, engrossed with his high and holy calling. He never mentioned Lucy; and the sister returned to her beloved home, satisfied that Cyril was at peace, if not happy.

And she was right. Sorrow that brings with it no self-reproach can be borne in time with patience. Cyril had in a great measure learned to look on life with less bitterness; he no longer suffered the uncontrollable anguish which had at first prostrated him in the dust; but he never again recovered the cheerful spirit of old. It has been said that men never love like women — that they soon recover from a loss such as Cyril had felt; but this is not true. Rarely does a man love with his whole soul, as a woman does; but when he does, the passion lasts for a lifetime, with an intensity unknown to most women. Cyril's love had engrossed every feeling of a sensitive nature, united to a delicate frame, and neither ever completely rallied from the shock.

Every year that passed over Cyril's head, his slight form became more bent, and his face more colourless and thin. When little past thirty, he looked like a man whose prime of life had gone by. Winter ever brought with it pain and failing health, so that he was obliged to relinquish many of his duties to his curate. For months he seldom went beyond the rectory and the church, where his voice was still heard, but fainter and more unearthly each Sabbath that came. He rarely visited Elmdale, for Mr. Morton had died not long after Lucy's marriage.

One Sunday, however, the then vicar requested Mr. Danvers to supply his place at Elmdale Church, and Cyril assented. It might be that he had a vague presentiment that it would be the last time he should lift his voice from the spot hallowed by many old recollections. As he stood in the little vestry, all looked the same as ten years before, when he was about to mount the pulpit for the first time. It was the same season too, and the June sun lighted up the old walls as it did then. As Cyril passed up the stairs, he almost expected to see Lucy Morton's face again in the rectory pew. In that pew, which was generally vacant, sat a lady and two blooming children. She raised her bowed head when the prayer was over, and Cyril beheld his first, his only, and lost love. Lucy sat in matronly grace, with her babes by her side, happiness and peace shining in every feature of her still beautiful face. A mournful shade passed over it when she looked at him whose love she never knew. What a contrast was there between the two now!

Cyril preached with a voice that was hardly more tremulous than usual. He shut out all earthly love from his eyes and his heart. But as he descended the pulpit his very lips had an ashen hue, and the retiring congregation heard with pity and regret that he had fainted on reaching the vestry. The old sexton — who was living still — said that the long walk had been too much for poor Mr. Danvers; and the farmers' wives shook their heads, and said that he was always too good for this world. Meanwhile Cyril went home, and never recrossed his own threshold more.

But though, in a few days, he lay down on his bed to rise no more, it was some weeks before the dread Shadow folded its still arms round its prey. Frances came to her brother, and Cyril talked with that calmness and peace which the near approach of death often gives of all the past. His mind was clear and joyful. He spoke of Lucy; and with the quick ear of sickness, distinguished her voice and footstep in the room below, where she came almost daily to inquire about him, and to see her former friend. At first Frances could hardly bear to look upon her; but then she thought how wrong such feelings were, and listened to Lucy as she spoke of her beloved and kind husband, and her beautiful children, though it gave her many a pang when she remembered him who was now fast departing.

One morning Lucy came earlier than usual. She sat many minutes alone, and then Frances' footsteps sounded slow and heavily on the stairs, and she entered.

Lucy's eyes asked the question her tongue could not utter.

"All is well with him now," said Frances, and her voice was strangely calm. "My brother is at rest."

Cyril had died that morning.

A few days after, Lucy and Frances sat together in the darkened house. It was the night before all that was mortal of poor Cyril was given to earth. They could now speak of him without tears; and they talked of old times and old pleasures shared with him who was no more.

Frances took the hand of her former companion. "All is changed with us now, Lucy; we are no longer young, and our feelings are different from what they once were. It can do no wrong, either to the living or the dead, if I tell you, now that you are a cherished and devoted wife, that he who is gone loved you with a passionate love which ceased but with life."

Lucy's face grew pale, and she burst into tears. "Why — oh, why did I never know this?"

"Because he could not hope to marry; and he was too honourable to drive his sisters from his home, or to bind the girl he loved by a doubtful engagement. He saw you did not love him."

"Because he never said one word of love to me, or I should soon have learned to love him, and then he might not have died!" said Lucy, still weeping.

"Hush, Lucy! All is best now. You are happy — you love your husband."

"I do love him; and he is worthy to be loved," answered the wife, earnestly. "But poor, poor Cyril!" and again she wept.

"Do not mourn for him," said Frances; "he might never have had a long life; and who shall say that he did not feel the sweet peace of duties fulfilled, and of knowing that his self sacrifice was not in vain? Lucy, I, Cyril's sister, amidst all my grief, still love you, and feel that you have done no wrong. Yet it is very bitter!" cried Frances, as her composure forsook her, and she bowed herself in agony. "Oh, would that I had died for thee, my brother — my only brother!"

THE DOCTOR'S FAMILY.

A STORY OF THE NEW YEAR.

In the country towns and villages of England there is not, from January to December, a merrier festival than the New Year. In London, and in those large commercial towns which ape the great metropolis, it is not so. There Christmas, with its accompaniments of plum-pudding and mince-pie, is all-in-all to the holiday lovers. The Old Year steals out and the New Year creeps in, like a neglected friend or a poor relation after its more honoured predecessor, glad enough to pick up the crumbs and fragments of the latter's feast of welcome. No one seems to care about the New Year in London. A few peals rung at midnight by the church-bells tell to some wakeful invalid or late reveller that the Old Year, with all its hopes and its pains, has gone by for ever; and perhaps next morning some man of business looking over his diary, or some lady glancing at her pictured almanack, remembers the fact; or friend meeting friend in the street just turns to wish a "happy New Year," but that is all. Christmas is gone by, with all its feasting and merry-making, and no one cares to welcome New Year's Day.

But in the rural districts of England, and throughout Scotland, it is very different. There the festival of New Year's Day is of as great importance as that of old Father Christmas himself. Young people look forward joyfully to "dancing the Old Year out, and the New Year in." It is held unlucky that the New Year should first dawn upon sleeping eyes; so in every house all sit up until midnight to let the young stranger in. Then, as the clock strikes twelve, the family and guests rise up and go in a mingled and noisy procession to the hall-door, which is opened with formal solemnity by the host; and thus the New Year is "let in."

It was New Year's Eve in the family of Dr. James Renwick. They were keeping it merrily, as befitting the good old times, though it was not many new years before this one of 1847. (May blessings attend those whose eyes meet this! says the writer in a parenthesis — wishing to all a happy New Year.) But before we enter Dr. Renwick's mirthful house, let us describe its exterior.

The doctor's house was at the entrance of a little village, situated just on the bounds of a manufacturing region, yet far enough in the country to make it pleasant and quiet without being dull. It stood on a turn of the road, the steep declivity of which was overlooked by its high garden walls. Over these walls many and many a time peeped children's curious faces, and little mischievous hands often dropped down flowers and pebbles on the stray passers-by. On the other side of the road a raised pathway led to the church — a Norman erection, old and quaint enough to charm Dr. Dryasdust himself. In the churchyard was a village school-room like a barn, and from thence rushed out daily a small troop of children, chasing the sheep that fed among the graves. Dr. Renwick's was the great house of the place, rich in the glories of a gravel entrance, and bay-windows — and oh, such an orchard! Never was seen the like for apples and pears! But now it looked cold and stately in the gloom of a December night — starry but moonless. A light covering of hoar-frost lay on the green plot, where, in early spring, snowdrops and crocusses peeped out from the grass, looking prettier than they ever do when set in the cold, brown mould of a garden-bed. A warm light streamed over the gravel walk through the half-drawn crimson curtains. Any passenger on the road would have said there was mirth and comfort within.

And so indeed there was; for it was the yearly gathering of the Renwick family, of which Dr. James Renwick was now the eldest son. Three generations were met once more in the eyes of the doctor's aged parents, who lived with him. They were now too old to have the care of an establishment of their own; and therefore this year the family meeting was held at Dr. Renwick's house, where they were spending the decline of life with their good and dutiful son.

Contrary to general English usage, the yearly gathering of the Renwicks was not held on Christmas-day; because it was on one Christmas-day that Death had first crossed the threshold and carried away their eldest-born from the young parents with bitter tears. It was many years since; but still they felt that to have a merry-making on that day would be treading in the shadow of a sorrow now gone by; so the day had ever since been changed from Christmas to New Year's Eve.

Old Mr. Renwick and his wife had been blessed with many children. Their quiver was full of arrows; and they wielded it joyfully, blessing God. Out of ten sons and daughters, five were with them that day; some wedded, with children of their own; one was travelling in foreign lands, and three had gone before them the way of all flesh — but the parents did not count these lost. One only — though still living — to use the touching words of a sorrowful father of old, "was not."

Dr. James Renwick, the eldest son, was a worthy man; and well did he occupy the station and fulfil the duties of a country physician. These duties are very different from those of a London practitioner. In a village "the doctor" is an important person, second only to the clergyman. He has more to do than merely to heal the bodies of his neighbours. If he be respected, he knows all the affairs of the parish; it is he to whom all come for advice in distress; he is the mediator between helpless poverty and benevolent but cautious wealth; and much good or much evil may he do, as his will leads him. Dr. Renwick chose the former path, and he was accordingly respected. He had married early a wife of like feelings to himself, and they had brought up a large family, the elder branches of whom were now almost men and women. Two brothers and a sister of the doctor were also round his table, with their flocks, few or many as it might be; so that the grandfather and grandmother Renwick looked on a tribe of juveniles as various in years, name, and appearance, as ever clustered round the chair of age since the patriarchal days.

The aged pair sat beside the fire, looking cheerfully around them. A dozen or more young cousins were dancing to the music of a piano and flute, while the elders played whist in an inner room. One or two quiet couples stole away into corners; they were too happy to dance and laugh with the rest. Among these was Isabel Renwick, the doctor's youngest and unmarried sister. The old parents looked at her as she stood with her betrothed in the shade of the crimson curtains.

"We shall have another fine tall son-in-law by this time next year, my dear," whispered the old man to his wife, with a merry smile.

"Don't talk nonsense before the children," answered Mrs. Renwick, trying to frown as she wiped her spectacles.

"Well, I always thought little Bell was the prettiest of all our children, and she will marry best though last," said the proud father. "Little Bell," was a beautiful young woman of three-and-twenty, whom no arguments could hitherto induce to quit her father's roof, until an old playmate returned from India, rich in money, and richer still in unaltered love. So Isabel was to be married at last.

The dance ended, and the various grandchildren sat down to rest, or walked idly about, arm-in-arm, talking and laughing.

"Do you know what a grand ball they are giving to-night at the Priory?" said Jessie Renwick to her cousin, William Oliphant.

"I doubt if they will be half so merry as we, nevertheless, with all Aunt Hartford's grandeur."

"Who is speaking of Mrs. Hartford — of my eldest daughter?" said the grandfather sharply. "Would that she had been no daughter of mine!"

"Hush, John, hush!" whispered his wife, laying her withered fingers on his arm.

"Jessie only said that there was a grand party at the Priory to-night," answered young Oliphant, for his cousin had drawn back, alarmed at her grandfather's harsh tone, so unusual to him.

"Let her go, with all her pride and her splendour! There is no blessing on an ungrateful child," said Mr. Renwick, sternly. "When she was born, her mother and I called her *Letitia*, out of the gladness of our hearts: but she has been to us a bitter sorrow, and no joy. Do not speak of her, my children."

The young people saw that there was deep sadness on their grandmamma's face, and that Mr. Renwick's tone, though severe, was tremulous; so they did not again mention Mrs. Hartford's name. The younger ones wondered; but many of the elder cousins knew the facts of their aunt's history — how she had married a prosperous man — how with increasing wealth had come pride, and with pride coldness and disdain, so that at last Mr. and Mrs. Hartford were self-exiled from the family circle, and only known by hearsay to the children.

After a season, the slight shadow which poor Jessie's unlucky speech had thrown over the circle passed away. William Oliphant, ever thoughtful in those little things which make the sum of home-happiness, adroitly brought to his grandmother's chair the two youngest of the flock, Mrs. Walter Renwick's bonnie little girl and boy. The old lady's attention was diverted. She took Bessie on her knee, and told Henry a fairy tale, and apparently thought no more of her own lost daughter.

Merrily passed the closing hours of the Old Year. The children danced again; then Aunt Isabel was entreated to sing, and the plaintive music of her voice changed the laughter into a pensive but pleasant silence. After a minute or two they all thanked her cheerfully. They did not know — the careless children! — that of all the merry troop around her, Isabel had sung but for *one*. After a while the mirth grew noisier; the light-hearted troop insist on chorussing Aunt Isabel's songs; and so those who could sing, and those who thought they could, all chimed in together, to the utter confusion of treble, tenor, and bass. But there was so much happiness and harmony in their hearts, that no one cared for a little musical discord.

Supper came, for "not even love can live upon air." Abundance of mirth was there; — particularly when the splendid dish of *trifle* came on, and little Bessie Renwick got the ring, and Aunt Isabel the ill-omened sixpence! It actually made her look grave for a minute — until her lover whispered something that made her smile and blush. There was little fear of Isabel's dying an old maid!

The time passed so quickly, that only just had the happy circle drunk the healths of grandpapa and grandmamma, and grandpapa had returned thanks in a few touching words, which made them grave in the midst of their fun, when, lo! the clock struck twelve.

And now came the grand cermony. Dr. James Renwick rose up with great solemnity of visage. Nothing made them laugh so much as to see the mock gravity of merry Uncle James. Bearing a light in each hand, the doctor went to his hall-door, followed by the whole troop. What a noise and

21*

confusion did they make in the narrow old-fashioned passage ycleped the hall! And now, the lights being resigned to the care of his eldest son, Dr. Renwick unfastened the bolts, and the door flew open, letting in, besides the New Year, such a gust of biting January night-wind as nearly extinguished the candles, and made the whole party shiver and hasten to the warm drawing-room with great celerity.

Just as Dr. Renwick was about to close the door, and retire also, some one called him from without.

"Wait a minute, doctor, pray. I want you, sir, if you please."

"Some patient, I suppose," said the doctor. "Well, come in, friend; it is too cold to stand talking outside."

The man came in, and Dr. Renwick and his untimely visitor retired to the study.

"What has become of Uncle James?" was soon the general cry, and some of the more daring of the youngsters rushed up and down the house in search of him. He was found in the study alone, but he looked very grave, and it was no pretence now.

"I cannot join you up-stairs again," he said; "I have to go out immediately." The children entreated, and Mrs. James Renwick expostulated, knowing that her husband had no patients on his list likely to require him at that time of night; until at last grandpapa sent down to know what was the matter.

"I am sure there is no need for you to leave us in this way, James," said the old man, rather querulously; "and at least you might tell us whither you are going."

"I had much rather not," said the plain-spoken James Renwick; "but if you still ask me, father, I will tell you."

"Do so, my son."

"Well, then, it is to my sister's; to Mrs. Hartford's."

"What business have you with her?" cried the angry old man. "It is an insult to your father and mother to cross the threshold of her heartless gaieties."

"There is no gaiety at the Priory to-night, but bitter sorrow," answered Dr. Renwick, gravely. "Arthur Hartford met with a dreadful accident to-night; he is still insensible, and his mother is almost frantic by the bedside of her only son."

There was a gloomy silence over the party at these words.

Old Mrs. Renwick began to weep; but her husband bade her be silent. "Did — did Mrs. Hartford send for you?"

"No; only old Ralph — you remember him? — came and begged me to go, for both Mr. and Mrs. Hartford are almost beside themselves with grief."

"You shall not go, James Renwick; no child of mine shall enter that ungrateful woman's door."

Dr. Renwick had been accustomed all his life to render obedience to his father; often, indeed, to a degree very unusual in a son who had himself long become the head of a family. Even when the old man's commands were harshly and unduly expressed, the good doctor seldom showed any open opposition, so strong was his habitual filial respect. Therefore he now only said, "Father, have you thought what you do in saying I shall not go? The boy has no proper assistance; he may die, and then ——."

Mr. Renwick's stern lineaments relaxed a little, but he made no answer. Then his aged wife took his hand, and looking at him with swimming eyes, said, "John, remember when our own Arthur died — twenty years ago; if any one had kept help away from him then! And Letty was his favourite sister; and she named her boy after him. Dear husband, do not be harsh; let James go!"

Many others joined their entreaties, and Mr. Renwick was softened; but still he would scarcely yield his authority.

"I will neither say yea nor nay; let James do as he pleases: only let me hear no more."

Dr. Renwick stayed not a moment, lest his father's mood should change, but was gone on his errand of mercy.

There was no more merriment for the young people that night; they were all too deeply touched. The aged pair soon retired, and the various families departed to their several homes. In an hour all was quiet in the doctor's house. Mrs. James Renwick alone sat waiting her husband's return, and thinking over in her kind heart how this might end. Every other eye was sealed in repose save one, and that was the aged mother's.

On New-Year's morning the family met as usual; Dr. James Renwick looked pale and careworn, but he did not speak of his last night's visit. Nor did the grandfather allude to it, and no one else dared mention the subject in his presence. At last the children separated to their various avocations, and Mr. and Mrs. Renwick were left alone with Dr. James and his wife. There was an uneasy silence, broken only by the clicking sound of the old lady's knitting, which she pursued busily, though her fingers trembled, and several heavy tears dropped on the work. At last the doctor rose and walked to the window, observed that it was a gloomy day, and began searching for his gloves.

"Before you go out, James," said his wife, with an evident effort at unconcern, "grandmamma might like to hear how the poor boy is — how that boy is?"

"You mean Arthur Hartford? He is better. I think he may recover."

"Thank God for that!" murmured the old lady, fervently.

"Did you see — Mrs. Hartford?" asked the father, after a pause.

"I did," answered the doctor, concisely.

"Dear James, tell us all that passed!" whispered the poor old mother. Her husband turned over the pages of a book, but he made no opposition; while the doctor sat down beside his mother, and began to tell his story.

"When I reached the Priory, all was confusion. Poor Letty was in violent hysterics. I heard her screams the moment I entered the house, so I knew it was of no use asking to see her. The father, they told me, was hanging over his insensible boy. I sent word to him that I had come to offer what assistance I could; and he was with me in a moment, wringing my hands, and imploring me to save poor Arthur. I never thought how misery could have bent the man's proud spirit. Mr. Hartford, who passed me but yesterday without a glance, would now have knelt to entreat me to forget the past, and do what I could for his son."

"And you did — you were successful, James?" said old Mrs. Renwick, anxiously.

"Yes; after a time the boy came to his senses: he is a fine fellow! He knew me directly, and looked so joyfully from me to his father, who had clasped my hand in overpowering gratitude."

"And poor Letty?" again asked the weeping mother.

"When she was a little calmer, I went to her room with Mr. Hartford. She started at seeing me: but her husband said, 'Letty, you must thank your brother for saving Arthur's life.'

And then she threw herself into my arms, and poured forth such a torrent of thanks, and blessings, and self-reproaches, that it almost made a child of me. Poor Letty! she is much altered," added the good doctor, his voice growing husky. He ceased talking, and looked steadily into the fire.

All this time the stern old father had not uttered a word. For a few minutes none of the party spoke. At last old Mrs. Renwick glanced timidly at her husband, and whispered, "Did she say anything about us, James?"

"Yes, mother, she asked after you both; said how glad she always was to hear of you, in any possible way; and wept much when she spoke of you."

Mr. Renwick lifted up his head; he had bent it on his hands; and said, "What truth, think you, is there in that woman's tears, when, not a week since, she passed us in the road; she riding in her splendid carriage, and the mother that bore her trudging wearily on foot; yet she never looked towards us, but turned her head another way? Do you think I can forgive that, James Renwick?"

"I have forgiven her, John," said the old lady. "She is our own child, and she is in trouble; she may repent now for the past."

"I know she does," added James, earnestly. "She told me how she longed to see you; even her husband said the same: he seems a kind husband to her, though people say he is so proud."

"And they expect that your mother and I will go humbly to their fine house to beg for reconciliation!"

"No, father; that was not what my sister said. She told me to say she prayed you to forget the past, and let her come and see you here, and be your daughter Letty once more."

Dr. Renwick stopped, for he saw that his father was actually weeping. He looked at his wife, and she left the room. For several minutes the aged couple sat with their hands clasped together in silence; then Mr. Renwick said in a broken voice, "Tell Letty she may come."

"She will come — she is come! my dear father," cried James, as he opened the door. Letty, entering, flung herself on her knees before her parents, and was clasped to both their hearts with full and free forgiveness. The erring child was pardoned — the lost one was found!

Dr. Renwick and his wife went silently away together, with

full and thankful hearts for the good which had been effected that day. It was their best reward.

There was deep joy throughout the whole of the Renwick family when they heard the news. Some of the younger and gayer spirits thought how pleasant it would be to visit now at Aunt Hartford's beautiful house, and ride Cousin Arthur's fine horses, when he recovered. But with more sincerity and disinterested pleasure did the elders rejoice that there was now no alienation to wound their aged father and mother in their declining years, but that they would now go down to the grave in peace, encircled by a family of love.

Arthur Hartford recovered speedily under his uncle's care. He was indeed a noble boy, resembling, both in person and character, the lost Arthur; so no wonder that he soon became the darling of the grandparents. The leaves were hardly green on the trees before there was a joyful family meeting; for it was the wedding of Aunt Isabel; and there were now no absent ones to mar the happiness of the festivity, for even the soldier had returned.

"'That speech of yours turned out not so very unlucky after all," whispered William Oliphant to his cousin Jessie, who hung on his arm as of old: they were always great friends.

"No," answered the laughing girl; "I dare speak of Aunt Hartford now without fear."

"And see how happy grandmamma looks! I heard her say that Aunt Hartford looks almost as handsome as the bride, though I think Aunt Isabel is much superior."

"Well, never mind, William; we are all very happy; it has all turned out like a fairy tale; and I am sure we can say with truth that this has been for us all a happy New Year."

ALL FOR THE BEST

A TALE.

I do not think there could be found in the three kingdoms a blither old maid than Miss Mellicent Orme, otherwise Aunt Milly, for so she was universally called by her nephews and nieces, first, second, and third cousins — nay, even by many who could not boast the smallest tie of consanguinity. But this sort of universal aunthood to the whole neighbourhood was by no means disagreeable to Miss Milly, for in a very little body she had a large heart, of a most India-rubber nature; not indeed as the simile is used, in speaking of female hearts, that "never break, but always stretch." But Miss Milly's heart possessed this elastic nature in the best sense — namely, that it ever found room for new occupants; and, moreover, it was remarkable for its quality of effacing all unkindness or injuries as easily as India-rubber removes pencil-marks from paper.

Aunt Milly — I have some right to call her so, being her very own nephew, Godfrey Escourt — was an extremely little woman. She had pretty little features, pretty little hands and feet, a pretty little figure, and always carried with her a pretty little worked bag, in whose mysterious recesses all the children of the neighbourhood loved to dive, seldom returning to the surface without some pearl of price, in the shape of a lozenge or a sugarplum. Her dress was always neat, rather old-fashioned perhaps, but invariably becoming; her soft brown hair — it really was brown still — lay smoothly braided under a tiny cap; her white collar was ever snowy; indeed Aunt Milly's whole attire seemed to have the amazing quality of never looking worn, soiled, or dusty, but always fresh and new. Yet she was far from rich, as every one knew; but her little income was just enough to suffice for her little self. She lived in a nutshell of a house, with the smallest of small handmaidens; indeed everything about Aunt Milly was on the diminutive scale. She did not abide much at home, for she was everywhere in request — at weddings, christenings, &c. And to her credit be it spoken, Aunt Milly did not turn her feet from the house of mourning. She could weep with those that wept, yet somehow or other she contrived to infuse hope amidst despair. And in general her blithe nature converted all life's minor evils into things not worth lamenting about.

Every one felt that Aunt Milly's entrance into their doors brought sunshine. She was a sunbeam in herself; there was cheerfulness in her light step, her merry laugh: the jingling of the keys in her pocket, dear little soul! was musical. She had a word of encouragement for all, and had an inclination to look on the sunny side of everything and everybody. No one was more welcome in mirthful days, no one more sought for in adversity, for she had the quality of making the heaviest trouble seem lighter; and her unfailing motto was, "All happens for the best."

All my schoolboy disasters were deposited in Aunt Milly's sympathizing ear; and when I grew up I still kept to the old habit. I came to her one day with what I considered my first real sorrow: it was the loss, by the sudden failure of a country bank, of nearly all the few hundreds my poor father had laid up for me. My sad news had travelled before me, and I was not surprised to see Aunt Milly's cheerful face really grave as she met me with, "My dear boy, I am very sorry for you."

"It is the greatest misfortune I could have," I cried. "I wish that wretch Sharples ——."

"Don't wish him anything worse than he has to bear already, poor man, with his large family," said Aunt Milly, gently.

"But you do not know all I have lost. That — that Laura ——," and I stopped, looking, I doubt not, very miserable, and possibly very silly.

"You mean to say, Godfrey, that since, instead of having a little fortune to begin the world with, you have hardly anything at all, Miss Laura Ashton will not consider that her engagement holds. I expected it."

"Oh, Aunt Milly, she is not so mean as that; but we were to have been married in two years, and I could have got a share in Mortlake's office, and we should have been so happy! All that is over now. Her father says we must wait, and

Laura is to be considered free. Life is nothing to me! I will go to America — or shoot myself."

"How old are you, Godfrey?" asked Aunt Milly, with a quiet smile that rather annoyed me.

"I shall be twenty next June," I said. Young people always put their age in the future tense: it sounds better.

"It is now July, so that I may call you nineteen and a month. My dear boy, the world must be a horrible place indeed for you to grow tired of it so soon. I would advise you to wait a little while before you get so very desperate."

"Aunt Milly," I said, turning away, "it is easy for you to talk — you were never in love."

A shadow passed over her bright face, but Aunt Milly did not answer my allusion.

"I do not think any boy of nineteen is doomed to be a victim to loss of fortune or hopeless love," she said, after a pause. "My dear Godfrey, this will be a trial of your Laura's constancy, and of your own patience and industry. Depend upon it, all will turn out for the best."

"Oh!" I sighed, "you talk very well, Aunt Milly; but what can I do?"

"I will tell you. You are young, clever, and have been for two years in a good profession. It will be your own fault if you do not rise in the world. Every man is in a great measure the architect of his own fortunes; and where, as in your case, the foundation of a good education is laid, so much the easier is it to raise the superstructure. You may yet be a rich man by your own exertions, and the best of fortunes is a fortune self-earned."

This was the longest and gravest speech I had ever heard from Aunt Milly's lips. Its truth struck me forcibly, and I felt rather ashamed of having so soon succumbed to disaster: it seemed cowardly, and unworthy the manly dignity of nearly twenty years. Aunt Milly, with true feminine tact, saw her advantage, and followed it up.

"Now, as to your heart-troubles, my dear nephew. To tell the truth, I hardly believe in boyish love; it is often so much of a dream, and so little of a reality. Do not be vexed, Godfrey; but I should not be surprised if, five years hence, you tell me how fortunate it was that this trial came. Men rarely see with the same eyes at nineteen and twenty-five."

I energetically quoted Shakspeare —

"Doubt that the stars are fire,
Doubt that the sun doth move,
Doubt truth to be a liar,
But never doubt I love."

Aunt Milly laughed. "As both these astronomical facts are rather questionable, you must excuse my doubting the final fact also. But time will show. Meanwhile, do not despair; be diligent, and be careful of the little you have left. Matters might have been worse with you."

"Ah, Aunt Milly, what a cheerful heart you have! But trouble never comes to you, as it does to other people."

"You are a little mistaken, for once, Godfrey. By Sharples' failure I have lost every farthing I had in the world."

I was struck dumb with surprise and regret. Poor dear Aunt Milly! when she was listening to my lamentations, and consoling me, how little did I know that she was more unfortunate than myself! And yet she neither complained nor desponded, but only smiled — a little sadly perhaps — and said she knew even this disaster was "all for the best," though she could not see it at the time. She calmly made preparations for quitting her pretty home, confided her little hand-maid to one cousin, in whose kitchen the tidy Rachel was gladly admitted, gave her few household pets to another, and prepared to brave the wide world. Some unfeeling people forgot Aunt Milly in her trouble; but the greater part of her friendly circle proved how much they esteemed and valued her. Some asked her to visit them for a month, three months, a year: indeed, had she chosen, Aunt Milly might have spent her life as a passing guest among her friends; but she was too proud to do any such thing.

At last a third or fourth cousin — a widower of large fortune — invited Miss Milly to reside at his house, as chaperon to his two daughters, young girls just growing up into womanhood. This proposal, kindly meant, was warmly accepted; and Aunt Milly set forward on her long journey, for Elphinstone Hall was some hundred miles off — a formidable distance to one who had never been a day's journey from her own home; now, alas! hers no more! Still, neither despondency nor fear troubled her blithe spirit, as little Miss Milly set out with her valorous nephew; for I had pleaded so earnestly my right to be her squire to Mr. Elphinstone's door, that the concession was yielded at last.

Of all the gloomy-looking old avenues that ever led to baronial hall, the one we passed through was the gloomiest. It might have been pretty in May, but on a wet day in October it was most melancholy. Poor Aunt Milly shivered as the wind rustled in the trees, and the dead leaves fell in clouds on the top of the postchaise. We alighted, and entered a hall equally lugubrious, and not much warmer than the avenue. The solemn old porter was warming his chilled hands at the tiny fire: he and the house were in perfect keeping — dreary, dull, and melancholy. The master was much in the same style: a tall black figure, with a long face and a white neckcloth, was the personified idea left behind by Mr. Elphinstone. When he was gone, I earnestly entreated Aunt Milly to return with me, and not stay in this desolate place; but she refused.

"My cousin seems kind," she said: "he looked and spoke as though he were glad to see me." (I was too cold to hear or see much, certainly, but I declare I did not notice this very friendly reception.) "My dear Godfrey," Aunt Milly continued, "I will stay and try to make a home here: the two girls may be amiable, and then I shall soon love them: at all events, let us hope for the best."

My hopes for poor Aunt Milly all vanished into thin air when, at the frigid dinner-table, where the very eatables seemed made of stone, I saw two young ladies of fifteen or thereabouts: one the wildest and rudest hoyden that ever disgraced feminine habiliments; the other, a pale stooping girl, with sleepy blue eyes, and lank fair hair, who never uttered a word, nor once lifted her eyes from the tablecloth.

"What will become of poor Aunt Milly?" I thought internally. Yet there she was, as cheerful as ever, talking to that solemn old icicle, Mr. Elphinstone; listening patiently to the lava-flood of Miss Louisa's tongue; and now and then speaking to Miss Euphemia, whose only answer was a nod of the head, or a stare from her immense blue eyes. "Well!" I mentally ejaculated, "Aunt Milly's talent for making the best of everything will be called into full requisition here, I suspect."

Nevertheless, when we parted, she assured me that she was

quite content; that she would no doubt be very comfortable at the Hall.

"But those two dreadful girls, how will you manage them, Aunt Milly?" and a faint vision of the tall stout Louisa going in a passion and knocking my poor little aunt off her chair, came across my mind's eye.

"Poor things! they have no mother to teach them better. I am sorry for them: I was a motherless child myself," said Aunt Milly, softly. "They will improve by and by: depend upon it, Godfrey, all will turn out well for both you and me."

"Amen!" said I in my heart; for I thought of my own Laura. How different she was from the Miss Elphinstones! And the image of my beloved eclipsed that of desolate Aunt Milly, I fear, before I had travelled many miles from the Hall.

Aunt Milly's epistles were not very frequent: for, like many excellent people, she disliked letter-writing, and only indulged her very particular friends with a few lines now and then, in which she fully acted up to the golden rule, "If you have anything to say, say it: if nothing — why, say it too." Thus my information as to how matters were going on at Elphinstone Hall was of a very slender nature. However, when a few months had rolled by, chance led me into the neighbourhood, and I surprised Aunt Milly with a visit from her loving nephew.

It was early spring, and a few peeping primroses brightened the old avenue. Underneath the dining-room windows, was a gay bed of purple and yellow crocuses which I thought bore tokens of Aunt Milly's care; she was always so fond of flowers. I fancied the Hall did not look quite so cheerless as before; the bright March sunbeams enlivened, though they could not warm it. In a few moments appeared Aunt Milly herself, not in the least altered, but as lively and active as ever.

She took me into her own little sitting-room, and told me how the winter had passed with her. It had been rather a gloomy one, she acknowledged: the girls were accustomed to run wild; Louisa would have her own way; but then she was easily guided by love, and her nature was frank and warm. Phemie, the pale girl, who had been delicate from her cradle, was rather indolent, but — (oh, what a blessing these charitable *buts* are sometimes!) — but then she was so sweet and gentle. I own when I again saw the young damsels, thus leniently described by Aunt Milly, I did not perceive the marvellous change: Louisa seemed nearly as talkative, and her sister nearly as insipid, as ever; still there was a slight improvement even to my eyes, and I gladly allowed Aunt Milly the full benefit of that loving glamour which was cast by her hopeful creed and sweet disposition.

"But now, Godfrey, how fares it with you?" said my good aunt. "How is Laura? and how are you getting on in the world?"

I could give but a melancholy answer to these questions; for I had to work hard, and law was a very dry study. Besides, many people looked coldly on me after they knew I was poorer than I had been; and even Laura herself was not so frank and kind. Vague jealousies were springing up in my heart for every smile she bestowed elsewhere; and these smiles were not few. I was, in truth, far from happy; and so I told Aunt Milly, adding, "If Laura does not love me, I don't care what becomes of me."

Aunt Milly smiled, and then looked grave. "My dear Godfrey, if Laura married to-morrow, you would recover in time."

"No, never! To lose the girl I love is to lose everything in the world."

"It may be you do not yet know what real love is, my dear nephew. The strength and duration of a man's attachment depend chiefly upon the character and disposition of the woman he loves. For your Laura —. But we shall see. Once more, have a good courage: work hard at your profession, and grieve as little about Laura as you can. If she ever did love you she does so still, and will as long as you keep constant to her, otherwise she is not worth the winning."

I did not agree with Aunt Milly's theory; but I said no more; my heart was too sore. She took me over the house and grounds: both looked cheerful under the influence of the soft spring; and then she told me how kind Mr. Elphinstone was, and how he had been gradually weaned from his solitary life to take pleasure in the society of his daughters.

"And I hope he is grateful to you, who have made it at all endurable?" I said.

Aunt Milly smiled. "Yes, I believe he is: but I have only

done what I ought: the girls both love me dearly, and it is sufficient reward to see them improved."

I did not see Mr. Elphinstone, but I earnestly hoped the solemn, coldly polite, middle-aged gentleman had shared in the general amelioration and reform effected by the cheerful-hearted Miss Milly.

Months had glided into years ere I again saw Aunt Milly. Everything had changed with me: from a boy I had grown a man, from toying to struggling with the world. I had followed Aunt Milly's advice, and had begun to reap the fruit of it, in the good opinion of those whose opinion was worth having. I had proved also the truth of her old saying, "How sweet is bread of one's own earning!" Another of her prophecies, alas! had come but too true. Laura Ashton had married — but I was not her husband: a richer man stole the jewel of my boyhood's fancy; but — and this was the saddest to bear — not before I had found it to be a false pearl, unworthy my manhood's wearing. But I will not speak of this; in spite of Aunt Milly's sage speeches, no one can quite forget his first love.

When I next visited Elphinstone Hall, it was in the golden days of midsummer. I thought I had never beheld a more lovely place. The old trees were so bowery and full of leaves; the grassy lawn so very green; the flower-garden so bright with blossoms. Age and youth were not more different than the ancient cheerless Hall of former times and the beautiful spot I now looked upon. Even Aunt Milly seemed to share in the general rejuvenescence. The two years which had changed me so much, had not made her look a day older. She had the same clear, fresh, cheerful face, and neat little figure: both perhaps a little rounder, the result of a happy life and few cares. Her dress was as tasteful as ever, but not quite so precise, and it was of richer materials. She wore, too, various handsome articles of jewellery; a remarkable circumstance for unpretending Aunt Milly. I thought her pupils must be very generous in presents.

We had not sat talking long when a very graceful girl crossed the lawn to the French window of Aunt Milly's room.

"I will come soon: go and take your walk, Phemie dear," said Aunt Milly.

Wonder of wonders! Could that beautiful fair face and golden ringlets which I saw through the open window belong to the lackadaisical Miss Euphemia of old? I absolutely started from my chair.

"You don't mean to say, Aunt Milly, that that lovely girl is Miss Elphinstone?"

"Most certainly," said Aunt Milly, laughing heartily — her own musical laugh.

"Well, if I ever saw such a transformation! You are as much a fairy as Cinderella's godmother."

"Not at all; I only did as a gardener does with half-cultivated ground; I pulled up the weeds, and nurtured the flowers. As for Phemie's beauty, I never thought her ugly, though you were too much occupied with your disgust at the place to perceive that she really had a fair skin and pretty features. I have only made the best of what I found."

"And how has Miss Louisa turned out in your hand?" I asked, smiling.

"Look at her; she is coming up the avenue on horseback."

And a very graceful, fearless horsewoman the quondam hoyden seemed: her wildness was subdued into sprightly, but not unladylike manners; in short, Louisa had become what many men would admire as a fine, lively girl.

"Why, Aunt Milly," I said, "you must have grown quite attached to these girls; it will really be painful for you to leave them."

"I do not think of leaving them very soon," said Aunt Milly, casting down her eyes, and playing with her gold watch-chain, while a very faint rosiness, deepening on her still fair cheek, and a scarcely perceptible smile hovering round her mouth, were distinctly visible.

"Indeed!" said I, inquiringly.

"Yes; Mr. Elphinstone is very kind; he does not wish me to go; the girls love me very much: and my cousin ——"

"Follows his daughters' good example!" I cried, at last arriving at the truth. "Well, I don't see how he could possibly help it; and so, dear Aunt Milly, I wish you joy."

Aunt Milly muttered something in return, blushed as prettily as a girl of fifteen, and at last fairly ran out of the room.

"After all, everything *was* for the best!" thought I, as I attended the quiet wedding of Mr. Elphinstone and his second wife — loved and loving sincerely; though to both the affection was but the Indian summer of their lives. He did not look half so grave and austere as I fancied, and really was a very noble looking man, in spite of his half-century; and if his winning little wife trod only ten years behind him in the road of life, why, I have seen many older-looking brides who were not thirty by the church register. After all, what matter years when the heart is still young? They both did right in marrying, and the Indian summer shines peacefully on them still.

I have nothing more to add, except that I have been for these two years a married man myself; and therefore fully sympathized with Aunt Milly's keeping of her seventh wedding anniversary last week. I may just mention, *en passant*, that I rarely call her Aunt Milly now, happening to be her son-in-law as well as nephew. Perhaps, to clear up all mysteries, I had better confess that my wife has fair hair, sweet blue eyes, and that her name is Euphemia.

THE END.